Lecture Notes
in Business Information Processing   178

T0212827

Lazaros Iliadis
Michael Papazoglou
Klaus Pohl (Eds.)

Advanced Information Systems Engineering Workshops

CAiSE 2014 International Workshops
Thessaloniki, Greece, June 16-20, 2014
Proceedings

 Springer

Volume Editors

Lazaros Iliadis
Democritus University of Thrace
Department of Forestry and Management of the Environment
Orestiada, Greece
E-mail: liliadis@fmenr.duth.gr

Michael Papazoglou
University of Tilburg
Department of Computer Science
Tilburg, The Netherlands
E-mail: mikep@uvt.nl

Klaus Pohl
University of Duisburg-Essen
Department of Software Systems Engineering
Essen, Germany
E-mail: klaus.pohl@paluno.uni-due.de

ISSN 1865-1348   e-ISSN 1865-1356
ISBN 978-3-319-07868-7   e-ISBN 978-3-319-07869-4
DOI 10.1007/978-3-319-07869-4
Springer Cham Heidelberg New York Dordrecht London

Library of Congress Control Number: 2014940063

Typesetting: Camera-ready by author, data conversion by Scientific Publishing Services, Chennai, India

Printed on acid-free paper

Springer is part of Springer Science+Business Media (www.springer.com)

Preface

A continuous challenge in modern information systems engineering (ISE) is to provide significant aid toward the improvement of the design, implementation, and fielding of advanced information systems. However, a timely daunting task is to employ ISE approaches to real-world, large-scale, adaptable systems that can have a potential impact in various diverse aspects of people's life. All of these topics and potential roadmaps toward innovation that might lead to development and welfare were discussed in the workshops that took place under the framework of the 26th CAiSE held in Thessaloniki, Greece, June 16–20.

It is a long-standing tradition of the International Conference on Advanced Information Systems Engineering to be accompanied by an ensemble of high-quality workshops. Their aim is to serve as a discussion forum between stakeholders in this domain, to exchange innovative ideas on new approaches, techniques or tools, covering a wide range of specific thematic areas. This year, CAiSE had two associated working conferences (BPMDS and EMMSAD) and seven workshops. Several workshop proposals were received initially and those accepted were chosen after a careful consideration by the corresponding chairs, based on maturity and compliance with our usual quality and consistency criteria.

This volume contains the proceedings of the following five 2014 workshops (in alphabetical order):

- First International Workshop on Advanced Probability and Statistics in Information Systems (APSIS)
- First International Workshop on Advances in Services Design based on the Notion of Capability (ASDENCA)
- Second International Workshop on Cognitive Aspects of Information Systems Engineering (COGNISE)
- Third New Generation Enterprise and Business Innovation Systems (NGEBIS)
- 4th International Workshop on Information Systems Security Engineering (WISSE)

The CAiSE 2014 workshop 10th EOMAS decided to publish their proceedings in a separate LNBIP volume. The 7th iStar workshop decided to publish the proceedings in the *CEUR Workshop Proceedings* series. Each workshop complied with the CAiSE 2014 submission and acceptance rules. The paper acceptance ratio across all workshops was approximately 40%.

As workshop chairs of the 26th CAiSE 2014 we would like to express our gratitude to all organizers and to all corresponding scientific committees for their invaluable contribution. We hope that this volume will offer a comprehensive and timely view on the evolution of advanced information systems engineering and that it will stimulate potential authors toward participation in future CAiSE events.

June 2014   Lazaros Iliadis
                                                                    Mike Papazoglou
                                                                       Klaus Pohl

First International Workshop on Advanced Probability and Statistics in Information Systems (APSIS 2014)

Preface

The rapid and continuous evolution of technology and especially the evolution of the Internet are changing the problems related to the development, the application, and the impact of information systems. Modern information systems are associated with the collection, management, processing, analysis, and production of massive amounts and different types of data. Although research in computer science has produced highly advanced methodologies for analyzing them, new complex research challenges appear.

Probability theory and statistics are considered well-defined and mature disciplines that have evolved through centuries and have become powerful based on the foundations of mathematics. Probabilities and statistics have offered innumerable theories, techniques, and tools to all aspects of data analysis with applications to all areas of information systems.

The aim of the First International Workshop on Advanced Probability and Statistics in Information Systems (APSIS), which was organized in conjunction with the 26th International Conference on Advanced Information Systems Engineering (CAISE 2014), was to bring together scientists from different branches of information systems who use or develop statistical or probabilistic methods in their research.

For this first year of the workshop, we received eight high-quality submissions from researchers in different fields of information systems, which were each peer-reviewed by at least two reviewers. Out of these submissions, three contributions were selected as full papers, while one short paper with promising research was also accepted.

The accepted papers are indicative of the wide applicability of probabilities and statistics in information systems research. Specifically, Yazdi et al. apply time series in order to describe and analyze the evolution of software systems at the abstraction level of models. Liparas and Pantraki propose a combination of the statistical Mahalanobis–Taguchi strategy with a Genetic Algorithm for Intrusion Detection Systems. Shoaran and Thomo use probabilistic methods for privacy mechanisms in social networks. Finally, Mavridis uses probabilistic notions to measure the quality evolution of open source software.

June 2014

Lefteris Angelis
Ioannis Stamelos
Apostolos N. Papadopoulos

APSIS 2014 Organization

Organizing Committee

Lefteris Angelis	Aristotle University of Thessaloniki, Greece
Ioannis Stamelos	Aristotle University of Thessaloniki, Greece
Apostolos N. Papadopoulos	Aristotle University of Thessaloniki, Greece

Program Committee

Apostolos Ampatzoglou	University of Groningen, The Netherlands
Andreas Andreou	Cyprus University of Technology, Cyprus
Paris Avgeriou	University of Groningen, The Netherlands
Stamatia Bibi	Aristotle University, Greece
Pavlos Delias	TEI of Kavala, Greece
Jesus M. Gonzalez-Barahona	University Rey Juan Carlos, Spain
Anastasios Gounaris	Aristotle University, Greece
Panagiotis Katsaros	Aristotle University, Greece
Stefan Koch	Bogazici University, Turkey
Stephen MacDonell	Auckland University, New Zealand
Emilia Mendes	Blekinge Institute of Technology, Sweden
Tim Menzies	West Virginia University, USA
Nikolaos Mittas	TEI of Kavala & Aristotle University, Greece
Maurizio Morisio	Politecnico di Torino, Italy
Efi Papatheocharous	Swedish Institute of Computer Science, Sweden
Evaggelia Pitoura	University of Ioannina, Greece
Grigorios Tsoumakas	Aristotle University, Greece
Athena Vakali	Aristotle University, Greece
Claes Wohlin	Blekinge Institute of Technology, Sweden
Michalis Xenos	Hellenic Open University, Greeece
Israel Herraiz	Technical University of Madrid, Spain

Keynote by Magne Jorgensen*

Abstract. The keynote addresses a selection of questionable statistical practices commonly observed in empirical software engineering research. This includes a discussion of the topics: "p-values considered harmful", "inflated effect sizes", "publication bias in regression analysis", "how much can we trust the outcome of statistical tests in software engineering studies?", "regression-towards-the-mean in non-random samples", "the fixed variables assumption is essential" and "Simpson's paradox". The topics will be illustrated with observations on how questionable statistical practices have produced misleading and incorrect results in software engineering research. We should never use a statistical method without understanding it thoroughly and never violate a statistical assumption without understanding the likely consequences of doing so. Several changes in statistical practice in software engineering research are suggested.

---

* Subject: Things you were never told, did not understand, forgot, or chose to ignore in statistics.

First International Workshop on Advances in Services Design Based on the Notion of Capability (ASDENCA 2014)

Preface

Lately the notion of *capability* is gaining much presence within the field of information systems engineering, due to a number of factors: the notion directs business investment focus, it can be used as a baseline for business planning, and it leads directly to service specification and design. Historically, it has been examined in economics, sociology, and management science. More recently, it has been considered in the context of business-IT alignment, in the specification and design of services using business planning as the baseline, in enterprise architecture, and in service-oriented architecture.

Capability is commonly seen as an *ability* or *capacity* for a company to deliver value, either to customers or shareholders, right beneath the business strategy. It consists of three major components: business processes, people, and physical assets. In recent academic proposals, such as of the Open Group Standard, capability is seen as originating from competence-based management and military frameworks, offering a complement to traditional enterprise modelling approaches by representing organizational knowledge from a result-based perspective. Thus it is an abstraction away from the specifics of how (process), who (agent), and why (goals), i.e., with a focus on results and benefits. At the same capability should allow fairly straightforward integrations with the aforementioned established bodies of knowledge and practices, such as goals (through "goal fulfillment"), processes (through "modelling"), and services (through "servicing").

The latter relation, specific to service-oriented engineering, has been described in service-oriented architecture, i.e., capability is seen as existing business functionality that enables a well-defined need, implemented through a service accessible through an interface. The business drive approach to service identification provides a solution for typical challenges of alignment between business and IT in this engineering context. Service design based on business capabilities is seen as an alternative to process-based service design, especially useful in cases of varying business contexts, where different capabilities address different contexts.

Traditionally, methods, approaches, theories, and applications of business–IT alignment have been vividly discussed by practitioners and researchers in IT. The idea for this first edition of the ASDENCA workshop came from the academic and industrial community gathered in the recently launched EU/FP7 project – CaaS.

Furthermore, the special theme of the 26th edition of CAiSE was "Information Systems Engineering in Times of Crisis." Capability orientation in IS design may play an important role in planning and reacting to crises of different kinds perceived as different contexts in which businesses may be found, and requiring efficient shifts to the services capable of sustaining these contexts.

ASDENCA 2014 attracted 21 submissions out of which the Program Committee selected nine high-quality papers for presentation at the workshop, which are included in this proceedings volume. The results of submitted proposals clearly demonstrate an increasing interest in the topic, and more specifically in service engineering emphasizing the use of capability notion. Divided into three sessions, the program of the workshop reflects different topics of capability-oriented service design, including modeling of capabilities, the practices of capability-based approaches, as well as variability and context modeling.

We owe special thanks to the Workshop Chairs of CAiSE 2014 for supporting the ASDENCA workshop, as well as for providing us with facilities to publicize it. We also thank the Program Committee for providing valuable and timely reviews for the submitted papers.

June 2014   Jelena Zdravkovic
                                                         Oscar Pastor
                                                      Peri Loucopoulos

ASDENCA 2014 Organization

Organizing Committee

Jelena Zdravkovic   Stockholm University, Sweden
Pericles Loucopoulos   University of Manchester, UK
Oscar Pastor   Universitat Politècnica de València, Spain

Program Committee

George Bravos	Greece
Jaelson Castro	Universidade Federal de Pernambuco, Brazil
Lawrence Chung	The University of Texas at Dallas, USA
Martin Glinz	University of Zurich, Switzerland
Sergio España	PROS Research Centre, Spain
Xavier Franch	Universitat Politècnica de Catalunya, Spain
Brian Fitzgerald	University of Limerick, Ireland
Janis Grabis	Riga Technical University, Latvia
Yousef Hassouneh	Birzeit University, Palestine
Zhi Jin	Key Peking University, China
Paul Johannesson	Royal Institute of Technology, Sweden
Dinitris Karagiannis	University of Vienna, Austria
Vagelio Kavakli	University of the Aegean, Greece
Kalle Lyytinen	Case Western Reserve University, USA
Julio Leite	PUC-Rio, Brazil
Nikolay Mehanjiev	Manchester Business School, UK
Haralambos Mouratidis	University of Brighton, UK
Antoni Olive	Universitat Politècnica de Catalunya, Spain
Andreas Opdahl	University of Bergen, Norway
Naveen Prakash	MRCE, India
Jolita Ralyte	University of Geneva, Switzerland
Gil Regev	Ecole Polytechnique Fédérale de Lausanne, Switzerland
Barbara Russo	Free University of Bolzano/Bozen, Italy
Kurt Sandkuhl	The University of Rostock, Germany
Jorge Sanz	IBM Research, USA
Isabel Seruca	Universidade Portucalense, Porto, Portugal
Keng Siau	Missouri University of Science and Technology, USA
Pnina Soffer	University of Haifa, Israel
Janis Stirna	Stockholm University, Sweden
Francisco Valverde Giromé	Universidad Politécnica de Valencia, Spain

Alain Wegmann   École Polytechnique Fédérale de Lausanne,
                           Switzerland
Hans Weigand   Tilburg University, The Netherlands
Carson Woo   University of British Columbia, USA
Eric Yu   University of Toronto, Canada

Keynote by Janis Stirna, Pericle Loucopoulos, Oscar Pastor and Jelena Zdravkovic subject: "Designing Business Capabilities: Challenges and Outlooks".

Second International Workshop on Cognitive Aspects of Information Systems Engineering (COGNISE 2014)

Preface

Cognitive aspects of information systems engineering is an area that is gaining interest and importance in industry and research. In recent years, human aspects and specifically cognitive aspects in software engineering and information systems engineering have received increasing attention in the literature and conferences, acknowledging that these aspects are as important as the technical ones, which have traditionally been in the center of attention. This workshop was planned to be a stage for new research and vivid discussions involving both academics and practitioners.

The goal of this workshop is to provide a better understanding and more appropriate support of the cognitive processes and challenges practitioners experience when performing information systems development activities. By understanding the challenges and needs educational programs as well as development supporting tools and notations may be enhanced for a better fit to our natural cognition, leading to better performance of engineers and higher systems quality. The workshop aimed to bring together researchers from different communities such as requirements engineering, software architecture, and design and programming, who share an interest in cognitive aspects, for identifying the cognitive challenges in the diverse development-related activities.

The second edition of this workshop included four full research papers and three short position papers. The papers presented at the workshop provide a mix of novel research ideas, some presenting completed research and others research in progress or research plans.

The full research papers included the following papers. "Low-Cost Eye-Trackers: Useful for Information Systems Research?" by Stefan Zugal and Jakob Pinggera explores whether low-cost eye-trackers are of use for investigating cognitive aspects of information systems research and, specifically, examines the accuracy of the low-cost eye-tracker Gazepoint GP3 in an empirical study. Their results show that Gazepoint GP3 is well suited for respective research, given that experimental material acknowledges the limits of the eye-tracker. "Supporting BPMN Model Creation with Routing Patterns" by Idan Wolf and Pnina Soffer proposes routing patterns combined with a decision guidance tool to support BPMN model creation, in order to overcome cognitive difficulties that may be encountered when using BPMN, due to the large number of constructs and the lack of ontological clarity of this language. The proposed set of patterns builds on an existing set of routing behaviors and operationalizes these behaviors by providing their BPMN representations. Testing the impact of this support in a study showed a significantly positive effect on the quality of the produced models, but longer modeling durations as compared with unsupported modeling. "Coupling Elements of a Framework for Cognitive Matchmaking with Enterprise Models" by Sietse Overbeek addresses the issue of the excessive cognitive load actors working in knowledge-intensive organizations need to cope with and its negative influence on the quality of knowledge-intensive task fulfillment. The paper discusses how elements from a cognitive matchmaking framework can be coupled with an example enterprise model to partly provide a solution for reducing cognitive load. This exercise enables one to achieve a better understanding of the cognitive fit of actor types and the knowledge-intensive task types they have to fulfill. "Investigating Differences Between Graphical and Textual Declarative Process Models" by Cornelia Haisjackl and Stefan Zugal reports on an investigation focusing on the question of whether a notation that does not contain graphical lookalikes, i.e., a textual notation, can help to avoid problems in understanding declarative process models, and particularly aspects that are present in both imperative and declarative process modeling languages at a graphical level, while having different semantics. The results indicate that even though a textual representation does not suffer from lookalikes, it performed worse in terms of error rate, duration, and mental effort.

The short position papers included the following papers. "Reducing Technical Debt: Using Persuasive Technology for Encouraging Software Developers to Document Code" by Yulia Shmerlin, Doron Kliger, and Hayim Makabee discusses the phenomenon of developers' reluctance to document code, which leads to increased costs of software systems maintenance. It searches for efficient ways of using persuasive technology to encourage programmers to document their code, thus assisting software practitioners and project managers to control and reduce documentation debt. "Conceptual Understanding of Conceptual Modeling Concepts: A Longitudinal Study Among Students Learning to Model" by Dirk van der Linden, Henderik Proper, and Stijn Hoppenbrouwers reports on a longitudinal study investigating the conceptual understanding that students have of common concepts used for conceptual modeling (e.g., actors, processes, goals), as well as if and how these understandings may change over time while a student progresses through the academic curriculum. The authors discuss the seeming lack of connection found between educational stimuli and such changes, and reflect on what this means for the training of people in conceptual modeling. Finally, "What Do Software Architects Think They (Should) Do?" by Sofia Sherman and Naomi Unkelos-Shpigel explores software architects and their perceptions regarding their role and responsibilities. Perception, being a part of and having an effect on cognitive processes and decision making, is explored in order to gain a deeper understanding of what tasks architects find to be included in their role and responsibility. The results highlight several differences between the role of the architect as defined in the existing literature, and the way architects perceive their role.

We hope that the reader will find this selection of papers useful to be informed and inspired by new ideas in the area of cognitive aspects of information systems engineering, and we look forward to future editions of the COGNISE workshop following the two editions we had so far.

June 2014   Irit Hadar
                                                                    Barbara Weber

COGNISE 2014 Organization

Organizing Committee

Irit Hadar   University of Haifa, Israel
Barbara Weber   University of Innsbruck, Austria

Program Committee

Daniel M. Berry   University of Waterloo, Canada
Xavier Franch   Universidad Politecnica de Catalunya, Spain
Marcela Genero   University of Castilla-La Mancha, Spain
Joel Lanir   University of Haifa, Israel
Meira Levy   Shenkar College of Engineering and Design,
                              Israel
Jan Mendling   WU Vienna, Austria
Jeffrey Parsons   Memorial University, Canada
Hajo Reijers   TU Eindhoven, The Netherlands
Pnina Soffer   University of Haifa, Israel
Irene Vanderfeesten   TU Eindhoven, The Netherlands
Stefan Zugal   University of Innsbruck, Austria

Keynote by Stijn Hoppenbrouwers "Pragmatics, Cognition, and Conceptual Modelling; why Process Modelling and Process Mining may Converge"

Third Workshops on New Generation Enterprise and Business Innovation Systems (NGEBIS 2014)

Preface

Innovation is one of the major drivers for enabling European enterprises to compete in global markets, especially in a severe economic downturn. Yet innovation is an elusive term that is often used in an imprecise or generic way. If we consider widely accepted definitions, we can see that they capture only part of the essence of innovation. Furthermore, an innovation process is different from a "usual" business process we find in an enterprise that is (supposedly) well defined in its activities, committed resources, time plan, etc. Conversely, innovation is a creative activity that falls in the category of "wicked problems," i.e., problems difficult to solve because of incomplete, contradictory, and changing requirements.

The New Generation Enterprise and Business Innovation Systems (NGEBIS) workshop, now in its third edition, intends to address the area of information systems dedicated to enterprise and business innovation, traditionally considered too fuzzy and ill-defined to be systematically tackled by using existing information systems and information engineering methods. We expect that the ideas discussed in the workshop will contribute to the development of methods to be used in the implementation of a new generation of information systems capable of supporting innovation, with particular attention to networked enterprises.

In this frame, NGEBIS 2014 included an interesting scientific program with the presentation of the research papers contained in this volume. This edition of NGEBIS received 12 submissions, each of which was reviewed by at least two Program Committee (PC) members in order to supply the authors with helpful feedback. The PC decided to accept four contributions as full papers and two as short papers. The workshop tackled the key issues in the field. The content of innovation and methods to support creation and management of content are addressed in "Leveraging User Inspiration with Microblogging-Driven Exploratory Search" and "Towards Semantic Collective Awareness Platforms for Business Innovation." The paper "Data Mart Reconciliation in Virtual Innovation Factories" considers the problem of monitoring innovation that takes place in the context of networked enterprises, where also decision making is a strategic issue, as discussed in "Cooperative Decision Making in Virtual Enterprises." Important architectural issues are illustrated in "System Architecture of the BIVEE Platform for Innovation and Production Improvement." Finally, the point of view of the end user is addressed in "A Methodology for the Set-Up of a Virtual Innovation Factory Platform." The scientific program of NGEBIS was completed by demo and poster papers, plus a final panel dedicated to the discussion of the hot issues that emerged in the workshop and in the dedicated NGEBIS Forum on LinkedIn.

We would like to thank all authors for their contributions and the members of the Program Committee for their excellent work during the reviewing phase. We would also like to thank the organizers of the CAiSE 2014 conference for hosting the workshop and the BIVEE European Project that is the initiator of this venture that we expect to continue in the future.

June 2014

Michele Missikoff
Johann Eder
Paul Johannes

NGEBIS 2014 Organization

Organizing Committee

Michele Missikoff	Università Politecnica delle Marche, Italy
Johann Eder	Alpen Adria Universität, Austria
Paul Johanneson	Royal Institute of Technology, Sweden

Program Committee

Arne Berre	SINTEF, Norway
Gash Bhullar	TANet, UK
Massimo Canducci	Engineering, Italy
David Chen	UB1, France
Martine Collard	University of the French West Indies and Guiana, France
Claudia Diamantini	Marche Polytechnic University, Italy
Asuman Dogac	SDRC, Turkey
Anders Hjalmarsson	Victoria Institute, Sweden
Nenad Ivezic	NIST, USA
Bernhard Katzy	LIACS, The Netherlands
Larry Kerschberg	GMU, USA
Peter Lindgren	University of Aalborg, Denmark
Leszek Maciaszek	WUE, PL
Simon Schlosser	University of St. Gallen, Switzerland
Erich Schwarz	AAU, Austria
Fabrizio Smith	CNR, Italy
Janis Stirna	KTH, Sweden
Francesco Taglino	CNR, Italy
Konstantinos Zachos	City University London, UK
Martin Zelm	CIMOSA, Germany

4th International Workshop on Information Systems Security Engineering (WISSE 2014)

Preface

As modern information systems support significant areas of the human society, which require storage and processing of sensitive personal and organizational information, security problems of information systems are currently a widespread and growing concern. The scientific community has realized the importance of aligning information systems engineering and security engineering in order to develop more secure information systems.

The International Workshop on Information System Security Engineering (WISSE) aims to provide a forum for researchers and practitioners to present, discuss, and debate on one hand the latest research work on methods, models, practices, and tools for secure information systems engineering, and on the other hand relevant industrial applications, recurring challenges, problems, and industrial-led solutions in the area of secure information systems engineering.

This fourth edition of the workshop, held in Thessaloniki (Greece) on June 17, 2014, was organized in conjunction with the 26th International Conference on Advanced Information Systems Engineering (CAiSE 2014). In order to ensure a high-quality workshop, following an extensive review process, four submissions were accepted as full papers and two as short papers addressing a large variety of issues related to secure information systems engineering.

We wish to thank all the contributors to WISSE 2014, in particular the authors who submitted papers and the members of the Program Committee who carefully reviewed them. We express our gratitude to the CAiSE 2014 workshop chairs, for their helpful support in preparing the workshop. Finally, we thank our colleagues from the Steering Committee, Nora Cuppens, Jan Jürjens, Carlos Blanco, and Daniel Mellado, for initiating the workshop and contributing to its organization.

June 2014

Nadira Lammari
David G. Rosado
Haralambos Mouratidis

WISSE 2014 Organization

General Chair

Haralambos Mouratidis   University of Brighton, UK

Program Chair

Nadira Lammari   Conservatoire National des Arts et Métiers, France

David G. Rosado   University of Castilla-La Mancha, Spain

Steering Committee

Nora Cuppens   Telecom-Bretagne, France

Jan Jürjens   Technical University of Dortmund, Germany

Nadira Lammari   Conservatoire National des Arts et Métiers, France

Haralambos Mouratidis   University of Brighton, UK

David G. Rosado   University of Castilla-La Mancha, Spain

Carlos Blanco   University of Cantabria, Spain

Daniel Mellado   Spanish Tax Agency, Spain

Publicity Chairs

Shareeful Islam   University of East London, UK

Luis Enrique Sánchez   University of Castilla-La Mancha, Spain

Frédéric Gervais   Université Paris-Est Créteil, France

Program Committee

Alban Gabillon   Université de Polynésie Française, Polynésie Française

Antonio Maña   University of Malaga, Spain

Brajendra Panda   University of Arkansas, USA

Carlos Blanco   University of Cantabria, Spain

Christophe Bidan   Supélec, France

Christos Kalloniatis   University of the Aegean, Greece

Daniel Mellado   Spanish Tax Agency, Spain

David G. Rosado	University of Castilla-La Mancha, Spain
Djamel Benslimane	LIRIS, Claude Bernard Lyon I University, France
Eduardo Fernández-Medina	University of Castilla-La Mancha, Spain
Eduardo B. Fernández	Florida Atlantic University, USA
Eric Dubois	CRP Henri Tudor, Luxembourg
Ernesto Damiani	Università degli Studi di Milano, Italy
Esma Aïmeur	Université de Montréal, Canada
Fabio Massacci	Università degli Studi di Trento, Italy
Frédéric Cuppens	Telecom Bretagne, France
Frédéric Gervais	Université Paris-Est Créteil, France
Günther Pernul	University of Regensburg, Germany
Haralambos Mouratidis	University of Brighton, UK
Isabelle Comyn-Wattiau	Cnam Paris, France
Jacky Akoka	Cnam Paris, France
Jan Jürjens	Technical University of Dortmund, Germany
Kamel Adi	Université de Québec en Outaouais, Canada
Luis Enrique Sánchez	University of Castilla-La Mancha, Spain
Mahmoud Barhamgi	LIRIS, Claude Bernard Lyon I University, France
Marc Gondree	Naval Postgraduate School, USA
Mohammad Zulkernine	Queen's University, Canada
Nadira Lammari	Cnam Paris, France
Nineta Polemi	University of Pireaus, Greece
Nora Cuppens	LUSSI/SERES Telecom-Bretagne, France
Paolo Giorgini	University of Trento, Italy
Régine Laleau	LACL, Université Paris-Est Créteil, France
Sabrina De Capitani di Vimercati	Università degli Studi di Milano, Italy
Sakurai Kouichi	Kyushu University, Japan
Shareeful Islam	University of East London, UK
Stefanos Gritzalis	University of the Aegean, Greece
Steven Furnell	Plymouth University, UK
Yves Ledru	LIG, University of Grenoble, France

Auxiliary Reviewers

Ludwig Fuchs	University of Regensburg, Germany
Manolis Maragkoudakis	University of the Aegean, Greece

Keynote by Sokratis Katsikas, University of Piraeus.

Table of Contents

Analysis and Prediction
of Design Model Evolution Using Time Series

Hamed Shariat Yazdi[1], Mahnaz Mirbolouki[2], Pit Pietsch[1],
Timo Kehrer[1], and Udo Kelter[1]

[1] Software Engineering Group, University of Siegen, Germany
{shariatyazdi,pietsch,kehrer,kelter}@informatik.uni-siegen.de
[2] Department of Mathematics, IA University of Shahre-Rey, Iran
m.mirbolouki@srbiau.ac.ir

Abstract. Tools which support Model-Driven Engineering have to be
evaluated and tested. In the domain of model differencing and model
versioning, sequences of software models (model histories), in which a
model is obtained from its immediate predecessor by some modification,
are of special interest. Unfortunately, in this application domain adequate
real test models are scarcely available and must be artificially created.
To this end, model generators were proposed in recent years. Generally,
such model generators should be configured in a way that the generated
sequences of models are as realistic as possible, i.e. they should mimic
the changes that happen in real software models. Hence, it is a necessary prerequisite to analyze and to stochastically model the evolution
(changes) of real software systems at the abstraction level of models. In
this paper, we present a new approach to statistically analyze the evolution of models. Our approach uses time series as a statistical method to
capture the dynamics of the evolution. We applied this approach to several typical projects and we successfully modeled their evolutions. The
time series models could predict the future changes of the next revisions
of the systems with good accuracies. The obtained time series models
are used to create more realistic model histories for model versioning
and model differencing tools.

1   Introduction

Tools, algorithms and methods in the context of Model Driven Engineering
(MDE) have to be evaluated and tested. In this regard test models, which are
concrete artifacts, should be used in order to test various desirable aspects such
as correctness, quality, efficiency and scalability. The problem is that real test
models are scarce and the available ones usually lack the properties which are
required by the tests. The only solution is to employ artificial test models and
to this end, test model generators have been proposed recently. To deliver a test
model, a base model (which can be an empty or a non-empty model) is usually
manipulated using a set of defined edit operations [13]. The manipulation step

L. Iliadis, M. Papazoglou, and K. Pohl (Eds.): CAiSE 2014 Workshops, LNBIP 178, pp. 1–15, 2014.

and the definition of the edit operations are done in a way that the resulting model(s) meets the requirements of the given testing scenario.

In the domain of model differencing [9] and model versioning systems [1], sequences of test models are of great importance and interest. By sequences, we mean revisions $r_1, r_2, \cdots, r_n$ of test models, where each revision is obtained from its immediate predecessor by applying some changes in terms of edit operations. The generated sequences should be "realistic" i.e. they should mimic the "real evolution" that we observe in real software models, otherwise the generated test models are of little value. By evolution, we mean the amount of changes that happen between subsequent revisions of software models. To achieve the goal of creating realistic sequences of test models, we need to (i) properly capture the "evolution" at the abstraction level of design models (class diagrams) in real software systems (ii) stochastically model the evolution (changes) and (iii) finally reproduce the real evolution in the generated sequences.

This paper particularly addresses the steps (i) and (ii). In this regard, we have to answer questions like: Is there time dependency in changes at the abstraction level of design models or the amount of changes between revisions of models are not correlated? If correlation exists, how can we mathematically model it? We prove that there is time dependency in observed changes between design models and the amount of change in one revision is dependent to the previous amount of changes. We show that ARMA time series models are capable of stochastically model such evolution. The results of this work are directly used in our test model generator called the SiDiff Model Generator [12] for producing realistic sequences of test models for MDE tools. Additionally, we will show that the presented time series models can be used for the prediction of future changes in design models of software systems with quite good accuracies.

We believe that the prediction power provides an effective method for planning the evolution of software systems as well as for maintenance of resources; when a large number of changes is predicted, more time and budget can be allocated to a project and testing efforts can be adjusted accordingly. Thus, the proposed time series models can be effectively used in this regard.

The rest of the paper is structured as follows. Section 2 presents how we capture the evolution of design models, while Section 3 explains how the projects that were used for our analysis were selected. Section 4 introduces the time series methodology to stochastically model the evolution of design models in software systems. Section 5 explains how we transform our raw data to make them appropriate for our time series analysis. We also discuss the detail of our analysis there and we show that ARMA models are quite successful to capture the evolution as well as to predict the future changes in design models of software systems. Threats to the validity of our work are discussed in Section 6 and related work is reviewed in Section 7. The conclusion and the summary of our work is provided in Section 8.

2 Usage of Design Models to Capture the Evolution of Java Systems

State-of-the-art approaches to understand the evolution of software systems are based on software metrics and similar static attributes. For example, research which is focused on the growth behavior of software systems is often based on software metrics reflecting the size of a system, e.g. SLOC (Source Lines of Code). In such cases the extent of the changes between revisions (or versions, depending on the granularity of the research) of a software system is expressed as a difference between values of metrics (e.g. see [19]). All further analyses are based on these differences. Unfortunately, such approaches reflect the dynamics of changes in a software system neither completely nor correctly. For instance, if we use the static metric *Number of Classes* (NOC) of a software system and if we observe an increase of 2 of this metric between two subsequent revisions, the actual amount of change might be much larger e.g. 4 existing classes were deleted, 6 new classes were added and 3 classes were moved to other packages. Thus, differences between values of metrics often underestimate the actual amount of change.

This error can be avoided by computing a precise specification of all changes between two revisions, i.e. a **difference**, and by computing metrics of this difference [23]. In our above example we would use the difference metrics *NOC-Deleted*, *NOC-Added* and *NOC-Moved* in which we get 13=(4+6+3) changes in total rather than an increase by 2 of the NOC metric. In other words, to fully understand the evolution of a system in detail, one has to count the occurrences of edit operations that have been applied between subsequent revisions.

To successfully implement the above approach, the differences should be appropriately derived. Obviously, textual differences consisting of insertions and deletions of lines of source code will not be a basis for computing meaningful difference metrics and we have to consider the semantic of the system into account. Thus, we reverse-engineered a set of carefully selected open-source Java systems into their design models.

The meta model which represents this design level information is similar to the class diagrams. The core of the meta model is depicted in Fig. 1. A revision is represented by the root element of type *Project*. Each project can contain several *Packages*. Packages can contain other packages, *Classes* and *Interfaces*. Both interfaces and classes, can contain *Methods* and *Constants*, while a class can furthermore contain *Fields*. Finally, methods can contain *Parameters*. For the sake of more readability, seven element types were omitted from Fig. 1. These elements represent specific constructs used by the Java language. The detailed description of the full meta model is presented in [16].

Having design models at hand, we can compare them using a model differencing tool. A survey of the existing approaches and tools for the problem of model comparison and difference derivation is given in [9]. Many model comparison approaches rely on persistent identifiers to trace model elements in subsequent revisions. However, reverse engineered models do not have persistent identifiers, and there are no other known information about the applied edit operations.

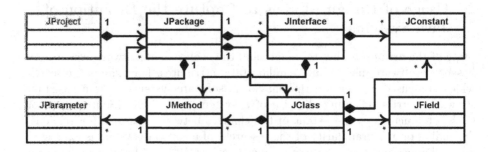

Fig. 1. (Simplified) Meta Model for Design Models of Java Source Code

Thus, we used a similarity-based model comparison engine known as the SiDiff model differencing framework [7] to compute differences. This generic matching engine was carefully adapted to handle our design models. The matching engine basically produces a set of correspondences between elements, which is called a *matching*. Model elements not reported in the matching are considered to be created or deleted between the compared revisions. SiDiff defines five different kinds of edit operations (changes) that might have been applied between two subsequent revisions of r_i and r_{i+1}: **Additions:** An element is inserted in r_{i+1}. **Deletions:** An element is removed from r_i. **Moves:** An element is moved to a different position, i.e. the parent element is changed in r_{i+1}. **Attribute Changes:** An element is updated in r_{i+1}, e.g. the name or visibility of a class is changed. **Reference Changes:** A reference of an element is changed, e.g. a method has a different return type in r_{i+1}.

For each element type ET (see Fig. 1) in our design model and for each edit operation OP defined as above, the corresponding **difference metric**, DM, is the count of occurrences of OP on all model elements of the type ET. The difference metrics represent the structural changes between two models. Since our model representation consists of 15 element types (ETs) and we distinguish 5 edit operations (OPs), a total of 75=(15*5) different difference metrics (DMs) were counted. Thus, between two revisions of design models, the changes are reflected in terms of 75 difference metrics. For design models of a software system, we compute the total number of changes between each two subsequent revisions, as the sum of all difference metrics between them. In this way we obtain a sequence of total numbers of changes. Such sequences are our data sets and our future statistical analyses of evolution will be based on them.

3 Sample Project Selection

For comprehension of evolution of software models and for generalizing the results of our statistical analysis, it is required that we appropriately select our sample space. Therefore, we defined three properties for selection of a project: (P1) The project must be an open-source Java system which is actively used by end users. (P2) The project must be or have been actively developed over a long enough period of time. (P3) For each revision, its design model representation must consist of at least 100 elements, preferably more. These requirements exclude small and trivial projects. We found out that the Helix Software Evolution Data Set (HDS) [20] has 55 projects which meet our requirements.

Eight projects were randomly selected from the HDS. All revisions of each project were checked out from the respective repositories. Then, a parser was used to generate the design model representation of each revision according to the meta model in Fig. 1. If the design models of two consecutive revisions were equal, the second model was ignored. Such cases occurred if only documentation was changed or if the changes affected only the code within a method; i.e. parts of the system which are not represented in the design models. In total 3809 different design models were created. Columns 1-3 of Table 1 contain basic information about the selected projects, respectively the name of the project, mean of the number of elements in models and the number of observations (revisions).

4   Time Series

In this section we provide the theoretical background which is required by our time series analysis. *Time Series* (TS) are sequential measurements or observations of a phenomenon of interest through time [3]. The time dependency of the data gives time series a natural ordering which is used to study them. Having N successive observations at times $t_1, \ldots, t_N$, the TS is denoted by $x = x_{t_1}, \ldots, x_{t_N}$.

In order to extract useful information and statistics out of the data and to discover its underlying dynamics, TS methods are employed. These methods are also used in order to forecast the future of the system. In TS methods, it is usually assumed that the data obey some underlying parametric stochastic processes (i.e. a sequence of random variables) and the parameters are estimated in order to describe the dynamics of the system. Principally it is assumed that an observed time series of $x_1, x_2, \ldots, x_N$ is a sample realization from an infinite population of such time series that could have been generated by such stochastic process $\{X_1, X_2, \ldots, X_k, \ldots\}$ [3][1].

In the study of TS, it is generally assumed that the underlying stochastic process is weakly stationary. Roughly speaking, a process is weakly stationary when there is no change in the trend of the data and also there is no change in the variance of the data through time, i.e. in the TS plot, the data are fluctuating around a fixed level with constant variation. Formally, a stochastic process is *Weakly Stationary* when it is mean and covariance stationary [4]. The variance stationary property is resulted from the covariance stationary as its special case.

There are some methods for transforming non-stationary processes to stationary ones in order to stabilize mean and variance, e.g. trend elimination methods, differencing, seasonal differencing, logarithm and power transformations, etc.

---

[1] When the underlying stochastic process is identified, this property is used by our test model generator [12] in order to create many number of model histories all with the same stochastic behavior.

4.1   ARMA Models

Autoregressive Moving Average models (ARMA) have been successfully used to analyze and stochastically model weakly stationary TS [3]. There, the behavior of the system is assumed to be dependent on: (i) previous observations and (ii) random disturbances in the past. Let $\{x_t\}$ be a weakly stationary TS with mean of μ and let $\tilde{x}_t = x_t - \mu$. Using $ARMA(p, q)$, with p degree of dependency to the past observations and q degree of dependency to the past disturbances, the current state of the model, i.e. $\tilde{x}_t$, is defined by:

$$\tilde{x}_t = \sum_{i=1}^{p} \phi_i \, \tilde{x}_{t-i} + a_t + \sum_{i=1}^{q} \theta_i \, a_{t-i} \tag{1}$$

where $\tilde{x}_{t-i}$; $i = 1, \ldots, p$ are the past observations, a_{t-i}; $i = 1, \ldots, q$ are the past disturbances and a_t is the current disturbance. $\{a_t\}$ is a *White Noise* process i.e. a weakly stationary process with mean 0 and constant variance σ_a^2 and no correlation [4]; additionally when $\{a_t\}$ is normally distributed it is called *Gaussian White Noise*. By definition, we have $\phi_p \neq 0$ and $\theta_q \neq 0$. Equation (1) has $p + q + 2$ unknowns that should be estimated from data: ϕ_i's, θ_i's, μ and σ_a^2 [3].

4.2   Methodology for Time Series Modeling

The methodology for TS modeling can be described by the following steps [11]:

Phase I - Model Identification

M1) *Data Preparation:* In this step, the original data should be investigated for adequacy of use in TS analysis. Data should be transformed into weakly stationary, by possibly removing trend for mean stabilization and also possibly some transformation for stabilizing the variance.

M2) *Model Selection:* The degrees of the $ARMA(p, q)$, i.e. p and q, should be estimated by investigating the *Autocorrelation* (ACF) and the *Partial Autocorrelation* (PACF) functions of the transformed data. In this step some candidates for p and q are suggested by examining the plots of the functions. Let S_{AR} and S_{MA} be the sets of values suggested for p and q respectively. The set of candidate models are created as [11]:

$$M = \{ARMA(p, q) \mid (p, q) \in S_{AR} \times S_{MA} - \{(0, 0)\}\}.$$

A more accurate approach is considering $S_{AR} = \{0, \ldots, p_{max}\}$ and $S_{MA} = \{0, \ldots, q_{max}\}$. Values of p_{max} and q_{max} can be specified by the user or can be estimated using the ACF and the PACF.

Phase 2 - Model Estimation and Testing

M3) *Estimation:* Getting M as the set of candidate models, $p+q+2$ parameters for each model should be estimated (Sec. 4.1) e.g. by using the *Maximum Likelihood Estimation* (MLE) method [3].

M4) *Diagnostics:* The residuals of candidate models should be examined to decide if they are appropriate candidates or not. Ideal residuals are Gaussian white noise with almost no correlation [4] (Sec. 4.1).

   Anderson-Darling Test can be used to check the normality of residuals. The ACF and the PACF of the residuals as well as *Ljung-Box Test* are used to test, if there are correlation between the residuals or not [18].

   If a model is adequate in this respect, it will remain in M. If $M = \{\}$ we can go to Step M2 and try to find new candidates or stop and concluding that there is no TS model capable of describing the dynamics of the data.

M5) *Best Model Selection:* If there is more than one candidate in M, we will have some suitable models to describe the dynamics of the data. The superior model in M is the one with lower *Akaike Information Criterion* (AIC). AIC rewards the goodness of fit and accuracy and penalize the overfitting or complexity of models [18,3].

Phase 3 - Applications

M6) *Forecasting and Simulation:* The best model can be used to predict the future of the system or it can be used to simulate the dynamics of the system and produce infinite similar time series all obeying the same characteristics. More information about forecasting and their calculation as well as their errors rates and bands can be found in [3,4].

4.3   Accuracy of Forecasts

Due to high volatility in our observations (see e.g. Fig. 2 in Sec. 5), the relative error is not suitable for assessing the accuracy of our TS forecasts. The same problem is also reported in [26] when predicting highly volatile Internet traffic. A remedy similar to ours is proposed there as well. In this section we describe the appropriate way of assessing the forecasts' accuracy.

Let x be an observation and $\hat{x}$ be the forecast of x. The relative error, in percent, is defined by $\delta_x = |x - \hat{x}|/|x| \times 100$ where $x \neq 0$. To clarify the problem, now suppose that $x = 1, \hat{x} = 2$ and $y = 100, \hat{y} = 101$ then $\delta_x = 100\%$ and $\delta_y = 1\%$ although for both the absolute error is 1. Therefore, in our case, the Mean Relative Error (MRE) [11] which is defined as $MRE = \frac{1}{N} \sum_{i=1}^{N} \delta_{x_i}$ is not a good interpretation for error rates of forecasts.

To solve this, *Normalized Relative Error* (NRE) is defined. Suppose that X is the set of possible outcomes for x and x is approximated by $\hat{x}$, then the NRE, in percent, is defined as:

$$\eta_x = \frac{|x - \hat{x}|}{max\,(X) - min\,(X)} \times 100 \tag{2}$$

Similarly, let X be the set of all possible outcomes for observations $x_1, \ldots, x_N$ and x_i is approximated by $\hat{x}_i$. The *Normalized Mean Squared Error* (NMSE) is defined by [10]:

$$NMSE = \frac{1}{N} \sum_{i=1}^{N} \frac{(x_i - \hat{x}_i)^2}{(max\,(X) - min\,(X))^2} \tag{3}$$

Equations (2),(3) are used to assess the quality of TS forecasts in Sec. 5.

5 Time Series Models of Changes

As discussed in Sec. 2, we distinguish 5 types of changes, namely additions, deletions, moves, reference changes and updates, for all 15 different model element
types. In each difference between two revisions of a software system, the total
number of changes reflects the extent of evolution of the system.

We use the sequence of the total numbers of changes in each revision as the
basis of our analysis. Although in the theory of TS analysis, the steps M4 and
M5 in Sec. 4.2, i.e. the "diagnostics" and the "best model selection", are enough
to use a TS model in practice, we additionally demonstrate the validity of our
approach and prove the goodness of the proposed TS models, by partitioning
our measured data, $\{x_1, \ldots, x_N\}$, into two disjoint subsets. The first set, called
the "base-set", consists of the observations of x_1 up to x_{N-3}. The second one,
which is called the "hold-out set", consists of the last three observations. We try
to estimate our TS models on the base-set. The fitness of the proposed models is
then checked by comparing their three step forecasts with the actual observations
in the hold-out set. The more the predictions and the actual observations are
close together, the better the model is for simulation and forecasting.

For our analyses, we used the Wolfram Mathematica® 9.0.1 computational
engine and in what follows, we will take the ASM project as the exemplary
project for describing the details of our approach. In total, we had 259 observations for the ASM project. The base-set of this project consists of the first 256
observations, the hold-out set contains the observations 257, 258 and 259.

Figure 2 shows the total number of changes for ASM, observed in its base-set.
The data show high degree of volatility and both big and small changes are
observable. For the sake of comprehension in Fig. 2, we limited the top of the
y-axis to 130, but we do have many bigger changes which are not visible there e.g.
the two biggest peaks with 1973 and 956 changes, respectively at 75th and 189th
observations. Additionally, we observe time periods in which more changes occur
in comparison to other time periods. Such a behavior is a significant obstacle
for applying some simpler statistical methods such as regression analysis. Since
the variance of the data is not stable and the process is not stationary, ARMA
models can not be applied and we first have to make the data weakly stationary
by suitable transformations (Step M1 in Sec. 4.2).

We used the *Box-Cox Transformation* (BCT) for stabilizing the variance[2] of
the data [22,14]. BCT has a transformation parameter (λ) which is obtained by
maximizing the logarithm of the likelihood function of the data. For stabilizing
the mean of data and for removing its trend, *differencing* can be used in which
instead of the original series, $\{x_i\}$, the series $\{x_i - x_{i-1}\}$ is used (Sec. 4).

All of our sample projects were successfully transformed into weakly stationary by subsequently applying the following three transformations: (T1) A
Box-Cox transformation using the optimum λ [3]. (T2) A Difference transformation of degree "one". (T3) The series mean of the previous step is subtracted.

---

[2] Alternative, but in our work less suitable methods is the logarithmic transformation.

[3] For each project, the optimum value of λ is given in the website of the paper at [16].

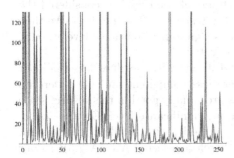

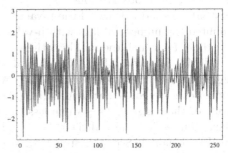

Fig. 2. ASM project - Total number of changes in the hold-out set. For better comprehension, the y-axis is limited to 130 and bigger values are not visible.

Fig. 3. ASM project - Fully transformed series using T1 to T3 transformations

In our exemplary project, Fig. 3 shows the transformed series after application of the three transformations. Apparently, the variance is more stable and the data are fluctuating around the mean of zero. Thus, the transformed series is stationary and meets the requirements of the ARMA process.

As mentioned earlier in Sec. 4.2 (Step M2), investigating the ACF and the PACF of a TS suggests some possible degrees for p and q in $ARMA(p, q)$. But here, in order to prove the applicability of our approach we deliberately used the more accurate way and we chose $p_{max} = q_{max} = 9$. The choice of the value 9 is due to the fact that for all projects, there is no significant correlation after the 9th lag in their ACFs and PACFs. Thus, $S_{AR} = S_{MA} = \{0, \ldots, 9\}$ and the set of our candidate model, M, consists of 99 ARMA models.

For all 99 ARMA models considered for each project, first their parameters were estimated using the MLE method and later their residuals were calculated[4]. If the residuals of a model is Gaussian white noise with almost no correlation, it stays in the candidate set M (Step M4 in Sec. 4.2). For normality of the residuals we used the Anderson-Darling test with the significance level of 0.01.

At first, we disregarded the models with non-normal residuals. Then we discarded the models with significant correlations in residuals. We used the ACF and the PACF considering the first 40 lags and the 0.95 confidence band. In the end we came up with 10 possible candidate models[5] for the ASM project.

To select the best model out of our candidate set, we additionally used the Ljung-Box test. The test is designed to check if the residuals are correlated or not. $\mathcal{H}_0$ states that data are independently distributed i.e. there is no correlation between them and $\mathcal{H}_1$ declares that they are not independently distributed. The number of lags which should be examined affects the power performance of the test. The minimum number of lags is usually approximated by $ln(N)$ where N

---

[4] For each project, the website of the paper [16] contains estimated parameters of all ARMA models, their residual and error bands.

[5] ARMA(1,4), ARMA(2,1), ARMA(2,3), ARMA(2,4), ARMA(3,2), ARMA(3,5), ARMA(3,7), ARMA(6,1), ARMA(6,2) and ARMA(6,4).

is the length of observations [18][6]. For each model, we therefore considered the first 40 lags and calculated the p-value of the test for each of the lags. We then counted the number of lags with p-value less than our significance level of 0.05, i.e. those for which the null hypothesis is rejected.

ARMA(3,5) and ARMA(6,4) had 4 and 9 lags with p-values less than our significance level respectively, so they were less competent and both were no longer considered. Other candidate models are equally good in this respect since none of their lags has a p-value less than our significance level. For the rest of 8 candidates, we checked their AICs and the model with smallest AIC was our final best model (Sec. 4.2, Step M5). We therefore selected ARMA(2,3)[7] as our best model for the ASM project.

In order to additionally prove the usability of our best model, we tried to compare the actual observations in the hold-out set with the three step forecasts of the model. The forecasts can be transformed back to their original form by reversing the order of three steps transformations (T1 to T3) and employing the inverse of the Box-Cox transformation. This respectively results in 5.96, 5.56 and 5.17 as forecasts of the hold-out set of the ASM project.

Since our aim is to forecast "changes" and we assume that there should be some changes to predict, we can round up our real valued forecasts to integers using the ceiling function i.e. $\lceil x \rceil$. Thus, we have 6, 6 and 6 as our final forecasts which is quite close to real observations of 5, 4 and 1 (see Table 1 for the NREs). Therefore, the suitability of our ARMA(2,3) model for capturing the dynamics of design model evolution of the ASM project is approved (see Step M5 in Sec. 4.2).

Generally it is shown that the errors are accumulated for k-step forecasts of ARMA models lose their prediction power as well as their accuracy quickly for farther predictions [3]. Table 1 shows the best chosen model for each project with their three step forecasts as well as the actual number of changes observed in their hold-out sets. The last column of the table (**#LB Lags**) contains the number lags out of 40 considered lags[8], for which their p-value of the Ljung-Box are less than our significance level.

In Table 1, the error rates of forecasts, i.e. NRE and NMSE, are given. They are calculated based on (2) and (3) in which they require the true max of observed changes for each project. For each of NRE and NMSE, first we calculated the errors based on the true max of observed changes as suggested by the formulas. Additionally since very big changes are not very frequent, we tried to be more conservative and used the 0.98-quantile (Q98) of observations instead of the true max in (2) and (3). The reason for choosing Q98 is the fact that it can properly disregard, for all projects, the less frequent big changes. Alternatively, one can exclude big changes using clustering techniques and calculate the max on the rest. Therefore, in Table 1 we report two sets of error rates for NRE and NMSE. The first sub-row shows the error rates calculated based on the true

---

[6] For the CheckStyle project which has the most number of observations, we have $N = 1010$ and $ln(N) \approx 6.918$.

[7] Parameters: $\phi_1 = 0.8207$, $\phi_2 = -0.6621$ & $\theta_1 = 1.7559$, $\theta_2 = 1.3910$, $\theta_3 = -0.5903$.

[8] For DataVision, we had 28 observations. So instead of 40 lags, we considered 28.

max of observations and the second sub-row delivers the results of our more conservative approach using Q98. For example in the ASM project, using true max, NRE and NMSE are $0.05\%, 0.10\%, 0.25\%$ and 2.5715×10^{-6} respectively. When we use Q98 we get $0.37\%, 0.74\%, 1.84\%$ and 1.3616×10^{-4}. Error rates in either of two approaches are quite good typically below 3%.

Generally the error rates of forecasts for the hold-out sets are quite small which proves the appropriateness of our approach in order to capture the true dynamics of design model evolution. The only exception is the Struts project in which its last prediction is not very good. This has two reasons: first, it is the third and the farthest forecast which is the least accurate and second, 9 lags out of 40 did not pass the Ljung-Box test and the residuals are little twisted from the ideal Gaussian white noise (Sec. 4.2, Step M4). These two factors degrade the prediction power of the proposed model for its farthest forecast.

Table 1. All projects - Forecasts vs observations

Project	Mean #Elem	#Obs.	Max of Obs.	Q98 of Obs.	(p,q) of Best ARMA	Obs./ Pred.	NRE: Max/Q98	NMSE: Max/Q98	AIC	#LB Lags
ASM	3635	259	1973	272	(2,3)	5, 4, 1	$0.05\%, 0.10\%, 0.25\%$	2.571×10^{-6}	-0.304	0
						6, 6, 6	$0.37\%, 0.74\%, 1.84\%$	1.362×10^{-4}		
CheckStyle	3181	1010	1366	99	(9,5)	9, 9, 16	$0.22\%, 0.29\%, 0.073\%$	4.651×10^{-6}	-0.307	0
						12, 5, 15	$3.06\%, 4.08\%, 1.02\%$	9.024×10^{-4}		
DataVision	5520	28	105	105	(2,1)	2, 3, 1	$0.96\%, 0.96\%, 7.7\%$	2.034×10^{-3}	-0.691	0
						3, 4, 9	$0.96\%, 0.96\%, 7.7\%$	2.034×10^{-3}		
FreeMarker	6895	339	851	189	(4,7)	2, 2, 2	$0.23\%, 0.0\%, 0.0\%$	1.845×10^{-6}	0.130	0
						4, 2, 2	$1.06\%, 0.0\%, 0.0\%$	3.772×10^{-5}		
Jameleon	3139	285	1107	85	(7,5)	12, 1, 5	$0.54\%, 1.99\%, 1.36\%$	2.030×10^{-4}	0.531	0
						18, 23, 20	$7.14\%, 26.19\%, 17.86\%$	3.519×10^{-3}		
JFreeChart	21583	366	599	244	(9,0)	4, 2, 32	$0.50\%, 1.34\%, 3.51\%$	4.791×10^{-4}	-0.094	0
						7, 10, 11	$1.23\%, 3.29\%, 8.64\%$	2.901×10^{-3}		
Maven	3786	781	2735	346	(8,8)	1, 10, 1	$0.0\%, 0.15\%, 0.0\%$	7.135×10^{-7}	-0.203	0
						1, 6, 1	$0.0\%, 1.16\%, 0.0\%$	4.481×10^{-3}		
Struts	4323	737	715	188	(8,9)	39, 5, 10	$3.22\%, 0.14\%, 30.11\%$	3.057×10^{-2}	-0.134	9
						16, 6, 225	$12.30\%, 0.53\%, 114.97\%$	4.457×10^{-1}		

Due to space limitation, we have put the detailed material of our analysis on the accompanied website of our paper [16]. Estimated parameters for all of the 99 models of each project, residuals of each model, error rates, confidence bands and error bands of the models are all available there.

6   Evaluation and Threat to Validity

In this section we discuss the evaluation of our work and the threats to validity to this research.

Evaluation: The evaluation of our work boils down to the appropriateness of our approach in order to successfully capture the evolution of design models. From the TS theory perspective, correctly performing steps M1 to M5 proves the appropriateness of a TS model to capture the dynamics of the data. In order to additionally prove the usability of the proposed TS models, as we discussed in Sec. 5, we divided our observations into the base and the hold-out sets. The usability of the TS models then additionally approved by comparing their forecasts with the hold-out sets. The forecast error rates were quite small (see Table 1) which approves the use of the proposed TS models in practice.

For the run-time evaluation, one might argue that estimating 99 ARMA models is time-expensive. As we mentioned in Sec. 4.2, the order of promising models can be estimated by investigating the ACF and PACF of the data. This will significantly reduce the number of possible candidate models to just a few. In this paper, we deliberately used 99 ARMA models to generally prove our proposed approach, but in practice much fewer models have to be investigated.

Threat to Validity: The first threat to validity is the accuracy in capturing the evolution of design models. As discussed in Sec. 2, difference metrics have advantages compared to static software metrics. Therefore, the evolution of design models is more accurately described by difference metrics rather than variation in values of static metrics.

The second threat is the accuracy of the calculation of difference metrics. Due to the heuristic nature of the model comparison algorithms, there is no guarantee that the established correspondences between elements are always correct. Error rates for class diagrams were calculated for the SiDiff algorithm which is used in this research [23]. These error rates were generally less than 2%. Because the model type used to represent our design models is similar to a class diagram, we expect similar error rates in our correspondence calculation. They do not have any significant effect on our results and the findings are not distorted.

The third threat is the selection of hold-out sets of length "3". As we mentioned earlier, our primary focus was to suitably capture the evolution dynamics of design models. We used the prediction power as an extra evaluation (see Sec. 4.2) for the suitability of our TS models. Therefore, to this end, a hold-out set with the length of 3 is sufficient. Additionally, it is known that for ARMA models the errors are accumulated for k-step forecasts [3] and the models quickly loose their prediction power and their accuracy. In the case that we have periodic or seasonal effect, the predictions are usually considered with a length equal to k times (usually $k=1,2$) of the length of the period. Since our data does not have any periodic effect, again, hold-out sets with length of 3 are justifiable.

The fourth threat is the external validity, i.e. how our results can be generalized. Our sample set of open source Java projects are quite diverse with respect to application domains, number of revisions, number of elements etc. The process described in this paper is independent of a specific programming language, though. It can be easily applied and used to analyze the evolution of projects which are coded in a different programming language. The only two constraints are: 1) a suitable design model representation for the respective language exists and 2) there is a model differencing tool capable of comparing these models.

It is not clear if comparable results will be observed considering closed source systems, especially where specific programming discipline is practiced. Hence, closed source systems as well as other object-oriented programming languages such as C++ can be the subjects of further research.

7   Related Work

In our previous work [17], we studied how observed frequencies of edit operations can be statistically modeled by statistical distributions. We showed that the Waring and the Beta-Negative Binomial distributions were able to statistically model the frequencies. In that work, we did not considered the "evolution" in real model histories and no time series analysis were considered either.

The following papers used time series analysis to answer research questions in the context of software maintenance and evolution. None of these paper addresses the topic of this paper, i.e. how (design) models of software systems evolve over a long period of time.

Fuentetaja et al. [5] applied time series analysis on growth data of released versions of software systems. They were able to validate the third and eighth law of software evolution, i.e. *Self Regulation* and *Feedback Systems*. Caution is advised when considering the presented results though, because for most systems less than 30 releases were considered, the base data is therefore limited.

Herraiz et al. [6] used time series to analyze the growth of open source software system based on simple size metrics. They concluded that time series analysis is the best method to forecast the evolution of software projects. Their findings showed that design decisions and changes in the history of a project have more influence on its future development than external events.

Kenmei et al. [8] analyzed the connection between change request in large-scale open source software and lines of code to identify trends in the change patterns of large software systems. Based on the trends they were able to predict the need for the number of developers for the next 2 to 6 weeks.

Antoniol et al. [2] presented a time series based method for monitoring and predicting the evolution of clones in a software systems. At first clones were detected within a system based on software metrics, then the identified clones were modeled as time series in a second step. They were able to predict the number of clones in the next release very accurately with this method.

Wu et al. [24] used ARIMA time series models to predict the number of bugs in large software systems on a monthly basis. The results of their prediction were acceptable. Furthermore they could show in their data, that software bug number series are to a certain extent dependent on seasonal and cyclical factors.

Raja et al. [15] used time series approach to predict defects in software evolution. They used monthly defect reports for eight open source projects and built up time series models to predict and analyze software defects.

The following papers address research questions in the area of system evolution which are similar to the one addressed in this paper. However, these works did not use time series or any other advanced mathematical concepts.

Vasa et al. [21] studied the evolution of classes and interfaces in open-source Java software. They analyzed the evolution based on static metrics of released versions of the systems. Their findings suggests that the average metric values are almost stable over histories, i.e. the average size of classes does not change much between released versions. This work also analyzes which types of classes change more than average and concludes that large, complex classes change more. This work does not use time series and makes no attempt to model time-dependency. In [19] Vasa presented an extended and more detailed version of his research.

Xing et al. [25] count the occurrences of language specific edit operations and categorize change levels according to 5 specific profiles, i.e. intense evolution, rapidly developing, restructuring, slowly developing and steady-state. To identify the edit operations they use a model differencing tool known as UMLDiff. Their findings suggest that different change categories are related to different phases of the software development process. Their findings are consistent with ours in that phases of low development activity alternate with phases with high development activity (see Fig. 2). Time series analysis was not used in their research.

8   Summary and Conclusion

In this paper we presented a new approach to statistically analyze the time-dependency of changes in design models of open source Java software systems. This allows us to precisely describe the past evolution of a system as well as to forecast the amount of changes which is to be expected in the next revisions. We applied this approach to several software systems. The evaluation showed that our models could very accurately predict the actual amount of changes in the last 3 revisions of each system; usually with error rates as low as 3% and less. This information can be used to control the time and budget allocated for a project in the near future or to plan regression testing activities. In our own work, we use these stochastic models to configure a test model generator which generates realistic histories of models; these histories are used to test and evaluate various tools which support model driven development.

Acknowledgment. The authors of this paper would like to thank Prof. Lefteris Angelis, head of Statistics and Information System Group at the Aristotle University of Thessaloniki, for his valuable comments and feedback.

The work of the first author, Hamed Shariat Yazdi, is supported by the German Research Foundation (DFG) under grant KE 499/5-1.

References

1. Altmanninger, Seidl, Wimmer: A survey on model versioning approaches. Inter. Journal of Web Information Systems 5(3) (2009)
2. Antoniol, Casazza, Penta, Merlo: Modeling clones evolution through time series. In: Proc. Inter. Conf. Software Maintenance, ICSM (2001)

3. Box, Jenkins, Reinsel: Time series analysis, forecasting and control, 4th edn. Wiley (2008)
4. Brockwell, Davis: Introduction to time series and forecasting, 2nd edn. Springer (2002)
5. Fuentetaja, Bagert: Software evolution from a time series perspective. In: Proc. Inter. Conf. Software Maintenance, ICSM (2002)
6. Herraiz: A statistical examination of the evolution and properties of libre software. In: Proc. Inter. Conf. Software Maintenance ICSM (2009)
7. Kehrer, Kelter, Pietsch, Schmidt: Adaptability of model comparison tools. In: Proc. 27th Inter. Conf. Automated Software Engineering, ASE (2012)
8. Kenmei, Antoniol, Di Penta: Trend analysis and issue prediction in large-scale open source systems. In: Software Maintenance and Reengineering (2008)
9. Kolovos, Ruscio, Paige, Pierantonio: Different models for model matching: An analysis of approaches to support model differencing. In: Proc. ICSE Workshop Comparison & Versioning of Software Models CVSM (2009)
10. Lughofer: Evolving Fuzzy Systems - Methodologies. Advanced Concepts and Applications. Springer (2011)
11. Makridakis, Wheelwright, Hyndman: Forecasting methods and applications, 3rd edn. Wiley (1998)
12. Pietsch, Yazdi, S., Kelter: Generating realistic test models for model processing tools. In: Proc. 26th Inter. Conf. Automated Software Engineering (2011)
13. Pietsch, Yazdi, S., Kelter: Controlled generation of models with defined properties. In: Proceedings of Software Engineering Conference (SE 2012), Berlin, Germany (2012)
14. Porunov: Box-Cox transforamtion and the illusion of the Normality of macroeconomics series. Business Informatics 2 (2010)
15. Raja, Hale, Hale: Modeling software evolution defects: a time series approach. Journal of Software Maintenance and Evolution 21(1) (2009)
16. Yazdi, S., Pietsch: Accompanied material and data for the APSIS 2014 paper (2014), http://pi.informatik.uni-siegen.de/qudimo/smg/APSIS2014
17. Yazdi, S., Pietsch, Kehrer, Kelter: Statistical analysis of changes for synthesizing realistic test models. In: Proc. of Multi-conf. Software Engineering 2013 (SE 2013), Aachen, Germany (2013)
18. Tsay: Analysis of financial time series, 2nd edn. Wiley (2005)
19. Vasa: Growth and change dynamics in open source software systems. Ph.D. dissertation, Swinburne University of Technology (2010)
20. Vasa, Lumpe, Jones: Helix - Software Evolution Data Set (2010), http://www.ict.swin.edu.au/research/projects/helix
21. Vasa, Schneider, Nierstrasz: The inevitable stability of software change. In: Inter. Conf. Software Maintenance, ICSM (2007)
22. Viktor: The Box-Cox transforamtion (March 2010), http://www.mql5.com/en/articles/363
23. Wenzel: Unique identification of elements in evolving models: Towards fine-grained traceability in MDE. Ph.D. dissertation, Uni. Siegen (2011)
24. Wu, Zhang, Yang, Wang: Time series analysis for bug number prediction. In: 2nd Inter. Conf. Software Engineering & Data Mining, SEDM (2010)
25. Xing, Stroulia: Analyzing the evolutionary history of the logical design of object-oriented software. IEEE Trans. Software Engineering 31(10) (2005)
26. Zhou, He, Sun: Traffic predictability based on ARIMA/GARCH model. In: 2nd Conf. Next Generation Internet Design and Engineering (2006)

An Evolutionary Improvement
of the Mahalanobis – Taguchi Strategy
and Its Application to Intrusion Detection

Dimitris Liparas and Evangelia Pantraki

Department of Informatics
Aristotle University of Thessaloniki
54124, Thessaloniki, Greece
{dliparas,pantraki}@csd.auth.gr

Abstract. The Mahalanobis - Taguchi (MT) strategy is a statistical methodology combining various mathematical concepts and is used for diagnosis and classification in multidimensional systems. MT is a very efficient method and has been applied to a wide range of disciplines so far. However, its feature selection phase, which uses experimental designs (orthogonal arrays), is susceptible to improvement. In this paper, we propose a methodology that incorporates MT and a Genetic Algorithm (MT-GA), with the latter being used both for optimizing the feature selection step of MT and for determining the most suitable training set. As an application domain for testing the proposed methodology, we utilized Intrusion Detection Systems (IDS). IDS play an increasingly important role in network security technology nowadays and more and more research is being directed towards building effective diagnostic models. We test the effectiveness of MT-GA by applying it to a well-known intrusion detection dataset and by comparing its performance to that of the typical MT strategy and of other classifiers. The results indicate the benefits of using MT-GA.

Keywords: Mahalanobis – Taguchi strategy, Genetic algorithm, Data mining, Intrusion detection systems.

1 Introduction

The Mahalanobis-Taguchi (MT) strategy, proposed by Genichi Taguchi, is a rather new methodology used for diagnosis and classification in multidimensional systems [35]. It combines various mathematical and statistical concepts like Mahalanobis distance (MD), Gram-Schmidt orthogonalization process and experimental designs. Principally, the MT strategy develops a univariate measurement scale from a group of "normal" or "healthy" observations. The scale is then used to signify the level of abnormality of a set of "abnormal" cases in reference to the "normal" population. The scale is assessed for its ability to effectively recognize the abnormal cases in the way that larger values of the scale indicate abnormality. The selection of an optimal subset of the most important variables from the original variable set is a very essential part of the MT strategy.

L. Iliadis, M. Papazoglou, and K. Pohl (Eds.): CAiSE 2014 Workshops, LNBIP 178, pp. 16–30, 2014.

Feature selection as a procedure can influence the classification process in various ways. [40] indicate that the choice of features used to represent patterns that are presented to a classifier affects, among other things, the accuracy of the learned classification algorithm, the time needed for learning a classification function, the number of examples needed for learning and the cost associated with the features. Within the framework of the typical MT strategy, feature selection is achieved with the use of experimental designs (orthogonal arrays-OA) and a measure called signal-to-noise (S/N) ratio. Through the selection of the most useful variables the final measurement scale is formulated. Although the primary goal of the methodology is the construction of a measurement scale, the strategy can also serve as a binary classifier with the determination of a proper abnormality threshold.

Despite the fact that the MT strategy has been successfully applied to an extensive range of disciplines, such as manufacturing and financial crisis forecast (see for example [5,19]), [39] have provided a review, analysis and criticism of MT strategy. Among other things, they illustrate that the use of OA and experimental design methods does not ensure that the optimal feature subset is obtained. Moreover, they suggest that the MT strategy could be modified to include a better dimensionality reduction algorithm. In a response discussion to [39], [1] express doubts about whether the OA method is the most suitable for feature selection within the MT strategy. A solution to these concerns and suggestions would be the development of a hybrid methodology, consisting of the MT strategy and a feature selection technique as a replacement for the OA-S/N ratio method. [24] have proposed an approach that uses binary particle swarm optimization for the feature selection problem.

In this study, we propose the use of a Genetic Algorithm (GA) for optimizing the procedure of selecting the most useful variables. In addition, we proceed further in the application of the GA by formulating a GA-based refinement of the training set as well. In other words, the GA is used both for selecting the optimal variable subset and for extracting the best training subset, in terms of classification accuracy. In order to explore the potential of the proposed hybrid methodology, we opted to apply it to the intrusion detection domain.

With the enormous growth of computer networks usage and the huge increase in the number of applications running on top of it, network security is becoming increasingly more important [36]. Intrusion detection systems (IDS) are devices that monitor network or system activities for known or potential threats and make reports on any intrusion attempts. A system that possesses all the features of an IDS, but also has the ability to try and stop intrusions, is called intrusion prevention system (IPS). Because of the increasing dependence on information systems and the potential impact of intrusions against those systems, IDPSs (Intrusion detection and prevention systems) have become a necessary addition to the security infrastructure of nearly every organization [29].

Over the years, a wide range of machine learning techniques have been applied, in order to propose and build efficient IDS. [37] have provided a thorough literature review of the different methodologies employed for intrusion detection purposes. Among others, Neural Networks [28], Naïve Bayes [30], Decision Trees [7] and Support Vector Machines [41] can be listed. Other studies focus on the idea of proposing hybrid (for example [31]) or ensemble classifiers (see for instance [23,8]) that combine several algorithms, in order to improve the performance of an intrusion detection model.

In order to evaluate MT-GA in the intrusion detection domain, we apply it to a benchmark intrusion detection data set. However, our intention is not to limit the use of the method simply as an intrusion detection model, but to provide a way of demonstrating the benefits of using MT-GA, by utilizing intrusion detection as an application domain. The application results show that it compares successfully to other MT-related and intrusion detection methods.

The rest of the paper is organized as follows: In Section 2 we provide the theoretical background of our study. We describe the notions and steps of MT strategy, as well as some basic GA concepts. In Section 3 we present the proposed MT-GA methodology. In Section 4 we provide the experimental results from the application of MT-GA and of other methods to the NSL-KDD intrusion detection data set. Finally, concluding remarks are provided in Section 5.

2   Theoretical Background

In 2.1 and 2.2 we present briefly the MT strategy's key features and operational steps. For more details see ([35]).

2.1   The Mahalanobis Distance

The Mahalanobis distance (MD) forms the basis of MT. In the MT strategy's context, there are two different ways to calculate the MD: the Mahalanobis Taguchi System (MTS) and Mahalanobis Taguchi Gram-Schmidt process (MTGS). Here we work only with the MTGS version of the strategy, because of the fact that it can handle cases of multicollinearity (a term that refers to strong linear correlations between the variables). Hence, in the MTGS version of the MT strategy the MD is calculated as follows:

Assume that a sample dataset consists of k variables and n cases (the size of the sample). Let x_{ij} be the value of the ith variable ($i = 1, ..., k$) on the jth case ($j = 1, ..., n$). These variables are standardized by

$$z_{ij} = (x_{ij} - m_i)/s_i \tag{1}$$

whereby m_i and s_i we denote the sample mean and standard deviation respectively of the ith variable.

The matrix of the standardized values z_{ij} is then transformed by the Gram-Schmidt orthogonalization process ([15]) and the MD is calculated using the derived Gram-Schmidt vectors u_{ij} as in the following equation:

$$MD_j = (1/k)\sum_{i=1}^{k}(u_{ij}^2/s_i'^2) \tag{2}$$

whereby s_i' we denote the standard deviation of the ith variable after the application of the Gram-Schmidt orthogonalization process. MD_j expresses the distance of the jth case from a reference (zero) point.

2.2   Steps of MT Strategy

The MT strategy consists of the following steps:

Step 1: Construction of the measurement scale.
First we must determine the variables that define which cases are considered "healthy" or "normal" and which are not. Then we collect all the necessary data from all the variables in the data set. Next, we standardize the values of the variables. Finally, we compute the Mahalanobis distance (MD) values only for the healthy cases using the Gram-Schmidt orthogonalization process.

Step 2: Validation of the scale.
In the next step, we compute the MD values for the "abnormal" cases (observations that do not belong to the "healthy" group). The values of the variables in these "abnormal" cases are standardized by using the mean values and standard deviations of the corresponding variables from the "healthy" group. The effectiveness of the scale is validated with the use of a simple rule: the MD values for the "abnormal" observations must be higher than those for the "healthy" ones (they must be further from the center of the group of "healthy" cases than any of the "healthy" cases are).

Step 3: Feature selection.
In this step, we use orthogonal arrays (OAs) and signal-to-noise (S/N) ratios in order to determine and select the most important variables from the original variable set.
    An OA is an experimental design matrix ([12]). Each row represents an experimental run and contains the levels of various factors in order to study the effects of the factors on a prespecified response variable. Each column of the OA represents a factor of the experiment. In the context of MT strategy, we consider the inclusion or exclusion of each variable as a factor with two levels. Hence, the experiment considers k factors and the level of a factor shows when a variable participates or not in the analysis. For each of these runs, the MD values are calculated for the "abnormal" cases as in step 2, but using only the specified variables. The MD values are then used to calculate the value of a S/N ratio, which is the response variable for each different run. The set of the most

important variables is obtained by computing and evaluating the gain in the values of the S/N ratios. For a variable, the gain in S/N ratio is the difference between the average S/N ratio when the variable is used in OA and the average S/N ratio when the variable is not used in OA. If the gain is positive, then that variable is useful ([34]).

Step 4: Reconstruction of the scale.
After selecting the subset of the most useful features, the measurement scale is reconstructed using only these variables. The reconstructed scale is used to compute the MD values for any unknown cases, in order to take any corrective actions, if necessary. The final measurement scale can be used for future diagnosis after defining an appropriate threshold.

2.3   Genetic Algorithm

The Genetic algorithm (GA) is a part of the field of evolutionary computing, which is an artificial intelligence area dealing with combinatorial optimization problems. Its theory is based on the process of natural selection and uses procedures inspired by biological evolution (mutation, selection and crossover). The basic idea behind GA is that it tries to evolve a group of candidate solutions (*population*) towards a globally optimal solution. The possible solutions are expressed by coded representations called *chromosomes*. Although there are quite a few encodings for the chromosomes, most usual is the binary one ([38]). In the binary encoding, every chromosome corresponds to bits of 0s and 1s. For example, in the feature selection context, the value 0 shows that a feature does not participate in the computations and the value 1 shows that it does. In this way, a candidate solution can easily be transformed into its representing chromosome.

The process of optimizing the problem's solution is evolved through a number of successive computational runs of the algorithm, called *generations*. In each generation, after all the candidate solutions have been processed, their *fitness* is evaluated by an appropriate function, called *fitness function*. The best solutions (in terms of fitness) are selected, in order to generate the next generation's population. There are many methods for the selection of the fittest solutions, such as roulette wheel selection, tournament selection, elitism and others. Elitism is the process of retaining some of the best solutions unaltered to the next population. This method increases the performance of GA and enables it to converge quicker to the optimal solution. In the next step, genetic operators such as *crossover* and *mutation* are used for the creation of the next population. In crossover, we exchange parts between two or more chromosomes (called *parents*) in order to produce a new chromosome (called *offspring*). A user-defined parameter called *crossover probability* or *crossover rate* indicates the frequency of the crossover operator. There are many crossover techniques, such as one point crossover, two point crossover and others. In mutation, parts of the chromosome are altered with a new chromosome as a result. In binary encoding, for example, bit values of 1 are changed to 0 and vice versa. Again, a parameter called *mutation probability* or *mutation rate* influences the frequency of the mutation operator.

The GA is executed until a stopping condition is satisfied (for instance, the maximum number of generations is reached or the fitness function's value no longer improves). For more details about the basic notions of GA, see ([9]).

In the relevant literature, there are various GA applications for feature selection (see for example [13,22]). Moreover, we find several studies dealing with hybrid GA-based methodologies in intrusion detection (see for example [32,18]).

3   Description of the Proposed MT-GA Methodology

The proposed MT-GA methodology is largely based on US Patent 2006/0230018 A1, published by [11]. The inventors describe a method that, among other things, is suitable for identifying a desired variable subset from a plurality of variables. The basic notion of the method is the application of a genetic algorithm on a set of data records, which have been defined as "normal" data or "abnormal" data based on predetermined criteria. The Mahalanobis distance values for the "normal" and "abnormal" data are calculated using the variable subsets derived from the application of the genetic algorithm. The fitness function evaluates the deviation of the Mahalanobis distance values between the "normal" and "abnormal" data records. The goal of the genetic algorithm is to maximize this deviation. Predetermined parameters, like an improvement rate, may be used to decide whether the genetic algorithm converges to the optimized variable subset.

The approach of the above-described procedure was incorporated into our MT-GA methodology. However, we expanded the idea by not only applying the genetic algorithm to the variables of the training data set (MT-GA$_{variables}$), but to the cases as well (MT-GA$_{variables-cases}$). In this way, we are able to reduce the size of the training set substantially, while at the same time aiming to maximize the classification accuracy of the model. The issue of suitably reducing the number of cases in the training set was addressed in two previous studies ([20,21]). We proposed the use of the MT strategy in conjunction with two clustering algorithms, the two step cluster analysis and the PAM (Partitioning Around Medoids) algorithm. For details about the two step cluster analysis and the PAM algorithm see ([4,16]) respectively. The two clustering algorithms are used in our studies for determining the most suitable training set, in terms of training classification accuracy, with very satisfactory results. In this study, by choosing to apply the GA to the training set's group of cases, we are essentially aiming to expand this notion. The procedures of MT-GA are described as follows.

Regarding MT-GA$_{variables}$, we start by setting up the GA with a proper input parameter set (population, number of generations, crossover rate, mutation rate, etc). We then proceed to initialize the GA feature selection procedure with the random selection of a population of candidate solutions and the encoding of the solutions into the equivalent chromosomes. In our case, the binary encoding method was used. Therefore, a chromosome bit of value 1 indicates that the corresponding variable is selected and a bit of value 0 indicates that it is not. After the population of the chromosomes is formulated, we construct the MD measurement scales from the "healthy" cases, using the feature subset derived from each chromosome. Then the measurement scales are validated by computing the MD values for the training set's "unhealthy" cases. The GA's fitness function evaluates each variable subset. The basic idea behind the fitness function in our method is to minimize the overlapping MD distributions in the "healthy" and "unhealthy" groups. It is almost certain that, for a particular problem, it is very difficult to select an appropriate group of "healthy" cases, able to construct a MD measurement scale that effectively distinguishes between the "healthy" and "unhealthy" groups. As a consequence, we end up with MD distributions with overlapping regions, e.g. many "normal" observations with extreme MD values are identified as "abnormal" and vice versa. Hence, we designed a fitness function aiming to maximize the percentage of the "unhealthy" cases, whose MD values are higher than the maximum MD value of the "healthy" group. The equation for the fitness function is given as follows:

$$Fitness function = (n(u > maxMDh)/n(u)) \qquad (3)$$

where
$n(u > maxMDh)$ = number of "unhealthy" cases with MD values higher than the maximum MD value of the "healthy" group's cases
$n(u)$ = total number of "unhealthy" group's cases.

After the evaluation of the solutions, if a predetermined rule for the termination of the GA is not satisfied, the method proceeds to create the next generation's population. This is achieved with the use of the proper selection strategy and the application of the GA operators (crossover, mutation). When the algorithm has converged to the optimal variable subset, the procedure ends.

With the use of the optimal variable subset, we are able to construct the final MD measurement scale from the "healthy" cases and validate it with the "unhealthy" cases. Furthermore, we plot the training set's Receiver Operating Characteristic (ROC) curve ([17]) and based on it, we define an appropriate threshold, meaning that we choose a MD value that provides a reasonable trade-off between sensitivity and specificity (see Section 4.2). With the use of the threshold, we determine the classification accuracy results for the training and test sets.

Finally, regarding the MT-GA$_{variables-cases}$ method, after the GA application to the training set's variables and the determination of the optimal variable subset, we apply exactly the same GA procedure, but this time to the training set's cases. The flowchart of MT-GA$_{variables}$ is depicted in Figure 1.

4   Application of MT-GA Method to Intrusion Detection Data

4.1   Data Set Description − Experimental Design

KDDCUP'99 is an intrusion detection benchmark data set, having been extensively used during the last decade for the evaluation of intrusion detection

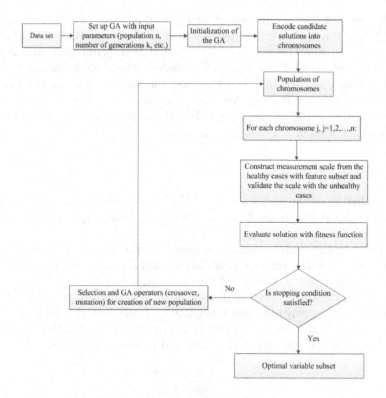

Fig. 1. Procedure of MT-GA$_{variables}$

systems. However, in a recent study [36] some of the underlying problems of KDDCUP'99 that affect the performance and evaluation of the systems have been highlighted. Hence, they proposed a new data set, NSL-KDD, which does not include any duplicate records in the training and test sets and therefore, the classifiers will not be biased towards more frequent records.

The NSL-KDD data set, as provided in http://nsl.cs.unb.ca/NSL-KDD/, is already split into training and test sets and consists of 25192 (13449 normal/"healthy" and 11743 attack/"unhealthy") training cases and 22544 (9711 normal/"healthy" and 12833 attack/"unhealthy") test cases. Each case is comprised of 41 features and 1 binary class attribute (normal/"healthy" or attack/"unhealthy"). More specifically, from the set of 41 variables/features, 38 are numeric and 3 are categorical. We note that in this study we chose to work only with the group of numeric variables.

Apart from applying the original MT and the proposed MT-GA methods to the NSL-KDD data set, we also employed the version that combines the original methodology with the PAM clustering algorithm (which is used for refining the training data set). In this way, we are able to make a direct comparison of the MT-GA results to the corresponding results of a methodology that employs similar concepts.

Finally, we selected a number of well-known machine learning classifiers, namely Naïve Bayes ([14]), J48 decision tree ([25]), Support Vector Machine (SVM) ([3]), Random Forest ([2]) and Multilayer Perceptron ([27]) and applied them to the NSL-KDD data set as well, in order to form a comparison basis to the MT-GA method. All the algorithms were implemented using functions in the statistical language R ([26]). We note here that for a fair comparison, the 5 machine learning classifiers were applied to the reduced data set that resulted from the application of MT-GA$_{variables-cases}$.

4.2   Accuracy Measures

For the evaluation of the performance of MT-GA, as well as of the other methods employed in this study, we used two basic accuracy measures, namely sensitivity and specificity.

Sensitivity in the study's context estimates the proportion of "unhealthy" or attack cases, which are correctly identified as such (i.e. number of true attack / (number of true attack + number of false normal)).

Specificity on the other hand estimates the proportion of "healthy" or normal cases, which are correctly identified (i.e. number of true normal / (number of true normal + number of false attack)). Moreover, we used the Relative Sensitivity (RS) measure, which was proposed by [33] and is defined as

$$RS = \frac{sensitivity}{specifity} \tag{4}$$

The above metric is used to determine whether a classifier's ability to predict the two different (positive and negative) classes is balanced or not. If the RS value is much higher or much lower than 1, then this is an indication that the method is biased. Generally, we are looking for RS values around 1.

Finally, for each classifier we plotted the ROC curve for the corresponding test set and used the Area Under the Curve (AUC) to measure the discriminability between the test set's different classes and consequently, to evaluate the performance of each method.

4.3   Genetic Algorithm Parameters

One issue concerning the GA's context is the selection of the optimal control parameters for a given problem. The performance of the GA is dependent on the configuration of these parameters. Although there have been some studies addressing this matter (see for instance [6,10]), there is no general theory or rules that one should follow.

In order to determine the best GA setting for our study, we opted to conduct several experiments with different input parameters for each one. Then we selected the setting that gave us the best results (in terms of training accuracy) and fitted best into the problem. The GA parameter setting that we selected to use is the following: population size 100, number of generations 150, crossover

rate 0.8, mutation rate 0.01, one-point crossover and elitism (20% of the population size). The stopping condition for the GA is that the algorithm reaches the
maximum number of generations (150) or that the fitness function's value does
not improve during the last 50 generations.

4.4   Experimental Results

Table 1 summarizes the results from the application of all MT-related methods
described in the previous Sections. The second and third rows contain the number of variables and cases (respectively) in the training set, after the application
of each method. We notice that:

- The original MT method achieves a 47.3% reduction in the number of variables (20 out of 38), due to the application of the OA-S/N ratio feature
  selection method. The same proportion of feature reduction is attained by
  MT-PAM.
- MT-GA$_{variables}$ reduces the size of the original variable set by 73.6% (10 out
  of 38).
- Regarding the cases, the application of the PAM clustering algorithm results
  in only a few discarded cases (54 cases out of a total of 25192).
- The application of GA to the cases, using only the optimal feature subset
  derived from the initial GA application to the variables of the training set,
  keeps only 8.6% (2158 cases out of 25192) of the training set's cases, i.e. we
  achieve a reduction of 91.4% in the cases.

Regarding the accuracy results for the training and test sets (fourth and
fifth row of Table 1 respectively): MT-GA$_{variables-cases}$ is very robust when
compared to the other methods. It outperforms them both in terms of training
(96.1%) and test accuracy (91.8%), while using a greatly reduced training set.
In the sixth and seventh row of Table 1 the sensitivity and specificity results

Table 1. Performance comparison for MT-related methods

Results/Method	MT$_{original}$	MT-PAM	MT – GA$_{variables}$	MT-GA variables−cases
Number of variables (optimal subset)	20	20	10	10
Number of cases (training set)	25192	25138	25192	2158
Training accuracy	93.6%	93.7%	92.3%	96.1%
Test accuracy	84.7%	87.3%	91%	91.8%
Sensitivity	79.6%	84.2%	91.6%	93.4%
Specificity	91.4%	91.5%	90.2%	89.7%
AUC	0.947	0.951	0.949	0.954
Relative Sensitivity	0.87	0.92	1.01	1.04

for all MT-related methods are given. We observe that although the specificity performance of MT-GA$_{variables-cases}$ is a little bit lower than that of the other methods, the improvement in the sensitivity value (MT$_{original}$: 79.6% ; MT-GA$_{variables-cases}$: 93.4%) is evident. Finally, in the eighth and ninth rows of Table 1 we provide the AUC and the Relative Sensitivity results, respectively. The four methods perform very highly in terms of the AUC, yet we do not notice great differences between them. Furthermore, we see that the two MT-GA methods are almost perfectly balanced in their ability to predict the "healthy" and "unhealthy" cases, since they achieve RS values very close to 1.

In Table 2 we compare the results of MT-GA$_{variables-cases}$ (which performed the best among the four MT-related methods) to these of five well-known machine learning methods (namely Naïve Bayes, J48, Random Forest, SVM and Multilayer Perceptron). First of all, we observe that while Random Forest achieves perfect training classification accuracy, it does not perform equally well in the test accuracy measure. As for the other methods, they yield quite promising test classification accuracy results, but still MT-GA$_{variables-cases}$ outperforms them all. In general, the five machine learning methods predict the positive class (specificity values > 90%) with greater effectiveness than the negative class (sensitivity values ranging from 69.6% - 88.7%). This is also obvious from their RS values, ranging from 0.75 to 0.85 (except for J48, whose RS value is very close to 1). Essentially, with the exception of the training accuracy and specificity measures, MT-GA$_{variables-cases}$ yields better results than the selected machine learning techniques in all performance aspects.

Table 2. Performance of MT-GA method vs. other machine learning algorithms

Results/Method	MT-GA variables−cases	Naïve Bayes	J48	Random Forest	SVM	Multilayer Perceptron
Training accuracy	96.1%	95.1%	99.7%	100%	98%	99.8%
Test accuracy	91.8%	79.3%	89.9%	81.4%	81.1%	84.2%
Sensitivity	93.4%	69.6%	88.7%	73.3%	72.1%	78.3%
Specificity	89.7%	92.1%	91.5%	92.3%	92.9%	92%
AUC	0.954	0.858	0.884	0.941	0.825	0.936
Relative Sensitivity	1.04	0.75	0.97	0.79	0.77	0.85

In Figure 2, a bar chart depicting the test accuracy of each method, sorted in descending order, is displayed. It is evident that both of the MT methods that use GA perform in this regard better.

In order to test whether the test accuracy of all the methods under comparison has statistically significant differences, we conducted a Cochran's Q-test which is suitable for multiple related binary samples. Here the samples are essentially the results of classification (1=Correct/0=False) of each one of the 9 methods (4 MT-based methods and 5 machine learning classifiers). Since all methods are

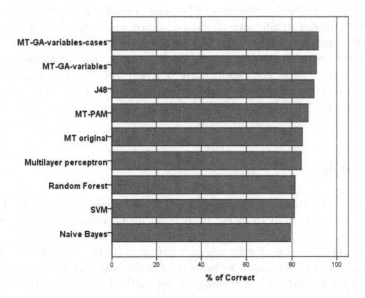

Fig. 2. Percentage of correct classifications of all methods (test accuracy)

Table 3. Results of the pairwise test for significant differences between method's test accuracy (MTGA/V/C: MT-GA$_{variables-cases}$; MTGA/V: MT-GA$_{variables}$)

	MTGA/V	J48	MT-PAM	MT original	Multilayer Perceptron	Random Forest	SVM	Naïve Bayes
MTGA/V/C	no dif	√	√	√	√	√	√	√
MTGA/V	–	no dif	√	√	√	√	√	√
J48		–	no dif	√	√	√	√	√
MT-PAM			–	no dif	no dif	√	√	√
MT$_{original}$				–	no dif	√	√	√
Multilayer Perceptron					–	√	√	√
Random Forest						–	no dif	√
SVM							–	√

applied to the same test set, the classification results are considered related. The test gave significance p<0.001, showing that overall, the 9 methods have statistically significant differences in their test accuracy. In order to locate the pairs of methods that are significantly different, we accompanied the Cochran's test with a pairwise test (as implemented in the statistical software SPSS/PASW). This pairwise test uses a correction for the significance of multiple comparisons in order to control the family-wise error. The pairs of methods that have significant differences (adjusted significance<0.05) are shown with a tick in Table 3.

We notice that, for example, the test performance of Naïve Bayes has significant differences with all the other methods. It is also important to mention that MT-GA$_{variables-cases}$ is not significantly different only from MT-GA$_{variables}$. But despite this we must note that the application of MT-GA$_{variables-cases}$ has the advantage of reducing the size of the training set even more than MT-GA$_{variables}$.

5   Conclusions

In this study, we propose the hybrid MT-GA methodology and we explore its capabilities and potential by using it to build an effective intrusion detection model. By combining a decision-making methodology based on simple statistical methods (MT strategy) with a search heuristic (GA), we build an effective classification model that improves both the classification accuracy and the size of the data set needed for the training of the method (optimal variable subset and reduced number of training instances).

It is important to note that the advantage of MT strategy is that it does not treat "abnormal" cases as if they belong to the same population, different from the population of normal cases. Instead, it implies that each "abnormal" case, which in our study is an intrusion, is a unique case. With all the different types of intrusion events that exist nowadays, the method maps well to intrusion detection problems and its philosophy is in accordance with realistic situations. Another advantage of MT is its ability to construct a scale of abnormality so as to characterize the degree of severity of "abnormal" conditions, which is also quite realistic in the intrusion detection area.

There are various suggestions that can be made for future work. For example, alternative fitness functions can be used for the GA, in order to investigate the behaviour of the algorithm in different settings and conditions. Furthermore, we can integrate the MT strategy with other feature selection techniques and test the performance of each resulting model. It will provide some insight into the capabilities of our proposed methodology, as well as a more direct comparison basis. Finally, the application of MT-GA to data sets that contain noise and require further data cleaning (for example, software engineering data sets) should also be investigated.

References

1. Abraham, B., Variyath, A.M.: Discussion paper to "A review and analysis of the Mahalanobis-Taguchi system". Technometrics 45(1), 22–24 (2003)
2. Breiman, L.: Random Forests. Machine Learning 45(1), 5–32 (2001)
3. Chang, C., Lin, C.: LIBSVM: a library for support vector machines (2001), Software available at http://www.csie.ntu.edu.tw/cjlin/libsvm

4. Chiu, T., Fang, D., Chen, J., Wang, Y., Jeris, C.: A robust and scalable clustering algorithm for mixed type attributes in large database environment. In: Proc. of the Seventh ACMSIGKDD International Conference on Knowledge Discovery and Data Mining, San Francisco, CA, ACM (2001)

5. Cudney, E.A., Paryani, K., Ragsdell, K.M.: Identifying Useful Variables for Vehicle Braking Using the Adjoint Matrix Approach to the Mahalanobis-Taguchi System. Journal of Industrial and Systems Engineering 1(4), 281–292 (2008)

6. DeJong, K.A., Spears, W.M.: An Analysis of the Interacting Roles of Population Size and Crossover in Genetic Algorithms. In: Schwefel, H.-P., Männer, R. (eds.) PPSN 1990. LNCS, vol. 496, pp. 38–47. Springer, Heidelberg (1991)

7. Depren, O., Topallar, M., Anarim, E., Ciliz, M.K.: An intelligent intrusion detection system (IDS) for anomaly and misuse detection in computer networks. Expert Systems with Applications 29, 713–722 (2005)

8. Giacinto, G., Perdisci, R., Rio, M.D., Roli, F.: Intrusion detection in computer networks by a modular ensemble of one-class classifiers. Information Fusion 9, 69–82 (2008)

9. Goldberg, D.E.: Genetic algorithms in search optimization and machine learning. Addison-Wesley, Reading (1989)

10. Grefenstette, J.J.: Optimization of Control Parameters for Genetic Algorithms. IEEE Trans. Systems, Man, and Cybernetics SMC-16(1), 122–128 (1986)

11. Grichnik, A.J., Seskin, M.: Mahalanobis Distance Genetic Algorithm (MDGA) Method and System. US Patent 2006/0230018 A1 (October 12, 2006)

12. Hedayat, A.S., Sloane, N.J.A., Stufken, J.: Orthogonal Arrays. Theory and Applications. Springer, New York (1999)

13. Huang, C.-L., Wang, C.-J.: A GA-based feature selection and parameters optimization for support vector machines. Expert Systems with Applications 31, 231–240 (2006)

14. John, G., Langley, P.: Estimating continuous distributions in Bayesian classifiers. In: Proc. of the Eleventh Conference on Uncertainty in Artificial Intelligence, pp. 338–345 (1995)

15. Johnson, R.A., Wichern, D.W.: Applied Multivariate Statistical Analysis. Prentice-Hall (1992)

16. Kaufman, L., Rousseeuw, P.J.: Clustering by means of Medoids. Statistical Data Analysis Based on the L1-Norm and Related Methods. In: Dodge, Y. (ed.), pp. 405–416. North-Holland (1987)

17. Krzanowski, W.J., Hand, D.J.: ROC Curves for Continuous Data. Chapman & Hall/CRC, London (2009)

18. Lee, C.H., Shin, S.W., Chung, J.W.: Network Intrusion Detection Through Genetic Feature Selection. In: Proc. of the Seventh ACIS International Conference on Software Engineering, Artificial Interlligence, Networking, and Parallel/Distributed Computing, SNPD 2006 (2006)

19. Lee, Y.C., Teng, H.L.: Predicting the financial crisis by Mahalanobis-Taguchi system - Examples of Taiwan's electronic sector. Expert Systems with Applications 36, 7469–7478 (2009)

20. Liparas, D., Angelis, L., Feldt, R.: Applying the Mahalanobis-Taguchi strategy for software defect diagnosis. Automated Software Engineering 19(2), 141–165 (2012)

21. Liparas, D., Laskaris, N., Angelis, L.: Incorporating resting state dynamics in the analysis of encephalographic responses by means of the Mahalanobis-Taguchi strategy. Expert Systems with Applications 40(7), 2621–2630 (2013)

22. Min, S.-H., Lee, J., Han, I.: Hybrid genetic algorithms and support vector machines for bankruptcy prediction. Expert Systems with Applications 31(3), 652–660 (2006)

23. Mukkamala, S., Sung, A.H., Abraham, A.: Intrusion detection using an ensemble of intelligent paradigms. Network and Computer Applications 28, 167–182 (2005)
24. Pal, A., Maiti, J.: Development of a hybrid methodology for dimensionality reduction in Mahalanobis-Taguchi system using Mahalanobis distance and binary particle swarm optimization. Expert Systems with Applications 37, 1286–1293 (2010)
25. Quinlan, J.: C4.5: Programs for Machine Learning. Morgan Kaufmann (1993)
26. R Development Core Team: R: A language and environment for statistical computing, R Foundation for Statistical Computing, Vienna, Austria (2005), http://www.R-project.org ISBN 3-900051-07-0
27. Ruck, D., Rogers, S., Kabrisky, M., Oxley, M., Suter, B.: The multilayer perceptron as an approximation to a Bayes optimal discriminant function. IEEE Transactions on Neural Networks 1(4), 296–298 (1990)
28. Ryan, J., Lin, M.-J., Miikkulainen, R.: Intrusion Detection with Neural Networks. In: Advances in Neural Information Processing Systems, vol. 10. MIT Press, Cambridge (1998)
29. Scarfone, K., Mell, P.: Guide to Intrusion Detection and Prevention Systems (IDPS), Computer Security Resource Center (National Institute of Standards and Technology) (800-94) (2007)
30. Scott, S.L.: A Bayesian paradigm for designing intrusion detection systems. Computational Statistics and Data Analysis 45, 69–83 (2004)
31. Shon, T., Moon, J.: A hybrid machine learning approach to network anomaly detection. Information Sciences 177, 3799–3821 (2007)
32. Stein, G., Chen, B., Wu, A.S., Hua, K.A.: Decision tree classifier for network intrusion detection with GA-based feature selection. Paper presented at the Proc. of the 43rd Annual Southeast Regional Conference, Kennesaw, Georgia (2005)
33. Su, C.T., Hsiao, Y.H.: An evaluation of the robustness of MTS for imbalanced data. IEEE Trans. Knowl. Data Eng. 19(10), 1321–1332 (2007)
34. Taguchi, G., Rajesh, J.: New trends in multivariate diagnosis. Sankhya 62, 233–248 (2000)
35. Taguchi, G., Jugulum, R.: The Mahalanobis-Taguchi strategy - A pattern technology system, p. 234. John Wiley and Sons (2002)
36. Tavallaee, M., Bagheri, E., Lu, W., Ghorbani, A.: A detailed analysis of the KDDCup 1999 dataset. In: Proc. of 2009 IEEE International Symposium on Computational Intelligence in Security and Defense Applications (CISDA 2009), USA (2009)
37. Tsai, C.-F., Hsu, Y.-F., Lin, C.-Y., Lin, W.-Y.: Intrusion detection by machine learning: a review. Expert Systems with Applications 36(10), 11994–12000 (2009)
38. Whitley, D.: A genetic algorithm tutorial. Statistics and Computing 4(2), 65–85 (1994), doi:10.1007/BF00175354
39. Woodall, W.H., Koudelik, R., Tsui, K.L., Kim, S.B., Stoumbos, Z.G., Carvounis, C.P.: A review and analysis of the Mahalanobis-Taguchi system. Technometrics 45(1), 1–30 (2003)
40. Yang, J., Honavar, V.: Feature subset selection using a genetic algorithm. IEEE Intelligent Systems 13(2), 44–49 (1998)
41. Zhang, Z., Shen, H.: Application of online-tradining SVMs for real-time intrusion detection with different considerations. Computer Communications 28, 1428–1442 (2005)

Zero-Knowledge Private Computation
of Node Bridgeness in Social Networks

Maryam Shoaran[1] and Alex Thomo[2]

[1] University of Tabriz, Tabriz, Iran
mshoaran@tabrizu.ac.ir
[2] University of Victoria, Victoria, Canada
thomo@cs.uvic.ca

Abstract. We introduce a bridgeness measure to assess the influence of a node in the connectivity of two groups (communities) in a social network. In order to protect individual privacy upon possible release of such information, we propose privacy mechanisms using zero-knowledge privacy (ZKP), a recently proposed privacy scheme that provides stronger protection than differential privacy (DP) for social graph data. We present techniques to compute the parameters required to design ZKP methods and finally evaluate the practicality of the proposed methods.

1 Introduction

For many years, complex graphs of real world networks have been studied from different aspects. One major line of research is devoted to the study of the role of nodes and edges in the functionality and structure of networks. Various indices have been proposed to characterize the significance of nodes and edges. Centrality measures like *degree*, *closeness*, and *betweenness* (cf. [30,12] are used to determine the role of a node in maintaining the overall and partial connectivity of networks. Various definitions of *bridgeness* are proposed to measure the role of nodes or edges [28,5]. Here we define another notion of bridgeness to measure the effect of a node (particularly a linchpin[1]) on the connectivity of two groups (communities) in a social graph.

Graph characteristics like bridgeness, similar to other aggregate information, are usually released to the third parties for different purposes. The release of such information can violate the privacy of individuals in networks. Among the wide range of definitions and schemes presented to protect data privacy, ϵ-Differential Privacy [11,9,10] (DP for short) has attracted significant attention in recent years. By adding appropriate noise to the output of a function, DP makes it practically impossible to infer the presence of an individual or a relationship in a database using the released information. While DP stays resilient to many attacks on tabular data, it might not provide sufficient protection in the case of

---

[1] Highly active members of networks usually act as linchpins. For example, highly active authors or actors in collaborative networks play an essential role in connecting sub-units (*communities* or *clusters*) [25].

L. Iliadis, M. Papazoglou, and K. Pohl (Eds.): CAiSE 2014 Workshops, LNBIP 178, pp. 31–43, 2014.
© Springer International Publishing Switzerland 2014

graph data, particularly social networks (c.f.[13,19]). Because of the extensive correlation between the nodes in social networks, not only the participation of a node (or relationship), but also the evidences of such participation have to be protected. And this requires a higher level of protection than DP (cf. [19]).

We explain the matter using an example. Suppose there are two groups of nodes g_1, g_2, and a node p in a social graph G. We want to publish the number of triangles between these three disjoint components of G. Suppose that there is a triangle between Bob in g_1, Alice in g_2, and p. As a consequence of such relationship, some friends of Bob make connections to Alice and to p, thus creating new triangles. What we want to protect is Bob's edge to Alice. From a counting perspective the existence or not of this edge can change the answer by 1. DP works in this case by ensuring that for any true answer, c or $c-1$, the sanitized answer would be pretty much the same. However, this is not strong enough; the existence of Bob's edge influenced the true number of triangles not just by 1, but by a bigger number as it caused more triangles to be created by Bob's and Alice's friends.

In order to provide sufficient data privacy for social graphs, Gehrke, Lui, and Pass proposed "zero-knowledge privacy" (ZKP) in [13]. The definition of ZKP is based on classes of aggregate functions. ZKP guarantees that any additional information that an attacker can obtain about an individual by having access to the privatized output is indistinguishable from what can be inferred from some sampling-based (approximate) aggregates. The level of privacy in ZKP mechanisms is defined using the sample complexity of aggregates. For instance, suppose in the Bob's example above the network size is 10000 and the sample size is $\sqrt[3]{10000^2} = 464$. With such a sampling rate of almost 0.05 the evidence provided by say 10 more triangles caused by Bob's connections will essentially be protected; with a high probability, none of these 10 triangles will be in the sample.

In this paper, we use ZKP to provide connection privacy when releasing inter-community bridgeness of linchpin nodes. We define a natural notion of bridgeness in social graphs and present a ZKP mechanism for private release of bridgeness. Specifically, we propose methods to compute the sample complexity of the bridgeness function. In order to achieve this, we present techniques to express the function as averages of specially designed, synthetic attributes on the nodes of graphs. Then, we derive precise prescriptions on how to construct ZKP mechanisms for the function.

The rest of the paper is organized as follows. We discuss related work in Section 2. In Section 3, we define our notion of bridgeness. Section 4 contains an elaborate discussion of the background concepts related to zero-knowledge privacy. In Section 4, we present ZKP mechanisms for bridgeness measure. Also in this section, we present our methods to compute the sample complexity of bridgeness. Section 6 presents a numeric evaluation of the ZKP mechanism, and Section 7 concludes the paper.

2   Related Work

Massive networks, graphs, and graph databases have become very popular for more than a decade (c.f. [14,2,35,3,15,31,32,4]). Computing statistics and summarizations for graph data is very important as it is difficult to understand their structure using other means (c.f. [36,39,18,37,38,16,22]).

The common goal of privacy preserving methods is to learn from data while protecting sensitive information of the individuals. k-anonymity for social graphs (cf. [23,6,21,7]) provides privacy by ensuring that combinations of identifying attributes appear at least k times in the dataset. The problem with k-anonymity and other related approaches, e.g. l-diversity [24], is that they assume the adversary has limited auxiliary knowledge. Narayanan and Shmatikov [27] presented a de-anonymization algorithm and claimed that k-anonymity can be defeated by their method using auxiliary information accessible by the adversary.

Among a multitude of different techniques, differential privacy (DP) [1,8,11,9] has become one of the leading methods to provide individual privacy. Various differentially private algorithms have since been developed for different domains, including social networks [17,29]. However as already shown, DP can suffer in social networks where specific auxiliary information, such as graph structure and friendship data, is easily available to the adversary. Important works showing the shortcomings of DP are [19,20].

Gehrke, Lui, and Pass in [13] present the notion of zero-knowledge privacy that is appealing for achieving privacy in social networks. Zero-knowledge privacy (ZKP) guarantees that what can be learned from a dataset including an individual is not more than what is learned from sampling-based aggregates computed on the dataset without that individual.

Shoaran, Thomo, and Weber in [34], use ZKP to release connectedness statistics between groups in a social network. This is different from the current work, where we aim at privately releasing bridgeness statistics for linchpin nodes.

Regarding DP, [33] discusses the utility of the statistics distorted to satisfy DP. Here we consider the utility of the bridgeness statistics distorted to satisfy ZKP, and conclude that the utility is better than that of the ZKP mechanism in [34].

3   Graphs and Bridges

We denote a graph as $G = (V, E)$, where V is the set of nodes and $E \subseteq V \times V$ is the set of edges connecting the nodes. We consider $\mathcal{S} \subset 2^V$ to be a set of disjoint node groups of size r or more that a social network wants to release statistics about. Let g' and g'' be two groups in $\mathcal{S}$ and p be a node in G such that $p \notin g'$ and $p \notin g''$.

Definition 1. *The* bridgeness *of node p on two groups g' and g'' is defined as*

$$B_p(g', g'') = \frac{|\{(p, v', v'') : v' \in g', v'' \in g'', \ and \ \{(v', v''), (p, v'), (p, v'')\} \subseteq E\}|}{|g'| \cdot |g''|}$$

Intuitively, bridgeness $B_p(g', g'')$ is the fraction of the number of (p, v', v'') triangles that exist over the number of all possible (p, v', v'') triangles.

Throughout the paper, we will refer to the bridgeness as B_p whenever g' and g'' are clear from the context.

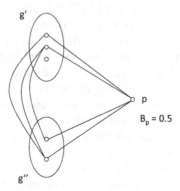

Fig. 1. Bridgeness

Example 1. Fig. 1 shows a graph G with two groups g' and g'', having three and two nodes, respectively. There are three edges connecting the nodes of g' and g'', and four edges connecting node p to the nodes of g' and g''. These edges form three triangles in total between p and two groups. The number of all possible such triangles is $3 \times 2 = 6$. Therefore, we have $B_p = \frac{3}{6} = 0.5$.

4   Background on ϵ-Zero-Knowledge Privacy

Zero-Knowledge Privacy (ZKP) introduced by [13] is an enhanced privacy scheme that guarantees stronger privacy protection, compared to other currently well-known methods such as differential privacy (DP), especially in social networks. Due to the extensive influence in such networks, the presence of a single element (node or connection) can lead to the creation of several new elements in the network. Therefore, in such settings a privacy mechanism needs to protect not only the participation of an element in the network, but also the evidence of such a participation, i.e. the presence of new elements created under the influence of the element in focus.

ZKP requires that whatever an intelligent agent (*adversary*) can discover from sanitized output of the mechanism is not more than what can be discovered by an assumed equally gifted agent that only has access to some sampling-based aggregate information. The latter agent is sometimes referred as *simulator*[2]. Thus, ZKP framework is defined based on a class of aggregate functions *agg*, such that the specification of those functions is used to define the privacy level of the ZKP mechanism. For example, the sample size in the class of aggregate

---

[2] In this context, adversaries and simulators are in fact some algorithms.

functions directly affects the accuracy of the output (as it will be defined later in this section). Using such parameters we can design a ZKP mechanism that can provide a similar privacy protection. The importance of agg functions in the definition of ZKP is that by sampling data, the evidence of participation is also protected.

Let G be a graph. We denote by G_{-*} a graph obtained from G by removing a piece of information (for example an edge). G and G_{-*} are called *neighboring graphs*.

Let M be the privacy mechanism that securely releases the answer to a query on graph G, and let A be the intelligent agent that operates on output $M(G)$, that is, privatized answer, trying to breach the privacy of some individual. Let S be a simulator as capable as A, that would have access to some aggregate information obtained by an algorithm $T \in agg$. Note that, the assumed algorithm T only would compute *approximate* answers to aggregate functions by sampling graph G_{-*}, i.e. the graph that misses the piece of information which should be protected.

Definition 2. *(Zero-Knowledge Privacy [13]) The mechanism M is ϵ-zero-knowledge private with respect to agg if there exists a $T \in agg$ such that for every adversary A, there exists a simulator S such that for every G, every $z \in \{0,1\}^*$, and every $W \subseteq \{0,1\}^*$, the following hold:*

$$Pr[A(M(G), z) \in W] \leq e^\epsilon \cdot Pr[S(T(G_{-*}), z) \in W]$$
$$Pr[S(T(G_{-*}), z) \in W] \leq e^\epsilon \cdot Pr[A(M(G), z) \in W]$$

where probabilities are taken over the randomness of M and A, and T and S.

This definition assumes that both the adversary and simulator have access to some general and easily accessible auxiliary information z, such as graph structures or the groups the individuals belong in.

Note that, based on the application settings the selection of k – the number of random samples – in agg algorithms is very important. It should be chosen so that with high probability very few of the elements (nodes or edges) related with the element whose information has to be private will be chosen. We will often index agg by k as agg_k to stress the importance of k. To satisfy the ZKP definition, a mechanism should use $k = o(n)$, say $k = \sqrt{n}$ or $k = \sqrt[3]{n^2}$, where n, the number of nodes in the database, is sufficiently large (see [13]). DP is a special case of ZKP where $k = n$.

Achieving ZKP. Let $f : \mathbf{G} \rightarrow \mathbb{R}^m$ be a function that produces a vector of length m from a graph database. For example, given graph G, the set of groups S, and a node p, f produces B_p measures for m pairs of groups. We consider the L_1-Sensitivity to be defined as follows.

Definition 3. *(L_1-Sensitivity) For $f : \mathbf{G} \rightarrow \mathbb{R}^m$, the L_1-sensitivity of f is*

$$\Delta(f) = \max_{G', G''} ||f(G') - f(G'')||_1$$

for all neighboring graphs G' and G''.

Another essential definition is that of "sample complexity".

Definition 4. *(Sample Complexity [13]) A function $f : Dom \to \mathbb{R}^m$ is said to have (δ, β)-**sample complexity** with respect to agg if there exists an algorithm $T \in agg$ such that for every $D \in Dom$ we have*

$$Pr[\|T(D) - f(D)\|_1 \leq \delta] \geq 1 - \beta.$$

T is said to be a (δ, β)-sampler for f with respect to agg.

This definition bounds the probability of error between the randomized computation (approximation) of function f and the expected output of f. Basically, functions with low sample complexity (smaller δ and β) can be computed more accurately using random samples from the input data.

When the released information, as typical, is real numbers, the ZKP mechanism *San* achieves the privacy by adding noise to each of the numbers independently.

Let $Lap(\lambda)$ be the zero-mean Laplace distribution with scale λ, and variance $2\lambda^2$. The scale of Laplace noise in ZKP is properly calibrated to the sample complexity of the function that is to be privately computed. The following proposition expresses the relationship between the sample complexity of a function and the level of zero knowledge privacy achieved by adding Laplace noise to the outputs of the function.

Proposition 1. *([13]) Suppose $f : \mathbf{G} \to [a, b]^m$ has (δ, β)-sample complexity with respect to agg. Then, mechanism*

$$San(G) = f(G) + (X_1, \ldots, X_m),$$

where $G \in \mathbf{G}$, and $X_j \backsim Lap(\lambda)$ for $j = 1, \cdots, m$ independently, is

$$\ln \left((1 - \beta)e^{\frac{\Delta(f) + \delta}{\lambda}} + \beta e^{\frac{(b-a)m}{\lambda}} \right)$$

$-$ZKP with respect to agg.

5   ZKP Mechanism for Bridgeness

In this section we design a ZKP mechanism to privately release B_p measures. Let f be the function that given graph G, set $\mathcal{S}$, and node p produces a c-dimensional vector of B_p measures (numbers), where $c = \binom{|\mathcal{S}|}{2}$.

Let $f = [f_1, \ldots, f_t]$ be the vector that is to be privately released. We apply a separate San_i (ZKP) mechanism, for $i \in [1, t]$, to each of the elements of f. Let us assume that each San_i provides ϵ_i-ZKP for f_i with respect to agg_{k_i}, where $k_i = k(n)/t$ and $n = |V|$. Then, based on the following proposition, f will be $(\sum_{i=1}^t \epsilon_i)$-ZKP with respect to $agg_{k(n)}$, where $k(n) = \sum_{i=1}^t k_i$.

Proposition 2. *(Sequential Composition [13]) Suppose San_i, for $i \in [1, n]$, is an ϵ_i-ZKP mechanism with respect to agg_{k_i}. Then, the mechanism resulting from composing[3] San_i's is $(\sum_{i=1}^n \epsilon_i)$-ZKP with respect to $agg_{(\sum k_i)}$.*

---

[3] A set of computations that are separately applied on *one* database and each provides ZKP in isolation, also provides ZKP for the set.

Consider G and G_{-e}, where G_{-e} is a neighboring graph of G obtained from G by removing edge e. The goal of our mechanism is to protect the privacy of the connections between the nodes of different groups. Therefore, we assume that the removed edge e is an edge between two nodes of two different groups in S. Removing such an edge from G can change by at most 1 the numerator of a B_p measure in G_{-e}. Note that this change affects only one B_p measure in the whole graph G_{-e}. Therefore, the sensitivity of any B_p function is $\Delta(B_p) = 1/r^2$, where r is the minimum group size in S.

Suppose $B_p(g, g')$ is an element of f, where g and g' are groups in S. Let $San = B_p(g, g') + Lap(\lambda)$ be a ZKP mechanism which adds random noise selected from $Lap(\lambda)$ distribution to the output of $B_p(g, g')$ in order to achieve ZKP. Our goal here is to come up with the right λ to achieve a predefined level of ZKP.

Based on the definition of ZKP, one should first know the sample complexity of B_p function. For this, without any change in semantics, we will express B_p so that it computes an average rather than a fraction of two counts. Then, using the *Hoeffding* inequality (cf. [26]) we compute the sample complexity of B_p.

Expressing B_p. In addition to regular node attributes (if any), we introduce $|S|$ new boolean attributes, one for each group in S. We denote each new attribute by upper-case I indexed by a group id. Each attribute I_g is a boolean vector of dimension $|g|$, where each dimension corresponds to a node in g. A node v in graph G will have $I_g(v)[u] = 1$, where $u \in g$, if $\{(v, u), (p, v), (p, u)\} \subseteq E$, and $I_g(v)[u] = 0$, otherwise. For each pair of groups g and g' we can show that

Proposition 3

$$B_p(g, g') = \frac{\sum_{v \in g, u \in g'} I_{g'}(v)[u]}{|g| \cdot |g'|}$$
$$= \frac{\sum_{v \in g', u \in g} I_g(v)[u]}{|g| \cdot |g'|}$$

Therefore, the $B_p(g, g')$ measure can be viewed as the average of $I_{g'}(v)[u]$'s or $I_g(v)[u]$'s.

ZKP Mechanism. Let $G = (V, E)$ be a graph enriched with boolean attributes as explained above. We would like to determine the value of $\lambda > 0$ for the $Lap(\lambda)$ distribution which will be used to add random noise to $B_p(g, g')$ measures included in f. For this, first we compute the sample complexity of B_p to be able to use Proposition 1 and establish an appropriate value for λ.

Let T be a randomized algorithm in agg_k, the class of randomized algorithms that operates on an input graph G. To randomly sample a graph G, algorithm T would uniformly select $k = k(n)/t$ random nodes from V, read their attributes, and retrieve all edges[4] incident to these k sample nodes.[5] Node p is assumed to be included in the set of randomly selected nodes.

---

[4] Clearly, only non-dangling incident edges, whose both end nodes have been sampled, will be retrieved.

[5] For other possible methods of graph sampling see for example [13].

With this sampling, the nodes in the groups of S, the edges between them, and the edges incident to node p would be randomly sampled as well. Let us assume that we have a sample of each group and edges between groups and the size of a sample group g is k_g. Then, algorithm T would approximate B_p using sampled graph data. For the sample complexity of $B_p(g, g')$, since we expressed it as averages, we can use the Hoeffding inequality as follows.

$$Pr[\|T(g, g') - B_p(g, g')\| \leq \delta] \geq 1 - 2e^{-2(k_g \times k_{g'})\delta^2}$$

From this and Definition 4, we have that B_p function has $\left(\delta, 2e^{-2K\delta^2}\right)$-sample complexity with respect to agg_k, where $K = (k_g \times k_{g'})$.

Now we make the following substitutions in the formula of Proposition 1: $\beta = 2e^{-2K\delta^2}$, $\Delta(B_p(g, g')) = 1/r^2$, $b - a = 1$, and $m = 1$. From this, we have that mechanism San is

$$\ln\left(e^{\frac{1/r^2 + \delta}{\lambda}} + 2e^{\frac{1}{\lambda} - 2K\delta^2}\right) \text{ -ZKP}$$

with respect to agg_k.

Similarly to DP, we set λ, the Laplace noise scale, to be proportional to "the error" as can be measured in ZKP method by the sum of the sensitivity and sampling error, and inversely proportional to the ZKP privacy level.

$$\lambda = \frac{\Delta(B_p) + \delta}{\epsilon} = \frac{1}{\epsilon}\left(\frac{1}{r^2} + \frac{1}{\sqrt[3]{K}}\right)$$

Regarding δ, we can consider for instance a sample size $k(n) = \sqrt[3]{n^2}$, and have $\delta = \frac{1}{\sqrt[3]{K}}$.

From all the above, the privacy level obtained will be

$$\ln\left(e^{\frac{1/r^2 + \delta}{\lambda}} + 2e^{\frac{1}{\lambda} - 2K\delta^2}\right) = \ln\left(e^\epsilon + 2e^{\frac{\epsilon}{1/r^2 + 1/\sqrt[3]{K}} - 2\sqrt[3]{K}}\right)$$

$$\leq \ln\left(e^\epsilon + 2e^{-\sqrt[3]{K}}\right)$$

$$\leq \epsilon + 2e^{-\sqrt[3]{K}}.$$

Thus, we have that by adding noise randomly selected from the $Lap\left(\frac{1}{\epsilon}\left(\frac{1}{r^2} + \frac{1}{\sqrt[3]{K}}\right)\right)$ distribution to B_p, San will be $\left(\epsilon + 2e^{-\sqrt[3]{K}}\right)$-ZKP with respect to agg_k.

Example 2. Let graph G be a social graph with ten million participants/nodes ($|V| = n = 10,000,000$), and g, g', and g'' be three node groups in S. Suppose the requested output vector is

$$f = \langle B_p(g', g''), B_p(g, g'') \rangle.$$

and suppose that the minimum group size in S is $r = 100$.

Assume we would like to have for f a ZKP mechanism expressed with respect to an acceptable agg_k, where

$$k(n) = \sqrt[3]{10,000,000^2} = 46,416.$$

To privately release the first output in f, a randomized algorithm T would uniformly select

$$k_1 = k(n)/2 = \sqrt[3]{10,000,000^2}/2 = 23,208.$$

nodes and approximate the value of $B_p(g', g'')$ using sample data.

The actual value of function $B_p(g', g'')$ is computed on G. Suppose that the size of the sample groups corresponding to g' and g'' are $k_{g'} = 500$ and $k_{g''} = 100$, respectively. Therefore, we have $K = 50,000$. Let (δ_1, β_1) be the sample complexity of $B_p(g', g'')$ where

$$\delta_1 = \frac{1}{\sqrt[3]{K}} = \frac{1}{\sqrt[3]{50,000}} = 0.0271.$$

$$\beta_1 = 2e^{-2K(\delta_1)^2} = 2e^{-2*(50,000)*(0.0271)^2} = 2.55 * 10^{-32}.$$

The sensitivity of f is

$$\Delta(f) = \frac{1}{r^2} = \frac{1}{100^2} = 0.0001.$$

Now, if we would like to use a mechanism which is 0.1-ZKP, we can add random noise selected from a Laplace distribution with scale

$$\lambda_1 = \frac{\Delta(f) + \delta_1}{\epsilon} = \frac{0.0001 + 0.0271}{0.1} = 0.272$$

to the actual value of $B_p(g', g'')$. With this noise scale, the ZKP privacy level of the mechanism is precisely

$$\epsilon_1 \leq \left(\epsilon + 2e^{-\sqrt[3]{K}}\right) = \left(0.1 + 2 * e^{-37}\right) \approx 0.1$$

with respect to agg_k.

6 Evaluation

In our methods, the amount of noise added to the output is independent of the database, and it only depends on the function we compute and their sensitivities. Therefore, the following analysis is valid for any database.

6.1   Parameters Affecting Noise Scale

Sampling error δ is an important factor specifying λ based on the formula of noise scale $\lambda = \frac{\Delta(f)+\delta}{\epsilon}$. The error in turn has reverse connection with the size of group samples and therefore, with the sample size and size of the database graph. Recall that throughout the paper we considered the error to be $\delta = \frac{1}{\sqrt[3]{K}}$, where $K = k_{g'} * k_{g''}$.

Fig. 2 illustrates the relationship between the noise scale λ and the parameter K. In this figure we assumed that the minimum group size is $r = 100$, and the ZKP-level ϵ is 0.1. The figure shows that as parameter K (the product of group sample sizes) decreases from five hundred thousand to one thousand the noise scale increases non-linearly to the amounts that are not practical in our setting. Therefore, our proposed ZKP mechanism is perfect for big databases with large sample sizes. Moreover, even $K = 500,000$ implies some sample group sizes, for example $k_{g'} = 1000$ and $k_{g''} = 500$, which are reasonable in social graphs with only millions of participants (see Example 2). Hence, we conclude that the proposed ZKP mechanism works well with small as well as large data graphs.

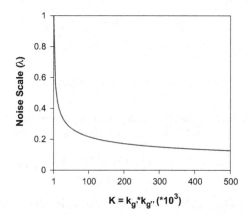

Fig. 2. Relationship between noise scale and sample group size

6.2   The Noise

We present the analysis in this section in order to provide a better understanding of the amount of noise added to outputs. The cumulative distribution function of Laplace distribution in an interval $[-z, z]$ is computed as follows,

$$Pr(-z \le x \le z) = \int_{-z}^{z} \frac{1}{2\lambda} e^{\frac{-|x|}{\lambda}} \, dx = 1 - e^{\frac{-z}{\lambda}}.$$

Let $pr = Pr(|x| \le z)$. Value z for a specified cumulative probability pr can be calculated using the above equation as

$$z = -\lambda \cdot \ln(1 - pr) = -\frac{\Delta(f) + \delta}{\epsilon} \cdot \ln(1 - pr).$$

Figure 3 illustrates the maximum absolute noise z as a function of cumulative probability pr for three different values of δ when $\epsilon = 0.1$ and $\Delta(f) = 0.0001$. Each point (pr, z) on the curve for a given δ means that

> pr percent of the time the random noise has an absolute value of at most z.

For example, for $\delta = 0.02$ we have that 50% of the time the absolute value of noise is at most 0.14, and 75% of the time it is at most 0.28. These values of δ are practical as our outputs are fractions.

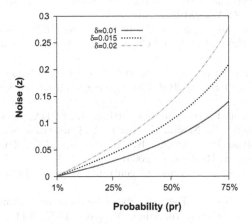

Fig. 3. Probability vs noise

7 Conclusions

We addressed zero-knowledge privacy for releasing the bridgeness measure of graph nodes. The application of our technique is crucial in order to have a secure public release of graph properties. We introduced methods to compute the ZKP parameters, specifically the sample complexity. We showed that the proposed technique is practically useful for large as well as small data graphs. This is different from the mechanism presented in [34], which is useful only for very large social graphs. As future work we aim at charting the landscape of other various graph statistics in order to determine their sample complexity and see for what sizes of graphs it makes sense to use ZKP from a utility point of view, i.e. without distorting too much the released statistics.

References

1. Blum, A., Dwork, C., McSherry, F., Nissim, K.: Practical privacy: the sulq framework. In: PODS, pp. 128–138 (2005)
2. Calvanese, D., De Giacomo, G., Lenzerini, M., Vardi, M.Y.: Reasoning on regular path queries. SIGMOD Record 32(4), 83–92 (2003)

3. Calvanese, D., De Giacomo, G., Lenzerini, M., Vardi, M.Y.: View-based query processing: On the relationship between rewriting, answering and losslessness. Theor. Comput. Sci. 371(3), 169–182 (2007)
4. Calvanese, D., De Giacomo, G., Lenzerini, M., Vardi, M.Y.: Query processing under glav mappings for relational and graph databases. PVLDB 6(2), 61–72 (2012)
5. Cheng, X., Ren, F., Shen, H., Zhang, Z., Zhou, T.: Bridgeness: A local indexon edge significance in maintaining global connectivity. J. Stat. Mech. 10, 10011 (2010)
6. Chester, S., Kapron, B.M., Ramesh, G., Srivastava, G., Thomo, A., Venkatesh, S.: k-anonymization of social networks by vertex addition. In: ADBIS, pp. 107–116 (2011)
7. Chester, S., Kapron, B.M., Ramesh, G., Srivastava, G., Thomo, A., Venkatesh, S.: Why waldo befriended the dummy? k-anonymization of social networks with pseudo-nodes. In: SNAM (2012)
8. Dwork, C.: Differential privacy. In: Bugliesi, M., Preneel, B., Sassone, V., Wegener, I. (eds.) ICALP 2006, Part II. LNCS, vol. 4052, pp. 1–12. Springer, Heidelberg (2006)
9. Dwork, C.: Differential privacy: A survey of results. In: Agrawal, M., Du, D.-Z., Duan, Z., Li, A. (eds.) TAMC 2008. LNCS, vol. 4978, pp. 1–19. Springer, Heidelberg (2008)
10. Dwork, C.: Differential privacy in new settings. In: SODA, pp. 174–183 (2010)
11. Dwork, C., McSherry, F., Nissim, K., Smith, A.: Calibrating noise to sensitivity in private data analysis. In: Halevi, S., Rabin, T. (eds.) TCC 2006. LNCS, vol. 3876, pp. 265–284. Springer, Heidelberg (2006)
12. Freeman, L.C.: A set of measures of centrality based on betweenness. Sociometry 40(1), 35–41 (1977)
13. Gehrke, J., Lui, E., Pass, R.: Towards privacy for social networks: A zero-knowledge based definition of privacy. In: Ishai, Y. (ed.) TCC 2011. LNCS, vol. 6597, pp. 432–449. Springer, Heidelberg (2011)
14. Grahne, G., Thomo, A.: Approximate reasoning in semistructured data. In: KRDB (2001)
15. Grahne, G., Thomo, A., Wadge, W.W.: Preferential regular path queries. Fundam. Inform. 89(2-3), 259–288 (2008)
16. Hassanlou, N., Shoaran, M., Thomo, A.: Probabilistic graph summarization. In: Wang, J., Xiong, H., Ishikawa, Y., Xu, J., Zhou, J. (eds.) WAIM 2013. LNCS, vol. 7923, pp. 545–556. Springer, Heidelberg (2013)
17. Hay, M., Li, C., Miklau, G., Jensen, D.: Accurate estimation of the degree distribution of private networks. In: ICDM, pp. 169–178 (2009)
18. Khezrzadeh, M., Thomo, A., Wadge, W.W.: Harnessing the power of "favorites" lists for recommendation systems. In: RecSys., pp. 289–292 (2009)
19. Kifer, D., Machanavajjhala, A.: No free lunch in data privacy. In: SIGMOD Conference, pp. 193–204 (2011)
20. Kifer, D., Machanavajjhala, A.: A rigorous and customizable framework for privacy. In: PODS, pp. 77–88 (2012)
21. Koochakzadeh, N., Sarraf, A., Kianmehr, K., Rokne, J.G., Alhajj, R.: Netdriller: A powerful social network analysis tool. In: ICDM Workshops, pp. 1235–1238 (2011)
22. Korovaiko, N., Thomo, A.: Trust prediction from user-item ratings. Social Netw. Analys. Mining 3(3), 749–759 (2013)
23. Liu, K., Terzi, E.: Towards identity anonymization on graphs. In: SIGMOD Conference, pp. 93–106 (2008)
24. Machanavajjhala, A., Kifer, D., Gehrke, J., Venkitasubramaniam, M.: L-diversity: Privacy beyond k-anonymity. TKDD 1(1) (2007)

25. Madey, G., Freeh, V., Tynan, R.: Modeling the free/open source software community: A quantitative investigation (2005)
26. Mitzenmacher, M., Upfal, E.: Probability and Computing: Randomized Algorithms and Probabilistic Analysis. Cambridge University Press, New York (2005)
27. Narayanan, A., Shmatikov, V.: De-anonymizing social networks. In: IEEE Symposium on Security and Privacy, pp. 173–187 (2009)
28. Nepusz, T., Petróczi, A., Négyessy, L., Bazsó, F.: Fuzzy communities and the concept of bridgeness in complex networks. Phys. Rev. E 77, 016107 (2008)
29. Rastogi, V., Hay, M., Miklau, G., Suciu, D.: Relationship privacy: output perturbation for queries with joins. In: PODS, pp. 107–116 (2009)
30. Sabidussi, G.: The centrality of a graph. Psychometrika 31(4), 581–603 (1966)
31. Shoaran, M., Thomo, A.: Fault-tolerant computation of distributed regular path queries. Theor. Comput. Sci. 410(1), 62–77 (2009)
32. Shoaran, M., Thomo, A.: Certain answers and rewritings for local regular path queries on graph-structured data. In: IDEAS, pp. 186–192 (2010)
33. Shoaran, M., Thomo, A., Weber, J.: Differential privacy in practice. In: Jonker, W., Petković, M. (eds.) SDM 2012. LNCS, vol. Secure Data Management, pp. 14–24. Springer, Heidelberg (2012)
34. Shoaran, M., Thomo, A., Weber-Jahnke, J.H.: Zero-knowledge private graph summarization. In: BigData Conference, pp. 597–605 (2013)
35. Stefanescu, D., Thomo, A.: Enhanced regular path queries on semistructured databases. In: Grust, T., et al. (eds.) EDBT 2006 Workshops. LNCS, vol. 4254, pp. 700–711. Springer, Heidelberg (2006)
36. Tian, Y., Hankins, R.A., Patel, J.M.: Efficient aggregation for graph summarization. In: SIGMOD Conference, pp. 567–580 (2008)
37. Zhang, N., Tian, Y., Patel, J.M.: Discovery-driven graph summarization. In: ICDE, pp. 880–891 (2010)
38. Zhao, P., Li, X., Xin, D., Han, J.: Graph cube: on warehousing and olap multidimensional networks. In: SIGMOD Conference, pp. 853–864 (2011)
39. Zhou, B., Pei, J., Luk, W.-S.: A brief survey on anonymization techniques for privacy preserving publishing of social network data. SIGKDD Explorations 10(2), 12–22 (2008)

Valuation and Selection of OSS with Real Options

Androklis Mavridis

Product Manager, b-Open S.A
andy@b-open.gr

Abstract. The selection of Open Source Software (OSS) applications is a complex and difficult task. The evolving nature of OSS with constant updates, as well as the vast number of available projects hampers the selection process. Advancements in evaluation methods offer assistance in measuring various quality aspects, but do not examine the financial implications of risks and uncertainties imposed by the frequent updates/modifications and by the dynamics of the OSS communities. We perceive the OSS applications as assets capable of generating value upon selection. The objective is to discover the uncertainty factors affecting the overall value, to measure the quality evolution and finally to quantify the expected generated utility value of the OSS candidates.

Keywords: Open Source Selection, Real options analysis.

1   Introduction

In the Open Source Software (OSS) realm, the enormous number of available projects and applications hinders the selection process. The available quality evaluation approaches provide a time static quality assessment and thus, are not able to handle the evolving nature of open source projects, the resulting changes in quality and the risks associated with these changes. Moreover, these approaches, do not examine the financial implications of risks and uncertainties imposed by the frequent updates/modifications and by the dynamics of the OSS communities.

Quality-based economic valuation approaches dealing with design rational, have been introduced recently providing reasoning in IT investments where uncertainty and changes are difficult to predict [1]. The value-oriented notion of software artefacts has been treated with the Real Options Analysis (ROA) perceiving these artefacts as assets capable of generating value when properly managing the inherent risks, as "exercise options". Inspired by previous endeavours of valuations [2], [3], [4], [5], in this paper we propose a method assisting the OSS applications selection, by managing the applications' quality evolution, and valuate the selection as option, in a similar approach to financial options.

The basic concept of our work is that a software development decision under uncertainty, such as the selection of an OSS application is comparable to a financial derivative. In financial markets a derivative is a financial instrument whose value depends on, or derives from, the values of basic underlying assets [6]. In our context

L. Iliadis, M. Papazoglou, and K. Pohl (Eds.): CAiSE 2014 Workshops, LNBIP 178, pp. 44–52, 2014.
© Springer International Publishing Switzerland 2014

these assets are the candidate applications OSS applications. In its classic application, ROA uses the expected revenue notion as a foundation [7] and perceives the assets under examination as revenue generators based on the initial investment/acquiring cost and on the expected profits volatility.

Our method proposes the employment of Real Options Analysis to exploit the OSS quality evolution and calculate the system's generated value, aiming to maximise the benefits of the selection decision. Doing so, we inject extra intelligence to OSS selection process.

The paper structure follows. In section two we provide the related research work followed by a detailed presentation of our method in section three. Finally in section four we discuss the threats to validity followed by the concluded remarks in section five.

2   Background

The OSS application selection process includes searching, locating, and evaluating processes based on pre-defined criteria, and deciding upon applications [8]. However, only a limited number of empirical studies on selection of OSS applications have been performed [9]. Even if successful applications of normative selection methods for both COTS and OSS exist, such methods are rarely applied [10]. In [11] authors attributed the situational nature of OSS, where project specific properties constrain the selection outcome, as one of the suspending factors limiting the adoption of normative selection methods.

The limitation of the OSS evaluation can be justified partially to the subjective measurements provided by the communities and to the absence of well-structured and standardized quality models [12] [13] [14]. To overcome this obstacle, various research efforts have been introduced aiming to measure OSS quality employing different methods and focusing on different perspectives, ranging from source code quality analysis to community based metrics analysis, often with impressive results. Initial cumulative efforts resulted in a number of quality models, the most indicative and well known are summarised below.

2.1   Software Quality Evaluation

In our work we focus on the OSS quality and its evolution over project's generations. We take advantage of the aforementioned efforts and we argue that quality evolution is generated and affected by the dynamic eco-system nature of OSS. In order to account for the uncertainties imposed by the dynamics inherent in OSS projects we perceive the OSS selection process as an investment under uncertainty that can be approached and formulated with different options.

We make the hypothesis that OSS quality carries economic value in the form of real options, expressed through the right, but not the obligation, to select an OSS in the future, where the OSS to be selected is treated as a real asset. Real options analysis can help in discovering how OSS value changes over time, as quality changes through project's releases. Our aim is to provide OSS stakeholders with a method able to translate in financial terms the impact of quality evolution to the OSS selection with respect to potentially uncertain future conditions.

2.2 Real Options

Real Options Analysis (ROA) is based on the analogy between investment opportunities and financial options. A real option is a right, but not an obligation, to make a decision for a certain cost within a specific time frame. A project is perceived as an option on the underlying cash flows with multiple associated investment strategies to be exercised if conditions are favourable. The big advancement is that ROA accommodates not only the value of the investment's expected revenues but also the future opportunities that flexibility creates. The inherent ability to react to market conditions increases the expected value of the investment by maintaining or improving the upside potential and limiting the downside loss. ROA overcomes the limitations of the traditional Discounted Cash Flow (DCF) method as it considers all possible price paths for the underlying project value and assumes a distribution for the underlying prices rather than a deterministic price assumption.

As option is an asset that provides its owner the right without a symmetric obligation to make an investment decision such as growth, exit, wait, and learning etc. If conditions to investing arise, the owner can exercise the option by investing the strike price defined by the option. A call option gives the right to acquire an asset of uncertain future value for the strike price. There are two option mechanisms, namely the *call* and *put.*

During the last decade Real Options theory found to be very attractive in IT investments [15], perceiving mainly the IT project from a holistic point of view, while in the same time efforts going a step further dealing with uncertainties inherent in software engineering practices were also introduced, such as in [16].

Based on these foundations, the central idea of our work is that a selection decision, such as *when to select a candidate OSS*, is analogous to a financial derivative expressed as a *call option,* where the owner (the person in charge of the OSS selection) has the right to decide when it is preferable to select the OSS candidate application. In financial markets a derivative is a financial instrument whose value depends on, or derives from, the values of basic underlying assets [17].

3   Proposed Method

Initially inspired by the work [18] where the author applies Real Options Analysis in COTS (commercial off-the- shelf) based software development scenario and encouraged by [19], highlighting the similarities of COTS and OSS in the context of OTS (Off-the-shelf) software development, we approach the application of Real Options in the context of OSS application selection/integration in a similar fashion to this analytically presented in [3].

Our method exploits the results of OSS quality assessments, as a basis for options based analysis. We keep the mechanisms as broad and flexible as possible in order to assure its applicability through various existing state of the art OSS quality assessment tools/frameworks and through various situational contexts. In authors' previous work [20] emphasis was given on the expected revenues each project could generate, while the application of Real Options was based on the simulated volatility of the most sensitive (the most affecting the Net Present Value) quality attributes. In this extended work we split the OSS applications selection process in three consecutive steps. The first step commences with the quality assessment of the candidate applications against the selected attributes. In the second we calculate the volatility of the scores of quality attributes in the form of (%) standard deviation, and finally in the third step we calculate the call options for each OSS candidate and we compare the results. In the following sections we analytically present these steps.

3.1   Quality Assessment

The majority of the available state of the art quality assessment methods can be used, for evaluating the desired quality attributes, as long as they provide weighted measurable metrics. The requirement in this step is to assess each candidate application against the same list of attributes. In this method we focus on fairly measurable attributes such as *number of downloads per week*, *number of major releases*, *project maturity*, *Community adoption*, etc. As the selection process of a candidate OSS can involve different stakeholders ranging from managers to software developers, different views of quality might be of concern. For example for an IT manager, factors influencing the evolution of the project, such as project downloads, From the other hand, for a software developer wishing to integrate an OSS to an existing system, the evolution of community adoption would provide more insights. For this reason above all, the proposed method should be constructed in a manner able to cope with different scenarios of use depending on the quality characteristics chosen.

3.2   Calculate Quality Volatilities

To perform the quality assessment and make inferences about the quality attributes, we employ available hierarchical quality models like the ones proposed in [21], [22], [23], [24]. The aim is to provide as much of automation as possible, through the analysis of source code and associated community metrics over the project's releases, and calculate the evolution of quality in the next future release in the form of standard deviation. We cope with situations where the information available for making judgement concerning quality evolution is collected by activities initiated/performed by the project's developer team and the involved community.

This information, like number of downloads or number of reported/fixed bugs can be extracted through the statistics services offered by OSS repositories (i.e. Sourceforge[1]) or more accurately through automatically extracting data from the project's web pages and especially the source code control system, in the form of CVS [23]. The aim is to analyse the offered statistical data, and provide experts' judgements about the evolution of the quality attributes [25]. For example by calculating the standard deviation –over the project's releases- a judgement on several quality attributes could be made. Though we acknowledge the fact that the analysis is characterised by subjectivity due to its highly dependability on experts opinion [13] [26], we believe that as long as it provides better understanding to stakeholders involved [27], and is able to infuse experts' tacit knowledge into measures associated with the achievement level of software quality attributes [28], it is useful and can be used supportively to provide extra reasoning in the context of OSS selection.

3.3   Calculating the Value of a Call Option

The investment opportunity can often be seen as a call option on the present value of the expected cash flows from the investment. The value of an option of the underlying asset depends on a number of variables:

a)   Current Value of the Underlying Asset: As option generates value from the underlying asset, changes in the value of the underlying asset affects the value of the option, an increase in the value of the asset will increase the value of the call option.

b)   Volatility of the Underlying Asset Value: The higher the variance in the value of the underlying asset, the greater the value of the option.

c)   Dividends on the Underlying Asset: The value of the underlying asset can be expected to decrease if dividend payments are made on the asset during the life of the option. Hence, the value of a call option decreases when the size of the dividend payments increases.

d)   Strike Price of Option: The value of the call option will decline as the strike price increases.

e)   Time to Expiration: Options tend to become more valuable as towards expiration time, as the longer the time to expiration the more the value of the asset to move.

f)   Riskless Interest Rate: As the buyer of an option pays the price of the option up front, an amortization of the cost is involved depending on the level of interest rate and the expiration time. Increases in the interest rate will increase the value of a call option.

We extend the Option valuation mechanism to accommodate the specificities and constraints of the OSS realm. To proceed with the Options analysis we need the following input:

Stock Price: The Stock Price for a candidate is expressed as the expected total cash flows or the utility value resulted from the successful adoption of the OSS for a given time frame.

---

[1] www.Sourceforge.net

Strike Price: This is the accumulation of the costs Total Cost of Ownership (TCO) for the transition to the OSS application for the given period until option expiration date [29]. Training/learning, software and Support costs are included here.

Time interval: This is the time until the opportunity disappears for making the selection.

Volatility: Represents the quality fluctuation – evolution over project releases.

Risk Free Rate: Assumed to be a known market value specific to the market domain [30].

Evolution Steps: The number of binomial steps to be calculated.

For the calculation of the Stock Price we adopt the notion of *utility* from the works of [31]. In a similar approach to this described in [3], we assume that this value is totally due to the utility provided by each attribute. Thus, the total Stock Price (Value) for a given candidate (*i*) is given by the equation (1):

$$SP_i(t) = \sum_j Vj(t) \tag{1}$$

Where Vj is the utility attributed to the jth quality attribute.

The objective here is to calculate the *Total Utility Value* (the total utility expected to be obtained until the expiration date) and the *Call Option Value* (the value of the option). In our context this translates to: *What is the total expected utility gain in the given time interval until selection and what is the option value in waiting until the time for making the selection expires?* To calculate the option value for each candidate we apply binomial options pricing model [32].

We build for each candidate application two binomial lattices based on the American call option fashion, which dictates that the option (the selection) can be exercised at any given time until the expiration. The first lattice calculates the expected total OSS value, while the second calculates the option value, the amount by which a call option is in the money (utility), in other words "how far" it is profitable to wait until making the selection of an OSS candidate.

To clarify the mechanisms of the binomial pricing model, lets consider an application whose value is initially So and an option on the application's selection whose current value is f. Suppose that the option lasts for time T (time to select). During the life of the option, the application value (due to its quality) can either move up i.e. the project community enhances the quality of the given application, from So to a new level, Su or down, i.e the community stops supporting the application and thus its quality value decreases, to a new level Sd.

The proportional increment in the application's value when there is an up movement is u-1; the proportional decrement when there is a down movement is 1-d. If the application value moves up to Su, the payoff from the option is assumed to be fu; if the stock price moves down to Sd, the payoff from the option is assumed to be fd.

From this point we calculate the binomial options value by applying the following equation (2):

$$\text{Value} = ([p * \text{Option up} + (1\text{-}p) * \text{Option down}] * \exp(\text{-} r * \Delta t)), \tag{2}$$

where r is the risk free rate corresponding to the life of the option, p is the probability of an up movement factor,

$$p = \frac{e^{(r-q)\Delta t} - d}{u - d} \tag{3}, \text{ with } u = e^{\sigma\sqrt{t}} \tag{4}$$

the up movement factor, d=1/u the down movement factor, and σ expressing in % the percentage of the quality volatility. Hence, similarly to equation (1), the total option value TOV for a given candidate *(i)* application will be given by the following equation (5):

$$\text{TOV}_i(t) = \sum_j OVj(t) \tag{5}$$

Where OVj is the option value attributed to the jth quality attribute.

It is to be noted here that we limit our focus on a simple selection process and do not consider in this work staged developments, upgrades and migrations of OSS applications which require a more in depth analysis. These cannot be dealt adequately with the simple call option mechanism but rather with combined option schemes. Nevertheless the binomial pricing model can effectively handle the simple selection process, framed as a call option regardless of the number of candidates.

4   Applicability

Several factors need to be taken into consideration when applying the proposed quality-valuation method to realistic settings. Our method is based on the premise that calculation of volatility is always possible regardless of the scenario of use and the information at hand, as it is suggested that a fair amount of releases should be examined in order to obtain enough insights of quality's evolution over the project's life time. This requirement limits the method's applicability only to mature and established projects.

Another limitation is the assumption that it is feasible to calculate the expected revenues and the costs attributed to qualities examined for the OSS application under analysis. Even though, the employment of the notion of "utility" provides a handy workaround to contexts with inadequate financial historical data, it remains a difficult task and should be handled by experienced project managers.

The calculated volatility strongly depends on the hierarchical quality model used. Different models could produce different estimates of volatility. Additionally, it is not always possible to efficiently perform structural analysis on the source code mainly due to tools' constraints to code size.

Our approach currently does not perform any kind of analysis on the correlations that naturally exist between quality attributes. The addition of a mechanism addressing the tradeoffs at quality level would increase the validity of the measured volatility limiting at the same the experts' subjectivity.

Lastly even though the mechanisms and the variables required performing the binomial lattice practices are simple enough, clear instructions on the methodology and the associated tools should be given prior to analysis.

5   Discussion - Conclusions

We have presented a method assisting the OSS applications selection process. Assumptions were made in order to simplify our approach and to increase its applicability. We proposed a blend of evaluation methodologies and valuation analysis able to give insights to risks anticipated due to future uncertainties on the qualities of OSS applications.

Our method provides an alternative view to the selection process in the uncertain Open Source Software realm. It is capable of shedding light to the mechanisms introducing uncertainty and manages this uncertainty to maximise the profits of our decisions. Nevertheless, we do not suggest that this proposed OSS application selection approach should be treated as panacea. Intuition and other factors should be taken always into account in the OSS selection process.

Perceiving the selection decision as call option bearing monetary value introduces a link between the worlds of software technology and finance and thus, the results can easily be exploited by both developers and managers.

References

[1] Shaw, M., Arora, A., Butler, S., Poladian, V., Scaffidi, C.: In search of a unified theory for early pre-dictive design evaluation for software, Technical Reports CMU-ISRI-05-114, Carnegie Mellon University (2005)

[2] Sullivan, K.J., Chalasani, P., Jha, S., Sazawal, V.: Software Design as an Investment Activity: A Real Options Perspective, Real Options and Business Strategy: Applications to Decision Making. In: Trigeorgis, L. (ed.) Risk Books (1999)

[3] Ozkaya, I., Kazman, R., Klein, M.: Quality-Attribute Based Economic Valuation of Architectural Patterns, Technical Report CMU/SEI CMU/SEI-2007-TR-003 (2007)

[4] Meinhausen, N., Hambly, B.M.: Monte Carlo Methods for the Valuation of Multiple-Exercise Options. Mathematical Finance 14(4), 557–583 (2004)

[5] Erdogmus, H.: Valuation of Learning Options in Software Development under Private and Market Risk. The Engineering Economist 47(3), 308–353 (2002)

[6] Hull, J.C.: Options, Futures, and Other Derivatives. Pearson Prentice Hall (2006)

[7] Amram, M., Kulatilaka, N.: Real Options: Managing Strategic Investment in an Uncertain World. Harvard Business School Press, Boston (1999)

[8] Mandanmohan, T.M., De' Rahul: Open Source Reuse in Commercial Firms. IEEE Software, No-vember-December 21(6), 62–69 (2004)

[9] Li, J., Conradi, R., Bunse, C., Torchiano, M., Slyngstad, O.P.N., Morisio, M.: Development with off-the-shelf applications: 10 facts. IEEE Software 26(2), 2–9 (2009)

[10] Torchiano, M., Morisio, M.: Overlooked Aspects of COTS-Based Development. IEEE Soft-ware 21(2), 88–93 (2004)

[11] Hauge, O.: An Empirical Study on Selection of Open Source Software - Preliminary Results. In: FLOSS 2009, Vancouver, Canada, May 18 (2009)

[12] Sung, W.J., Kim, J.H., Rhew, S.Y.: A Quality Model for Open Source Software Selection. In: Sixth International Conference on Advanced Language Processing and Web Information Technology, ALPIT 2007 (August 2007)

[13] del Bianco, V., Lavazza, L., Morasca, S., Taibi, D., Tosi, D.: An investigation of the users' perception of OSS quality. In: Ågerfalk, P., Boldyreff, C., González-Barahona, J.M., Madey, G.R., Noll, J. (eds.) OSS 2010. IFIP AICT, vol. 319, pp. 15–28. Springer, Heidelberg (2010)

[14] Lincke, R., Lundberg, J., Löwe, W.: Comparing Software Metrics Tools. In: ISSTA 2008, Seattle, Washington, USA, July 20-24 (2008)

[15] Schwartz, S., Trigeorgis, L.: Real options and Investment Under Uncertainty: Classical Readings and Recent Contributions. MIT Press, Cambridge (2000)

[16] Erdogmus, H.: Valuation of Complex Options in Software Development. In: First International Workshop on Economics-Driven Software Engineering Research, EDSER-1, Los Angeles, May 17 (1999)

[17] Hull, J.C.: Options, Futures, and Other Derivatives. Pearson Prentice Hall (2006)

[18] Erdogmus, H.: Management of License Cost Uncertainty in Software Development: A Real Options Approach. In: 5th Annual Conference on Real Options: Theory Meets Practice, Los Angeles (2001)

[19] Jingyue, L., Conradi, R., Bunse, C., Torchiano, M., Slyngstad, O., Morisio, M.: Development with Off-the-Shelf Components: 10 Facts. IEEE Software 26(2), 80–87 (2009), doi:10.1109/MS.2009.33

[20] Mavridis, A., Stamelos, I.: Options as Tool Enhancing Rationale of OSS Components Selection. In: IEEE-DEST 2009, Istanbul, Turkey, May 31-June 2 (2009)

[21] ISO/IEC TR 9126-(1-4). Software engineering – Product quality. International Standardisation Organisation (2003-2004)

[22] McCall, J.A., Richards, P.K., Walters, G.F.: Factors in Software Quality, Nat'l Tech. Information Service, volumes 1,2 and 3, AS/A-049-014/015/055. Springfield, Vancouver (1977)

[23] Dormey, G.R.: A Model for Software Product Quality. IEEE Transactions on Software Engineering 21(2), 146–162 (1995)

[24] Bansiya, J., Davis, C.: A Hierarchical Model for Object-Oriented Design Quality Assessment. IEEE Transaction on Software Engineering 28(1), 4–17 (2002)

[25] Moses, J.: Benchmarking quality measurement. Software Quality Journal 15(4), 449–462, doi: 10.1007/s11219-007-9025-4

[26] Moses, J., Farrow, M.: Tests for consistent measurement of external subjective software quality attributes. Empirical Software Engineering 13(3), 261–287, doi:10.1007/s10664-007-9058-0

[27] Wohlin, C., Andrews, A.A.: Assessing Project Success Using Subjective Evaluation Factors. Software Quality Journal 9(1), 43–70, doi:10.1023/A:1016673203332

[28] Rosqvist, T., Koskela, M., Harju, H.: Software Quality Evaluation Based on Expert Judgement. Software Quality Journal 11(1), 39–55, doi:10.1023/A:1023741528816

[29] Russo, B., Braghin, C., Gasperi, P., Sillitti, A., Succi, G.: Defining the Total Cost of Ownership for the Transition to Open Source Systems. In: Proceedings of the First International Conference on Open Source Systems, Genova, July 11-15 (2005)

[30] Hull, J.C.: Options, Futures, and Other Derivatives, 6th edn. Prentice Hall, Upper Saddle River (2006)

[31] Kazman, R., Asundi, J., Klein, M.: Making Architecture Design Decisions: An Economic Approach Technical Report CMU/SEI-2002-TR-035 ESC-TR-2002-035

[32] Copeland, T., Antikarov, V.: Real Options: A Practitioner's Guide. TEXERE, New York (2001)

State of the Art in Context Modelling – A Systematic Literature Review

Hasan Koç, Erik Hennig, Stefan Jastram, and Christoph Starke

University of Rostock, Albert-Einstein-Straße 22, 18059 Rostock, Germany
{hasan.koc,erik.hennig,stefan.jastram,
christoph.starke}@uni-rostock.de

Abstract. Due to the dynamic changes in business environments enterprises adjust their business services and information technology systems. This is a prerequisite to deliver an enhanced business capability to the customers. Such needs address that the information systems should be aware of the context that they are operating in. This work explores context modelling research domain conducting a systematic literature review (SLR) in a limited time frame and literature resources. The work concludes that although the term context is widely used in computer sciences, there is no methodology or a common language to model context in identified articles.

Keywords: Systematic Literature Review, Context Modelling, Context Awareness.

1 Introduction

Enterprises are operating in rapidly changing environments therefore they should be able to adjust their business services to secure competitive advantage in existing markets or to shift directions towards new business opportunities. Such contextual changes in business environments must be monitored and mapped quickly to the information technology systems. This is a prerequisite to deliver an enhanced business capability to customers, as business capability delivery needs to be based on the application context [9]. Capabilities as such are directly related to business processes that are affected from the changes in context like regulations, customer preferences and system performance.

The notion of context plays an important role in many areas, both theoretical and applied, such as Formal Logic, Artificial Intelligence, Philosophy, Pragmatics, Computational Linguistics, Computer Science, Cognitive Psychology [1]. In today´s enterprises broad parts of the reality is designated by means of abstracted models. Such models have the duty to represent the situation at hand as precise as possible and yet the task of modelling is determined via the goals and application domains. This work investigates the domain of context modelling research conducting a systematic literature review (SLR). For this purposes, four research questions (RQ) are formulated to analyse and evaluate the activities in this domain. After introducing the

L. Iliadis, M. Papazoglou, and K. Pohl (Eds.): CAiSE 2014 Workshops, LNBIP 178, pp. 53–64, 2014.
© Springer International Publishing Switzerland 2014

notions and definitions of context, section 2 presents the underlying research approach. Then in section 3 the design of the systematic literature review is explained. Next in section 4, the data from the relevant papers is extracted and analysed to answer the four research questions formulated in section 2. Finally section 5 concludes our analysis and points out future work.

1.1   Notions of Context

In computer science the notion of context have appeared first in operating systems field where contexts are regarded as states about the processes, i.e. running, blocked or waiting. Several areas, such as artificial intelligence, software development, databases, data integration, machine learning, and knowledge representation fields also used their own definitions of context, mainly perceiving it as a collection of things associated to some specific situation [2]. A useful classification about the notion of context in computer sciences is provided by [3]. In accordance with this classification, the notion of context appears in software development and databases as views, aspects and roles. In machine learning contextual information is used to classify environmental concepts. In the data integration area the notion of context is used to exchange or adapt value from local information sources to the global applications. Artificial intelligent field understands under the notion of context as logical constructs that facilitate reasoning activities by partitioning knowledge into manageable sets. Finally in the knowledge representation area context appears as an abstraction mechanism for partitioning an information base.

Different than computer science, sociological approaches typically regard context as networks of interacting entities (people, agents or actors and artefacts) created and continually updated by the interactions among them [2]. Cognitive sciences define context as the set of all entities that influence human (or system's) behaviour on a particular occasion [4].

1.2   Definitions of Context

Various definitions of context arise due to its widespread use in different domains as explained in the above section. According to the framework of context use, the definitions and characteristics vary [5]. It is important that one should speak of the context in reference to its use [6], since there is no real consensual definition. Hence interpretation of context depends on the field of knowledge that it belongs to [7]. As an example, in computer sciences linguistic context focuses on texts to disambiguate meaning of words and sentences using the surrounding paragraphs. Situational context has a wider-concept and includes any information that characterizes the state of the entity, whereas an entity can be represented by a person, location or an object [8]. Organizational context describes mostly static information about a person. Such information includes things like roles, positions, tasks, titles etc. and can be provided for instance by an employee database and by a workflow management system [12].

Mostly cited definition given by [10] describes context as "any information that can be used to characterize the situation of any entity". According to [13] this definition is too broad since *"something is context because of the way it is used in interpretation, not due to its inherent properties"*. Although having a common definition of context is a challenging issue, [5] identifies invariant characteristics of the context such as (i) context relates always to some entity, (ii) is used to solve a problem (iii) depends on the domain and (iv) is a dynamic process. Last but not least [7] identifies main components of the concept "context" by examining a corpus of 150 definitions. The study concludes that context definitions can be analysed in terms of six parameters like "constraint, influence, behaviour, nature, structure and system".

2   Research Approach

The research approach used by this paper is a systematic literature review (SLR) performed according to the guidelines defined by Kitchenham et al. [14]. A SLR is a review process of research results with a structured and comprehensible procedure that aims to accumulate all "existing evidence concerning a treatment or technology", "identify gaps in current research", and provide "background in order to appropriately position new research activities" [14]. Kitchenham recommends six steps that are reflected in the "Review Design" section. Following the guidelines of systematic literature reviews by [14], we formulated four research questions (RQ):

- RQ 1: How much activity in the field of context modelling has there been since 2005? Who is active in this research area?
- RQ 2: What research topics are being investigated? How can these topics be classified?
- RQ 3: What research paradigms & research methods are being used?
- RQ 4: Which topics on the field of context modelling need further research according to the authors?

3   Review Design

3.1   Literature Sources

As a first step, an initial search on online databases (IEEE Xplore, ACM DL, Taylor & Francis Online, AISeL, Science Direct and EBSCOhost) was executed to identify the conferences and journals that are proceeding in context modelling. In this phase, two terms namely "context modelling" and "context representation" were searched in keywords or abstracts of the publications. Then, according to the relevancy of findings, the resulting conferences and journals were narrowed down utilizing the following criteria:

- The selected resources had to publish the articles in German or English
- The selected resources had to provide their publications on databases that are freely accessible with the possibilities given by the University of Rostock.
- The selected resources had to publish papers on a regular basis and cover recent research topics and trends.

As a result, we were able to identify one conference and four journals, which formed the basis of our systematic literature review. These are illustrated in Table 1. Moreover, we have decided to cover the publications from 2005 to 2013 since the SLR was conducted as a part of the research seminar, which was limited to 10 weeks. The AISeL database has also returned a number of relevant publications but due to the membership restrictions we had to exclude these findings.

Table 1. List of included Sources

Resource Name	Available via	Initial Search
CONTEXT Conference[1]	SpringerLink	34
Information Systems Journal	Science Direct	5
Journal of Systems and Software	Science Direct	1
Information Systems Management	Taylor&Francis	1
Information Systems and e-Business Management	SpringerLink	11
Σ		52

3.2   Paper Selection

The four search terms used in the conference and journals was "context", "context awareness", "context modelling" and "context modeling". If these terms appeared in the title, abstract or keywords of the publications, then the article was primarily classified as relevant. As a result, the search returned 52 papers in total allocated to resources as illustrated in Table 1. In order to investigate our research questions, we narrowed down this number mainly by reading abstracts to 24 papers. If the abstract reading did not help much concerning the relevancy to our research questions, then a complete reading was conducted. After working the whole text through, we eliminated further six papers. This brought us to a total number of 18 papers that would be used as the basis of further analysis.

As depicted in Fig. 1, the major source in our systematic literature review was the Conference on Modeling and Using Context (CONTEXT). A total of 13 relevant articles were published in a time frame of 2005 to 2013 in this conference. The search in journals "Information Systems" and "Journal of Systems and Software" has returned two relevant articles. Finally, one paper was detected in "Information Systems and e-Business Management" journal.

4   Data Analysis

In this section we present the collected data to answer the RQ's from section 2. At first, we identify the years the most publications about Context Modelling were published at and active researchers in this area, i.e. the authors' names, their institution and their nationality. After that we identify what research topics were

---

[1] Modeling and Using Context, International and Interdisciplinary Conference CONTEXT.

investigated and how they can be classified. The third question deals with the different research methods and designs that are being used. For the last RQ, we will discuss the topics on the field of context modelling that need further research according to the authors of selected papers.

4.1 Activity in Context Modelling

In four sources we found 18 papers from 2005 to 2013 dealing with context modelling. The years 2007 and 2013 should be emphasized as a result of 13 published papers. On the other hand in 2006, 2009 and 2010 no articles regarding the context modelling were published. As a matter of fact this statement relates to the organization frequency of Conference on Modeling and Using Context (CONTEXT) which is only held at uneven years and did not gather in 2009. We were not able to identify any reasons for this. Finally in 2005 and 2008 one and in 2011 three papers were detected. In conclusion, we did not find enough evidence to support a hypothesis that the research in context modelling increases or decreases through the years. In a broader connection, where the researcher extends the time frame as well as resources including diverse conferences and journals, a wider observation can be made. Fig. 1 illustrates the respective number of papers by including conference/ journals and years of publication.

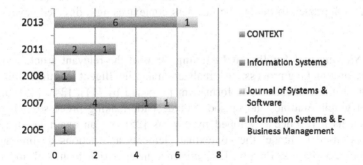

Fig. 1. Allocation of Relevant Papers to Resources

81% of the contributions to the context modelling came from European institutions. In this respective the European universities are most active institutions, as per to their high share (88%) in articles written in European institutions. Specifically we identified a total of 15 European educational institutions, 8 of which are located in France. The most active author appears to be Patrick Brézillion of University Pierre and Marie Curie (UPMC), Paris, who collaborated to five papers, mostly in the area of decision making (see the following subsection). As a consequence the French institutions are the most active in context modelling topic. A detailed illustration for the locations of institutions can be retrieved under following link[2].

---

[2] https://mapsengine.google.com/map/
edit?mid=zt6P_78RGC40.kLp7gVY7n-Yg

4.2   Research Topics and Approaches in Context Modelling

Within the relevant sources of paper the following research topics were identified:

Context Modelling in Software Engineering. 39% of the relevant articles are concerned with the Context Modelling in Software Engineering. These papers utilize Context Modelling to produce development methods and tools for context-aware software systems. In this respective, [15] presents an editor (NexusEditor) to model and manage complex context information. [16] proposes a generic framework to adapt applications to the context in a pervasive computing environment. [17] and [18] present Model Driven Development approaches (MDD) to design context-aware applications. [5] is the only paper that introduces a methodology in the development of context-aware systems. [19] proposes a model to use context in human computer interaction area. Finally [20] suggests an architecture and a prototype for querying and visualising context information.

Modelling Context in Software Organizations. 17% of the relevant articles cover the organizational aspects in context modelling. [21] investigates the role of context in practice-based organizational learning and performance improvement. [22] presents a semantic model to describe collaboration processes in dynamic environments and contextual process information. [23] extends the Unified Context Model[3] (UCM) and represents an approach to model the business context using a directed acyclic graph (DAG).

Decision Making and Intelligent Learning. 28% of the relevant articles cover the area of decision-making process, task realization and intelligent learning. This area is dominated by the context-graphs formalism proposed by [11], [24], [25] and [26]. Contextual graphs outlines the episodes of decision-making processes where each path represents a practice developed by experts [25]. As an example, in [26] the formalism is used to model the contextual elements and actions dealing with the behaviour of car drivers. Finally, [27] presents an approach to model and use the context of learning in intelligent learning environments, which aims to individualise learning by aligning the resources with the learner´s needs.

Modelling and Formalizing Context Information. 33% of the relevant articles cover the areas of modelling, structuring, using and formalizing context information. Proposing a general framework, [3] investigates the possibilities of structuring context information using the traditional abstraction mechanisms like classification, generalization and attribution. In this respective the article presents a theory for contextualized information bases. [17] presents a Domain Specific Language (DSL) to model context information. Based on the interactive learning of activity traces, [28] models context information surrounding objects concerned by activity to support interactive knowledge discovery. [15] and [20] also covers subjects related to context information modelling, which were described above.

---

[3] UN/CEFACT: Standard used to manage representations and applications of business context.

Meta Articles. This area comprises of literature researches and theoretical work in the field of context modelling. The main characteristic of these papers is that they conduct research "about context modelling", whereas the four areas introduced above resemble research "with context modelling". In this respective 11% of all articles are classified into this group. [29] presents a literature review about the concept of context investigating the use of term in different disciplines and suggests that context modelling needs a systematic approach, since it is a complex phenomenon. Finally [3] presents a theory that "includes a set of validity constraints, a model theory, as well as a set of sound and complete inference rules".

In order to classify the approaches for context modelling we use the six classes that are described in [30]. These approaches consist of (i) key-value modelling, (ii) mark-up scheme modelling (*Comprehensive Structured Context Profiles, Pervasive Profile Description Language, ConteXtML,* etc.), (iii) graphical modelling (*UML, Object Role Modelling, ER,* etc.), (iv) object oriented modelling (*cues, Active Object Model*), (v) logic-based modelling and (vi) ontology-based modelling (*Context Ontology Language, CONtext Ontology,* etc.). The same article concludes that ontology-based modelling is the most suitable approach for context modelling for ubiquitous computing environments.

As depicted in Fig. 2, the graphical modelling was the most frequent approach in our pool of 18 papers. Nearly half of the works (45%) proposed approaches or modelled context utilizing graphical models. Specifically the works of Brézillion in terms of context-graphs adopted this approach. Alongside with ontology-based approaches, logic-based approaches are the second most used technique in modelling context. Only two works adopt combined approaches, i.e. object oriented/or graphical modelling with logic-based modelling. We were not able to identify any modelling approach in 2 papers, since the first one conducts a literature review and the latter one describes the dimensions of context more than modelling it.

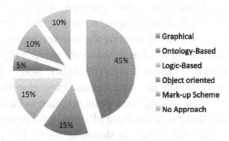

Fig. 2. Approaches for Modelling Context

4.3   Research Paradigms and Research Methods in Context Modelling

We mainly identified three research paradigms that were applied in relevant articles, i.e. Design-science research (DSR), conceptual research and empirical research. DSR answers questions relevant to human problems via the creation of innovative artefacts, thereby contributing new knowledge to the body of scientific evidence. Unlike the natural sciences, the design science research is fundamentally a problem-solving paradigm whose end goal is to produce an artefact, which must be built and then evaluated [31]. To be classified as design-oriented, the articles should follow the seven guidelines provided [32], that is, they have to develop useful solutions by creating and evaluating an artefact relevant to an IS problem. For development and evaluation of the design artefact, rigorous methods have to be used and the contributions must be communicated to audiences. Articles that lack one of these steps were accepted to utilize empirical research paradigm that make use of qualitative (e.g., case studies, action research, grounded theory), and quantitative research methods (e.g., surveys, experiments). Last but not least, conceptual research develops an artefact of the designer´s creative efforts, which is only to a very small extent grounded in empirical data [33]. Inline with [34] a research activity in this work is classified as conceptual, if the developed artefact has not been verified or evaluated.

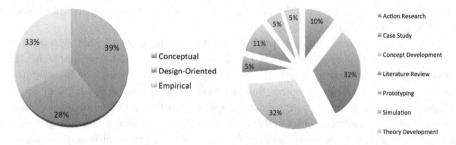

Fig. 3. Research Designs in Context Modelling   **Fig. 4.** Research Methods in Context Modelling

As Fig. 3 shows context modelling research adopts with a narrow majority conceptual research paradigm. The main research methods used in conceptual research design are the concept development and literature review (non-systematic); the methods like surveys, case studies, interviews, action research etc. are rarely used. As a result context modelling approaches developed conceptually might suffer a lack of proper validation of their structure and applicability. 40% of papers conducting conceptual research do not evaluate their models and 60% plan for further evaluation. This negative consequence of adopting conceptual research is illustrated in Fig. 5.

Our findings show that there is a balanced allocation between the design-oriented and empirical research paradigms, which is shown in Fig. 3. Obviously the benefit of adopting such paradigms lies in artefact evaluation. As illustrated in Fig. 5 all articles utilizing design-oriented or empirical research evaluated their models. In this respective, articles adopting empirical research design utilize only qualitative evaluation methods, more specifically case studies. Design-oriented publications use both qualitative and quantitative evaluation methods i.e., grounded theory, prototyping, simulation, field study and action research. Regarding the evaluation methods 50% of our findings evaluated their models via qualitative methods and 11% used quantitative methods. The remaining 39% either do work on further evaluation or do not evaluate their model at all.

Concerning the research methods in context modelling, case studies and concept development are the most applied forms as depicted in Fig. 4. As mentioned above, this might be a problem from the evaluation point-of view, since concept development is characterized as a method in conceptual research. On the other side, case studies are applied in various domains like medicine, transportation, intelligent learning and agent-based environments, which emphasizes the wide-spread application of context.

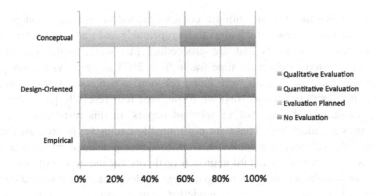

Fig. 5. Evaluation Methods vs. Research Designs

4.4   Further Research Areas in Context Modelling

The most significant result derived from the relevant works in the context modelling in software engineering research topic is the aim to extend, develop or integrate the artefacts or models. As an example [15] extend the editor developed to model and manage complex information, [16] work on a benchmark to evaluate performance of modelling approaches and develop multi-domain development platform. Future work in [19] includes also the development of a context tool. Finally [17] find quality parameters for context sources. The authors alone should not realize this type of development; also the practitioners and academia are kindly asked to contribute to gain better results.

Nearly the half of the papers (43%) adopting conceptual research does not point out further research. Moreover three out of five articles concerning the context-graphs outline the problems of their approach but do not plan any further work. In contrast to that, there are some works that plan to evaluate their models or approaches. [21] aims to evaluate its proposal by conducting case studies with organizations. [35] purposes an evaluation to extend the semantic model. Similarly [28] will formalize its method and test it in the transportation field to understand the impact of driving behaviour on fuel consumption. [3] is concerned with a framework development to query contextualized information bases and methodological issues, i.e. the criteria of qualifying as "context information". [5] will apply the developed methodology to the different types of applications in various fields. [18] introduce rules to support ontologies better by deducing new rules. In this respective [11] plans to extend the work by adding integrity constraints and inference rules and [20] plans to integrate more context information such as users´ profiles and interests.

5   Conclusion and Outlook

This work investigates the domain of context modelling research conducting a systematic literature review, which aims to be repeatable and transparent. To identify the conferences and journals that are proceeding in context modelling, first we described some criteria and set the time frame from 2005 to 2013. As a consequence one conference and four journals were found relevant, which could form the basis of our systematic literature review. Next we formulated four research questions, which were used to analyse the total of 18 relevant papers. In this respective five main research topics are identified. These are not mutually exclusive; in contrast they are closely interrelated, since the main focus is to develop a context-aware artefact. Nonetheless, there is not a standard approach or theory for the notion of context [2], apparently methodologies how to develop context models lack. Still it should be noted that nearly half of the works (45%) modelled context utilizing graphical models. Regarding the research designs, there seems to be a balanced allocation between conceptual, design-oriented and empirical research. The articles adopting design-oriented or empirical research have obviously evaluated their artefacts whereas the adoption of conceptual research results in a lack of evaluation. There is a significant part of works that have not evaluated their artefacts yet (17%) or plan future evaluation (22%). It is our view that the developed artefacts should be evaluated in order to reach more stable models or even standards.

The SLR was conducted as a part of the research seminar, which had to be by definition concluded in 10 weeks. This had major limitations on the choice of resources and defining a larger timespan. Moreover, the SLR proposed by [14] considers only conferences and journals; hence other set of works might be out of the scope due to this limitation. Obviously using a different setting for the time frame and including more conferences, journals and other works would make it possible to examine wider perspectives. For instance, the trends in context modelling, the reasons, why there is not a common language for context modelling and seminal works in this domain can be added to the body of knowledge, the research topics can be more generalized. Still a moderate number of 18 papers provide a starting point to classify research topics as well as research methods used in the area of context modelling which surely can be extended in the future.

Acknowledgments. This work has been performed as part of the EU-FP7 funded project no: 611351 CaaS – Capability as a Service in Digital Enterprises.

References

1. Bouquet, P., Serafini, L., Brézillon, P.: Preface. In: Bouquet, P., Serafini, L., Brézillon, P., Benercetti, M., Castellani, F., et al. (eds.) CONTEXT 1999. LNCS (LNAI), vol. 1688, pp. v–vi. Springer, Heidelberg (1999)
2. Zacarias, M., Pinto, H.S., Magalhães, R., et al.: A 'context-aware' and agent-centric perspective for the alignment between individuals and organizations. Information Systems 35(4), 441–466 (2010), doi:10.1016/j.is.2009.03.014
3. Analyti, A., Theodorakis, M., Spyratos, N., et al.: Contextualization as an Independent Abstraction Mechanism for Conceptual Modeling. Information Systems 32, 24–60 (2007)
4. Kokinov, B.: Dynamics and Automaticity of Context: A Cognitive Modeling Approach. In: Bouquet, P., Serafini, L., Brézillon, P., Benercetti, M., Castellani, F., et al. (eds.) CONTEXT 1999. LNCS (LNAI), vol. 1688, pp. 200–213. Springer, Heidelberg (1999)
5. Ben Mena, T., Bellamine-Ben Saoud, N., Ben Ahmed, M., Pavard, B.: Towards a Methodology for Context Sensitive Systems Development. In: Kokinov, B., Richardson, D.C., Roth-Berghofer, T.R., Vieu, L. (eds.) CONTEXT 2007. LNCS (LNAI), vol. 4635, pp. 56–68. Springer, Heidelberg (2007)
6. Brézillon, P., Cavalcanti, M.: Modeling and Using Context. Knowl. Eng. Rev. 13(2), 185–194 (1998), doi:10.1017/S0269888998004044
7. Bazire, M., Brézillon, P.: Understanding Context Before Using It. In: Dey, A.K., Kokinov, B., Leake, D.B., Turner, R., et al. (eds.) CONTEXT 2005. LNCS (LNAI), vol. 3554, pp. 29–40. Springer, Heidelberg (2005)
8. Hoffmann, P.: Context-based Semantic Similarity Across Ontologies (2008)
9. Zdravkovic, J., Stirna, J., Henkel, M., Grabis, J.: Modeling Business Capabilities and Context Dependent Delivery by Cloud Services. In: Salinesi, C., Norrie, M.C., Pastor, Ó. (eds.) CAiSE 2013. LNCS, vol. 7908, pp. 369–383. Springer, Heidelberg (2013)
10. Dey, A.K.: Understanding and using context. Personal and Ubiquitous Computing 5(1), 4–7 (2001)
11. Brézillon, P.: Context Modeling: Task Model and Practice Model. In: Kokinov, B., Richardson, D.C., Roth-Berghofer, T.R., Vieu, L. (eds.) CONTEXT 2007. LNCS (LNAI), vol. 4635, pp. 122–135. Springer, Heidelberg (2007)
12. Klemke, R.: The Notion of Context in Organisational Memories. In: Bouquet, P., Serafini, L., Brézillon, P., Benercetti, M., Castellani, F., et al. (eds.) CONTEXT 1999. LNCS (LNAI), vol. 1688, pp. 483–486. Springer, Heidelberg (1999)
13. Winograd, T.: Architectures for Context. HCI 16(2), 401–419 (2001)
14. Kitchenham, B., Pearl Brereton, O., Budgen, D., et al.: Systematic literature reviews in software engineering – A systematic literature review. Information and Software Technology 51(1), 7–15 (2009), doi:10.1016/j.infsof.2008.09.009
15. Cipriani, N., Wieland, M., Großmann, M., et al.: Tool support for the design and management of context models. Information Systems 36(1), 99–114 (2011)
16. Chaari, T., Ejigu, D., Laforest, F., et al.: A comprehensive approach to model and use context for adapting applications in pervasive environments. Journal of Systems and Software 80(12), 1973–1992 (2007), doi:10.1016/j.jss.2007.03.010
17. Hoyos, J.R., García-Molina, J., Botía, J.A.: A domain-specific language for context modeling in context-aware systems. Journal of Systems and Software 86(11), 2890–2905 (2013), doi:10.1016/j.jss.2013.07.008
18. Ayed, D., Delanote, D., Berbers, Y.: MDD Approach for the Development of Context-Aware Applications. In: Kokinov, B., Richardson, D.C., Roth-Berghofer, T.R., Vieu, L. (eds.) CONTEXT 2007. LNCS (LNAI), vol. 4635, pp. 15–28. Springer, Heidelberg (2007)

19. Grill, T., Tscheligi, M.: Towards a Multi-perspectival Approach of Describing Context. In: Beigl, M., Christiansen, H., Roth-Berghofer, T.R., Kofod-Petersen, A., Coventry, K.R., Schmidtke, H.R., et al. (eds.) CONTEXT 2011. LNCS, vol. 6967, pp. 115–118. Springer, Heidelberg (2011)

20. Zhou, E., Wu, B., Wu, J., Ding, Y.: An Architecture and a Prototype for Querying and Visualising Recorded Context Information. In: Beigl, M., Christiansen, H., Roth-Berghofer, T.R., Kofod-Petersen, A., Coventry, K.R., Schmidtke, H.R. (eds.) CONTEXT 2011. LNCS, vol. 6967, pp. 321–334. Springer, Heidelberg (2011)

21. Hegarty, J., Brézillon, P., Adam, F.: The Role of Context in Practice-Based Organizational Learning and Performance Improvement. In: Brézillon, P., Blackburn, P., Dapoigny, R. (eds.) CONTEXT 2013. LNCS, vol. 8175, pp. 59–72. Springer, Heidelberg (2013)

22. Brézillon, P., Blackburn, P., Dapoigny, R. (eds.): CONTEXT 2013. LNCS, vol. 8175. Springer, Heidelberg (2013)

23. Novakovic, D., Huemer, C., Pichler, C.: Context Model for Business Context Sensitive Business Documents. In: Brézillon, P., Blackburn, P., Dapoigny, R. (eds.) CONTEXT 2013. LNCS, vol. 8175, pp. 336–342. Springer, Heidelberg (2013)

24. Brézillon, J., Brézillon, P.: Context Modeling: Context as a Dressing of a Focus. In: Kokinov, B., Richardson, D.C., Roth-Berghofer, T.R., Vieu, L. (eds.) CONTEXT 2007. LNCS (LNAI), vol. 4635, pp. 136–149. Springer, Heidelberg (2007)

25. Brézillon, P.: Context-Based Development of Experience Bases. In: Brézillon, P., Blackburn, P., Dapoigny, R. (eds.) CONTEXT 2013. LNCS, vol. 8175, pp. 87–100. Springer, Heidelberg (2013)

26. Brézillon, P., Brézillon, J.: Context-sensitive decision support systems in road safety. Inf. Syst. E-Business Management 6(3), 279–293 (2008)

27. Akhras, F.N.: Modelling the Context of Learning Interactions in Intelligent Learning Environments. In: Dey, A., Kokinov, B., Leake, D., Turner, R. (eds.) CONTEXT 2005. LNCS (LNAI), vol. 3554, pp. 1–14. Springer, Heidelberg (2005)

28. Traoré, A., Tattegrain, H., Mille, A.: A Trace Analysis Based Approach for Modeling Context Components. In: Brézillon, P., Blackburn, P., Dapoigny, R. (eds.) CONTEXT 2013. LNCS, vol. 8175, pp. 371–380. Springer, Heidelberg (2013)

29. Alshaikh, Z., Boughton, C.: Notes on Synthesis of Context between Engineering and Social Science. In: Brézillon, P., Blackburn, P., Dapoigny, R. (eds.) CONTEXT 2013. LNCS, vol. 8175, pp. 157–170. Springer, Heidelberg (2013)

30. Strang, T., Linnhoff-Popien, C.: A Context Modeling Survey. In: Workshop on Advanced Context Modelling, Reasoning and Management, UbiComp 2004 - The Sixth International Conference on Ubiquitous Computing, Nottingham/England, pp. 31–41 (2004)

31. Hevner, A.R., Chatterjee, S.: Design research in information systems. Theory and practice. Integrated series in information systems, vol. 22. Springer, London (2010)

32. Hevner, A.R., March, S.T., Park, J., et al.: Design Science in Information Systems Research. MIS Q. 28(1), 75–105 (2004)

33. Niehaves, B., Simons, A., Becker, J., et al.: Maturity Models in Information Systems Research: Literature Search and Analysis. Communications of the Association for Information Systems 29(1) (2011)

34. Wendler, R.: The maturity of maturity model research: A systematic mapping study. Information and Software Technology 54(12), 1317–1339 (2012), doi:10.1016/j.infsof.2012.07.007

35. Knoll, S.W., Lukosch, S.G.: A Context-Sensitive Intervention Approach for Collaboration in Dynamic Environments. In: Brézillon, P., Blackburn, P., Dapoigny, R. (eds.) CONTEXT 2013. LNCS, vol. 8175, pp. 115–128. Springer, Heidelberg (2013)

On the Applicability of Concepts from Variability Modelling in Capability Modelling: Experiences from a Case in Business Process Outsourcing

Kurt Sandkuhl and Hasan Koc

University of Rostock, Albert-Einstein-Straße 22,
18059 Rostock, Germany
{kurt.sandkuhl,hasan.koc}@uni-rostock.de

Abstract. Efficient and effective value creation and service delivery processes are considered as the key factor to competitiveness in a globalized market environment. Capability management contributes to this goal by considering an integrated view of the ability to deliver a certain service with the capacity to do so. In this paper, we focus on the aspect of variability in capabilities. Starting from an industrial case from business process outsourcing, we propose to introduce concepts from variability modelling, i.e. variation points and variation aspects, into modelling and representation of capabilities. The main contributions of this paper are the introduction of variability points into capability modelling, a proposal for further formalizing the term capability, and an industrial case showing the use of variability points.

Keywords: capability, variability modelling, variation point, enterprise modelling, business process outsourcing.

1   Introduction

In many industrial sectors, efficient and effective value creation and service delivery processes are considered as the key factor to competitiveness in a globalized market environment. Systematic management of enterprise architectures including the technical, application and business architecture is emerging into a key discipline in enterprises. One of the objectives of this discipline is to manage and systematically develop the capabilities of an enterprise, which often are reflected in the business services offered to customers and the technical services associated to them. In this context, networked enterprises [1], value networks [2] and extended enterprises [3] massively use service-oriented and process-oriented architectures.

The term capability is used in various industrial and academic contexts with often different meanings (see section 2.1 for a discussion). Most conceptualizations of the term agree that capability includes the ability to do something (know-how, organisational preparedness, appropriate competences) and the capacity for actual delivery in an application context. This indicates that flexibility, dynamics and variation are attributes associated with capability. In this paper, we focus on the aspect of variability in the context of capabilities and we propose to introduce

L. Iliadis, M. Papazoglou, and K. Pohl (Eds.): CAiSE 2014 Workshops, LNBIP 178, pp. 65–76, 2014.
© Springer International Publishing Switzerland 2014

variation points and variation aspects into modelling and representation of capabilities. For this purpose, a certain degree of formality is required in capability models, which will also be subject of the paper. The main contributions of this paper are the introduction of variability points into capability modelling, a proposal for further formalizing the term capability, and an industrial case showing the use of variability points.

The remaining part of the paper is structured as follows: Section 2 will give a brief overview to background for this work including existing capability modelling approaches, a meta-model proposed for formalizing capabilities and feature modelling. Section 3 presents an industrial case for motivating extension and formalization of capability definition. Section 4 introduces the concept of variation points in capability modelling including a formalization and an example from the industrial case illustrating the context of business service delivery together with the variation points. Finally, section 5 summarizes the work and discusses future work.

2   Background

This section summarizes the conceptual background including capability definitions and existing modelling approaches (2.1), variability modelling in product lines (2.3) and an analysis of improvement potential of a selected capability meta-model (2.2).

2.1   Capability Definitions

The term capability is used in different areas of business information systems. In the literature there seems to be an agreement about the characteristics of the capability, still there is no generally acceptance of the term. The definitions mainly put the focus on "combination of resources" [8], "capacity to execute an activity"[7], "perform better than competitors" [10] and "possessed ability [6]".

The capabilities must be enablers of competitive advantage; they should help companies to continuously deliver a certain business value in dynamically changing circumstances [11]. They can be perceived from different organizational levels and thus utilized for different purposes. According to [12] the firm performance is the greatest, when the enterprises map their capabilities to IT applications. In this perspective the capabilities are provided as Business Services, i.e. they are designed and delivered in a process-oriented fashion. Capabilities as such are directly related to business processes that are affected from the changes in context such as regulations, customer preferences and system performance. As companies in rapidly changing environments need to anticipate variations and respond to them [9], the affected processes/ services need to be adjusted quickly. In other words the changes in context can be realized if the variations to the standard processes are promptly instantiated.

A capability definition is proposed by the EU-FP7 project Capabilities-as-a-Service in Digital Enterprises (CaaS)[1]. In the CaaS project capability is defined as *the*

---

[1] See http:// http://caas-project.eu/

ability and capacity that enable an enterprise to achieve a business goal in a certain context. Ability refers to the level of available competence, where competence is understood as talent intelligence and disposition, of a subject or enterprise to accomplish a goal; capacity means availability of resources, e.g. money, time, personnel, tools. This definition focuses on the components of enterprise modelling such as goal modelling and utilizes the notion of context, thus stresses the variations of the standard processes.

2.2   Improvement Needs in Existing Capability Meta-models

Since textual definitions leave room for ambiguity some capability modelling approaches define meta-models. Meta-models in general define the elements of a modelling language with their relationships and structural constraints. The meaning of relationships often is expressed by the name of the relationship, which leaves room for interpretations. An exception might be the taxonomic and aggregation relationships, which are available in many modelling languages and established with respect to their meaning. Some meta-models also include behavioural constraints to be observed during runtime, like the meta-model of MEMO [4]. However, even the existence of behavioural constraints does not fully specify how the model language elements have to be interpreted at runtime, i.e. the operational semantics (or runtime semantics) also should be defined, if the model is meant to be enactable.

In the area of capability modelling a recently published meta-model was proposed by Stirna et al. [13] together with the capability definition from the CaaS project presented above. Figure 1 depicts an excerpt from this meta-model, which shows all concepts directly related to Capability. The capability notion is the core element of this approach and related to other important components. In order to provide a capability some goals have to be fulfilled. These goals are operationalized via processes. As a result, capabilities require processes to be executed. During the capability delivery context indicators are measured in order to adjust the delivery to anticipated changes. This implies that the capability must be adequately delivered for certain context situations represented as context set. In order to react to the anticipated changes in context and to adjust the capability delivery process variations are used. These are modelled as specialisations of the processes.

Although this meta-model contains a quite detailed conceptualization of capability, some aspects need to be further specified in order to avoid ambiguities. Examples are:

- Each Capability "requires" at least one Process and exactly one ContextSet and one Goal. Semantically, this indicates that a capability cannot exist if there either is no Process or no Goal or no ContextSet, but it does not further specify the exact meaning of the relationship between Capability and these other concepts. From the textual definition of capability, it could be concluded that the ContextSet, the Process and the Goal specify the capability or are even part of it, but this cannot be derived from the meta-model.
- A Capability is supported by exactly one Pattern. Each Pattern is an aggregation of ProcessVariants, which in turn are specializations of Process. What is the

relation of the ProcessVariants of the Processes required for a Capability and the ProcessVariants aggregated in the one Pattern supporting a Capability? One interpretation would be that all ProcessVariants of all Processes required by a Capability have to be aggregated in the one Pattern required by the Capability. Other interpretations would be that only selected ProcessVariants or only one ProcessVariant per Process would be part of the one Pattern for a Capability.

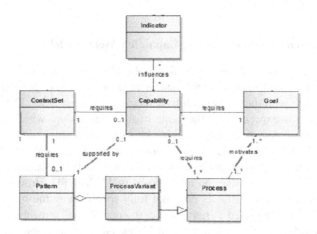

Fig. 1. Excerpt of the Capability Meta-Model introduced by [13]

- Not only Capability but also Process has a relation to Goal, which is that each process is motivated by one or many goals and that each goal motivates one ore many processes. Has the one Goal "requiring" a certain Capability to be among the Goals motivating the Processes required by the same Capability? Intuitively, this seems to be obvious, but it again is not expressed in the model.

The above examples show the general problem of most meta-models, the insufficient expressivity when it comes to runtime and behavioural characteristics also applies for the given meta-model. As a contribution and first step to address this issue, we propose to further specify the relations between Capability, Process and Context.

2.3   Variability Modelling in Product Line Engineering

Discussion of the term capability and existing meta-models in capability modeling indicates that capturing and representing variations in processes, business services or other elements of capability including the relationships or dependencies to context sets is an essential task in capability modeling. The area of variability modeling offers concepts how to deal with variability in complex systems, which might be applicable for capability modeling and will be briefly presented in this section.

   Variability modeling offers an important contribution to limit the variety of the variants of systems by capturing and visualizing commonalities and dependencies between features and between the components providing feature implementations.

Since more than a decade, variability is frequently used in the area of technical systems and as element of software product line implementations. Among the variability modeling approaches, feature models are considered as in particular promising. The purpose of a feature model is to extract, structure and visualize the commonality and variability of a domain or set of products. Commonalities are the properties of products that are shared among all the products in a set, placing the products in the same category or family. Variability are the elements of the products that differentiate and show the configuration options, choices and variation points that are possible between variants of the product, aimed to satisfy customer needs and requirements. The variability and commonality is modelled as features and organized into a hierarchy of features and sub features, sometimes called feature tree, in the feature model. The hierarchy and other properties of the feature model are visualized in a feature diagram. Feature diagrams express the relation between features with the relation types mandatory, optional, alternative, required and mutually-exclusive. The exact syntax of feature diagrams is explained in [5].

3   Industrial Case

Work in this paper is motivated by an industrial case originating from the EU-FP7 project "Capability-as-a-Service in Digital Enterprises (CaaS)". This section introduces the case with its general characteristics (3.1) and shows an example for a business service offered (3.2)

3.1   Business Process Outsourcing of Energy Distribution Companies

SIV.AG from Rostock (Germany) offers business process outsourcing services to a variety of medium-sized utility providers and other market roles of the energy sector in Germany, Bulgaria, Macedonia and other European countries.

Energy distribution companies are facing a continuously changing business environment due to new regulations and bylaws from regulating authorities and due to competitors implementing innovative technical solutions in grid operations or metering services. In this context, both the business processes in organizations and information systems supporting these processes need to be quickly adaptive to changing organizational needs.

Business process outsourcing, i.e. the performance of a complete business process for a business function by a service provider outside an organization, has to offer and implement solutions for different cases. One variation is inherent in the business process as such. Even though core processes can be defined and implemented in standard software systems, configurations and adjustments for the organization in question are needed. The second cause of variation is the configuration for the country of use, which not only includes the usual localization, but also includes implementation of the actual regulations and bylaws. The third variation is related to the resource use for implementing the actual business process for the customer, i.e. the provision of technical and organizational capacities and capabilities.

3.2   Business Service MSCONS

The MSCONS (Metered Service Consumption Report Message) use case is viewed from a global perspective. The purpose of the global process in MSCONS use case is the transmission of energy consumption data from one market role to another role. By regulatory requirement, all data must be sent by e-mail and its format must comply with the international UN/EDIFACT standard. In addition to this requirement, national variants of the EDIFACT standard may exist that add further constraints to the syntactical structure of exchanged messages. Thus, messages must not only comply with the international but also with the national EDIFACT standard, which are subject to periodical change by the regulatory authorities, with usually two releases per year.

The process is triggered with a received MSCONS message after which the first syntax check happens. The second check is the examination of model error. In this task the rules force the declaration of a unique transaction ID between communicating partners. If there is no model error, the messages are classified. After this, a processability error check per message is performed. Messages may be invalid though syntactically correct. An invalid message causes an exception to be thrown. Currently, all of these exceptions are treated manually, involving the role of a knowledge worker. In the future it is possible to offer dynamic capabilities that routes the exception handling processes depending on the context in which the exception is thrown (see also section 4.2). If the message is processable, then the reading reason has to be determined since the MSCONS message is triggered due to a change of meter, installation of meter or period meter reading. Each reading reason has specific processes, still some components are recurring. After all messages are processed, they have to be archived. Fig. 2 illustrates only the "happy path" in the process of MSCONS Validation excluding the error conditions. For the sake of brevity the activities specifying which tasks should be executed when exceptions occur are omitted from the use case description and model.

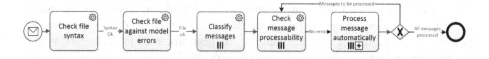

Fig. 2. Process of MSCONS Validation

4   Variation Points for Capability Modelling

This section contains a proposal how to apply concepts from variability modelling, i.e. variation points and variation aspects, for modelling capabilities. At the same time, a formalization of relationships between the core concepts of a capability is proposed (section 4.1) which extends what is defined in the meta-model introduced in section 2. Section 4.2 and 4.3 show the use of variation points and aspects in the industrial case; section 4.4 discusses initial experiences.

4.1 Variation Points and Variation Aspects in Capability Models

As discussed in section 2.2, a further formalization of the term capability and its relations to related concepts is supposed to reduce ambiguities and improve preciseness. At the same time, variability is considered an important aspect in capability modelling and management. This is why we will focus our proposal for a more detailed formalization on aspects related to variability. The basic idea of our approach is inspired by variability modelling in general and feature modelling in particular (see section 2.3). We propose to identify those aspects in business services of an enterprises where alternative flows, functions or procedures are possible and to identify cause and type of variations. For this purpose, we introduce *variation aspects* as the cause of variations and *variation points* as the locations of the variations in the business service model. Variations in behavior, functionality or content can be caused by different aspects, like performance indicators, exception types or information input. Since the context of a capability and its elements already have been introduced as characteristics of adapting capabilities, our approach is that these variation aspects correspond to context elements. Variation aspects can be relevant for different business services and at different positions in the business service model. A variation point identifies the business service model element where a variation with respect to a specific variation aspect occurs.

The formalization introduced in the following reflects the above ideas and starts with defining capability, context, business service, pattern and variant. Based on this definition, we introduce variation aspects and variation points and interlink them. Regarding the variants, our proposal is to also consider the fact, that variants can be composed of different alternating, optional or mandatory sub-variants. Decomposing variants in such a way will ease adaptation to different context.

A capability structure is a tuple $Cap := \{B, C, P, V, BT, CT, PT, VAss, VS, type\}$, consisting of

- disjoint sets B and BT whose elements are called business service model elements and business service model element types respectively; and a function $type_B : BT \rightarrow B$, that assigns a type $bt_i \in BT$ to an element $b_i \in B$

  We assume that an enterprise's services offered to their customers can be modelled. B represents the different elements of such a model and BT the types used. The inner structure of the model could be further specified, for example using OMG's MOF. We by intention do not further specify the content of B since this is not required for our approach. B could be a business process model with attached web services or a software specification in UML, to just name two examples. With respect to the meta-model from section 2.1, B represents the Process concept.

- disjoint sets C, and CT whose elements are called context elements and context element types, respectively; and a function $type_C : CT \rightarrow C$, that assigns a type $ct_i \in CT$ to each $c_i \in C$. C and CT represent the ContextSet concept from the meta-model.

- disjoint sets P, and PT whose elements are called pattern elements and pattern element types, respectively, with $PT \subseteq BT$ and a function $type_P : PT \rightarrow P$, that assigns a type $pt_i \in PT$ to each $p_i \in P$. P and PT represent the Pattern concept from the meta-model.
- a set of variants V with $\forall v_i \in V : v_i \subset B \vee v_i \subset P$. V represents the ProcessVariant concept from the meta-model.

Based on the above capability structure, we define a variability assignment as a tuple $VAss := \{VA, VP, VPT, R, var\}$, consisting of

- Sets of variation aspect VA with $VA \subseteq C$ which means that each $va_i \in VA$ consists of one or several $c_i \in C$.
- Sets of variation point types VPT with $VPT \subseteq PT$ and set of variation points VP with $VP \subseteq P$ and $\forall vp_i \in VP : type_V (vp_i) \in VPT$
- Set of relations R and a function $var : R \mapsto VA \times VP$ with $\forall vp_i \in VP : \exists va_i \in VA : var(R)(va_i, vp_i)$. This function relates variation aspects from the context to variation points in a pattern or variant. With var(R) = (va_i,vp_j) we define vp_j as a variation dependant on va_i.

Furthermore, we define a variability specification as a tuple $VS := \{V, R, man, opt, alt, req, excl\}$, consisting of

- the variation set V introduced above and a set R whose elements are called relations; V and R are disjoined sets.
- A function $man : R \mapsto V \times V$ that relates mandatory variants. With man(R) = (V_1,V_2) we define V_2 as a mandatory sub-variant of V_1.
- A function $opt : R \mapsto V \times V$ that relates optional variants. With opt(R) = (V_1,V_2) we define V_2 as an optional sub-variant of V_1.
- A function $alt : R \mapsto V \times V$ that relates alternative variants. With alt(R) = (V_1,V_2) we define V_2 as an alternative sub-variant of V_1.
- A function $req : R \mapsto V \times V$ that relates required features. With req(R) = (V_1,V_2) we define V_2 as a required variant for V_1.
- A function $excl : R \mapsto V \times V$ that relates mutually-exclusive features. With excl(R) = (V_1,V_2) we define V_2 is mutual-exclusive to V_1.

The functions are inspired by the relation types used in feature modeling for expressing relations between features (see section 2.3).

4.2   Context of Business Service Delivery

Context is a term that is used in many domains of computer science like artificial intelligence, operating systems, software engineering, databases, knowledge representation etc. The concept of context is also adapted by different disciplines other than computer sciences such as cognitive or social sciences. Thus the various definitions of context arise due to its widespread use. According to the framework of context use, the definitions and characteristics vary [14]. It is important that one should speak of the context in reference to its use [15], since there is no real consensual definition. Hence interpretation of context depends on the field of knowledge that it belongs to [16]. In accordance with [17] context is defined in this work as "any information that can be used to characterize the situation of any entity".

In the business process outsourcing use case described above, it is possible to identify context sets that consist of different context elements. These context elements define variation aspects introduced in section 4.1 and are related to the variation points in the process models (see section 4.3). For instance in order to execute the process "check file syntax" properly, the information about the country where the company operates is needed so that the appropriate service of the application is activated and parses the message. In addition other information like the role of the issuer and the addressee, the type of the message, the message version as well as the energy commodity needs to be acquired to "classify messages" before checking their processability (see also Fig. 2). The affects of the context elements to the process execution are demonstrated in the following section.

The values of such context elements form a context set, which is required to realize the capability "MSCONS processes supporting automated validation & exception handling". This capability is required to ensure correct exchange of messages between market roles. Different context sets arise due to various constellations of context elements. Since these context sets require the adoption of process variations, they are the main causes of process variability. This list of context elements derived from the use case and their ranges are illustrated in Table 1.

Table 1. Context Elements as Causes of Variability

ContextElement	Range
Country	{EU, Non EU}
Role	{Grid Operator, Balance Supplier}
Service Contract	{Types of Exceptions, Backlog size}
Application Reference	{LG, EM, VL, TL}
Process Execution	{Cloud, Customer, SIV}
Commodity	{Gas, Electric, Water}
Message Type	{MSCONS, UTILMD}
Message Version	{2.2a, 2.2b, 5.0, 5.1}
Exception Handling	{Routine, Knowledge Worker}

4.3   Variation Points in the Industrial Case

This section aims at applying the idea of variation points and variation aspects to the industrial case presented in section 3. Since the business services in the case are defined and modelled in a process-centred way, we will consider processes and process variants instead of business services in general.

Process variations are used to react to the anticipated changes in context and to adjust the capability delivery process as the following scenario demonstrates: the system imports an MSCONS message sent from the market role "grid operator" to another market role "balance supplier" with the message type "change of balancing area". In this case the application does not execute the standard process that changes the balancing area, but instead it changes the tariff that the customer uses. If the same message type was sent from the balance supplier to grid operator, then the standard process that changes the balancing area had to be executed. Thus two context elements "market role" and "message type" form the context set "CS1". The context set information is applied to complex gateway in Fig. 3.

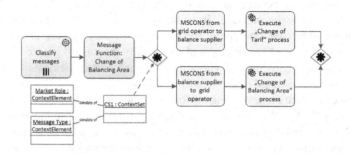

Fig. 3. Variation Points and Context Set

Regarding the formalization of capability structure, following observations were made. The business service model elements (B) are activities in MSCONS Validation processes. The context elements (C) that are required to realize the capability are listed in Table 1. In accordance with the actual values of context elements, different process variants (V) can be executed to deliver the capability. In order to deliver the capability, the variability should be assigned ($VAss$) by applying patterns (P). The variability assignment was also defined as a tuple. The variation points (VP) are those activities in the process model directly affected by the context set, hence they are related to one or more context elements. Moreover, the context set defines the variation aspects (VA). In this example we have a variation aspect of a "process execution" depending on context elements like roles and message types. This shows that the variation aspects are related to the variability points via context. Last but not least, different relations between process variants can be specified (VS), e.g. the process variants in Fig. 3 are mutually exclusive, since only one of them can occur at a time.

4.4   Discussion

The application of variation points and variations aspects in the industrial case confirmed that these concepts originating from feature modelling in principle can be transferred to capability modelling. Variation aspects, which in feature modelling are the characteristics deciding about mandatory, optional, mutually-exclusive or required features correspond to context elements in capability modelling; variation points in feature models are the different feature nodes which corresponds to business service model elements in capability models, e.g. activities in the process models of the industrial use case. However, the utility of variant hierarchies from feature modelling intuitively makes sense, but still has to be investigated in capability modelling.

The formalization of the relations between context, process, pattern, variant and capability resolves some of the ambiguities discussed in section 2, but not all of them. The definition of operational semantics still is required if capability models are meant to transformed to executable or enactable representations. The way of formalization presented in section 4.1 is not the only possibility. Using OCL constraints or other formal languages as annotations to the existing relationships between concepts in combination with further refinement of the concepts' attributes would be another option.

Although the formalization does not assume a process-oriented perspective on business services, the practical use with other business service representations, e.g. in functional or declarative paradigms, will have to be investigated in future work, since the industrial case only confirmed the use process-oriented business services.

5   Summary

New situations in business environments arise due to changes in regulations, bylaws and customer preferences. The capabilities help companies to continuously deliver a certain business value in these dynamically changing circumstances by adjusting the service delivery to different contexts. This paper focuses on the variation aspects of the business services which are triggered by the changes in context. As a starting point the capability meta-model introduced in [13] is taken.

In section 2 the relations between the concepts concerning the capability are discussed. These discussions addressed the need to contribute to capability modelling by specifying the relations of the meta-model components, particularly Capability, Process and Context. At the same time, we suggested that variability is considered as important aspect in capability modelling and introduced an example from an industrial use case. The variation aspects are mainly reflected on the business processes since the use case is modelled in a process-centred way. In the future, the relation between variation aspects and different paradigms such as service-oriented-architectures can be further investigated.

Another contribution of this work is an initial formalization approach that is proposed to increase preciseness of the term capability and to specify how the term is related to the aspects in the meta-model concerning variability. In that way we aim to avoid ambiguities identified in the underlying capability meta-model and enumerated in section 2.2. Future challenges may include attempts to specify or extend the formal capability definition to emphasize the semantics of associations between the capability components.

Acknowledgments. This work has been performed in the EU-FP7 funded project no. 611351 CaaS - Capability as a Service in Digital Enterprises.

References

1. Gunasekaran, A., McGaughey, R., Wolstencroft, V.: Agile Manufacturing: Concepts and Framework. In: Gunasekaran, A. (ed.) Agile Manufacturing: The 21st Century Competitive Strategy, pp. 25–49. Elsevier (2001)
2. Tapscott, D., Lowy, A., Ticoll, D.: Digital capital. Harnessing the power of business webs. Harvard Business School Press, Boston (2000)
3. Fong, M.W.L.: E-collaborations and virtual organizations. IRM Press, Hershey (2005)
4. Frank, U.: Multi-perspective enterprise modeling: foundational concepts, prospects and future research challenges. Softw. Syst. Model. (2012), doi:10.1007/s10270-012-0273-9
5. Thörn, C., Sandkuhl, K.: Feature Modeling: Managing Variability in Complex Systems. In: Tolk, A., Jain, L.C. (eds.) Complex systems in knowledge-based environments. SCI, vol. 168, pp. 129–162. Springer, Heidelberg (2009)
6. Open Group Standard TOGAF Version 9.1, http://pubs.opengroup.org/architecture/togaf9-doc/arch/chap03.html (accessed March 06, 2014)
7. Jiang, Y., Zhao, J.: An empirical research of the forming process of Firm inter-organizational e-business capability: Based on the supply chain processes. In: 2010 2nd International Conference on Information Science and Engineering (ICISE), pp. 2603–2606 (2010)
8. Antunes, G., Barateiro, J., Becker, C., et al.: Modeling Contextual Concerns in Enterprise Architecture. In: 2011 15th IEEE International Enterprise Distributed Object Computing Conference Workshops (EDOCW), pp. 3–10 (2011)
9. Eriksson, T.: Processes, antecedents and outcomes of dynamic capabilities. Scandinavian Journal of Management (2013), doi: 10.1016/j.scaman, 05.001
10. Boonpattarakan, A.: Model of Thai Small and Medium Sized Enterprises' Organizational Capabilities: Review and Verification. JMR 4(3) (2012), doi: 10.5296/jmr.v4i3.1557
11. Stirna, J., Grabis, J., Henkel, M., Zdravkovic, J.: Capability Driven Development – An Approach to Support Evolving Organizations. In: Sandkuhl, K., Seigerroth, U., Stirna, J. (eds.) PoEM 2012. LNBIP, vol. 134, pp. 117–131. Springer, Heidelberg (2012)
12. Chen, J., Tsou, H.: Performance effects of 5IT6 capability, service process innovation, and the mediating role of customer service. Journal of Engineering and Technology Management 29(1), 71–94 (2012), doi:10.1016/j.jengtecman.2011.09.007
13. Zdravkovic, J., Stirna, J., Henkel, M., Grabis, J.: Modeling Business Capabilities and Context Dependent Delivery by Cloud Services. In: Salinesi, C., Norrie, M.C., Pastor, Ó. (eds.) CAiSE 2013. LNCS, vol. 7908, pp. 369–383. Springer, Heidelberg (2013)
14. Ben Mena, T., Bellamine-Ben Saoud, N., Ben Ahmed, M., Pavard, B.: Towards a Methodology for Context Sensitive Systems Development. In: Kokinov, B., Richardson, D.C., Roth-Berghofer, T.R., Vieu, L. (eds.) CONTEXT 2007. LNCS (LNAI), vol. 4635, pp. 56–68. Springer, Heidelberg (2007)
15. Brézillon, P., Cavalcanti, M.: Modeling and Using Context. Knowl. Eng. Rev. 13(2), 185–194 (1998), doi:10.1017/S0269888998004044
16. Bazire, M., Brézillon, P.: Understanding Context Before Using It. In: Dey, A.K., Kokinov, B., Leake, D.B., Turner, R. (eds.) CONTEXT 2005. LNCS (LNAI), vol. 3554, pp. 29–40. Springer, Heidelberg (2005)
17. Dey, A.K.: Understanding and using context. Personal and Ubiquitous Computing 5(1), 4–7 (2001)

Capability Sourcing Modeling

A High-Level Conceptualization Based on Service-Dominant Logic

Laleh Rafati and Geert Poels

Center for Service Intelligence
Faculty of Economics and Business Administration, Ghent University,
Tweekerkenstraat 2, 9000 Gent, Belgium
{laleh.rafati,geert.poels}@UGent.be

Abstract. Companies need to acquire the right capabilities from the right source, and the right shore, at the right cost to improve their competitive position. Capability sourcing is an organizing process to gain access to best-in-class capabilities for all activities in a firm's value chain to ensure long-term competitive advantage. In this paper, capability sourcing modeling is introduced as a technique to create sourcing alternative solutions to facilitate strategic sourcing decision making. Our approach is applying conceptual models as intermediate artifacts which are schematic descriptions of sourcing alternatives based on organization's capabilities. Therefore, a high-level conceptualization based on Service-Dominant Logic (S-D Logic) is proposed as a language to create capability sourcing conceptual models.

Keywords: strategic sourcing, capability sourcing, capability sourcing modeling, capability sourcing conceptual models, service system, dynamic capability, competitive advantage.

1 Introduction

"For years, sourcing has just been another word for procurement — a financial material, but strategically peripheral, corporate function. Now, globalization, aided by rapid technology innovation, is changing the basis of competition [1]. *It's no longer a company's ownership of capabilities that matters but rather its ability to control and make the most of critical capabilities, whether or not they reside on the company's balance sheet"* [1].

"Sourcing is evolving into a strategic process for organizing and fine-tuning the value chain" [1]. Companies should be looking for alternative sourcing of business capabilities to seize new market opportunities. Yet few companies are taking full advantage of the cost and flexibility opportunities in the new global arena [1].

Strategic sourcing is a systematic and fact based approach for optimizing an organization's supply base and improving the overall value proposition. *"Strategic sourcing allows companies to take full advantage of cost, flexibility and new capability opportunities; whether delivered by traditional suppliers, trading partners, distributors, agents and even customer self-service models"* [2].

L. Iliadis, M. Papazoglou, and K. Pohl (Eds.): CAiSE 2014 Workshops, LNBIP 178, pp. 77–87, 2014.
© Springer International Publishing Switzerland 2014

Strategic sourcing is rooted in the idea that a business must have a set of explicitly defined capabilities in order to execute its strategy successfully [2]. *"Leaders often mistake the course of action and pursue a wrong path — diverting attention from the intended strategy. A root cause is often that strategic intent and objectives are not articulated in clear operating language for better execution. A written strategy does not ensure strategic action"* [2].

Sourcing decisions are strategic decisions at the management level of organization. These decisions are related to the organizing process of an organization. Organizing is defined as the process of arranging resources to work together to accomplish a goal [3]. The organizing process formulates corporate strategies to achieve competitive advantage through arranging the firm's resources and configuring the firm's capabilities within a changing environment. In the organizing process, strategic decisions are made about choosing the right sourcing solutions like outsourcing, insourcing or co-sourcing. Sourcing decisions include the commitments, decisions and actions required for a firm to achieve strategic competitiveness on resources and organizational capabilities.

At the strategic management level in an organization, decision makers need to share a common ground or a common language to facilitate their discussions [4]. A common language is needed to define and articulate concepts that facilitate the description of objects of strategic interest and that improve the strategic discussions and enhance related decision making [5]. We introduce capability sourcing modeling as a technique to create sourcing alternative solutions. Capability sourcing models can facilitate strategic sourcing decision making to choose the right sourcing solution for the organization. Our approach is applying a conceptualization based on service system as a language for modeling the relevant concepts of strategic capability sourcing. This conceptualization can serve as a common language to facilitate discussions about sourcing at the strategic management level in an organization.

A theoretical background of strategic sourcing and competitive advantage is explained in the next section. In the third section, the capability sourcing process and modeling are introduced as an approach to improve the firm's competitive position. Finally, in the last section, conceptualization as a solution is proposed for capability sourcing modeling.

2   Theoretical Background

Strategy is the direction and scope of an organization over the long term, which achieves competitive advantage for the organization through its configuration of resources and capabilities within a changing environment. Companies need to leverage right *strategic sourcing* (the right capability at the right cost from the right source and the right shore) to improve their competitive position. *Competitive advantage* is the ability to create more economic value than competitors. It is a firm's profitability that is greater than the average profitability for all firms in its industry. Furthermore, sustained competitive advantage is a firm maintaining above average and superior profitability and profit growth for a number of years. Competitive advantage results in *superior profitability.* The primary objective of strategic sourcing is to achieve a sustained competitive advantage which in turn results in superior profit and profit growth [6].

The firm's resources, capabilities and competencies are the main factors driving the strategic sourcing. *Resources* are the assets that organizations has or can call upon (e.g. from partners or suppliers), that is, 'What the firm Has'. Two categories of resources are tangible resources and intangible resources.

According to the Resource-Based View (RBV) theory, a firm is able to achieve sustained competitive advantage if it can acquire and control Valuable, Rare, Inimitable, and Non-substitutable (VRIN) resources [7]. *Valuable resources* need to deliver a product or service that is not currently available from a competitor. Only value-adding resources can lead to competitive advantage, whereas non-value-adding resources may lead to competitive disadvantage. *Rare resources* are those possessed uniquely by one organization or by a few others only (e.g. a company may have patented products, have supremely talented people or a powerful brand). Rarity could be temporary (e.g. patents expire, key individuals can leave or brands can be de-valued by adverse publicity). Valuable common resources can lead to competitive parity but no advantage. Valuable rare resources can provide, at best, temporary competitive advantage. *Inimitable resources* are those that competitors find difficult to imitate or obtain, usually due to unique historical conditions, causal ambiguity or social complexity. They are things such as culture, partnerships and working relationships perhaps underpinned by recruitment, training, motivating and rewarding staff. Valuable, rare, but imitable resources provide temporary advantage. Only valuable, rare and hard-to-imitate resources can provide sustained competitive advantage. *Non-substitutable resources* do not have strategic equivalents, such as firm-specific knowledge or trust-based relationships. Valuable, rare, hard-to-imitate resources and non-substitutable resources can also provide sustained competitive advantage [8].

VRIN resources if managed by unskilled people will provide no benefit to the firm. The resources themselves do not confer any advantage for a company if they are not organized to capture the value from them. A firm must organize its management systems, processes, policies, organizational structure and culture to be able to fully realize the potential of its valuable, rare, hard-to-imitate and non-substitutable resources. Only then the companies can achieve sustained competitive advantage. Therefore, VRIN framework is modified to VRIO framework [9]. For a firm's resources to be the basis of a competitive advantage, they must have VRIO attributes: valuable (V), rare (R), costly to imitate and non-substitutable (I) and Organization (O). Also the firm must be able to organize (O) in order to capture the value of the resources. The organization (O) means *"how is a firm organized to develop and leverage the full potential of its resources base"* [9].

The concept of *capability* represents the firm's capacity or ability to integrate the firm's tangible and intangible resources to achieve a desired objective, that is "What the firm Does". So, capabilities can be considered as the Organization (O) in VRIO, as the firm's capacity and ability to capture the value of resources [9].

The concept of Competency captures the essence of what makes an organization unique in its ability to provide value to customers. Competencies are "What a firm

Does that is strategically valuable" (e.g. product design skills, cooperative relation-ships). *Distinctive competency* is something that an organization does particularly well relative to its competitors. It is a unique firm-specific strength that allows a company to better differentiate or achieve lower cost than rivals [6]. These arise from VRIN resources and capabilities.

Summarizing, strategic sourcing is the direction of an organization to achieve competitive advantage through its configuration of VRIN resources, capabilities and distinctive competencies within a changing environment. (Fig.1)

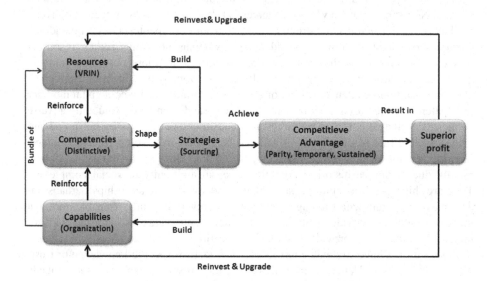

Fig. 1. Competitive advantage through strategic sourcing

To complete the theoretical foundation of our proposed solution, one more concept is needed. The *Dynamic Capability (DC)* of an organization is defined as "*the capacity of an organization to purposefully create, extend, and modify its resource base*" [10]. The resource base includes the tangible, intangible resources as well as capabilities which the organization owns, controls, or has access to on a preferential basis [10]. The concept of DC has evolved from the RBV theory. RBV proponents argue that VFIN resources can be a source of superior performance, and may enable the firm to achieve sustained competitive advantage. DC has lent value to the RBV arguments as it transforms what is essentially a static view into one that can encompasses competitive advantage in a dynamic context [11], [12],[13]. Therefore, the "O" in VRIO should refer to DC as the organization (O) needed to transform bundles of resources into competitive advantage [9].

Three cluster of capabilities can be realized by DC: 1) Sensing capability - dynamic capability of opportunity identification; 2) Seizing capability - dynamic capability of opportunity investment; and 3) Transforming capability - dynamic capability of recombination and reconfiguration. The enterprise will need sensing, seizing, and reconfiguring capabilities to be simultaneously developed and applied for it to build and maintain competitive advantage [14].

The roots of competitive advantage are thus found in DC, as shown in Fig 2. The Dynamic Capability lets a firm arrange and develop its resources to create and capture value. This ability leads to achievement of competitive advantage. For creating and capturing value, two basic strategies are low cost (similar product at lower cost) and differentiation (price premium from unique product) [6].

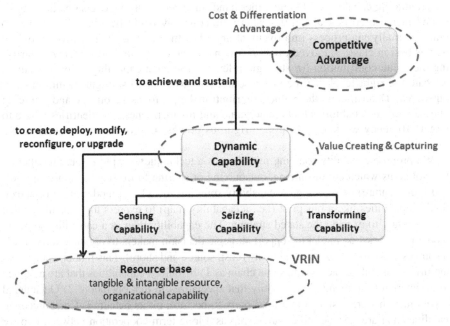

Fig. 2. Dynamic capability to achieve and sustain competitive advantage

3   Solution Approach

Capability sourcing began as a cost-cutting measure, but companies that create real sustained value routinely use it for far more strategic ends to gain capabilities that they don't have in-house, or to strengthen capabilities they do have, for everything from developing world-class talent to bringing new products to market faster and enabling business model innovation [15]. The capability sourcing process improves a company's competitive position by ensuring that processes and functions are obtained from the right source at the right cost. Greater focus on capability sourcing can improve a company's strategic position by reducing costs, streamlining the organization, and improving quality [15]. Also it can support companies for finding more-qualified partners to provide critical functions that usually allow to enhance their core capabilities that drive competitive advantage in their industries [1].

Capability sourcing is a process of gaining access to best-in-class (sensing, seizing, and reconfiguring) capabilities in a company's value chain to ensure sustained competitive advantage. Right sourcing of sensing, seizing, and reconfiguring capabilities improves the competitive position of firm across the value chain and within a changing environment. Right sourcing means leveraging the right capability at the right cost from the right source and the right shore to improve the competitive position. Capabilities are the key to alignment and successful strategy execution. Capabilities exist across the value chain and in order to achieve high-performance a business must learn to manage capabilities that other parties in the value chain perform. They must learn to govern a network of capabilities. Right sourcing allows sharper focus on differentiating capabilities. On the other hand, incorrect sourcing decisions limit agility and increase costs. Capabilities where the company is not best in class can be, 1) built internally via process improvement and investment; 2) outsourced to a provider who is best in class; 3) moved offshore when cost and/or quality are superior. Clarifying the value contribution (or strategic relevance) of each capability helps a business allocate the right level of time and resources — whether to strengthen, minimize or outsource. Determining the value contribution helps focus resources and sourcing alternatives on capabilities that create value and distinctiveness, or identifies where to target efficiency work, either through rigorous process improvement or sourcing to a low cost provider [2].

We propose capability sourcing modeling as a technique to explore sourcing alternative solutions which are insourcing, outsourcing or sharing forms (e.g. in-house, spin-off and joint venture) of sourcing. A capability sourcing model is a model of an organization's capabilities like a blueprint (i.e., a capability map) to express the capabilities that are necessary to execute the stated strategy. The capability map as a capability sourcing model is a black-box model to support strategic decision makers to organize their firm's resources and capabilities in a right way (cost, source and shore). This model can express the firm's capabilities across the value chain as 1) Insourced capabilities that are assigned to an internal (but 'stand-alone') entity that specializes in that operation. 2) Outsourced capabilities that are assigned to a third party to perform on its behalf. 3) Co-sourced capabilities that are assigned to a partnership as a long-term cooperation between two (or more) business partners. Therefore, the capability map can facilitate decision making to choose the right sourcing forms as in Table 1.

Table 1. Sourcing alternatives based on a capability map

Capability	Sourcing alternatives (forms)
Insourced capabilities	▪ Shared service center (SSC) ▪ Captive center
Outsourced capabilities	▪ Nearshore outsourcing ▪ Offshore outsourcing ▪ Business Process Outsourcing (BPO) ▪ Build Operate Transfer (BOT)
Co-sourced capabilities	▪ Selective sourcing ▪ Joint venture ▪ Strategic alliance

Our approach to create a capability sourcing model as a part of sourcing solutions is applying conceptual modeling. "*Conceptual modeling is a widely applied practice and has led to a large body of knowledge on constructs that might be used for modeling and on methods that might be useful for modeling"* [16]. The main purpose of conceptual modeling is extraction of a high-quality conceptual schema of a system.

"Conceptual models are used as intermediate artifact for system construction. They are schematic descriptions of a system, a theory, or a phenomenon of an origin thus forming a model" [17], [18]. A conceptual model is a model enhanced by concepts. Conceptual models use a language as a carrier for the modeling artifact and are restricted by the expressiveness of this carrier [17], [18]. This language is often also used for the description of the concepts that are incorporated into a modeling result.

Therefore, for capability sourcing modeling, we use conceptual models as intermediate artifacts which are schematic descriptions of sourcing alternatives based on organization's capabilities. We propose the Service-Dominant Logic (S-D Logic) as a language and the service system abstraction as a high-level conceptualization [19] for modeling the intermediate artifacts in capability sourcing conceptual modeling.

4   Proposed Solution

"Conceptualization aims at collection of objects, concepts and other entities that are assumed to exist in some area of interest and the relationships that hold among them. It is thus an abstract, simplified view or description of the world that we wish to represent. Conceptualization extends the model by a number of concepts that are the basis for an understanding of the model and for the explanation of the model to the user" [17].

S-D Logic provides a framework for thinking more clearly about the service system and its role in competition (competitive advantage) [20], [21]. The S-D Logic views a service system as a dynamic value co-creation configuration of resources, including at least one operant resource, all connected internally and externally to other service systems by value propositions [22]. Service system as a dynamic value co-creation configuration of resources is related to the concept of Dynamic Capability that is defined before (in section 2) as the capacity of an organization to purposefully reconfigure its resource base. More specifically, the concept of service system can be used for modeling the bundle of VRIN resources that can be used to provide services to other service systems in order to create value and then to achieve the sustained competitive advantage. (Fig. 3)

S-D Logic views service as the application of operant resources – for example skills and knowledge that are capable of acting and producing effects in other resources – for the benefit of another party. Service is the fundamental basis of exchange. *"Competing through service is about applying operant resources better than the competition"* [20], [21]. The concept of service can be used for modeling the connection between service systems as the "service-for-service exchange" that is needed to create value.

S-D Logic represents a shift in focus from operand to operant resources. Operand resources are resources upon which an operation or act is performed to produce an effect like primarily physical resources, goods, etc. Operant resources are resources that produce effects e.g., primarily knowledge and skills. Operant resources are active resources that are capable of creating value [23]. Competitive advantage is a function of how one firm applies its operant resources to meet the needs of the customer relative to how another firm applies its operant resources. Since applied operant resources are what are exchanged in the market, they are the source of competitive advantage. *"Operant resources are the fundamental source of competitive advantage"* [20], [21]. The concept of operant resource can be used for modeling the VRIN resources and capabilities (resource base) that have potential to achieve the sustained competitive advantage. (Fig. 3)

The ability to integrate operant resources between organizations increases the ability to gain competitive advantage through innovation. Firms gain competitive advantage by engaging customers and value network partners in co-creation activities. One opportunity for organizations to compete through service is to identify innovative ways of co-creating value. The central idea of S-D Logic is the concept of resource integration as a key mechanism for value co-creation. The individual firms need a network-to-network conceptualization of relationships that converge on value creation through a web of resource integration. Resource integration is therefore a multidirectional network-oriented process with parties integrating multiple resources for their own benefit and for the benefit of others [20], [21]. Resource integrating is a process for value co-creation through a value network of actors that results in a competitive advantage. The concepts of value co-creation and resource integration can be used for modeling the collaborative relationships between a firm and its value network partners to achieve the sustained competitive advantage. (Fig. 3)

The core concepts of S-D Logic like service exchange, value co-creation, resource integration, and collaborative relationships point to a generic actor conceptualization in which all actors engaged in exchange (e.g., firms, customers, etc.) are viewed as service provider or value creator. In other words, all social and economic actors are essentially doing the same thing: creating value for themselves and others through reciprocal resource integration and service provision [24]. S-D Logic views the social and economic actors as an operant resource – a resource that is capable of acting on other resources, a collaborative partner who co-creates value. *"The value network member (actor) that is the prime integrator is in a stronger competitive position"* [20], [21]. The concept of actor (resource integrator or value co-creator) can be used for modeling internal and external service providers. (Fig. 3)

Value comes from the ability to act in a manner that is beneficial to a party. Value is subjective and always ultimately determined by the beneficiary, who in turn is always a co-creator of the value. Value creation is at the heart of competitive advantage. A firm is said to have a competitive advantage only if it can create more economic value than its competitors. The concept of value can be used for modeling value creating (value-in-use) and value capturing (value-in-exchange) to achieve the sustained competitive advantage [25]. (Fig. 3)

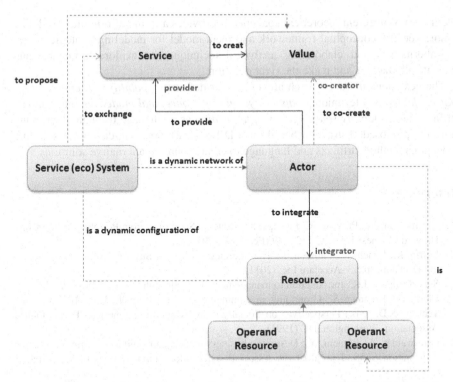

Fig. 3. A high level conceptualization for capability sourcing modeling

The proposed conceptualization (Fig. 3) can be applied to build capability sourcing conceptual models as intermediate artifacts which are schematic descriptions of sourcing alternatives based on organization's capabilities. Service system can be used for modeling the bundle of (operand/operant) resources which are able to exchange services through value propositions. The bundle of resources in a service system can be available internally or externally. Therefore, it can be provided through internal providers (firm) or external providers (market). Determining the value contribution of a service system can be used to analyze whether resources are able to provide a (sustained, temporary, parity) competitive advantage within an capability or not. This analysis may be a step toward a decision on making, buying or sharing this capability.

5   Conclusion

Capability sourcing conceptual models as intermediate artifacts are schematic descriptions of sourcing alternatives based on organization's capabilities. These models help decision makers to choose the right sourcing alternatives for capabilities such as insourcing forms (e.g. in-house, captive center), outsourcing forms (e.g. spin- off, divestment) and sharing forms (e.g. strategic alliance, joint venture). S-D Logic is introduced as a language and conceptualization for modeling these intermediate artifacts in capability sourcing. The proposed 'high-level' conceptualization is more an integration of different theoretical concepts. It provides a frame of reference to define a more specific conceptual framework and meta-model for modeling strategic sourcing alternatives and elaborating analytical techniques to explore, compare, and evaluate alternatives and make the right decision.

The next steps in our research are 1) Further defining *capability sourcing conceptual modeling* as a technique, *capability sourcing conceptual models* as intermediate artifacts and *capability sourcing conceptualization* as a language through elaborating more the proposed abstraction based on S-D Logic; 2) Applying capability sourcing conceptual method, artifacts and language to create sourcing alternative solutions.

References

1. Gottfredson, M., Puryear, R., Phillips, S.: Strategic Sourcing: From Periphery to the Core. Harvard Business Review, 132–139 (February 2005)
2. Loftin, R., Lynch, R., Calhoun, J.: The Sourcing Canvas: A Strategic Approach to Sourcing Decisions, p. 13. Accelare Inc. (2011)
3. Schermerhorn, J.R.: Introduction to management, 12th edn. John Wiley & Sons (2012)
4. Clark, H., Brennan, S.: Grounding in communication. In: Resnick, L.B., Levine, J.M., Teasley, S.D. (eds.) Perspectives on Socially-shared Cognition, American Psychological Association, Washington, DC (1991)
5. Osterwalder, A., Pigneur, Y.: Designing business models and similar strategic objects: the contribution of IS. Journal of the Association for Information Systems 14(5), Article 3 (2013)
6. Hill, C., Jones, G.: Strategic Management: an integrated approach, 10th edn. Cengage Learning (2012)
7. Barney, J.B.: Gaining and sustaining competitive advantage, 2nd edn. Prentice Hall, Upper Saddle River (2002)
8. Barney, J.: Firm resources and sustained competitive advantage. Journal of Management 17(1), 99–120 (1991)
9. Cardeal, N., António, N.: Valuable, rare, inimitable resources and organization (VRIO) resources or valuable, rare, inimitable resources (VRI) capabilities: What leads to competitive advantage? African Journal of Business Management 6(37), 10159–10170 (2012)
10. Helfat, C., Finkelstein, S., Mitchell, W., Peteraf, M., Singh, H., Teece, D., Winter, S.: Dynamic Capabilities: Understanding Strategic Change in Organizations. Blackwell, Malden (2007)
11. Ambrosini, V., Bowman, C., Collier, N.: Dynamic capabilities: An exploration of how firms renew their resource base. British Journal of Management 20(S1), S9-S24 (2009)
12. Barney, J.B.: Is the resource-based view a useful perspective for strategic management research? Yes. Academy of Management Review 26, 41–56 (2001a)
13. Barney, J.B.: Resource-based theories of competitive advantage: a ten year retrospective on the resource-based view. Journal of Management 27, 643–650 (2001b)
14. Teece, D.J.: Explicating dynamic capabilities: The nature and micro foundations of sustainable enterprise performance. Strategic Management Journal 28(13), 1319–1350 (2007)
15. Capability Sourcing / Outsourcing/ Offshoring - Bain & Company, http://www.bain.com/consulting-services/ performance-improvement/capability-sourcing.aspx

16. Thalheim, B.: Towards a theory of conceptual modelling. Journal of Universal Computer Science 16(20), 3102–3137 (2010)
17. Thalheim, B.: The science and art of conceptual modelling. In: Hameurlain, A., Küng, J., Wagner, R., Liddle, S.W., Schewe, K.-D., Zhou, X. (eds.) TLDKS VI. LNCS, vol. 7600, pp. 76–105. Springer, Heidelberg (2012)
18. Thalheim, B.: The theory of conceptual models, the theory of conceptual modelling and foundations of conceptual modelling. In: The Handbook of Conceptual Modeling: Its Usage and Its Challenges, ch. 17, pp. 547–580. Springer, Berlin (2011)
19. Poels, G., Van Der Vurst, G., Lemey, E.: Towards an Ontology and Modeling Approach for Service Science. In: Falcão e Cunha, J., Snene, M., Nóvoa, H. (eds.) IESS 2013. LNBIP, vol. 143, pp. 285–291. Springer, Heidelberg (2013)
20. Lusch, R.F., Stephen, L., Vargo, S.L., Matthew, O.: Competing through service: Insights from service-dominant logic. Journal of Retailing 83(1), 2–18 (2007)
21. Mele, C., Della Corte, V.: Resource-based view and Service-dominant logic: Similarities, differences and further research. Journal of Business Market Management 6(4), 192–213 (2013)
22. Lusch, R.F., Vargo, S.L., Wessels, G.: Toward a Conceptual Foundation for Service Science: Contributions from Service-Dominant Logic. IBM Systems Journal 47(1), 5–14 (2008)
23. Vargo, S.L., Lusch, R.F.: Service-Dominant Logic: Premises, Perspectives. Possibilities Naples Forum on Service (2013)
24. Wieland, H., Polese, F., Vargo, S., Lusch, R.F.: Toward a Service (Eco)Systems Perspective on Value Creation. International Journal of Service Science, Management, Engineering, and Technology 3(3), 12–25 2012)
25. Vargo, S.L., Akaka, M.A.: Value Cocreation and Service Systems (Re)Formation: A Service Ecosystems View. Journal of Service Science (2012)

Capability-Based Business Model Transformation

Martin Henkel, Ilia Bider, and Erik Perjons

DSV, Stockholm University, Forum 100, 164 40 Kista, Sweden
{martinh,ilia,perjons}@dsv.su.se

Abstract. Any organization in subject of changes in the environment, or having the desire to improve, needs to change their processes, personnel and their use of resources. Changes, may they be called for by external threats or opportunities or internal strengths or weaknesses, take their departure in an organizations existing capabilities. To support change, there is thus a fundamental need to understand and analyse an organizations capabilities in order to perform changes. In this paper we present an approach to support organizational change by the use of a capability based recursive analysis, and a set of improvement patterns. The recursive analysis is based on resource types, and capability sub-types. We illustrate the approach by using several examples taken from the industry.

Keywords: Dynamic Capability, Capability Engineering, Enterprise Modelling.

1   Introduction

Modern organizations work in ever changing environments. They constantly need to adopt their capabilities to meet new demands from customers and in order to increase their efficiency. Failure of an organization to adapt to radically changing environments can endeavour organizations profitability or even its existence [1]. There are no signs that the pace at which the organizations need to adapt to changes is slowing down. On the contrary, organizations that have a competitive advantage tend to keep that advantage for a shorter time [2]. Thus, to survive and grow in a dynamic environment with global competition for customers, capital and skilled workforce, a modern enterprise needs to quickly adapt its capabilities and business model to changes in the environment. If successful, organizations can use the opportunities these changes offer for launching new products and services.

Adapting to changes in the environment can be a complex task. First, an organization needs to know its current state. Secondly, there is a need to identify and understand the changes that need to be carried out.

There are several ways to describe an organizations current state. One established way is to describe an organization from a resource based view. Taking a resource based view [3] entails examining an organization's resources in the form of tangible and intangible assets under the control of the organization. These resources include the products an organization owns, its personnel skills, its processes, and the information it controls. An organization can, though, make use of its resources in

L. Iliadis, M. Papazoglou, and K. Pohl (Eds.): CAiSE 2014 Workshops, LNBIP 178, pp. 88–99, 2014.

different ways. Therefore, the concept of capability has been introduced. Capability can be defined as the ability of an organization to manage its resources to accomplish a task. The *capabilities* of an organization are thus tightly tied to the management of to its resources.

The resource based view has later been adopted to describe the necessity for organization to be dynamic, and thus develop skills to have "dynamic capabilities" [4]. The problem is, however, that little attention has been paid to providing organizations with a practical, easy-to use approach to analyse its existing capabilities, and to change them.

The long-term goal of our research is to provide a practical approach to model, and change an organization based on its existing capabilities. This paper presents an initial approach that achieves this, based on two main contributions, namely a *modelling approach* that allows the identification and description of organizational capabilities and *patterns* that facilitate change. We ground our approach in an industrial case, showing its initial viability.

The first contribution is a modelling approach that describes an organization as a recursive structure of capabilities, including the resources being used. The objective of having such a model is to help an enterprise to better understand its existing structure of capabilities so that it could be fully exploited and/or improved. Note that the creation of this form of model is not a trivial matter, as only the most visible processes usually catch attention of management and consultants. These easy-to-find processes represent only the tip of an iceberg of processes that exists in the enterprise, often in a half-documented, or in a totally undocumented form.

Our second contribution is a set of initial transformation patterns that allows an organization to find out possible new capabilities. These patterns rely on the previously defined model of capabilities. The approach presented in this paper fulfils one of the research topics as presented by the authors in [5]. In particular we introduce an approach tailored for identifying capabilities, and introduce new patterns for changing an organization.

This paper is structured according to the following. The next section sets this research in the context of related research. Section 3 gives and overview of the approach and defines its key concepts. Section 4 describes the first part of the approach, the recursive modelling of capabilities. Section 5 describes a set of patterns for discovering beneficial changes to the capabilities. Section 6 demonstrates the approach by applying it to an industrial case.

2   Related Research

Using capabilities as the foundation to describe organizations is not new, and can be found in the research domain of strategic management and enterprise architecture. Furthermore, recursive approaches to describe an organization, have been applied in the area of enterprise modelling. The research about these two concepts, capabilities and recursive approaches to describe an organization, are further described in this section.

In strategic management the notion of dynamic capability can be used to describe the key properties that makes and organization withstand and make use of change. Analysis of existing companies has revealed differences in how successful companies manage change [6]. Even though the concept of capability has fluctuated in the area of strategic management, there is a tendency to associate it with resources and their allocation [7]. We use this interpretation of capability, that is, we view resources and their use as an integral part of capabilities. Frameworks such as Barneys VRIN [3] (Valuable, Rare, In-imitable, Non-sustainable) has been suggested as a way to find the resources that constitutes a company's competitive advantage. In contrast to the VRIN framework, our target is not to only elicit the resources that are company unique, we rather provide a tool for analysing all capabilities of an organisation.

In the strategic management area several authors are focusing on business transformations. These transformations can target finding a non-competitive area for products [8], or more general changes to the business model [9]. However these transformations, or patterns, only work on a high-level and thus run the risk of missing business opportunities buried in the lower levels of an organization. The recursive approach presented in this paper can be combined with the above mentioned approaches, since it adds the possibility to in detail analyse an organization.

In the area of enterprise modelling and architecture, the concept of capability has been used as a mean to develop dynamic IT solutions [10], and also to describe an organizations readiness for using enterprise architecture. This is most notable in the open group TOGAF framework [11], where capability frequently refers the architecture readiness of an organization. In general enterprise models has been used before as a step-wise way to analyse and change an organisation [12]. Our modelling approach is however particularly focusing on capabilities and is applying a recursive structure.

Analysis of enterprises based on the idea of a recursive structure has been done by several researchers and practitioners using the concept of fractal organisations, e.g., [13], [14]. In essence, fractals are a high-level abstract idea of a structure with a recurring (recursive) pattern repeating on all levels. Hoverstadt [13] uses the viable system model (VSM) to unfold the fractal structure of the enterprise via the system - subsystems' relationships. Our long term goal is similar to Hoverstadt's: create an approach for modelling an enterprise as a multi-layered complex system. However, we use a different approach to enterprise modelling, instead of system subsystems relationships, we interleave capabilities and resources when building an enterprise model. Moreover, Sandkuhl and Kirikova [14] present the idea to find fractal structures in an enterprise model built when using a general modelling technique. The approach in [14] radically differs from that of ours. We have a hypothesis of a particular fractal structure to be found when analysing an enterprise, while [14] is trying to find any types of the fractal structures based on the generic characteristics of organizational fractals.

3 Overview of the Approach

The approach presented is this paper is based on the idea that an organization's capabilities can be used as a foundation for describing and changing the organisation. Following a resource based view [3], we define a capability as the ability of an organization to manage its resources to accomplish a task. As pointed out in [7] an organization can only be said to exhibit a certain capability if it is able to repeatedly apply it. In essence this also means that the organization must have the resources *and* that the right *capacity* of those resource to perform the tasks. In this paper we build on this view of capabilities and use the notion of resource types (e.g. people, infrastructure), and tasks in the form of execution templates (e.g. a documented manufacturing process).

The approach is built upon two main steps. The first step consists of uncovering an organisations structure by recursively applying the concepts of capabilities and resources. This is aided by the use of a set of *capability resource types* and a set of *capability sub-types*. The second main step consists of transforming the organizational structure to construct a more viable structure. This second step is aided by the use of a set of simple *transformation patterns*. These two steps are described in detail below:

Step1, uncovering the organizational structure, is performed according to the following procedure. One starts with the visible part of the iceberg, so-called main capability. Here, as main we count capabilities that produce value for which some of the enterprise external stakeholders are ready to pay, e.g., customers of a private enterprise, or a local government paying for services provided to the public. Typical examples of main capabilities are product manufacturing, or service delivery (e.g., educational process at a university). When the main capabilities are identified, one proceeds "under water" following up resources that are needed to run the main capability. Each resource type requires a set of so-called supporting capabilities to have the corresponding resources in "working order" waiting to be deployed in the main capability. To supporting capabilities belong, for example, human resources (HR) (e.g., hiring or retiring members of staff) that ensure the enterprise having right people to be engaged in its main activities.

To convert the procedure above into a procedure that could be easily used in practice, we introduce:

- *Capability resource types* that aid in the identification of the resources that are a part of a particular capability. This is especially important as a starting point to unwind an organizations main capability.
- *Capability sub-types* that aid the exploration of supporting capabilities that are needed for each resource that are being part of a (main) capability.

Having these resource types and capability sub-types will help us to unveil the dynamic structure of an organisation starting from the main capability and going downwards via repeating pattern capability, its resources, sub-capabilities for each resource, resources for the sub-capability and so on. As the result we will get an indefinite tree consisting of the same type of elements. Such kind of structures is known in the scientific literature under the name of fractal structures [15]. As the result we will get an indefinite tree consisting of the same type of elements. Such kind of structures is known in the scientific literature under the name of fractal structures [15].

Step 2 aims at transforming the structure identified during step 1. Essentially the aim is to identify sub-capabilities that can be transformed into more customer oriented capabilities, thereby creating a new business model for the organization. A part of this transformation process is to examine if there need to be a change in the resources being used, and the needed capacity of the resources. The transformation can be done in several different ways, however in this paper we focus on supporting an initial transformation by using transformation patterns:

- *A capability transformation pattern* describes a modification of a capability structure (see step 1) into a new structure.

Based on the description above, the goal of this paper is to introduce the resource types, capability sub-types and transformation patterns, and show how to use them in practice to untangle and improve the dynamic structure of an organisation.

The research presented in the paper is done in the frame of the design science paradigm. The goal of such kind of research is finding and testing a generic solution, or artefact, for a class of practical problems [16]. The resource types, capability sub-types and transformation patterns and procedure of using them suggested in this paper constitute the design science artefact.

4   Identifying Organisational Capabilities

In the previous section we gave an overview of the approach, in this section we go into details about the first step - uncovering the organizational structure. We thus first introduce (Section 4.1) how to identify capabilities and their resources before going into details on how to find sub-capabilities (Section 4.1).

4.1   Applying Capability Resources Types

We consider as enterprise any organization where the operational activities of which are financed by external stakeholders. It can, for example, be a private company that gets money for its operational activities from the customers, a head office of an interest organization that gets money from the members, or a public office that gets money from the taxpaying citizens or inhabitants. We consider a main capability of an enterprise to be a capability that produces value to the enterprise's external stakeholders for which they are willing to pay. Note here that the concept of capability includes the resources being used to produce value. Our definition of main capability is thus not the same as the concept of core capability. Core capability refers to the inner sub-capabilities that are unique within a market segment and gives an enterprise competitive advantage [17]. For example, we do not consider as main capability neither sales nor marketing processes, nor product development processes in a product manufacturing company.

To ensure that the enterprise can make use of its capabilities, it is essential that it got the necessary resources and that the capacity of the resources match the need. To describe the resources, is it practical to employ some form of classification scheme. An initial classification of resources coupled with enterprise capabilities is to divide resources into physical infrastructure resources, workforce in form of human capital, and organizational capital resources [3]. Organizational capital resources include the management plans and coordination to perform actions. In order to simplify the identification of resources we use this classification with the following additions: Firstly, in order to describe an enterprises relations to external stakeholders we introduce paying stakeholder (as described above), and partners. Moreover, to focus on the documented management procedures, we refer execution templates. We thus make use of the following resource types:

- *Paying stakeholders.* Examples: customers of a private enterprise, members of an interest organization, local or central government paying for services provided for the public.
- *Workforce* – people trained and qualified for employment. Examples: workers at the conveyor belt, physicians, researchers.
- *Execution templates* (ET). Plans of activities governing the use of resources, such as management policies and document methods. For example, for a production process in a manufacturing company, ET includes product design and design of a technological line to produce the product. For a software development company that provides customer-built software, ET could include a software methodology (project template) according to which their systems development is conducted.
- *Partners.* Partners provide the enterprise with resources needed for the organizational capabilities, e.g., electricity (power provider), money (banks or other type of investors), parts, etc. Partners get compensation for their products and services in form of payment, profit sharing, etc. Partners can be other enterprises or individuals, e.g., retired workers that can be hired in case there is temporal lack of skilled workforce to be engaged in a particular process instance.
- *Infrastructure* – equipment required for running the main task. Examples: production lines, raw materials, computers, communication lines, buildings, software systems etc.

The list of resources types can be extended, and made more fine granular. However, the above list makes a practical foundation for untangling an enterprise's structure. Below we give some additional clarification on the list of resources above.

- All resources are equally important, thus the order in which the resource types are listed is arbitrary.
- The resource types are mostly describing intangible resources. This can make them clash with the notion of resource as used in the world of finance [18]. Except the infrastructure, all resources listed above belong to the category of so-called *intangible* assets of the finance world.
- To be of use, each resource need to available in the right capacity. For example, hosting a niche website with few users may use a similar infrastructure as a popular website with high load, however the capacity of the infrastructure need to be vastly different.

To identify the main capability of an enterprise according to the above description an analysts can ask the question "What are the capabilities that produces value to the enterprise's external stakeholders for which they are willing to pay?". The resource types can then be used to drive the exploration of the main capability. Figure 1 contains an example in graphical form. The figure contains the main capability "Production manufacturing" in an ellipse and its constituent resources using rectangles. The arrows from the oval indicates the dependency that the capability need the resources to function, the *resource type* of each resource is indicated as a label on the arrows. If desired, the needed capacity of the resources could be indicated on the arrows (e.g. that the capability needs 10 workers). Note that the example includes two resources of type "Execution template".

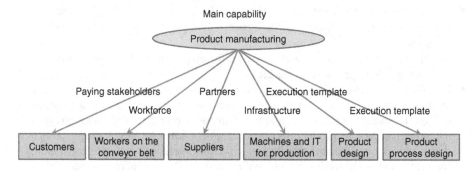

Fig. 1. An example of a main capability and its resources

As shown in the example, the resource types are used to detail the inner workings of a capability. The concept of capability is thus encompassing the resources and their correct configuration in the form of the needed capacities. To further explore an organization, we need to examine each resource in more detail.

4.2 Capability Sub-types

In the previous section we described how to identify main capabilities and their inherent resources. However each resource also needs to be managed to ensure that the overall capability is upheld. For example, an enterprise may need to work to promote their products in order to get new customers, or hire new workers if some workers leave. This handling of resources can be viewed as sub-capabilities. Indeed, some authors point out that this type of resource handling can be crucial for an enterprise and be an essential core capability of the enterprise [17].

To aid in the identification of sub-capabilities we make use of a simple acquire-maintain-retire resource lifecycle associated with each resource:

1. *Acquire* – capabilities that result in the enterprise acquiring a new resource of a given type. The essence of this capability depends on the type of resource, the type of the main capability in which it is used and the type of the enterprise. For a

product-oriented enterprise, *acquiring* new customers (paying stakeholders) is done through its marketing and sales capabilities. *Acquiring* skilled work force is a task completed inside a recruiting process. *Acquiring* a new product design (an execution template) for a product-oriented enterprise is a task of new product and new technological process development.

2. *Maintain* – capabilities that help to keep existing resources in the right shape to be useful in the capability of a given type. For customers (paying stakeholder resource type), it could be the capability to perform Customer Relationship Management (CRM). For workforce, it could be training. For an execution template, it could be process or policy improvements. For technical infrastructure, it could be a utilized cloud service provided by a partner.

3. *Retire* – sub-capabilities that phase out resources that no longer can be used as part of the capability. For customers, it could be discontinuing serving a customer that is no longer profitable. For execution templates, it could be phasing out a product design that no longer satisfies the customer needs. For workforce, it could be actual retirement.

Fig. 2. An example of applying the sub-capability types

The sub-capability types can be graphically presented in the form of figure 2. Figure 2 contains an example of a customer resource in a manufacturing company. Just as for figure 1, the resource is represented by a rectangle, and (sub-) capabilities by ovals. An arrow from the resource to a capability shows that the capability is aimed at managing the given resource. The label on the arrow shows the type of the capability in relation to its resource – *acquire*, *maintain*, or *retire*.

5   Changing Organisational Capabilities

The work with identifying capabilities lay the groundwork for proposing changes in the structure. The impetus for changing the structure of and enterprise can be both threats from competing enterprises and external business opportunities, such as a growing market segment. As pointed out by Chesbrough [19], experimentation is an essential part of changing the way an enterprise conducts its business. Moreover, Chesbrough argues that a suitable model of the enterprise can be used as a starting point for this experimentation. The presented structure of capabilities, resources and sub-capabilities can be used for this kind of experimentation. However, rather than having an ad-hoc approach for the experimentation itself we propose to use a set of generic capability transformation patterns. To illustrate their main use in this paper we here present two basic patterns that can be applied to the tree structure identified in the earlier step of the approach:

- Externalising a capability. This involves taking a capability that the enterprise has and market it toward its customers. For example, the well-known on-line book retailer Amazon has turned its internal IT platform into a service that customers can buy. In essence, what Amazon did was taking an internal sub-capability and turned it into one of its main capabilities (note that we defined a main capability to be the ones directly providing values to paying customers).
- Add value to a capability. While externalising a capability turns an existing capability into an organisation main capability, there is also the possibility to extend existing capabilities, or embed them into new main capabilities. For example, the ERP system provider Microsoft has plans to provide their ERP system Dynamic AX as a service hosted on Microsoft Azure based data centres. This move builds upon Microsoft capability to create ERP systems, combined with their capability to host cloud platforms.

To leverage the capability structure that was defined earlier, the above patterns can be applied to the identified capabilities. In practical terms this involves finding possible candidates for externalisation (the first pattern) by, for each capability, asking "Can this capability deliver values directly to customers?". The use of the added value pattern (the second pattern) can be assessed by in a similar manner asking "Can we combine this capability with other capabilities in order to provide value to our customers?". Examining the existing structure using the patterns provide a structured form of experimentation with an enterprises capabilities.

5.1 Recursively Analysing the Capabilities

By combining the described resource types with the capability sub-types it is possible to step-by step discover the organizational structure in form of capabilities. Potentially the resulting tree will grow in width and in breadth indefinitely. As an enterprise has a limited size, there should be some mechanisms that limit this growth and, eventually, stops it. We see several points at which the growth of the tree will stop:

- Outsourcing. Some capabilities, e.g., maintenance of infrastructure, can be outsourced to a partner. In this case, the partner will be responsible for a resource in the tree. If desired, the analysis could continue, to also cover the inner capabilities of the partner organisation. This could for example be useful if there is a doubt about the partners capacity.
- Reusing capabilities. A capability on an upper level of the tree can be employed as a supporting capability on the lower level, which terminates the growth from the corresponding node. For example, the capability to provide customer support for products could also be used internally within an organization.

The above points can be combined with other ways of limiting the scope of the analysis, for example by scoping the analysis to a certain domain within the organization.

6   Applying the Approach

To illustrate the approach presented in this paper we have applied it to describe the changes a software development company went through. One of the main authors previously worked in this software company, and thus has experience with its way of working and the organisational changes that was applied. The changes described here took several years to perform, so we thus simplify the description.

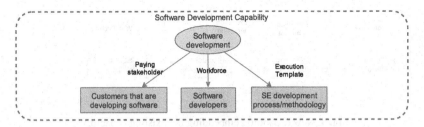

Fig. 3. Initial capability and its resources

Initially the company was a traditional software consulting company, working in several domains such as healthcare and financials. Its main capability (the main capability being defined as the one providing value to paying customers) was that of software development. Thus, the company worked as consultant for other organisation that developed custom made software. This capability consisted of the use of a set of resources as depicted in Figure 3. Most notably the organisation employed an execution template in form of a software development methodology (see figure 3).

As the time passed the company lost one of its main customers, leaving the company with several software developers without a project. To sustain, the company was thus in need of re-organising its capabilities. The re-organisation that was done can best be described using the added-value capability pattern described in the previous section. This means that the company looked for ways to build upon its existing capabilities by extending them. The extension in this case was to use the software development capability to develop a capability to build and distribute software packages. Figure 4 illustrates the new model describing this change.

The transformation that was made naturally also affected the use of the company's resources. As depicted in figure 4, the company could keep on utilising the main resources for software development, with the addition of procedures (execution templates) for generating new ideas for software products and their features. In addition to this the need for new capabilities to *maintain* and *retire* software products was added (see figure 4). The new main capability, software package distribution, also needed product delivery procedures (an execution template resource, see figure 4).

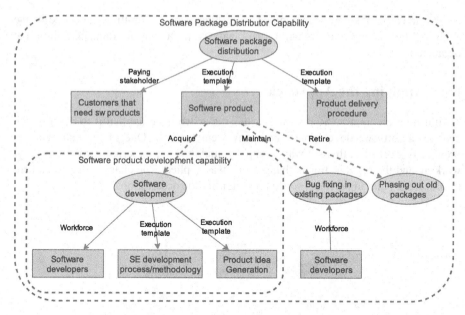

Fig. 4. New capability, embedding the existing capability

7   Conclusion

In this paper we presented an approach that help organisations to discover their inner structure and evolve it. The approach is based on that an organisation can be viewed as consisting of a multitude of capabilities, and that each capability requires specific resources of the correct capacity. To aid a recursive analysis of an organisation's capabilities, we introduce a set of capability resource types and a set of capability sub-types. Moreover, we presented two initial patterns that can help organisations to re-organise their capabilities in the event of threats or opportunities. The approach was illustrated by using an industrial case.

We see two possible ways for the future validation of the approach; discerning the utility by letting business consultant apply it to a real case and using historical-empirical validation in which the approach are used to explain existing organisational transformation.

Acknowledgements. This work has been partially supported by the EU-FP7 funded project no: 611351 CaaS - Capability as a Service in Digital Enterprises.

References

1. Audia, P.G., Locke, E.A., Smith, K.G.: The paradox of success: An archival and a laboratory study of strategic persistence following radical environmental change. Academy of Management Journal 43(5), 837–853 (2000)
2. Wiggins, R.R., Ruefli, T.W.: Schumpeter's ghost: Is hypercompetition making the best of times shorter? Strategic Management Journal 26(10), 887–911 (2005)

3. Barney, J.: Firm resources and sustained competitive advantage. Journal of Management 17(1), 99–120 (1991)
4. Teece, D.J.: Explicating dynamic capabilities: the nature and microfoundations of (sustainable) enterprise performance. Strategic Management Journal 28(13), 1319–1350 (2007)
5. Bider, I., Perjons, E., Elias, M.: Untangling the Dynamic Structure of an Enterprise by Applying a Fractal Approach to Business Processes. In: Sandkuhl, K., Seigerroth, U., Stirna, J. (eds.) PoEM 2012. LNBIP, vol. 134, pp. 61–75. Springer, Heidelberg (2012)
6. Miller, D., Hope, Q., Eisenstat, R., Foote, N., Galbraith, J.: The problem of solutions: balancing clients and capabilities. Business Horizons 45(2), 3–12 (2002)
7. Schreyögg, G., Kliesch, E.M.: How dynamic can organizational capabilities be? Towards a dual-process model of capability dynamization. Strategic Management Journal 28(9), 913–933 (2007)
8. Kim, W.C., Mauborgne, R.: Blue ocean strategy: How to create uncontested market space and make competition irrelevant. Harvard Business Press (2005)
9. Osterwalder, A., Pigneur, Y.: Business model generation: a handbook for visionaries, game changers, and challengers. John Wiley & Sons (2010)
10. Stirna, J., Grabis, J., Henkel, M., Zdravkovic, J.: Capability Driven Development – An Approach to Support Evolving Organizations. In: Sandkuhl, K., Seigerroth, U., Stirna, J. (eds.) PoEM 2012. LNBIP, vol. 134, pp. 117–131. Springer, Heidelberg (2012)
11. Open Group Standard, TOGAF - Enterprise Architecture Methodology, Version 9.1 (2011), http://www.opengroup.org/togaf/ (accessed March 01, 2014)
12. Henkel, M., Johannesson, P., Perjons, E.: An Approach for E-Service Design using Enterprise Models. International Journal of Information System Modeling and Design (IJISMD) 2(1), 1–23 (2011)
13. Hoverstadt, P.: The Fractal Oragnization: Creating Sustainable Oragnization with the Viable System Model. John Wiley & Son (2008)
14. Sandkuhl, K., Kirikova, M.: Analysing enterprise models from a fractal organisation perspective - potentials and limitations. In: Johannesson, P., Krogstie, J., Opdahl, A.L. (eds.) PoEM 2011. LNBIP, vol. 92, pp. 193–207. Springer, Heidelberg (2011)
15. McQueen, P.: Physics and fractal structures. Journal of Statistical Physics 86, 1397–1398 (1997)
16. Bider, I., Johannesson, P., Perjons, E.: Design Science Research as Movement Between Individual and Generic Situation-Problem–Solution Spaces. In: Designing Organizational Systems, pp. 35–61. Springer, Heidelberg (2013)
17. Schoemaker, P.J.: How to link strategic vision to core capabilities. Sloan Management Review (October 15, 1992)
18. Elliott, B., Elliott, J.: Financial Accounting and Reporting. Financial Times/Prentice Hall, London (2004)
19. Chesbrough, H.: Business model innovation: opportunities and barriers. Long Range Planning 43(2), 354–363 (2010)

Capability-Driven Development of a SOA Platform: A Case Study[*]

Sergio España[1], Tania González[2], Jānis Grabis[3], Lauma Jokste[3],
Raúl Juanes[2], and Francisco Valverde[1]

[1] Research Centre on Software Production Methods (PROS)
Universidad Politécnica de Valencia, Spain
{sergio.espana,fvalverde}@pros.upv.es
[2] everis, Spain
{tania.gonzalez.cardona,raul.juanes.pascual}@everis.com
[3] Information Technology Institute
Riga Technical University, Latvia
{grabis,lauma.jokste}@rtu.lv

Abstract. Capability-driven development (CDD) is a novel paradigm for organisational modelling and information technology development. Its cornerstones are capability modelling (including goals, context, processes), pattern-based design, and runtime context awareness and service delivery adjustment. There is a lack of empirical studies regarding the industrial application of CDD. This paper reports on a case study that focuses on capability modelling within a service-oriented architecture development project. We have collected lessons learned, as well as open challenges to feedback the improvement of the CDD methodology.

Keywords: Information systems, capability-driven development, enterprise architecture, case study, context modelling, business process modelling.

1   Introduction

Capability is a concept that has been used for some time in disciplines such as organisational management [1] and welfare economics [2], and it is used in defence technology development. However, when applied to information technology (IT) development, there is much debate on how the concept of capability relates to other widely used concepts, such as business process, business service, goals, etc. [3, 4].

Recently, a metamodel for capability modelling has been proposed [5]. Within the European Commission FP7 Project CaaS, a methodology and tools to support capability-driven development (CDD) are being developed.

Despite the growing use of the capability concept, there are no empirical validations of its application to IT developments. This paper presents a case study research that reports on a software project undertaken in everis, a multinational firm. everis applied a preliminary version of the CDD methodology and supported it with the modelling tools the team had at hand. The paper contributions are the following:

---

[*] This work has been partially supported by the EU-FP7 funded project no: 611351 CaaS – Capability as a Service in Digital Enterprises.

L. Iliadis, M. Papazoglou, and K. Pohl (Eds.): CAiSE 2014 Workshops, LNBIP 178, pp. 100–111, 2014.

- We report on the case study, its protocol and qualitative findings.
- We discuss the lessons learned about the application of capability modelling to IT development and we highlight challenges for improving the CDD methodology.

The rest of the paper is structured as follows. Section 2 overviews the CDD paradigm. Section 3 presents the research methodology. Section 4 reports on the case study (an e-government service platform), including a discussion on lessons learned and open challenges. Section 5 discusses the validity of the results. Section 6 concludes.

2   Capability-Driven Development of Information Technology

From the business perspective, a capability is the ability and capacity that enables an enterprise to achieve a business goal in a certain context. From the technical perspective, capability delivery requires dynamic utilisation of resources and services in dynamically changing environments. For instance, if we provide an e-government service to a given municipality, we need to react to changes that might happen throughout the year, and we may also want to provide the same service to other municipalities with a different context (e.g. different population, laws).

This principle of describing a reusable solution to a recurrent problem in a given context has been adopted in domains such as organisational design [6], business modelling [7], knowledge management [8], and workflow management [9]. Open challenges are the proper integration of conceptual reuse approaches (e.g. patterns, components) with business design and the provision of an adequate tool support.

The specification of context-aware business capabilities, by using enterprise modelling techniques, can be the starting point of the development process. Following this approach, business services are configured by enterprise models and built-in algorithms that provide context information. Capability-driven development (CDD) is a novel paradigm where services are customised on the basis of the essential business capabilities and delivery is adjusted according to the current context [5, 10]. For supporting CDD, the CaaS project has envisioned the following main components:

- *CDD methodology*: an agile methodology for identification, design and delivery of context aware business models. It formalizes the notion of capability by means of a metamodel that comprises the following elements [10]:
  - *Goal*: desired state of affairs that needs to be attained.
  - Key performance indicator (KPI): for monitoring the achievement of a goal.
  - *Context*: characterisation of situations in which a capability should be provided.
  - *Capacity*: resources (e.g. money, time, staff, tools) for delivering the capability
  - *Ability*: competence (i.e. talent, intelligence and disposition), skills, processes.
- *Capability delivery patterns*: they are generic organisational designs and business processes that can be easily adapted, reused, and executed.
- *CDD environment*: tool support for design (e.g. capability modelling) and runtime (e.g. the context platform monitors changes and the capability navigation delivery application calculates KPIs and selects the most suitable pattern) of CDD solutions.

3   Research Goal and Methodology

Our goal is gathering knowledge on the results of the application of capability modelling in industry. We specifically target the lessons learned during the application of the CDD methodology, as well as identifying current challenges that ought to be addressed in future improvements. We have structured the research methodology following the Design Science approach [11] (see Figure 1).

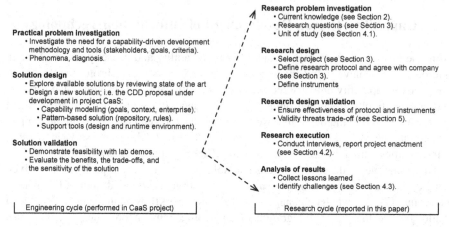

Fig. 1. Overall structure of the research methodology

The investigated project has been enacted in industry, so we have selected the case study research methodology. The actual interaction between the company and the researchers is closer to a case study research than to an action research since (i) the participation of the company in CaaS project meetings prior to the application of the CDD methodology made a method transfer process unnecessary, (ii) the company had much degree of freedom to apply the methodology, and (iii) the researchers mainly acted to solve some doubts formulated by the company and to conduct interviews and gather the data that is reported in Sections 4 and 5. The checklist by Runeson and Höst [12] served as guideline for conducting and reporting the case study research. The reader should consider the exploratory nature of this case study.

4   Case Study

4.1   The Company and the Project

The **case-study company** is everis, a multinational firm offering business consulting, as well as development, maintenance and improvement of IT. Within the public administration sector, everis has wide experience in projects related to modernisation of public procurement management, education, e-government, health, justice, etc.

The **unit of analysis** is a project to improve a service-oriented architecture (SOA) platform for e-government. It aligns with the Spanish administration goal of sharing human resources, software and hardware to support e-government. The most valuable feature of the SOA platform is offering electronic services provided by municipalities to citizens and companies. By the end of 2013, the platform provided a service catalogue of around 200 services (e.g. marriage registration application, public pool booking, taxes). Approximately 50 of them are in active use in 250 municipalities. As a result, over 1 million Spanish citizens benefit from using the SOA platform.

We selected this project because the platform context is complex and volatile; for instance, each municipality has a distinct profile, citizens have different interests, and laws and regulations change frequently. everis has to adapt the electronic services when the platform is deployed for a new municipality and whenever the context changes. For the time being, service customisation is done at code level.

The **main challenges** are (i) to perform organisational actions tailored for a specific municipality in a given moment in time (i.e. taking into account the period of the year, real-time usage indicators, calendar events, or most requested services in a certain period of time), and (ii) to automate the adaptation of the supporting IT.

By means of applying CDD methodology and tools, everis intends to adapt its way of working and to evolve the SOA platform into a context-aware, self-adaptive platform. In this first attempt to apply CDD, everis set up the following team:

- A *Public Sector and R&D Manager*, has over 12 years of experience in the IT sector for public administrations and that has led several innovation projects. This role has a mixture of knowledge about the SOA platform, the CDD methodology, and also of the results expected by public administrations. He is author number 5.
- A *Business Consultant*, with concrete expertise in the CDD methodology, who is willing to apply the CDD paradigm to several projects, and with little initial knowledge of the use case domain (i.e. the SOA platform). She is author number 2.
- A *Technological Consultant*, with concrete expertise in the SOA Platform, whose responsibility is improving the services provided by the SOA platform, but with no initial knowledge about the CDD Approach.

This team had the support of academic partners that are part of the CaaS consortium. Authors 1, 3, 4 and 6 are among them.

4.2   The Application of the CDD Methodology

During this project, everis has approached CDD from a goal-first perspective. This means that the goal model was created in the first place and then the rest of the models (e.g. stakeholders, context) were reasoned taking the goal model as input. However, this was not the initial intention and the approach rather emerged as capability modelling turned out to be more complex than expected. Initially, the Public Sector and R&D Manager and the Business Consultant organised a brainstorming session in which the overarching questions were: What type of new or adapted solutions can everis provide their customers by applying CDD? How can everis measure the accomplishment and the benefits of these solutions? Several staff members envisioned possible capabilities and specified them using a textual template.

Table 1. Initial capability drafts expressed during brainstorming

Capacity: IT infrastructure, monitoring tool, developers, technicians. *Ability*: being able to deploy a maintenance portal. *Enterprise*: everis *Goal*: keep services available despite platform errors. *Context*: loss of connectivity w. other subsystems. *Goal KPI*: time service available / time error in platform	*Capacity*: swimming pool facilities, swimming coaches. *Ability*: offer the electronic service to request swimming course registration. *Enterprise*: municipality *Goal*: reduce cost of service provision. *Context*: amount of requests. *Goal KPI*: amount of money saved

Table 1 shows a sample of two out of the eight capability descriptions. Such descriptions were sent to the academic partners in UPV, along with an invitation to meet in order to discuss goal modelling. The joint meeting clarified the different perspectives and granularities from which capabilities can be conceived. This discussion paved the way for everis to focus on the business goals and, therefore, a goal-first approach was adopted. Figure 2 depicts the resulting flow of capability modelling activities enacted during the project. For the moment, CDD methodology is notation-agnostic (e.g. for business process modelling one can use either BPMN, Activity Diagrams, Communicative Event Diagrams [13], etc.).

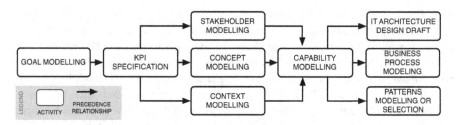

Fig. 2. Flow of activities enacted during the project

As first step towards clarifying the capabilities pursued in the SOA platform project, everis performed a modelling session in which the goals were elicited and modelled graphically (see Figure 3).

The model was mainly created from the perspective of everis objectives towards the project. Table 2 shows a sample of goal specifications. In order to facilitate reasoning, goals were classified into five categories:

- *Strategic goals* refer to improving services and their usage (G-1 to G-5).
- *Business goals* are mostly related to the ability to identify changes in usage of services and changes in services themselves (G-6 to G-9).
- *Technical goals* relate to service usage and platform collocation (G-10).
- *Design time goals* relate to service design requirements and to the identification of change patterns (G-11 to G-13).
- *Run-time goals* relate to the run time of the SOA platform, such as usage of patterns, dynamic adjustment, automated responses, etc. (G-14 to G-18).

In order to measure goal achievement, key performance indicators (KPIs) were defined using templates. For the sake of brevity, we include only a few in Table 2.

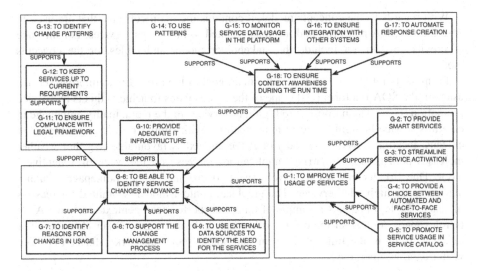

Fig. 3. Goal model of the project

Table 2. Sample of goals and KPIs of the SOA platform project

G-1. To improve the usage of the services
At the time being EVR provide up to 200 services for 250 municipalities, but only 100 services are in active use and not in all municipalities. The goal is to improve the usage of the services. This goal is supported by other strategic and business goals.
Category: Strategic goal   *Stakeholder*: S-3. EVR
KPIs: Percentage of citizens consuming the services (*target*=25%)
Percentage of completed service actions / submissions (*target*=90%)
G-6. To identify service changes in advance
The services provided by the SOA platform are affected by changes. These include changes in requirements, environment and other aspects. The goal is to proactively identify possible changes in the services. This goal includes sub-goals G-2, G-3 and G-4.
Category: Business goal   *Stakeholder*: S-3. EVR
KPIs: Frequency of change in current services

Stakeholders were identified from the current business processes. They are considered responsible for reaching the goals described above. Three important stakeholders are the *end users* (companies and citizens), the *project management office* (PMO, who is responsible for coordination in collaborative projects) and *municipalities* (a general-purpose administrative subdivision -as opposed to a special-purpose district- and the smallest administrative unit in a province). Municipalities carry out the services provided to end users (e.g. registering marriage applications).

With regards to the concepts model, it contains the main concepts that are used to describe the SOA platform, and not those related to individual services. For the sake of brevity, we do not include the stakeholder model and tables, or the concepts model.

From the point of view of everis, the main goal of the project is to improve service usage in the SOA platform (G-1); one of the mechanisms to achieve this is by service promotion (G-5). The purpose is to highlight services in the municipality homepage in case this service is highly used in municipalities with similar profile (e.g. number of citizens, location -coast or inland-) or if the context is favourable (e.g. hot weather increases pool booking, marriage applications increase on the week of Valentine's day). Due to technological development decisions, some homepages cannot automatically highlight services. The graphical context model is omitted for reasons of space. Table 3 presents a sample of three out the fourteen context elements. A set of rules maps contextual indicators with measurable properties. Other elements refer to the legislation, the time of the year and week, social network information, pool visitor data, weather, etc.

Table 3. Sample of context element specifications

Element	Values	Measur. prop.	Mapping rules
Municipality size	{Small, Medium, Large}	Number of citizens	If number of citizens <10 000 then 'small' If number of citizens 10000- 30000 then 'medium' If number of citizens >30000 then 'large'
Service usage in other muni- cipalities	{High, Medium, Low}	Percentage of municipalities using the service	If municipalities using service < 20%, then 'low' If municipalities using service between 20 and 50% then 'medium' If municipalities using service >50% then 'high'
Type of highlighting	{Automatic, Manual}	NA	NA (unknown at design time)

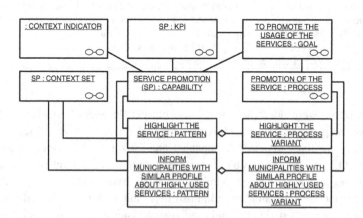

Fig. 4. Service promotion capability model

Figure 4 presents the service promotion capability model, which graphically summarises the capability by aggregating all its related elements. It includes the process Promotion of a service, which promotes services in one municipality whenever that service is being highly used in similar municipalities. This process is detailed in Figure 5 and has two main process variants:

- If the municipality homepage has automatic service highlighting then service highlight procedure is executed. Depending on different context data, service highlight procedure can be run once every 24 hours or once every 72 hours.
- If automatic highlighting is not possible or municipality with similar profile does not have that particular service, then an email is sent to municipality or to the PMO recommending service promotion.

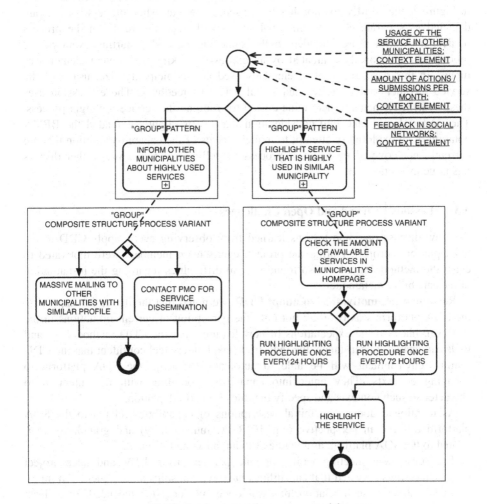

Fig. 5. Service promotion process model

Service usage context is monitored at run time:

- If service usage is high, then service can be highlighted in similar municipalities (similar size and profile);
- If the citizens feedback about service usage in social networks is positive, then the service is highlighted in similar municipalities (similar size and profile);
- If the municipality homepage is not able to automatically highlight the service, an email is sent to the municipality reporting on the high usage of services.
- If municipality A is not offering a specific service that has a high usage in other municipalities that have a similar profile to A, then the PMO is sent an email recommending deploying the service in A.

The process model with its process variants and capability delivery patterns is shown in Figure 5, the BPMN notation has been used. Note that, while process variants are depicted as separate elements in capability models (see Figure 4), in the process models the variants are included in the same diagram. The starting event of the process is conditionally evaluated by an expression taking the context elements as inputs. In this case, the context elements used are municipality size, usage of the service in other municipalities and social networks feedback. The expression uses these context elements to determine a need for running the service highlight process. The reader should take into consideration that everis slightly extended the BPMN notation in an exploratory attempt to model aspects of the capability solution that are currently not covered by business process modelling notations. We further discuss this issue in Section 4.3.

4.3   Lessons Learned and Open Challenges

We now discuss on some lessons learned from observing everis apply CDD to the SOA platform project. During the project, everis team members were motivated to enact the methodology, but also found several difficulties regarding the instantiation of the capability metamodel.

Regarding the **motivation to adopt CDD**, we noted that the driver for improving the SOA platform was twofold: not only the perception of current limitations in the platform, but also the expectations of new features that the CDD methodology and tools can enable. For instance, the industrial stakeholders feel confident that the CDD runtime environment will be able to automatically adapt the SOA platform to changing contexts. They enter into capability modelling with the intention to characterise such contexts and specify the rules for self-adaptation.

As mentioned above, the initial descriptions of capabilities related to the SOA platform differed in perspective (e.g. EVR vs. municipality) and granularity (e.g. related to the SOA platform as a whole or to an individual service).

The subsequent meeting with academic partners from UPV and later project plenary meetings revealed that capabilities have relationships among them. An initial characterisation of such relationships was done. We envision the need for at least three types of **relationships among capabilities** (see Figure 6). More research is needed regarding capability relationships related to:

- *Perspective.* For instance, municipalities are the owners of some capabilities (e.g. C1), while everis are the enablers of such capabilities and, in turn, owners of other capabilities related to the prior (C2).
- *Refinement.* Some capabilities (e.g. SOA1) must be refined in smaller ones (SOA1.1 to SOA1.3) in order to handle them more easily.
- *Context or quality levels.* Some capabilities need to be ordered because they refer to different levels of the context (e.g. high attendance to a cultural event vs. small events) or the agreed quality (C_SLA1 to CSLA3).

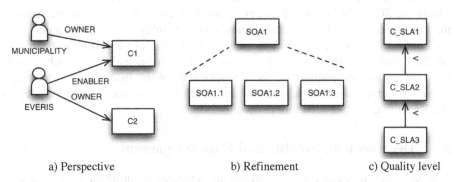

| a) Perspective | b) Refinement | c) Quality level |

Fig. 6. Illustration of types of capability relationships

The Public Sector and R&D Manager observed during the brainstorming that, depending on the profile of the analyst the outlined capability had a different perspective and granularity. His impression was that there is a need for guidelines.

By the time the goals model, the KPIs, the stakeholders model and the concepts model were created, the analysts had already realised that they could conceive capabilities (i) from the point of view of everis and (ii) from the point of view of the municipalities. The former are capabilities possessed by everis as PMO and the SOA platform provider; the later are capabilities possessed by the municipalities although delivered by everis using the SOA platform on behalf of the municipalities.

Based on our observations during this case study and comments of other CaaS industrial stakeholders during project meetings, there is an open challenge related to **how to start capability modelling**. everis performed a goal-first capability modelling, but one could also start CDD by modelling context or resources. Also, if current business process models exist, CDD enters a reengineering scenario that may differ in terms of the flow of modelling activities and guidelines. We plan to compare these starting points in future work.

In the SOA platform project, everis brought together a consultant that was knowledgeable in the CDD paradigm, a consultant that was knowledgeable in the SOA platform and its business process, and a manager who bridged the gap by standing somewhere in the middle. Although such collaboration for capability modelling worked well in this case, both the company and the researchers wonder whether this third role is needed. Also, in case it is indeed needed, an open question is who should play it (someone from the organisation, an external stakeholder) and whether his/her competence can be reused for different projects.

Regarding **modelling notations**, an open research challenge is discovering which notations are more suitable for each of the model views, whether different notations require specialised guidelines or extensions (e.g. everis connected context elements with elements of the BPMN diagram, see Figure 5), and whether situational guidelines are needed to adapt to project contingencies.

The identification and modelling of **variability** is key to CDD. To avoid manual customisation of services software code, everis intends to apply CDD so as to identify the variability in the context and, in design time, define solution patterns that deal with such variability. Following the CDD vision, at run-time, a context platform will enable the SOA platform to be context-aware and automatically select the patterns that suit the context. Above, we have shown the variability related to the automation (or lack of it) of service highlighting. Other main factors of variability in the project are the existence of different facilities provided by a municipality (e.g. public pool, marriage registration institution), the characteristics of the facilities (e.g. pool size, opening hours), and the legislation affecting the services. Variability brings challenges to CDD that need further investigation.

5   Discussion on Validity and Ethical Concerns

This case study is one of many milestones that are planned during the three-year span of CaaS project. Both the capability-modelling endeavour by everis and the case study research were of exploratory nature. Two facts make us cautious regarding everis perception of the utility of the approach. First, the development team is motivated to apply the CDD methodology. Second, they have high expectations towards the CDD runtime environment. Also, to obtain evidences and evaluate the benefits and drawbacks of CDD, further research is needed, especially when new versions of CDD are issued and applied. Instead, we focused on identifying the key lessons learned and future challenges.

As mentioned above, the SOA platform project was selected because its characteristics (project size, dynamic and changing context, high variability) suited our research goals. The interviews were not recorded; instead, the researchers made annotations using note-taking software (e.g. Evernote), conceived hypotheses (e.g. the consultants had troubles related to the perspectives of capabilities) and formulated additional questions to verify them. After every interview, the minutes were collaboratively edited. To mitigate threats to the validity of our conclusions, several researchers were involved in later discussions, so as to reduce researcher bias and achieve inter-subjective agreement. The lessons learned and open challenges were subjected for the consideration of the Public Sector and R&D Manager and the Business Consultant and they expressed their agreement.

We are aware that only one case has been analysed and, in order to avoid threats to the external validity of the results, other case study researches should be conducted. In any case, we argue that the results are a valuable feedback for CDD methodology improvement.

With regards to ethical concerns, everis team members and managerial staff were aware of the goals of this research and consented on publicly reporting the results.

6   Conclusions

Capability modelling is central to capability-driven development (CDD). We have conducted a case study research on the industrial application of capability modelling in a SOA platform project. By observing the process and the results, we can conclude that CDD facilitates a systematic analysis of organisational needs and designing an IT solution that is aware of the context so as to adjust the business services to changes in the environment. The CDD methodology still needs improvement and we have identified some open challenges, such as the need to provide relationships among capabilities, and the need for guidance with regards to the flow of modelling activities or how to use modelling notations.

As future work, we plan to design guidelines for goal-first capability modelling, to conduct a controlled experiment with students to validate some aspects of the guidelines and to conduct additional case studies to assess the evolution of the CDD.

References

1. Barney, J.: Firm resources and sustained competitive advantage. Journal of Management 17(1), 99–120 (1991)
2. Sen, A.: Development as freedom. Oxford University Press (1999)
3. Sharp, A.: Capabilities, agile and "process blindess". In: BPTrends (November 2011)
4. Sharp, A.: Peace accord reached! Process vs. capability debate ends with a whimper. BPTrends (October 2013)
5. Stirna, J., Grabis, J., Henkel, M., Zdravkovic, J.: Capability driven development – an approach to support evolving organizations. In: Sandkuhl, K., Seigerroth, U., Stirna, J. (eds.) PoEM 2012. LNBIP, vol. 134, pp. 117–131. Springer, Heidelberg (2012)
6. Niwe, M., Stirna, J.: Pattern approach to business-to-business transactions. In: International Conference for Internet Technology and Secured Transactions (ICITST 2009). IEEE, London (2009)
7. Business Model Innovation Hub (2013), http://businessmodelhub.com/ (cited March 2014)
8. Persson, A., Stirna, J., Aggestam, L.: How to disseminate professional knowledge in healthcare: the case of Skaraborg Hospital. Journal of Cases on Information Technology 10(4), 41–64 (2008)
9. Dumas, M., van der Aalst, W.M.P., ter Hofstede, A.H.M.: Process-aware information systems: bridging people and software through process technology. Wiley (2005)
10. Zdravkovic, J., Stirna, J., Henkel, M., Grabis, J.: Modeling business capabilities and context dependent delivery by cloud services. In: Salinesi, C., Norrie, M.C., Pastor, Ó. (eds.) CAiSE 2013. LNCS, vol. 7908, pp. 369–383. Springer, Heidelberg (2013)
11. Wieringa, R.: Design science as nested problem solving. In: 4th International Conference on Design Science Research in Information Systems and Technology, pp. 1–12. ACM, Philadelphia (2009)
12. Runeson, P., Höst, M.: Guidelines for conducting and reporting case study research in software engineering. Empirical Software Engineering 14(2), 131–164 (2009)
13. España, S., González, A., Pastor, Ó.: Communication analysis: A requirements engineering method for information systems. In: van Eck, P., Gordijn, J., Wieringa, R. (eds.) CAiSE 2009. LNCS, vol. 5565, pp. 530–545. Springer, Heidelberg (2009)

Modeling Enterprise Capabilities with $i*$: Reasoning on Alternatives

Mohammad Hossein Danesh[1] and Eric Yu[2]

[1] Department of Computer Science, University of Toronto, Toronto, Canada
[2] Faculty of Information, University of Toronto, Toronto, Canada
{danesh,eric}@cs.toronto.edu

Abstract. In a dynamic world, information technology (IT) systems are expected to provide capabilities that can be used to address evolving needs. Recent work has adopted notions of capability to model how IT systems meet enterprise goals. In this paper we draw upon theories of dynamic capabilities from strategic management to model enterprise capabilities, reason on their development choices, orchestration alternatives and deployment configurations. The modeling approach builds upon $i*$ and proposes to model capabilities as actors. $i*$ modeling supports reasoning about intangible and tangible requirements of capabilities and trade-offs among alternatives. We illustrate with examples from the insurance industry. The examples show how social and non-functional dependencies among capabilities affect decisions about development, orchestration and configuration alternatives.

Keywords: Enterprise Modeling, Capability Modeling, Dynamic Capability, Resource Orchestration, iStar.

1 Introduction

Today's rapidly changing business environment requires dynamically evolving IT enabled competencies [1]. This dynamic requirement has changed the focus of software architecture from functional composition to dynamic configuration [2]. Approaches such as Service-Oriented Architecture (SOA), Model Driven Development (MDD), and software ecosystems facilitate more agile system development to support dynamic requirements of enterprises [1,2]. However a gap still exists between enterprise-level business requirements analysis on the one hand, and software engineering approaches that produce IT artifacts on the other [1]. Technical approaches for achieving adaptability such as context-aware and service-oriented systems allow run-time configuration in response to dynamic functional and non-functional requirements. The focus of the adaptation is primarily based on technical performance criteria rather than on higher-level business values and strategies [1].

In this paper, we focus on the need for IT systems to respond to the dynamic nature of strategic business requirements. Concepts and theories from strategic management have been adopted in enterprise modeling, raising the level of abstraction to analyze

L. Iliadis, M. Papazoglou, and K. Pohl (Eds.): CAiSE 2014 Workshops, LNBIP 178, pp. 112–123, 2014.

IT architectures and to better achieve business-IT alignment [1]. Capabilities, defined as "an organization's ability to appropriately assemble, adapt, integrate, reconfigure and deploy valued resources, usually, in combination or co-presence", have been recognized as a primary source of business profitability and competitive advantage [3,4]. IT capabilities have been shown to create competitive advantage when they form rare, valuable and difficult to replicate orchestrations [5,6].

Enterprise "core" capabilities that lead to competitive advantage include knowledge and skills embodied in people, business processes, as well as technical systems. In developing capabilities, an enterprise faces many choices and alternatives. These alternatives and choices are limited and influenced by the organization's past, its environment, governance structure, and organizational cultures and norms [4], [7,8].

Based on a review of the literature, we consider alternatives that occur in three stages: (1) Capability Development: How to build or acquire resources to form a capability. The choice to either develop a sales system in-house, or to adopt a software-as-a-service solution is an example of such alternative. The skill sets and resources required for each are significantly different. (2) Capability Orchestration: How to bundle the capabilities and which bundles to choose. For example, use the enterprise data warehouse or data virtualization servers for the in-house sales system. (3) Capability Deployment Configuration: How to configure the capability at deployment time. For example, for in-house implementation, to rely on the existing IT department, or to allow the sales team to hire their own IT staff.

Recognizing the socio-technical nature of such reasoning, we aim to explore the potential of *i** to express and reason about the three types of capability alternatives. The *i** modeling framework has been developed to capture dependencies and rationales of actors' strategic interests [9]. The representation of actors, dependencies, intentions and their alternatives has the potential to illuminate the social context of capabilities, their reliance on one another to create competitiveness, and the alternate choices available. The analysis will include how capability development alternatives affect capability orchestration and whether *i** dependencies can effectively represent such relations.

In section 2, related work on capability modeling in enterprises is reviewed. In section 3, we illustrate why capability is important in strategic management and what are the management processes and drivers of decision making. Section 4 discusses the suitability of *i** to model enterprise capabilities and their alternatives. In section 5 we discuss hypothetical alternatives for capability development, orchestration and deployment configuration of an insurance service provider. The paper is concluded in section 6.

2   Related Work

Capability modeling has recently been used to represent business investment profile, facilitate business-IT alignment, and support service design and mapping. In this section we review recent approaches to capability modeling, and consider their capacity to analyze alternative decisions regarding capability development, orchestration and deployment configuration.

Iacob et al. [3] propose an extension to ArchiMate V2 and use capability and resource modeling to facilitate modeling business strategy concepts and architecture-based approaches to IT portfolio valuation. ArchiMate is an enterprise architectural modeling language that facilitates integration of business, application, and technology architectures. A recent extension proposed by Iacob et al. [3], aims to capture the business value of IT artifacts and projects in order to achieve better alignment with business strategy. The capability construct is used to facilitate the alignment. The modeling framework can model constraints imposed on capabilities and align implementation architecture accordingly. However reasoning on sources of the constraint is not modeled. The models cannot depict relations among capabilities, stakeholders and the value creation logic. Furthermore, reasoning on capability alternatives or the influence of the alternatives on one another is not considered.

The DoD Architecture Framework (DoDAF) version 2 [10] emphasizes the importance of capabilities and has dedicated a viewpoint to facilitate capability deployment planning, implementation, monitoring and preservation. This viewpoint consists of capability vision, taxonomy, phasing, dependencies, organizational development mapping, operational activity mapping and service mapping to business capabilities. DoDAF facilitates the description of capabilities and their dependencies, and their mapping to operational components and services, but does not facilitate reasoning on capability alternatives, their orchestration and intentions of the dependencies between capabilities.

Capability maps [11] are used to present a library of organizational capabilities at different levels of granularity. Capability heat maps use color codes to visualize hot spots within the capability landscape. The Value Delivery Model Language (VDML) [12] extends the use of capability maps and links capability offerings to organizational value network. Capabilities in VDML are mostly treated as resources required to perform an activity. The dependencies modeled in VDML do not illustrate why a dependency exists and what kind of dependencies are required. VDML treats capabilities as assets that are needed to realize a business model. However they do not consider challenges concerning integration of two or more capabilities [2], [7].

Barroero et al. [13] present a capability-centric Enterprise Architecture (EA) that extends TOGAF with a business capability viewpoint. The authors use capability and business component maps to identify a modularization of the enterprise business portfolio. They use business components as IT clusters that provide and consume services and propose modularizing IT architecture accordingly. The collaboration diagrams used to describe interactions and dependencies between business components does not capture intensions behind the collaboration. The approach does not facilitate reasoning on alternatives available and how they affect one another.

Capability Driven Development (CDD) aims to facilitate smooth (nearly automated) transition to software development by modeling capabilities and the contexts in which they operate. CDD facilitates run-time adjustments to changing requirements by implementing contextualized patterns of capability execution. This approach allows selection among different service providers at design-time or run-time based on functional and non-functional requirements specified in the context [1], [14]. However CDD does not capture the socio-technical notion of capabilities, their relations and dependencies, alternatives influence on other capabilities and business goals. Capabilities in CDD are considered in isolation but not all compositions of capabilities and software artifacts work seamlessly without social and managerial support [2], [15].

3   Dynamic Capability and Strategic Management

Current modeling approaches as discussed in section 2 lack the ability to facilitate reasoning on how capability alternatives affect one another and organizational value creation. For conceptual foundations, we draw on the literature in strategic management, which focus on sustainable competitive advantage. The Resource Based Theory (RBT) [16] argues that sustainable competitive advantages is obtained by creating Valuable, Rare, Inimitable and Non-substitutable (VRIN) resources. Within the RBT, the Dynamic Capability View (DCV) [4] argues that VRIN resources are not sufficient. Organizations require a dynamic capability that can continuously integrate and reconfigure an organization's resource base to create strategic capabilities that are valuable, rare and difficult to replicate. RBT and DCV have been used extensively to analyze the role of IT in creating competitive advantage [5,6], [15].

To attain competitive advantage, an enterprise is faced with choices in multiple stages of the capability lifecycle and development [12]. Decisions on capability development are shaped by available physical capital, human capital, social capital, cognition, and the history of capabilities [8]. Sirmon et al. [17] identify capability management as including acquiring, building and retiring capabilities; bundling resources and processes to form capabilities; analyzing the combination of capabilities to use; and leveraging the right deployment strategy. Over time, capabilities acquire social identity and autonomy, particularly in decentralized organizations [4], [8].

Evaluation of capabilities and their strategic fit is challenging, especially when the capability in question is intangible or contains intangible elements [18]. The complementary nature of capabilities and reliance on one another to create competitive advantage [4] complicates decision making further. The complementary nature plays a more significant role when reasoning on IT capabilities as studies indicate that synergetic relations of IT capabilities can be sources of sustained competitive advantage. Managerial and social support is required to successfully integrate diverse capabilities (such as IT and business capabilities) [5,6], [15].

4   Suitability of *i** to Model Enterprise Capabilities

Drawing on the strategic management literature as outlined in the preceding section, we treat capabilities as intentional autonomous bundles of organizational resources that are built and evolved over time. The enterprise needs to decide among: (1) capability development alternatives: what to include and exclude and what resources to bundle into a capability (2) capability orchestration alternatives: which capabilities are complementary and what coordination mechanism suits them, and (3) Deployment configurations. There are four criteria (adapted from Molloy et al [18]) to consider when deciding on each alternative at any stage. (1) How does it affect the value creation logic? (2) How does the generated value benefit stakeholders? (3) How will it influence other capabilities that depend on it or that the capability depends on? (4) In what context is the alternative viable?

In this section we explore whether *i**, a socio-technical modeling framework [9], can facilitate capability modeling, reason about development alternatives and deployment configurations, and study the influence of alternate choices on one another. The *i** framework facilitates socio-technical exploration of enterprises by providing a graphical depiction of actors, intensions, dependencies, responsibilities and alternatives. *Actors* including agents and roles and associations between them (*is-a, part-of, plays, covers, occupies, instantiates*) represent the social aspect of *i**. Actor intentions are expressed within the actor boundary in *i** using actor's desired *goals* and *softgoals*, performed *tasks* and available *resources*. Softgoals in *i** are goals without clear-cut satisfaction criteria. In an *i** Strategic Dependency (SD) model, actors *depend* on each other to accomplish tasks, provide resources, and satisfy goals and softgoals. The reasoning of each actor is revealed in more detail in the Strategic Rationale (SR) model. *Decomposition* of a task within the boundary of an actor depicts elements required to accomplish it. *Means-ends* links illustrate alternatives available to achieve a certain goal. *Contribution* links, which can be *Make/Break, Help/Hurt, Some+/Some-* or *unknown*, show the effects of *i** elements on softgoals [19]. Horkoff and Yu [19] propose a qualitative, interactive evaluation procedure to reason on *i** goal models and alternatives.

We use *i** goal models to reason about how capabilities are constructed and achieved. In particular, we use *i** actors to model core capabilities which embody an identity that can act independently and is built over time, as emphasized by the dynamic capability view of strategic management [4], [8]. Capabilities are modeled as specialized actors (indicated with intertwined circles added to the i* symbol for actor). A position within the enterprise is responsible for a capability (in case of collaborating partners the position can be in a partner enterprise). A role within the organization can be associated with the position that is responsible for a capability and be dependent or depend on a capability. Examples of such associations are provided in the following section in Figures 4 and 5. In addition, by using *i** actors to model capabilities, we can reason on how a capability can resist or facilitate a development choice which is inspired by Leonard-Barton [7] and is presented in the next section (Figure 4).

Modeling capabilities as *i** actors allows us to: (1) analyze how different capabilities relate to one another. A map of capabilities dependencies will facilitate understanding consequences of a change to the capability. (2) Model capability dependencies alongside the social relations of influential actors within an organization that will facilitate reasoning on IT capability alternatives. This is supported by research findings that indicate alignment of IT capabilities to other organizational capabilities can have significant contribution to competitive advantage [5,6], [15]. The social dynamics and collaboration required for such alignment can affect the flexibility of the capabilities dependencies and their performance [20]. (3) Use SD models of capabilities and their relation with stakeholders (modeled as roles, positions and agents) as a roadmap to analyze how capabilities participate in organizational value creation and how the value is appropriated to stakeholders. Both value creation logic and value appropriation are dimensions proposed by Molloy [18] for evaluating the contributions of capabilities.

5   Illustrative Example

We illustrate with an example from the inventory of insurance industry capabilities provided by ACORD [21]. Figure 1 shows the SD model for the *Product Management* capability of an insurance company. The *Sales Representative*, shown as an *i** Role, depends on the *Product Development* capability to deliver a new product. That product along with other insurance services is provisioned to the consumer. Later in Figure 5 we present how the *Sales Representative* depends on the *Sales Management* capability to be paid. Figure 5 also depicts how the insurance enterprise makes money from the premium paid by the consumer. The aim of the SD model is not to quantify value creation and appropriation as done in value-based modeling approaches, but to illustrate the strategic dynamics that can facilitate reasoning on alternatives.

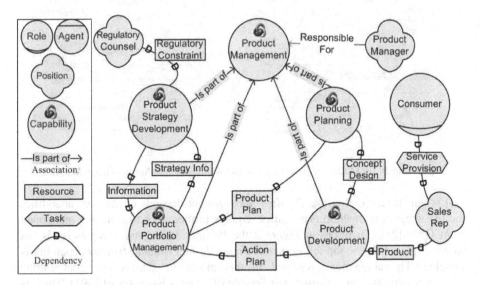

Fig. 1. Strategic Dependency Model - The Product Management Capability

Figure 2 depicts the *i** model of the *Product Management* capability and the sub-capabilities dependencies on one another. These dependencies are based on our understanding of the description provided by ACORD [21]. Some were explicitly mentioned and some were implicit. One would expect that some soft-goal dependencies exist between the capabilities but in the ACORD model none were specified. Such dependencies are exemplified in subsequent models in this paper.

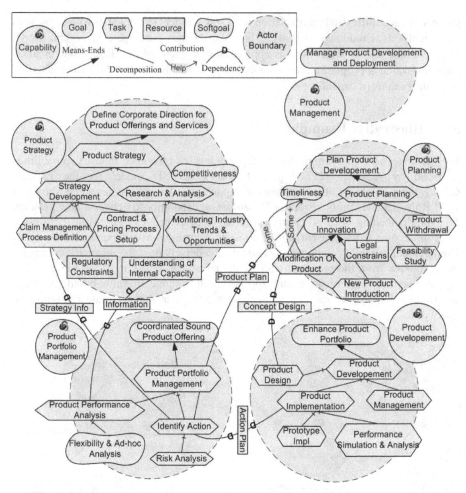

Fig. 2. Capability Model for Insurance Product Management - Adopted from ACORD

It is our understanding that *Product Management* depends on its sub-capabilities and the integration of these capabilities requires further steps that are not mentioned in ACORD [21]. Therefore in Figure 2 the *Product Management* capability is not further explored. In the top left corner of Figure 2, the *Product Strategy* capability is modeled. The alternative presented in this model to achieve the goal *Define Corporate Direction for Product and Service Offering* is based on ACORD. There is a potential to change this implementation and develop new alternatives to achieve the goal. *Product Strategy* has two sub-capabilities: *Product Strategy Development* and *Product Research and Analysis.* . These third layer capabilities can be modeled as *i** actors and associated with *Product Strategy,* if their social and capability dependencies are significantly different from their parent. In this model we show the sub-capabilities as tasks as they describe business processes. Modeling the sub-capabilities as tasks allows specification of their requirements through decomposition and analysis of their dependencies on other capabilities. The decomposition presented in Figure 2 depicts our understanding of the description provided for the sub-capabilities. The *Product Strategy* capability has to produce strategies that are able to compete in the industry hence the softgoal of *Competitiveness* was added as an element. The modeled resources *Understanding of Internal Capacity* and *Regulatory Constraints* were mentioned as skills and knowledge requirements. *Monitoring Industry Trends and Opportunities* was mentioned as the main activity of the research and analysis process. Assets required to perform capabilities are modeled as *i** resources

The capabilities and their alternatives presented from this point onwards are hypothetical and not adopted from ACORD. These examples illustrate how by modeling dependencies between capabilities and analyzing their relations, one can facilitate decision making on capability alternatives. Figure 3 depicts how Product Strategy Development depends on Social Media Analytics. Legends are same as provided in Figure 2.

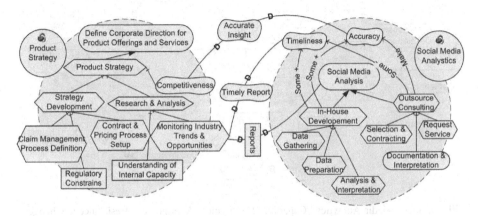

Fig. 3. Social Media Analytics - Capability Development Alternatives

The organization has two alternatives to satisfy its social media analytics requirements: (1) establish in-house processes that go through *Data Gathering, Data Preparation* and *Data Analysis and Interpretation;* or (2) hire a consulting firm that requires the following elements: *Request Service, Selection and Contracting* and *Documentation and Interpretation.* If the right consulting firm is chosen the accuracy of information would be guaranteed. On the other hand, following an in-house implementation will generate reports faster (softgoals of *Accuracy* and *Timeliness*). Considering dependencies in Figure 3, both alternatives can satisfy the reporting requirements. However the outsourcing option will provide better *Accuracy* and therefore better satisfy the *Competitiveness* of product strategy development. We would argue that since competitiveness plays a significant role in the organization's value generation, prioritizing its dependencies when making decision regarding capability development is justified. However in cases where their priority is not as trivial as competitive product offering, we need models that present a complete set of capabilities and trace value creation network. Such example is provided in Figure 5.

In this hypothetical case, it is assumed that the in-house *Social Media Analytics* capability exists in the organization (the left alternative in Figure 3). In this case it is highly likely that people behind the scenes will resist outsourcing. This resistance will harm the *Timeliness* softgoal in Figure 3 seriously which can cause interruption in product strategy development. Therefore when deploying the new alternative, the organization should use its in-house skill set to analyze and interpret data. How the *Social Media Data Analyst* within the organization would react towards each alternative is presented in Figure 4.

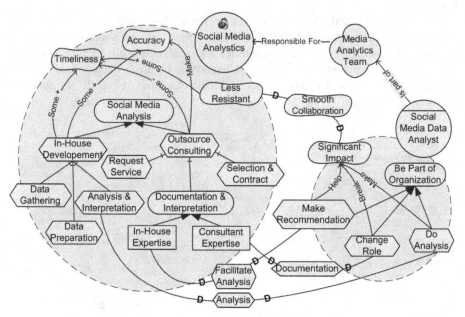

Fig. 4. Social Media Analytics - Capability Deployment Alternatives - Resistance to Change

In Figure 5, we introduce *Automated Sales Operation* which is an IT enabled capability that is part of sales management. The enterprise has two options: either purchase an *In-House* sales management product or use a *Software-as-a-Service* solution. If in-house implementation is chosen, the solution can rely on a *Data Virtualization Server* or the organization's *Data Warehouse*. The automated sales management is dependent on different IT capabilities in the two cases. The three alternatives also affect the softgoal dependency of the *Portfolio Management* capability. The decision in this case between software-as-a-service and in-house data virtualization is not trivial as both alternatives provide satisfactory levels of flexibility to access data. The *Sales Representative* depends on *Timely Operation* from the *Automated Sales Operation* capability which influences how the organization makes money as illustrated in Figure 5. This dependency will increase the importance of the *Fast Implementation* softgoal. If development and maintenance of this capability in the sales management department causes performance degradation in sales, then the software-as-a-service solution would be a better choice. In the presented analysis, one can further breakdown the alternatives (the two in-house implementation choices or software-as-a-service) if they influence decision making regarding capability development, orchestration or deployment configuration. However if no such influence exists, approaches such as CDD [14] (discussed in the related work section) can be used to facilitate design-time and run-time adaptation of capability implementation alternatives.

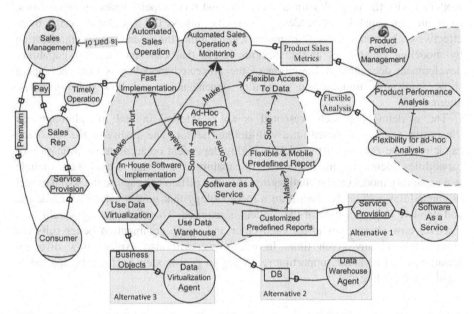

Fig. 5. Automated Sales Operation - Capability Development & Orchestration Alternatives

6   Discussion and Conclusion

Capability modeling is used to facilitate alignment of business architecture with IT artifacts and to identify associated risks with adoption of a certain capability deployment configuration [3]. Several approaches [1], [3], [10] aim to capture strategic intentions of capabilities through association to goals. Researchers propose monitoring Key Performance Indicators (KPIs) associated with goals to evaluate and maintain IT capabilities and projects [1], [3]. Mapping capabilities to service-oriented implementation is proposed to facilitate architectural alignment [3], [10]. Capability modeling is also used to identify capability context and allow run-time adaptation of alternatives [14]. However our review of the literature on the impact of IT on competitive advantage indicates the need to explore orchestration alternatives. Considering implementation alternatives for capabilities in isolation disregards such a need. Current approaches of capability modeling lack the ability to reason on the social dynamics, complementarities and influence of alternatives on one another. These approaches do not facilitate reasoning on alternatives with different quality outcomes to allow trade-off analysis.

In this paper we illustrated the *i** framework's potential to capture the socio-technical aspect of capabilities and allow expression of both top-down strategic intentions and bottom-up integration of organizational resources and skill sets. The *i** notion of softgoals allows expression of intangible drivers of capability alternatives. The mean-ends and decomposition links of *i** allow granular analysis of sub-capabilities. The social context in which capabilities are developed and evolve are modelled with the help of actor associations and their dependencies on capabilities. Reasoning on capability dependency alternatives allows the modeler to design more effective orchestrations. The *i** framework can capture the essence of decentralization by modeling capabilities as autonomous actors that can react to new capability development decisions. A limitation of the presented modeling is that one cannot show constraints imposed on capability dependencies and how they influence alternatives.

The modeling approach presented is not yet tested in real life although the illustrative example is based on a well-defined sector. The quality of the reasoning capacity of the *i** capability models is highly dependent on accurate identification of capabilities. Identifying the boundaries of capabilities and what to exclude or include in a capability model can be challenging. It is also difficult to capture the social aspect of capabilities accurately. Therefore a methodology that guides capability modeling and iterative improvements of the models is required. The methodology should help discover how alternatives affect each other and which combination better suits the organization at any given time. In future, we will also explore how different techniques and tools for supporting reasoning in goal models [22] can be applied to capability modeling.

References

1. Stirna, J., Grabis, J., Henkel, M., Zdravkovic, J.: Capability Driven Development – An Approach to Support Evolving Organizations. In: Sandkuhl, K., Seigerroth, U., Stirna, J. (eds.) PoEM 2012. LNBIP, vol. 134, pp. 117–131. Springer, Heidelberg (2012)
2. Bosch, J.: From Software Product Lines to Software Ecosystems. In: Proceedings of the 13th International Software Product Line Conference, pp. 111–119. Carnegie Mellon University, Pittsburgh (2009)
3. Iacob, M.-E., Quartel, D., Jonkers, H.: Capturing Business Strategy and Value in Enterprise Architecture to Support Portfolio Valuation. In: 16th International Enterprise Distributed Object Computing Conference (EDOC 2012), pp. 11–20. IEEE, Beijing (2012)
4. Teece, D.J.: Explicating dynamic capabilities: the nature and microfoundations of (sustainable) enterprise performance. Strategic Management Journal 28, 1319–1350 (2007)
5. Bhatt, G.D., Grover, V.: Types of Information Technology Capabilities and Their Role in Competitive Advantage: An Empirical Study. Journal of Management Information Systems 22, 253–277 (2005)
6. Nevo, S., Wade, M.: The Formation and Value of IT-Enabled Resources: Antecedents and Consequences. Management Information Systems Quarterly 34, 163–183 (2010)
7. Leonard-Barton, D.: Core capabilities and core rigidities: A paradox in managing new product development. Strategic Management Journal 13, 111–125 (1992)

8. Helfat, C.E., Peteraf, M.A.: The dynamic resource-based view: capability lifecycles. Strategic Management Journal 24, 997–1010 (2003)
9. Yu, E.S.: Social Modeling and *i**. In: Borgida, A.T., Chaudhri, V.K., Giorgini, P., Yu, E.S. (eds.) Mylopoulos Festschrift. LNCS, vol. 5600, pp. 99–121. Springer, Heidelberg (2009)
10. DoD, D.C.I.O.: Department of Defense Architecture Framework (DoDAF) Version 2.0. DoD Deputy Chief Information Officer (2010)
11. Keller, W.: Using capabilities in enterprise architecture management, White Paper, Object Architects (2009)
12. Berre, A.J., de Man, H., Lindgren, P.: Business Model Innovation with the NEFFICS platform and VDML. In: Short Paper Proceedings of the Second Workshop on New Generation Enterprise and Business Innovation Systems, pp. 24–30. CEUR-WS proceedings, Valencia (2013)
13. Barroero, T., Motta, G., Pignatelli, G.: Business Capabilities Centric Enterprise Architecture. In: Bernus, P., Doumeingts, G., Fox, M. (eds.) EAI2N 2010. IFIP AICT, vol. 326, pp. 32–43. Springer, Heidelberg (2010)
14. Zdravkovic, J., Stirna, J., Henkel, M., Grabis, J.: Modeling Business Capabilities and Context Dependent Delivery by Cloud Services. In: Salinesi, C., Norrie, M.C., Pastor, Ó. (eds.) CAiSE 2013. LNCS, vol. 7908, pp. 369–383. Springer, Heidelberg (2013)
15. Aral, S., Weill, P.: IT Assets, Organizational Capabilities, and Firm Performance: How Resource Allocations and Organizational Differences Explain Performance Variation. Organization Science 18, 763–780 (2007)
16. Barney, J.B., Ketchen, D.J., Wright, M.: The Future of Resource-Based Theory Revitalization or Decline? Journal of Management 37, 1299–1315 (2011)
17. Sirmon, D.G., Hitt, M.A., Ireland, R.D., Gilbert, B.A.: Resource Orchestration to Create Competitive Advantage Breadth, Depth, and Life Cycle Effects. Journal of Management 37, 1390–1412 (2011)
18. Molloy, J.C., Chadwick, C., Ployhart, R.E., Golden, S.J.: Making Intangibles "Tangible" in Tests of Resource-Based Theory A Multidisciplinary Construct Validation Approach. Journal of Management 37, 1496–1518 (2011)
19. Horkoff, J., Yu, E.: Evaluating Goal Achievement in Enterprise Modeling – An Interactive Procedure and Experiences. In: Persson, A., Stirna, J. (eds.) PoEM 2009. LNBIP, vol. 39, pp. 145–160. Springer, Heidelberg (2009)
20. Byrd, T.A., Turner, D.E.: Measuring the Flexibility of Information Technology Infrastructure: Exploratory Analysis of a Construct. Journal of Management Information Systems 17, 167–208 (2000)
21. Jones, D., Schmitz, D., France, N., Orlandi, M.: The ACORD Capability Model. ACORD Corporation (2010)
22. Horkoff, J., Yu, E.: Comparison and evaluation of goal-oriented satisfaction analysis techniques. Requirements Engineering 18, 199–222 (2013)

Service Functioning Mode in Variability Model

Peteris Rudzajs and Marite Kirikova

Institute of Applied Computer Systems, Riga Technical University, Latvia
{peteris.rudzajs,marite.kirikova}@rtu.lv

Abstract. Recently variability handling has become a very important research topic due to necessity to provide higher flexibility in business and software operations. Usually variability is discussed either at business operations level or at software operations level. However, often both types of operations must be taken into consideration, especially in information intensive tasks, where human actors as well as computer systems are handling the information. Information intensive tasks are common in information service systems. Therefore description and use of variability from information handling perspective is important when designing and implementing this type of systems. In the paper we consider variability in the context of information services and information service systems. The paper proposes extended feature model based approach for capturing key variability facets in information service systems. Practical application of the approach is illustrated by the education demand and offer monitoring service system.

Keywords: variability, multi-mode service, information service, information service system, monitoring system.

1   Introduction

Variability is the main factor in almost every system [1]. Many types of systems are built with the variability in mind, e.g., self-adaptive systems, open platforms, and service-oriented systems. Variability handling can be supported by different variability management tools, software configuration wizards and tools, software component configuration interfaces, as well as by infrastructure for dynamic service composition [1].

In this paper we consider variability in the context of information services and information service systems. Information service [2] is *"a component of an information system representing a well defined business unit that offers capabilities to realize business activities and owns resources (data, rules, roles) to realize these capabilities"*, whereas the information service system is a collection of interoperable information services. In software based information service system a human actor of an information service has to be considered because it can participate in service execution with different degrees of involvement up to the degree where only the human actor performs the service. We use concept "functioning mode of service" to denote the degree of human involvement in service execution.

L. Iliadis, M. Papazoglou, and K. Pohl (Eds.): CAiSE 2014 Workshops, LNBIP 178, pp. 124–135, 2014.
© Springer International Publishing Switzerland 2014

There are different types of variability, such as variability in features or in business processes [3]. In an information service system the variability in features, particularly, variability in functioning modes of services is one of the concerns that should be considered, since the services can be performed only by human actors (manually), automatically, or semi-automatically. Moreover, in some information service systems, one and the same abstract service can be instantiated in any of aforementioned functioning modes depending on the information handling situation. Currently most of variability models are designed to handle variability for systems and their components of single functioning mode. In this paper our goal is to focus on differences of functioning modes of services and analyze the impact of these differences on the variability representation. For variability representation we use well known feature model [4] to document and analyze the mandatory, optional, and alternative features of the system and to communicate them to stakeholders of the system. In feature model we represent services as features provided by the information service system. Our contribution in this paper is an approach to introduce functioning modes of services in the feature model that facilitates design and implementation of the information service system.

The paper is organized as follows: In Section 2, the basic concepts used in the paper are described and related work is briefly outlined. In Section 3, the approach for extending the feature model by assigning functioning mode properties to the services is proposed. In Section 4, extended feature model is discussed using practical example of education demand and offer monitoring service system [6]. Brief conclusions are stated in Section 5.

2   Basic Concepts and Related Work

Basic concepts used in the paper and related work are briefly outlined in the following subsections.

2.1   Basic Concepts

The following basic concepts are used in the paper:

- *Information service* [2] is a component of an information system representing a well defined business unit. This unit offers capabilities to realize business activities and owns resources (data, rules, roles) to realize these capabilities. We assume that the "business unit" here can own human performers only, artificial performers (software and hardware components) only, or both human and artificial performers.
- *Information service system* [2] is a collection of interoperable information services.
- *Variability* – in software engineering the variability usually is defined as ability of software or software artifact (e.g. component) to be changed so that it fits a specific context [7]; here we take an information handling perspective and define the variability as ability to change the information handling unit so that it fits a specific context, goal, or intention.

- *Variation point* denotes a particular place in a system where choices are made as to which variant to use [8].
- Variant is a particular option of a variation point [8].
- *Functioning mode* of service [9]: *manual* - the service is performed by human actor (perhaps, using some office software, but there are no specific software services or tools included in the service system for implementing this service); *automatic* - the service is performed by dedicated software and/or hardware that does not require human actor intervention; *semi-automatic* - the service is performed by dedicated software and/or hardware that requires human involvement, e.g., a human performer should provide the input data and review and approve data processed and/or generated by the tool.
- *Multi-mode service* (or service with mode variation) [9] - service that can be instantiated in different functioning modes.

2.2   Related Work

The approach of variability modeling discussed in this paper is based on related work on variability in service systems and software engineering. Mohabbati et.al. [10] identify the main variability research focus and its application points, namely, *service variability modeling*, service identification, service reuse, service configuration and customization, dynamic software product line, and adaptive systems. Galster et.al. [1] provide the classification of variability in different dimensions that capture key facets of variability. Classification can be used as the baseline from which the key aspects of variability of different types of software systems can be identified and compared. Galster et.al. [1] identify also the dimensions of variability that are organized in two clusters namely, the type and the mechanism. The type cluster includes *dimensions for introduction and specification of variability*, namely, requirement type, representation, artifact, and orthogonality dimensions. The mechanisms cluster of variability refers to the way variability is realized. Our work considers variability modeling [10] and the *representation* dimension for introduction and specification of variability [1]. For variability representation we use well known feature model [4]. Feature model is used to document and analyze the mandatory, optional, and alternative features of system and to communicate them to the stakeholders of the system.

Lamprecht et.al. [11] look at the variation in processes and provide variation realization approach to automatically implement and manage concrete process variants. All variants are described by means of domain model (consisting of services, ontologies, and constraints) and constructed by means of a synthesis algorithm. From this work we use the idea of constraining available (possible) process variants and extend it with respect to the automation of process variant generation in cases where multiple functioning modes of services are available from the information handling perspective.

Stollberg and Muth [12] propose method for service customization, by using model driven variability management. Service variability aspects (mandatory and optional operations, properties of message types and their dependencies) are described on the meta-model basis. Consistent variants are derived depicting only those features that are important for the customer. Meta-model design including the details of functioning modes of services could be used in our future work, but is not introduced in this paper.

Petersen et.al. [13] propose the model to support customer decisions by documenting alternatives in the feature model and to communicate alternatives to the customer. In this paper we use the idea that feature models can serve as simple means to document and communicate alternatives to particular stakeholders of the service system. We use the feature models to (1) document variability aspect in information service system, (2) to analyze the potential human involvement and service interfaces for particular functioning mode, and (3) to draw further implementation considerations.

Nguyen and Colman [14] propose feature-oriented approach for web service customization addressing three main challenges: reducing complexity, automatic validation and dynamic deployment. Authors of [15] and [16] provide six variability patterns for service oriented computing domain that can guide developers to solve different variability problems in practice. Patterns include Parameter Pattern, Routing Pattern, Service Wrapping Pattern, Variant/Template Pattern, Extension Points Pattern, Copy, and Adapt Pattern. Authors of [14], [15], and [16] focus only on automatic web services. In the context of information service systems we should consider services with other functioning modes, too; such as services performed manually or services performed semi-automatically by support of external tools or systems.

In general, we can conclude that in the related work the main focus is on services performed automatically by software components. There exist some researches that concern several automation levels of services, e.g., [17], [18], and [19], but they do not consider the mix of different levels of automation. Also none of the authors discuss the variation points and variants with different functioning modes.

In the remainder of the paper we will examine how consideration of service functioning modes can impact the variability representation model.

3   Functioning Modes in Feature Model

In this section we depict the functioning modes of services and describe how these modes could be represented. We use the feature model to show the variability in information service system (the initial design of the feature model is out of the scope of this paper). In the model we represent services as features provided by the information service system. Other representation types also could be considered (e.g., ontologies [11]), but they are out of the scope of this paper. In the feature model we distinguish between two types of services, namely, *abstract services* (represented as variation points in rectangular boxes in Fig. 1) and *concrete services* (represented as boxes with rounded corners in Fig. 1). These concrete services are supposed to implement abstract services. We use the abbreviation *AS* for abstract services and *CS* for concrete services. An abstract example of feature model consisting of one abstract service (variation point) and three concrete services (variants) is presented in part A of Fig. 1. We propose to assign a particular functioning mode to a particular concrete service as a property using functioning mode assignment (FMA) approach. The FMA approach uses the feature models and prescribes the following steps for functioning mode assignment (practical illustration of the approach is given in Section 4):

1. In the given feature model, review concrete services (see part A in Fig. 1) of each abstract service.
2. Add the property of functioning mode to each concrete service, if it cannot be instantiated in any other functioning mode (see part B in Fig. 1; for concrete services CS.1.1 and CS.1.3 the property of functioning mode is added, namely, for CS.1.1 functioning mode is automatic - A, for CS.1.3 it is manual – M).
3. Add variability to each concrete service by converting it into abstract service and identify new concrete services, if the concrete service (variant) can be instantiated in more than one functioning modes; and repeat Step 2. In our abstract example CS.1.2 can be instantiated in 2 functioning modes (see CS.1.2 in part A and AS.1.2 in part B in Fig. 1). After repeating Step 2, we have added functioning modes to CS.1.2.1 (automatic - A) and to CS.1.2.1 (semi-automatic - SA).
4. After the functioning modes are added to concrete services, interfaces designated for transition between services with different or the same functioning modes should be added (see part C in Fig. 1).

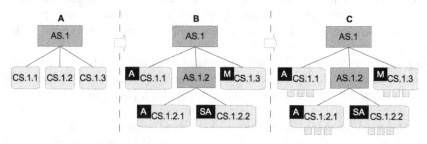

Fig. 1. Adding variability with respect to functioning modes of services. Abstract services (AS) are represented in rectangular boxes, concrete services (CS) – in boxes with rounded corners. Functioning modes are represented in concrete services as A (automatic), M (manual), SA (semi-automatic).

Since in information handling we should consider the functioning modes of concrete services, the representation of these modes will help designers or implementers of a service system to determine the types of service interfaces necessary for transition between services with the same or different functioning modes. This highlights the necessity to consider the variability in service interfaces. In Table 1 we briefly illustrate the need for (multiple) input and output interfaces or communication possibilities to be designated or provided for passing and retrieving information to/from services with particular functioning modes. The following transitions between services are considered A-A, A-M, M-A, M-M and any combinations where SA mode is involved. For each concrete service there should be considered three interfaces for transition to each of the possible functioning modes of the service (see concrete services in part C in Fig. 1).

Table 1. Interfaces between services of various functioning modes (A (automatic), M (manual), or SA (semi-automatic)) (adapted from [9])

Functioning modes	Interface involved	Human actor involved
A-A	Application level service interfaces should be established between services in transition	-
A-M	User interface should be established allowing particular stakeholder of service with manual (M) functioning mode to review the output of service with automatic (A) functioning mode	+
M-A	User interface should be established (usually as input forms) allowing the preparation of the result of service with manual (M) functioning mode for input into service with automatic (A) functioning mode	+
M-M	Specific application level interfaces are required (usually as input forms), business level communication could be possible	+
SA involved	Depending on the specifics of the service with semi-automatic (SA) functioning mode, it may require only application level interface, only business level communication, or both.	+

FMA approach allows adding the functioning mode for concrete services. Availability of this property provides basis for further decisions with respect to interfaces necessary in information service system for transitions between the services (to ensure proper service flow). While the feature model itself lacks the ability to represent the composition of services (service flow), since this is not the aim of the feature model, still, the feature model with depicted service functioning modes could serve as a solid basis for developing other models aimed at composing multi-mode services (see identified compositions for a particular example in Table 2).

Information service system can evolve; therefore it is necessary to deal with changes of features provided by the system. Potential changes include adding, removing, and updating of abstract and concrete services. When planning the changes of the system we should reflect the changes in the feature model and analyze the impact on the service compositions and service flows already available in the system. For instance, in case of adding new service to the system, (1) the feature model should be updated by adding this service to the model and (2) FMA approach should be applied to the service to assign to the functioning mode (or add variability to concrete service by converting it to abstract service and identifying new concrete services) and to assign the interfaces to it. We consider in this paper the assignment of functioning modes at the level of concrete services, however it could be done also at the level of abstract services. Then it would require another way for feature model change management, as well as the extension of FMA approach. The construction and examination of such feature model is one of our further research directions.

4   Practical Example and Discussion

In this section we define the feature model and apply FMA approach for education demand and offer monitoring system (EduMON) [6].

EduMON is information service system for information handling with respect to different information sources and stakeholders. EduMON service system is aimed at supporting education demand and offer monitoring process by the following activities (feature model of EduMON is provided in Fig. 2):

- *Providing* activity is for providing documents from available reachable information sources. The documents available in information sources should reflect the information about demanded and offered knowledge, skills, and competences and are retrieved from different types of textual sources (e.g., Web sites, databases, XML-based files).
- *Processing* activity aims at extracting education information (knowledge, skills, and competences) from the information sources (particularly, from the documents) available in the system and, by comparing information from different sources, to depict the education demand and offer correspondence.
- *Consuming* activity distributes the processed information to the stakeholders of the system via graphical and tabular reports.

In each above-mentioned activity, various stakeholders (e.g., teachers, students, employers, and others) are involved. Stakeholders interact via, with, and within EduMON to fulfill specific information handling intentions.

Providing and *Processing* activities are targeted to particular information sources and their documents (represented in part I of Fig. 2), however the *Consuming* activity is for representing the processed information from multiple information sources to users via graphical and tabular reports (part II of Fig. 2). In the feature model provided in Fig. 2, solid lines represent the types (mandatory or optional) and relationships (OR or XOR) of abstract services. Dashed lines represent "required by" relationship between abstract and/or concrete services. For instance, to execute any of the concrete services of *Extraction* abstract service (see 1.2 in Fig. 2), the execution of any of the concrete services of *Retrieval* abstract service is required.

In Fig. 3 we provide the feature model extended by FMA approach proposed in Section 3. First, we review the initial feature model provided in Fig. 2 (Step 1 of the FMA approach). By following Step 2 of the approach, 10 out of 12 initial concrete services were updated and additional property characterizing the functioning mode was added.

By following Step 3 of the approach, 2 out of 12 services showed additional variability in functioning modes; therefore these two initially concrete services were converted to abstract services (namely variants *Retrieval by database* 1.2.2. and *Retrieval by crawling* 1.2.3). For each of new abstract services two concrete services were introduced and additional property characterizing their functioning mode was added. *Retrieval by database* (1.2.2) variant was converted to variation point and two variants were added, namely, by browsing database manually (1.2.2.1) and by using SQL to automatically retrieve data from the database (1.2.2.2).

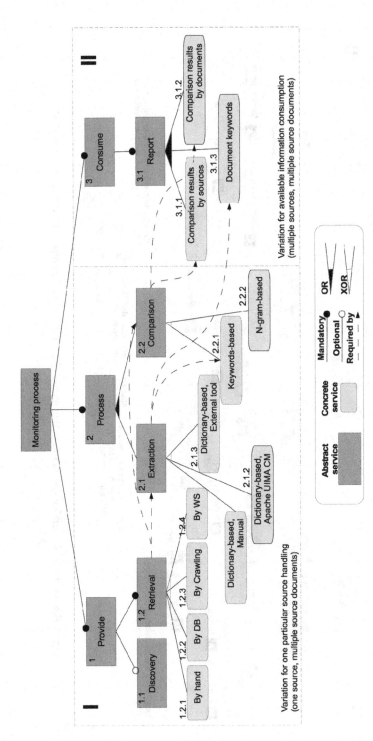

Fig. 2. Feature model for service system supporting monitoring process. Process is composed of three other information handling processes, namely, Provide, Process, and Consume. The features at the inner nodes represent groups of abstract services (variation points) realized by the concrete services (variants) at the leaves.

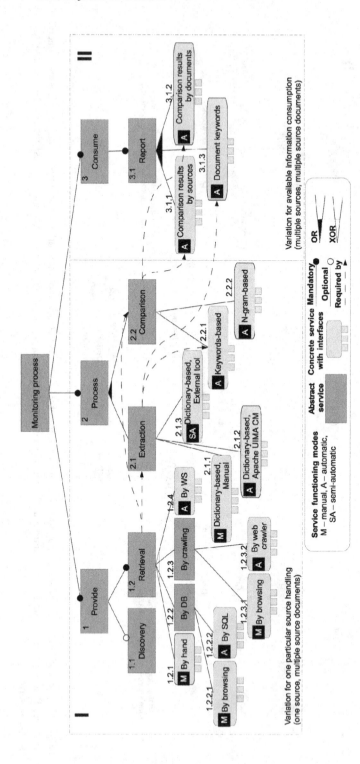

Fig. 3. Feature model for service system supporting monitoring process with the proposed FMA approach applied

As mentioned in previous section, service interfaces should also be analyzed for transition between services with the same or different functioning modes. In Table 2 we provide the variety of transitions available in EduMON system and illustrate particular modes of services in various compositions. Considering available functioning mode of the concrete service and its interfaces allows us to analyze the information service system more deeply to design or provide the input and output facilities or communication possibilities for passing and retrieving information to/from services with particular functioning mode. For instance, the service *Retrieval by hand* (see 1.2.1 in Fig. 3) with manual functioning mode is in transition with the service *Dictionary based extraction by Apache UIMA ConceptMapper* (see 2.1.2 in Fig. 3) with automatic functioning mode. In this case we should establish interface to allow the passing the retrieved document from service *Retrieval by hand* to the service *Dictionary based extraction by Apache UIMA ConceptMapper*. This interface can be implemented, e.g., as input form where the human actor passes the document, e.g., study course description, to automatic keyword extraction service. In this particular example, the extended feature model (see Fig. 3) and possible transitions between services (see Table 2) helped to reason and take decision about the potential human involvement necessary to perform particular services.

Table 2. Available transitions between multi-mode services in EduMON. Numbers in table relate to numbers of services in Fig. 3. In the intersection of the row and column, the functioning modes of services in transition are indicated.

	1.2.1 (M)	1.2.2.1 (M)	1.2.2.2 (A)	1.2.3.1 (M)	1.2.3.2 (A)	1.2.4. (A)	2.1.1 (M)	2.1.2 (A)	2.1.3 (SA)	2.2.1 (A)	2.2.2 (A)	3.1.1 (A)	3.1.2 (A)	3.1.3 (A)
1.2.1 (M)							M-M	**M-A**	M-SA	M-A	M-A			
1.2.2.1 (M)							M-M	M-A	M-SA	M-A	M-A			
1.2.2.2 (A)							A-M	A-A	A-SA	A-A	A-A			
1.2.3.1 (M)							M-M	M-A	M-SA	M-A	M-A			
1.2.3.2 (A)							A-M	A-A	A-SA	A-A	A-A			
1.2.4. (A)							A-M	A-A	A-SA	A-A	A-A			
2.1.1 (M)												M-A	M-A	M-A
2.1.2 (A)												A-A	A-A	A-A
2.1.3 (SA)												SA-A	SA-A	SA-A
2.2.1 (A)												A-A	A-A	
2.2.2 (A)												A-A	A-A	
3.1.1 (A)														
3.1.2 (A)														
3.1.3 (A)														

5   Conclusions

In the paper we discussed how variability could be modeled in situations where functioning modes of services must be taken into consideration. Such situations arise in information service systems, which include services that can be performed manually, semi-automatically, and/or automatically. To facilitate design and implementation of these information service systems, we suggest to model their variability by feature model and propose FMA approach for extending the feature model by assigning functioning mode properties to the services. The approach uses concepts of abstract and concrete services and can dynamically convert variants corresponding to concrete services into variation points corresponding to abstract services.

The application of the approach is limited to the already designed variability model, i.e., it does not prescribe the creation of initial variability model. When the initial model exists, the FMA approach facilitates deeper analysis in design and implementation of information service systems by considering the degree of human involvement. In FMA approach we represented functioning modes of services as properties for the concrete services. Functioning modes can be captured also at the level of abstract services. It would require another way for feature model change management and would allow structuring the feature model differently with respect to functioning modes. The construction and examination of such feature model is one of our further research directions. Direct benefit of using extended feature model would be in multi-mode service composition where the feature model can be used to allow automatically deriving the multi-mode service flows permitted in the information service system. The implementation of multi-mode service composition based on the feature model is another research direction.

References

1. Galster, M., Weyns, D., Tofan, D., Michalik, B., Avgeriou, P.: Variability in Software Systems - A Systematic Literature Review. IEEE Trans. Softw. Eng. (2014)
2. Ralyté, J., Khadraoui, A., Léonard, M.: From information systems to information services systems: Designing the transformation. In: Grabis, J., Kirikova, M. (eds.) PoEM 2013. LNBIP, vol. 165, pp. 69–84. Springer, Heidelberg (2013)
3. Galster, M., Avgeriou, P., Tofan, D.: Constraints for the design of variability-intensive service-oriented reference architectures – An industrial case study. Inf. Softw. Technol. 55, 428–441 (2013)
4. Kang, K.C., Cohen, S.G., Hess, J.A., Novak, W.E., Peterson, A.S.: Feature-oriented domain analysis (FODA) feasibility study (1990)
5. Kang, K.C., Lee, H.: Variability Modeling. In: Capilla, R., Bosch, J., Kang, K.-C. (eds.) Systems and Software Variability Management: Concepts, Tools and Experiences, pp. 25–43. Springer, Heidelberg (2013)
6. Rudzajs, P.: Towards automated education demand-offer information monitoring: The system's architecture. In: Niedrite, L., Strazdina, R., Wangler, B. (eds.) BIR Workshops 2011. LNBIP, vol. 106, pp. 252–265. Springer, Heidelberg (2012)
7. Van Gurp, J., Bosch, J., Svahnberg, M.: On the notion of variability in software product lines. In: Proceedings of the Working IEEE/IFIP Conference on Software Architecture, pp. 45–54 (2001)
8. Svahnberg, M., van Gurp, J., Bosch, J.: A Taxonomy of Variability Realization Techniques: Research Articles. Softw. Pr. Exper. 35, 705–754 (2005)

9. Rudzajs, P., Kirikova, M., Strazdina, R.: Configurative Alignment of Business and Application Services: A Work Systems Perspective. In: Abramowicz, W. (ed.) BIS Workshops 2013. LNBIP, vol. 160, pp. 100–111. Springer, Heidelberg (2013)
10. Mohabbati, B., Asadi, M., Gašević, D., Hatala, M., Müller, H.A.: Combining service-orientation and software product line engineering: A systematic mapping study. Inf. Softw. Technol. 55, 1845–1859 (2013)
11. Lamprecht, A.-L., Naujokat, S., Schaefer, I.: Variability Management beyond Feature Models. Computer (Long. Beach. Calif). 46, 48–54 (2013)
12. Stollberg, M., Muth, M.: Service customization by variability modeling. In: Dan, A., Gittler, F., Toumani, F. (eds.) ICSOC/ServiceWave 2009. LNCS, vol. 6275, pp. 425–434. Springer, Heidelberg (2010)
13. Petersen, K., Bramsiepe, N., Pohl, K.: Applying Variability Modeling Concepts to Support Decision Making for Service Composition. In: Service-Oriented Computing: Consequences for Engineering Requirements, SOCCER 2006, p. 1 (2006)
14. Nguyen, T., Colman, A.: A Feature-Oriented Approach for Web Service Customization. In: Proceedings of the 2010 IEEE International Conference on Web Services, ICWS 2010, pp. 393–400 (2010)
15. Khan, A., Kästner, C., Köppen, V., Saake, G.: Service variability patterns. In: De Troyer, O., Bauzer Medeiros, C., Billen, R., Hallot, P., Simitsis, A., Van Mingroot, H. (eds.) ER Workshops 2011. LNCS, vol. 6999, pp. 130–140. Springer, Heidelberg (2011)
16. Khan, A., Kästner, C., Köppen, V., Saake, G.: Service Variability Patterns in SOC (2011)
17. Sasa, A., Juric, M.B., Krisper, M.: Service-Oriented Framework for Human Task Support and Automation. IEEE Trans. Ind. Informatics 4, 292–302 (2008)
18. Šaša, A., Krisper, M.: Service-oriented architectural framework for support and automation of collaboration tasks. J. Inf. Organ. Sci. 35, 119–133 (2011)
19. Parasuraman, R., Sheridan, T.B., Wickens, C.D.: A model for types and levels of human interaction with automation. IEEE Trans. Syst. Man. Cybern. A Syst. Hum. 30, 286–297 (2000)

Towards a Computer-Aided Problem-Oriented Variability Requirements Engineering Method*

Azadeh Alebrahim, Stephan Faßbender, Martin Filipczyk,
Michael Goedicke, Maritta Heisel, and Marco Konersmann

Paluno – The Ruhr Institute for Software Technology, Germany
firstname.lastname@paluno.uni-due.de

Abstract. In theory, software product lines are planned in advance, using established engineering methods. However, there are cases where commonalities and variabilities between several systems are only discovered after they have been developed individually as single systems. In retrospect, this leads to the hindsight that these systems should have been developed as a software product line from the beginning to reduce costs and effort. To cope with the challenge of detecting variability early on, we propose the PREVISE method, covering domain and application engineering. Domain engineering is concerned with exploring the variability caused by entities in the environment of the software and the variability in functional and quality requirements. In application engineering, the configuration for a concrete product is selected, and subsequently, a requirement model for a concrete product is derived.

Keywords: Variability modeling, problem frames, software product lines (SPL), orthogonal variability modeling (OVM), UML profile.

1 Introduction

In our ongoing project GenEDA[1], we aim at extending our method for deriving design alternatives from quality requirements [11], which supports a single-system development to a product-line development addressing quality requirements. Software product line engineering (SPLE) represents an emerging paradigm to develop software applications which are tailored to individual customer's needs [12].

Software product lines (SPL) involve a set of common features as well as a set of variable ones. The first challenge we are facing is how to utilize and adjust conventional requirements engineering techniques for modeling and engineering SPL. Modeling and managing variability is the central concept in SPLE. Beyond the variability which is caused by variable requirements, there exist further variabilities, which might emerge because of changes in the environment in which the software will be located. Such kind of variability should be taken into consideration when developing SPL.

In this paper, we propose the PREVISE (**PR**obl**E**m-oriented **Var**Iability Require-ment**S** Engineering) method, which conducts requirements engineering in software

---

* This research was partially supported by the German Research Foundation (DFG) under grant numbers HE3322/4-2 and GO774/5-2.
[1] www.geneda.org

L. Iliadis, M. Papazoglou, and K. Pohl (Eds.): CAiSE 2014 Workshops, LNBIP 178, pp. 136–147, 2014.

product lines considering quality requirements. Our method is composed of four phases. It covers domain engineering (phases one and two) as well as application engineering (phases three and four).

The PREVISE method uses the problem frames approach [10] as a basis for requirements engineering and extends it for developing SPL. We use the problem frames approach, because 1) it takes the surrounding environment of the software into consideration. Therefore, it allows identifying variability, which is caused by the environment, 2) it allows decomposing the overall software problem into subproblems, thus reducing the complexity of the problem, 3) it makes it possible to annotate problem diagrams with quality requirements, 4) it enables various model checking techniques, such as requirements interaction analysis and reconciliation [1] or quality requirements elicitation [6] due to its semi-formal structure, and 5) it supports a seamless transition from requirements analysis to architectural design (e.g. [3]).

The remainder of this paper is organized as follows. An alarm system as a running example is introduced in Sect. 2. Section 3 gives a brief overview of the OVM, problem frames, and problem-oriented requirements engineering. Section 4 describes how we extend problem frames with a notation for variability. We introduce the PREVISE method in Sect. 5. Section 6 presents related work, while Sect. 7 concludes the paper and points out suggestions for future work.

2   Running Example

As our running example, we have chosen an alarm system. We will not elaborate on a full alarm system, but a very small and simple one, blanking many functionalities that such a system normally embodies. An initial problem description is given as follows: the *alarm system* is installed within a defined perimeter, such as a building. In this building alarm *buttons* and *signal horns* are installed. Whenever a person in the building witnesses a critical situation such as a fire, he / she shall warn others. A *witness* can *alert* others in the building, using the alarm buttons. The *alarm is given* using the signal horn. The alarm shall be given within one second. Additionally, every *alarm raised* is forwarded to an *alarm central*. The notification is repeated every 30 seconds. The *broadcast* to the alarm central is optional as not every owner of the alarm system needs or can afford using such an alarm central. When a communication to an alarm central is established, no third party shall be able to tamper with the communication. From this small scenario, we can derive two functional, one performance and one security requirement:

R1. A witness can alert others in a building using the alarm buttons. The alarm is given using the signal horn.
R2. Every alarm raised is forwarded to an alarm central. The notification is repeated every 30 seconds.
PR1. The alarm shall be given within one second.
SR1. When a communication to an alarm central is established, no third party shall be able to tamper with the communication.

3 Background

In this section, we give an overview of the concepts and methods our method relies on. OVM is described in Sect. 3.1, while the problem frames approach is given in Sect. 3.2.

3.1 Orthogonal Variability Modeling

In SPLE, OVM describes an approach to capture a product line's variability. In contrast to other approaches, which integrate variability into existing design artifacts, OVM explicitly captures variability in distinct models. Using traceability links, elements from OVM models can be connected to arbitrary design or development artifacts or elements within these artifacts, e.g. requirements, a state within a UML state machine, or implemented classes [12].

OVM comprises a set of model elements that allow for modeling variability. The central model element is the abstract *variation point (VP)*. A VP defines a place where single products may differ.

Since an OVM model defines the variability of an entire SPL, it provides a concept to derive products. Several model elements (including VPs) support a selection concept. A single product is defined through all elements that have been selected. To indicate a choice for the developer, selectable VPs may be *optional*. In contrast, if a VP is considered essential, it is declared *mandatory*. A mandatory VP must be selected for every product.

While VPs define where products may differ, *variants* define how they differ. Variants and VPs are linked through *variability dependencies (VD)*, while a variant has to be associated with at least one VP (in turn, a VP must be associated with at least one variant). Similar to VPs, variability dependencies may be either *optional* or *mandatory*. If a VP is selected and is associated with a variant through an optional VD, this very variant may be selected. However, if the association is a mandatory one, the variant must be selected in this case.

To ensure flexibility in the product derivation, OVM offers the possibility to define *alternate choices*. An alternate choice groups a set of variants that are associated with the same VP through optional dependencies and defines a minimum and a maximum value. Within product derivation, a number of n with $minimum \leq n \leq maximum$ variants have to be selected if their corresponding VP has been selected.

Since in practice relationships and interactions between variants and VPs can be observed, OVM allows for defining these relationships through *variability constraints*. Variability constraints can be set up between two variants, two VPs, or a variant and a VP. OVM provides two types of variability constraints: *requires* and *excludes*. The requires constraint is directed from a source to a target element and requires the target to be selected if the source has been selected. The excludes constraint is undirected and prevents selecting one element if the other element has been selected.

3.2 Problem Frames

Problem frames [10] proposed by Michael Jackson are a means to describe and classify software development problems. A problem frame represents a class of software problems. It is described by a *frame diagram*, which consists of domains, interfaces between

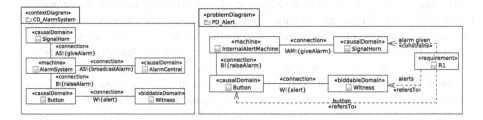

Fig. 1. Context diagram for the Alarm System (left) and problem diagram for R1 (right)

them, and a requirement. Domains describe entities in the environment. *Interfaces* connect domains, and they contain *shared phenomena*. Shared phenomena may, e.g., be events, operation calls or messages. They are observable by at least two domains, but controlled by only one domain, as indicated by "!". For example, the notation $W!\{alert\}$ (between *Witness* and *Button*) in Fig. 1 (right) means that the phenomenon *alert* is controlled by the domain *Witness*. The software to be developed is called *machine*.

We describe problem frames using UML class diagrams, extended by a specific UML profile for problem frames (UML4PF) proposed by Hatebur and Heisel [9]. A class with the stereotype ≪machine≫ represents the software to be developed. Jackson distinguishes the domain types biddable domains (represented by the stereotype ≪BiddableDomain≫) that are usually people, causal domains (≪CausalDomain≫) that comply with some physical laws, and lexical domains (≪LexicalDomain≫) that are data representations. To describe the problem context, a *connection domain* (≪ConnectionDomain≫) between two other domains may be necessary. Connection domains establish a connection between other domains by means of technical devices.

In UML4PF, requirements are a special kind of statement. When we state a requirement, we want to change something in the world with the machine to be developed. Therefore, each requirement expressed by the stereotype ≪requirement≫ constrains at least one domain. This is expressed by a dependency from the requirement to a domain with the stereotype ≪constrains≫. A requirement may refer to several domains in the environment of the machine. This is expressed by a dependency from the requirement to these domains with the stereotype ≪refersTo≫. The requirement *R1* on the right-hand side of Fig. 1 constrains the causal domain *Signal Horn*, and it refers to the causal domain *Button* and the biddable domain *Witness*.

Problem-oriented Requirements Engineering. Our method for problem-oriented requirements engineering involves the steps *problem context elicitation, functional requirements*, and *quality requirements modeling*.

The first step *problem context elicitation* aims at understanding the problem the system-to-be shall solve, and therefore understanding the environment it should influence according to the requirements. We obtain a problem description by eliciting all domains related to the problem, their relations to each other and the system-to-be. To elicit the problem context, we set up a *context diagram* consisting of the machine (system-to-be), related domains in the environment, and interfaces between these domains. The context diagram for our example is shown on the left-hand side of Fig. 1.

The second step *functional requirements modeling* is concerned with decomposing the overall problem into subproblems, which describe a certain functionality, as expressed by a set of related functional requirements. We set up *problem diagrams* representing subproblems to model functional requirements. A problem diagram consists of one submachine of the machine given in the context diagram, the relevant domains, the interfaces between these domains, and a requirement referring to and constraining problem domains. The problem diagram describing the functional requirement *R1* in our example is shown on the right-hand side of Fig. 1.

To analyze quality requirements in the software development process, they have to be addressed as early as possible in the requirement models. The functionality of the software is the core, and all quality requirements are related in some way to this core. Modeling quality requirements and associating them to the functional requirements is achieved in the step *quality requirements modeling*. We represent quality requirements as annotations in problem diagrams. For more information, see our previous work [4].

4   Extending Problem Frames with a Variability Notation

We extend the problem frames notation by introducing new elements for modeling variability in software product lines. We base our extension on the OVM terms. In Sect. 3.2, we briefly described the UML4PF profile, which enables us to use the problem frames notation in UML models. Our extension is a UML profile relying on the UML4PF profile.

The detailed usage of the stereotypes[2] will be explained in Sect. 5. The profile allows the creation of new kinds of diagrams and statements. The first new kind of *UML4PF diagrams* are *variability diagrams*. They capture the actual variation points. There are *requirement variability diagrams*, *domain variability diagrams*, and *phenomenon variability diagrams* as the variability can stem from requirements, domains, and phenomena. One special variability diagram is the *constraint variability diagram*, which captures constraints to variability. To the *context diagram* we add two new sub-types. First of all, a *variability context diagram*, which describes the context containing the variability. In contrast, the *product context diagram* describes the context regarding a particular product, which is defined by a *configuration*. The same distinction is made for *problem diagrams*. For problem diagrams we also have *variability problem diagrams* and *product problem diagrams*. The latter diagram is the *configuration diagram*, which describes a particular configuration for a product.

The first new statement introduced is the *variation point*. One can distinguish between *mandatory variation point* and *optional variation point*. Related to variation points are *variants*, which can represent an *optional variation* or a *mandatory variation*. A variation point indicates by its *min* and *max* properties how many of the variants have to be chosen for the variation point. The type of variation relation is indicated by a *variation dependency*. Variants and variation points can be related by a *constraint dependency*. The relation can be an *excludes* or a *requires* dependency.

---

[2] The meta-model is available in
http://www.geneda.org/pub/TechnicalReportPREVISE.pdf

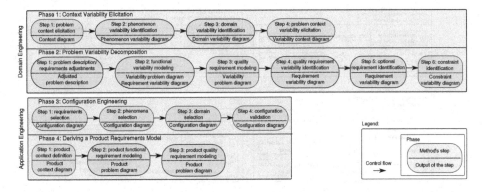

Fig. 2. PREVISE method and the outputs of each step

5 Problem-Oriented SPL Requirements Engineering Method

In this section, we present the PREVISE method, which defines the activities in the first phase of the domain and the application engineering, namely the requirements engineering. We describe how we extend our current problem-oriented requirements engineering method described in Sect. 3.2 for SPL. In Sect. 5.1, we describe the phases of domain engineering and the subsequent steps, in which we create a requirement model for the SPL. Then, we describe the phases of application engineering, in which we derive a concrete SPL product from the SPL requirement model in Sect. 5.2. Figure 2 shows an overview of the steps to be conducted in the PREVISE method and the corresponding outputs.

5.1 Product Line Requirement Model Creation

Phase 1: Context Variability Elicitation. In this phase, the context of the system-to-be is analyzed, and variation points in the environment of the machine are identified.

Step 1 - Problem context elicitation. For our method, it is not necessary to have a problem description, which already includes variability. Instead, one can start by giving a problem description for one possible product. The variability is identified and added in later steps. Hence, in step one we derive a context diagram from the problem description as proposed by Jackson [10]. *The context diagram is shown on the left-hand side of Fig. 1 and was already explained in Sect. 2.*

Step 2 - Phenomenon variability identification. In this step, every phenomenon of the context diagram has to be analyzed for two things. First, if the phenomenon at hand is a generic one, which has more than one possible concrete instances. For the case that it is not a generic one, there may be other alternatives for the phenomenon at hand. If one of these two cases holds, the generic phenomenon has to be added as a variation point and the concrete phenomena as variants. Additionally, one has to model if a variant or variation point is optional or not. Second, if a phenomenon is shared using a dedicated connection domain, this connection domain has to be added to the context diagram. *For our example, the phenomenon* alert *turns out to be a generic phenomenon, which*

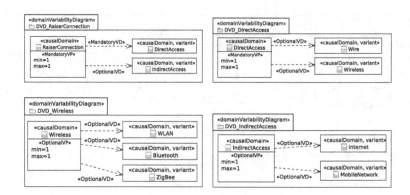

Fig. 3. Domain Variability Diagrams

has two variants. First, one can push *something to give the alert. Second, one can* shout *to give an alarm, which is a more advanced option for an alarm system.*

Step 3 - Domain variability identification. Similar to the phenomena, the domains of the context diagram have to be checked for variation points and variants. Note that it can occur that one variant is a variation point as the variant can be further refined.

One example for domain variability is shown in Fig. 3. The starting domain for this variability is the causal domain wire. *It connects the alarm raiser with the machine. The domain* wire *is abstracted to the causal domain* raiser connection, *which is a mandatory variation point. Variants for the raiser connection are a* direct access *connection, which is mandatory or an* indirect access *connection, which is optional. For direct access, one variant is the* wire. *The other variant is a* wireless *solution, which can be a* WLAN, *a* bluetooth, *or a* ZigBee *connection. The indirect access can be realized via* internet *or a* mobile network.

Step 4 - Problem context variability elicitation. This step uses the context diagram and the domain variability diagrams to generate the variability context diagram. The variability context diagram enables us not only to elicit all domains related to the problem to be solved, but also to capture, which domains represent variability and which ones commonality. The structure of the variability context diagram is similar to the *context diagram* from step 1. It differs from it in the way that we represent variation points for the problem domains and phenomena, which involve variability. The variability context diagram represents a context diagram for the SPL. Note that the variability context diagram can be automatically generated using the context diagram and the domain variability diagrams.

Figure 4 on the left-hand side shows the resulting variability context diagram for our example. The domains alarm system *and* witness *are directly taken from the context diagram as they are not variable. The signal horn is replaced by the variation point* notifier. *The alarm button is replaced by the variation point* raiser. *Additionally, the connection domains and their abstract variation points* raiser connection, *notifier* connection, *and* alarm central connection *are added to the variability context diagram.*

Phase 2: Problem Variability Decomposition. In this phase, the overall problem is decomposed into smaller subproblems according to the requirements of the system-to-be. The quality and functional requirements are adjusted in a way that they reflect the variability of the problem.

Step 1 - Problem description/ requirements adjustment. In this step, the textual requirements of the machine are derived from the problem description. As the initial problem description does not contain the variability identified in phase one, the textual description of the requirements has to be adjusted. *In Sect. 2 we already derived the textual requirements from the initial problem description. Now the wording has to be adjusted to the variability context diagram. For example, requirement R1 changes to "A witness can [alert] others in a building using [raisers]. The alarm is given using [notifiers]."*

Step 2 - Functional variability modeling. This step is concerned with decomposing the overall problem into subproblems, which accommodate variability. Each functional requirement has to be modeled as a problem diagram. Whenever the problem diagram contains at least one variation point, the requirement is variable, too. But variability in a requirement cannot only stem from phenomena or domains, which are variable. Sometimes requirements contain further variation points, which do not show up in the structure of a problem diagram. One reason might be a variability in behavior, for example in the sequence of phenomena. Hence, each requirement has to be checked for such variations not visible in the problem diagrams. Such variabilities are represented by a *requirement variability diagram (RVD)*, which represents the requirement as variation point and its alternatives as variants. *For our example, the functional requirement R2 contains further variability. The repetition of the alarm notification is optional. The according requirement variability diagram is shown in Fig. 4 on the right-hand side. Note that requirement R2.1 contains further variability regarding the time span between the repetitions. Figure 5 on the left-hand side shows the variability problem diagram for requirement R2.*

Step 3 - Quality requirement modeling. This step is concerned with annotating quality requirements, which complement functional requirements. In contrast to functional

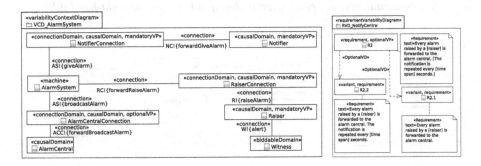

Fig. 4. Variability Context Diagram for the Alarm System (left) & Requirement Variability Diagram for R2 (right)

requirements, quality requirements are not modeled as problem diagrams on their own. Instead, they augment existing functional requirements.

Step 4 - Quality requirement variability identification. Variability in quality requirements can be caused when making trade-offs among quality requirements of different types. Such requirements are subject to interactions. Interactions among quality requirements can be detected by applying step 1 of the QuaRO method proposed in our previous work [1]. To resolve interactions, we generate requirement alternatives by relaxing the original requirement. To obtain such a variability in quality requirements, we apply the second step of the QuaRO method. The generated quality requirement alternatives provide variants for the original requirement. The requirement variability diagrams have to be updated according to the results of the QuaRO method. Sometimes, quality requirements introduce new domains, e.g., an attacker for security, and phenomena. Thus, one has to check these domains and phenomena for variability, too. *For our example, we have the security requirement SR1. It complements the functional requirement R2. It adds the biddable domain* attacker. *The domain attacker is a variation point as there can be different attackers distinguished by their abilities (see [1] for more information).*

Step 5 - Optional requirement identification. In this step, one has to identify the requirements, which are optional. They have to be modeled as optional variation point. *For the alarm system, the notification of the alarm central is optional, which is already reflected in Fig. 4 on the right-hand side, as* R2 *is annotated as an optional variation point (*optionalVP*).*

Step 6 - Constraint identification. This step is concerned with identifying constraint dependencies among requirement, phenomena, and domain variants. Dependencies caused by quality requirements interactions are identified as a result of the first step of the QuaRO method [1]. For functional requirements, one can use the RIT (Requirements Interaction Tables) as proposed in previous work [2]. Other kind of dependencies have to be checked manually. We distinguish between two types of dependencies, namely *requires* in which one variant or variation point requires another variant or variation point for a valid configuration, and *excludes* in which one variant or variation point is not allowed together with another variant or variation point in a valid configuration. *For example, the phenomenon* shoutToAlert *requires a* voice sensor. *The according constraint variability diagram is shown in Fig. 5 on the right-hand side.*

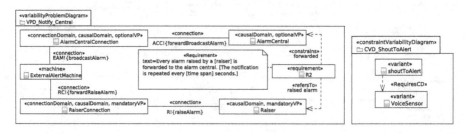

Fig. 5. Variability Problem Diagram for R2 (left) & Constraint Variability Diagram for alert to shout (right)

5.2 Deriving a Concrete Product Requirement Model

To derive requirements for a concrete SPL product, we make use of the artifacts generated in domain engineering. The aim of the application engineering is to get a coherent subset of requirements for a particular product from the overall set of requirements containing the variability. The application engineering is divided into two phases, which are explained in the following. Note that for the product engineering we do not elaborate the example for reasons of space. The example is explained in the accompanying technical report[3]

Phase 3: Configuration engineering. In this phase the configuration for the concrete product is selected. The following steps can be supported by a feature diagram and OVM diagrams derived from the domain requirements model. Note that this phase can be repetead to define more than one configuration. Step 1 - Requirements selection: The first step towards a configuration is to select the desired requirements among all optional requirements. This selection may reduce the phenomena and domains to select from in the next steps. The reason is that phenomena and domains, which are only bound to optional requirements that are not selected can be left out. For all requirements, which represent an optional variation point, one has to decide whether to include the requirement or not. Next, one has to select a variant for all requirements, which represent a variation point and which are included in the desired set of requirements. The desired set contains the selected optional and all mandatory requirements. The selected variants have to be documented in a configuration diagram. Step 2 - Phenomena selection: The second step is to select the variants for all phenomena, which are variation points. The reason for going first for the phenomena is that phenomena are the starting point of the interaction of end users with the system-to-be. Thus, we have the end user in focus. Additionally, the selected phenomena often constrain the set of domains to be chosen from. In many cases, specific phenomena exclude or require specific domains. Step 3 - Domain selection: In this step, one has to select for all domain variation points the according desired variants. Step 4 - Configuration validation: Last, one has to check if the constraints defined in the constraint variability diagrams are all satisfied. Additionally, one has to check whether the variation dependencies given by the variation diagrams and the min / max constraints of the variation points are satisfied.

Phase 4: Deriving a Product Requirements Model. In this phase, the concrete product requirements model is derived based on a given configuration. Note that one can define more than one configuration at a time and derive product requirement models for them. Step 1 - Product context definition: This step is concerned with deriving a *product context diagram* for a concrete product. To this end, we make use of a configuration diagram that defines, which requirement variants have to be achieved by the concrete product. Then, we derive the concrete SPL context diagram from the variability context diagram, replacing all variation points by the variants defined by the configuration. Variation points, which are not addressed by a variant in the configuration are removed. Step 2 - Product functional requirement modeling: In this step, we derive *product problem diagrams* for a concrete product. By means of the configuration we know which functional requirements have to be involved in the requirement models for the concrete SPL product. We use the *variability problem diagrams* for deriving *product problem diagrams*. The activities to

---

[3] http://www.geneda.org/pub/TechnicalReportPREVISE.pdf

be performed are like the ones for step 1. One additional step is the textual adjustment of the requirements. Step 3 - Product quality requirement modeling: For the product quality requirement modeling one has to perform the same activities as given for step 2.

6   Related Work

There exist several methods connecting SPL with requirements engineering approaches. We focus on methods, which connect problem frames and variability. Zuo et al. [14] introduce an extension of the problem frames notation that provides support for product line engineering. The extension for problem frames only supports variability in requirements and machines. In contrast to the PREVISE method, the authors do not consider the variability, which can be caused by domains and phenomena. Furthermore, the authors only provide a notation for domain engineering.

Ali et al. [5] propose a vision for dealing with variability in requirements caused by the environment. The authors propose an idea for a framework, which relates the three requirements engineering methods goal models, feature diagrams, and problem frames to the environmental context in order to use context information for product derivation. In contrast to PREVISE, it does not pay attention to the variability caused by the requirements and relies on preliminary knowledge about variability.

Variability, which emerges due to changes in the environment (contextual variability), is discussed by Salifu et al. [13]. The authors first set up problem diagrams and then identify a set of variables representing the contextual variations. Using the contextual variables, variant problem diagrams are derived. In their work, the authors provide no systematic approach on how to identify contextual variations in the environment and Application engineering is not considered.

An approach for integrating SPLE and the problem frame concept is proposed by Dao et al. [8]. The starting point is a feature model, which is mapped to a problem frames model to elicit functional requirements and domain assumptions. To take quality requirements into account, a goal model is adopted. The three different notations feature models, problem frames, and goal models are used, which might cause consistency problems among different models. In contrast, we provide one single model, which enables consistency checking and tool support.

Similar to our method, the approach proposed by Classen et al. [7] considers variability in requirements and phenomena. However, the authors do not treat variability in domains. Furthermore, quality requirements are not considered.

7   Conclusion

In this paper, we have presented an extension of the problem frames notation to enable variability modeling. The notation extension for variability is accompanied by a method called PREVISE for discovering variability, modeling variability, and deriving products from the variability models. The contributions of this paper are providing 1) an OVM-based notation for adding variability to requirements, which are expressed in the problem frames notation (see Sect. 4), 2) a method, which can be conducted without any previous knowledge about variability, 3) a structured method for conducting domain engineering in the requirements phase, which includes (see Sect. 5.1) discovering and modeling variability, 4) a structured method for conducting application engineering in the requirements phase, which includes (see Sect. 5.2) setting up configurations for products and deriving requirement models for products according to the configurations.   For the future, we plan to implement and improve the tool support.[4] We also plan to integrate PREVISE and QuaRO.   We will also integrate PREVISE into the GenEDA method, which will provide the software engineer with a method, which closely integrates requirements engineering, architecture and design, and patterns. Hence, the variability will not only be reflected in the requirements, but will also be integrated in the architecture generation. For the validation of the method , we will apply the method to a bigger case study.

References

1. Alebrahim, A., Choppy, C., Faßbender, S., Heisel, M.: Optimizing functional and quality requirements according to stakeholders' goals. In: Mistrik, I. (ed.) Relating System Quality and Software Architecture. Springer (to appear, 2014)
2. Alebrahim, A., Faßbender, S., Heisel, M., Meis, R.: Problem-Based Requirements Interaction Analysis. In: Salinesi, C., van de Weerd, I. (eds.) REFSQ 2014. LNCS, vol. 8396, pp. 200–215. Springer, Heidelberg (2014)
3. Alebrahim, A., Hatebur, D., Heisel, M.: A method to derive software architectures from quality requirements. In: APSEC, pp. 322–330. IEEE Computer Society (2011)
4. Alebrahim, A., Hatebur, D., Heisel, M.: Towards systematic integration of quality requirements into software architecture. In: Crnkovic, I., Gruhn, V., Book, M. (eds.) ECSA 2011. LNCS, vol. 6903, pp. 17–25. Springer, Heidelberg (2011)
5. Ali, R., Yu, Y., Chitchyan, R., Nhlabatsi, A., Giorgini, P.: Towards a Unified Framework for Contextual Variability in Requirements. In: IWSPM 2009, pp. 31–34. IEEE (2009)
6. Beckers, K., Faßbender, S., Heisel, M., Meis, R.: A problem-based approach for computer-aided privacy threat identification. In: Preneel, B., Ikonomou, D. (eds.) APF 2012. LNCS, vol. 8319, pp. 1–16. Springer, Heidelberg (2014)
7. Classen, A., Heymans, P., Laney, R.C., Nuseibeh, B., Tun, T.T.: On the Structure of Problem Variability: From Feature Diagrams to Problem Frames. In: VaMoS 2007, pp. 109–117 (2007)
8. Dao, T.M., Lee, H., Kang, K.C.: Problem frames-based approach to achieving quality attributes in software product line engineering. In: SPLC 2011, pp. 175–180. IEEE (2011)
9. Hatebur, D., Heisel, M.: A UML profile for requirements analysis of dependable software. In: Schoitsch, E. (ed.) SAFECOMP 2010. LNCS, vol. 6351, pp. 317–331. Springer, Heidelberg (2010)
10. Jackson, M.: Problem Frames. Analyzing and structuring software development problems. Addison-Wesley (2001)
11. Konersmann, M., Alebrahim, A., Heisel, M., Goedicke, M., Kersten, B.: Deriving Quality-based Architecture Alternatives with Patterns. In: SE. LNI, vol. 198, pp. 71–82. GI (2012)
12. Pohl, K., Böckle, G., van der Linden, F.: Software Product Line Engineering - Foundations, Principles, and Techniques, pp. 1–467. Springer (2005)
13. Salifu, M., Nuseibeh, B., Rapanotti, L., Tun, T.T.: Using Problem Descriptions to Represent Variabilities For Context-Aware Applications. In: VaMoS 2007, pp. 149–156 (2007)
14. Zuo, H., Mannion, M., Sellier, D., Foley, R.: An Extension of Problem Frame Notation for Software Product Lines. In: APSEC 2005, pp. 499–505. IEEE (2005)

---

[4] For more details see:
`http://www.geneda.org/pub/TechnicalReportPREVISE.pdf`

An Outlook on Patterns as an Aid
for Business and IT Alignment with Capabilities

Janis Stirna[1] and Kurt Sandkuhl[2]

[1] Department of Computer and Systems Sciences, Stockholm University
Forum 100, SE-16440, Kista, Sweden
js@dsv.su.se
[2] Institute of Computer Science, University of Rostock
Albert-Einstein-Str. 22, 18059, Rostock, Germany
kurt.sandkuhl@uni-rostock.de

Abstract. Patterns have established themselves as a useful and practicable instrument for capturing reusable solutions to reoccurring problems in a multitude of domains. This paper discusses three cases of pattern application – at Riga City Council, Kongsberg Automotive, and Proton Engineering, An outlook on how pattern based approaches should be developed to support business and IT alignment and the concept of capability as means to deliver context dependent organizational solutions is also presented.

Keywords: Patterns, alignment, best practices, capability.

1   Introduction

In the process of developing or customizing information systems (IS) we are frequently faced with questions such as: what is the best IT solution to this organizational problem, how should this piece of best practice or experience be used, is it of any value, what can it be used for, when can it be used and by whom. These questions address various aspects of IT use, from management, e.g. concerning IT governance frameworks, to development, e.g. how to customize a particular system component to support company's business process. To answer these questions two main aspects of a knowledge artifact are of importance – what is the problem it addresses and what is the solution it provides.

Alexander [1] defined such problem-solution pairs as patterns – "a problem which occurs over and over again in our environment and then describes the core of the solution to that problem, in such a way that you can use this solution a million times over, without ever doing it the same way twice". Following this principle patterns have been introduced in IS design, data modeling, and in IS analysis. The common objective is to capture, store and communicate reusable artifacts, such as fragments of code or models. Including a set of patterns in a text book on system analysis and design is a de facto standard nowadays. The pattern concept has also been successfully used in organizational development and knowledge management under

L. Iliadis, M. Papazoglou, and K. Pohl (Eds.): CAiSE 2014 Workshops, LNBIP 178, pp. 148–158, 2014.

the term organizational patterns. An overview of six such application cases can be found in [2]. Pattern users appreciate the problem-solution principle of structuring knowledge and can immediately relate their problems to what the patterns address. There are however challenges – at the moment patterns are to a large extent used by people with IT development knowledge, but to ensure efficient business and IT alignment they should also be used by domain experts and business developers.

The objective of this paper is to discuss how the existing drawbacks of pattern methodologies and tools can be improved to support business and IT alignment and the concept of capability.

The rest of the paper is structured as follows. Section 2 gives a brief overview to pattern use in information systems and computer science. Section 3 describes three pattern usage cases. Section 4 discusses the future use of patterns for business and IT alignment while section 5 outlines the main principles of Capability Driven Development and ponders on challenges pertinent to pattern use. Section 6 presents concluding remarks.

2   Pattern Use in Computer Science

Since more than a decade, patterns have been popular in Computer Science and have been used for numerous areas, such as software design, information modeling and business process design. Although there is no generally accepted definition of the term pattern, most publications in the field get some inspiration from Christopher Alexander's definition (see section 1). Whilst Alexander's focus is on the solution, many pattern approaches in computer science concentrate more on capturing proven practices or an advice for how to approach certain problems.

The seminal book on patterns in the area of information system engineering was published by the "Gang of Four" [3] and focuses on software design patterns. Many other books followed, basically offering patterns for all phases of the software development process, including analysis patterns [4], data model patterns [5], software architecture patterns [6, 7], test patterns, etc. The pattern idea was adapted in other areas of Computer Science, like workflow patterns [8], ontology patterns [9], groupware patterns [19] and patterns for specific programming languages [10].

Patterns have also been adopted for organizational design and knowledge management purposes, c.f. for instance [11] and [12]. Furthermore, patterns and anti-patterns have also been used to capture best practices of enterprise modeling in the attempt to improve model quality [13].

Despite the many different fields addressed by these different pattern types, they share certain common characteristics:

- They are based on experiences and deeply rooted in the practice of the field,
- They are not meant to be used blindly as they are. The core idea within the pattern must be understood first and the pattern adjusted or tailored for the specific application case
- They do not only help to build software, processes or models, but also to communicate work approaches within a team or among different stakeholders.

Different approaches can be taken in order to develop or to discover patterns. The existing literature in the field (see above for a selection) suggests at least four possible ways that can be used depending on the nature of the problem and the overall vision for pattern application:

- Pattern detection: use (a large number of) existing development in the area under consideration (e.g. enterprise models, software designs, etc.) and analyze them for recurring parts
- Pattern derivation: use knowledge from related areas (e.g. process models, information flow diagrams, enterprise models) and derive patterns from this knowledge
- Pattern construction: use expert knowledge in the domain and construct patterns based on this knowledge
- Community-based pattern development: use communities of people with knowledge in the field (on the web, wikis, in conferences (e.g. PLoP) or associations) to develop patterns.

In terms of working with patterns we have to consider that there are two dimensions of reuse - design for reuse and design with reuse. By design for reuse we mean the process of identifying valuable solutions in existing or newly created models and creating reusable components, i.e. patterns, from them. By design with reuse we mean the process of creating new organizational designs, e.g. enterprise models, by identifying existing patterns, adapting the solutions, and integrating them with the new solutions created in the project.

3   Examples of Pattern Application Cases

This section presents three pattern allocation cases – in Riga City Council (Latvia), Kongsberg Automotive (Sweden), and Proton Engineering (Sweden) exemplifying the diverse applicability of the pattern concept. All three organizations used patterns for capturing what can be regarded as organizational best practices or know-how. Hence, it is important to point out that the pattern repositories will only create the expected impact if the organizations have supporting processes and roles for knowledge capturing, packaging, storing, searching and applying. Without such a supporting foundation any pattern collection, no matter how competitive and initially innovative, will quickly become obsolete and forgotten. These cases also show that there is a strong demand for supporting the solutions proposed by patterns with information systems.

In 2002 patterns were applied in the Riga City Council (RCC). The RCC wanted to develop an employee knowledge sharing portal where best practices structured according to the pattern format would play a central role (see [14] for details). The RCC had six internal pilot cases located in different organizational units. Patterns were developed by modeling and pattern experts in consultation with stakeholders from the RCC. The resulting patterns included enterprise model fragments, general drawings as well as multimedia content. They were structured by a content management system (CMS) that was able to automatically suggest hyperlinks based on similar entries in the repository. The users interacted with the patterns via the web interface of the CMS.

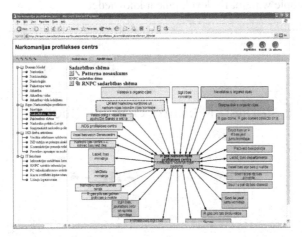

Fig. 1. An example pattern (in Latvian) showing collaborating organizations of the Riga Drug Abuse Prevention Centre

Figure 1 shows an example pattern that explains the collaboration structure within the RCC and how it is supported by various information systems of the involved organizations. This is described by text and conceptual models in the pattern (not shown in the figure). The objective of these patters was to document and share the existing knowledge about RCC's work processes and different best practices used. Some patterns described which information is available in which information system of the RCC or its municipal companies. Beyond that it was up to the pattern users to elaborate the needed connections themselves or ask the RCC's IT department to do it. This can be seen as a drawback that probably contributed to low usage of the pattern repository.

Kongsberg Automotive used patterns from 2006-2008 within the EU-FP6 project MAPPER (Model-adapted Process and Product Engineering) for supporting collaborative engineering in networked manufacturing enterprises by capturing reusable organizational knowledge with Active Knowledge Models (AKM). MAPPER developed c.a. 20, so called, task patterns, which included process, product, organization structure and resources for specific recurring organizational tasks (see [15] for details). The significant difference of the MAPPER project is that the patterns developed were linked to IS components in the METIS tool and the AKM platform, which made the organizational solutions achieved by applying patterns executable. The more or less instant transition from a pattern to a running system was one of the advantages of the MAPPER approach. Figure 2 shows a pattern for establishing a material specification on the left and a functioning workflow system the behavior of which is defined by the pattern.

The drawbacks hindering the adoption of the approach were: (1) the patterns developed in the project only covered a limited area of company's needs and (2) development of new patterns by the domain experts was considered to be too advanced for people without IT development knowledge.

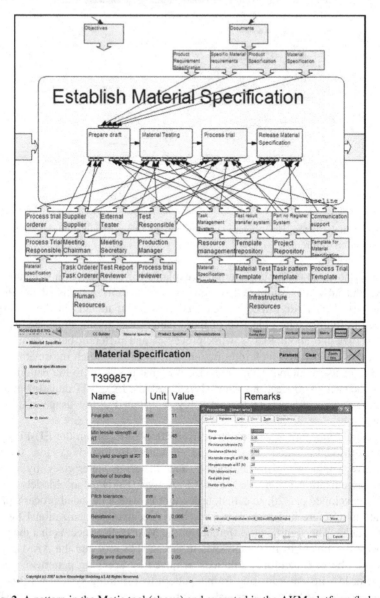

Fig. 2. A pattern in the Metis tool (above) and executed in the AKM platform (below)

Proton Engineering developed and applied information demand patterns within the infoFLOW project during 2009-2012. Proton is a sub-supplier to different first-tier suppliers in automotive and telecommunication industries who performs various surface treatment services of metal components. Surface treatment in this context includes different technical or decorative coatings to achieve certain functionality or appearance. The patterns were developed for engineering change management (ECM) in the production process. The challenge is to handle the continuously incoming change specifications for products manufactured for many different OEMs in the automotive industry. Not implementing the changes in time would lead to products with wrong characteristics and economic consequences.

An information demand analysis of a specific part of the ECM process (from quotation to production planning) was performed, which resulted in several information demand patterns. *An information demand pattern addresses a recurring information flow problem that arises for specific roles and work situations in an enterprise, and presents a conceptual solution to it.* An information demand pattern consists of a number of essential parts used for describing the pattern: pattern name, organisational context, problems addressed, conceptual solution (consisting of information demand, quality criteria and timeline), and effects.

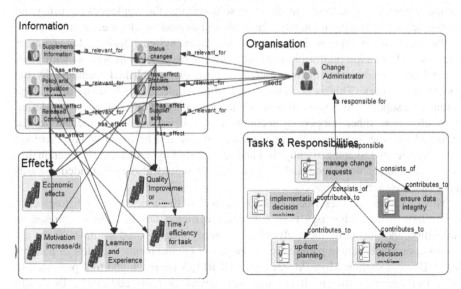

Fig. 3. Visual model of the information demand pattern for the role "change administrator"

Figure 3 shows an example of the information demand pattern for the change administrator role, which is represented as textual description accompanied by a visual model fragment. The advantage of these patterns can also be seen as a disadvantage: they are intended for decision makers in enterprises and focuses on transferring knowledge about how to solve organizational problems related to information flow. Hence, the patterns can be easily understood by domain experts who get hints for how to their problems. However, the domain experts can only take the basic structure of the solution for the problem and have to design the implementation of the solution without the pattern providing details regarding how this should be done.

4   Challenges for Pattern Use in Business and IT Alignment

Sections 2 and 3 discussed the current state of pattern usage in organizations. This section summarizes the current challenges and discuses issues for future work.

There are patterns that present relatively stable knowledge that is unlikely to change soon, e.g. the Gang of Four patterns [3] present a set of foundational solutions for object-oriented design. But there also are other kinds of patterns that are only useful if they take into account the latest IT developments, e.g. the Yahoo pattern case in [16]. Consequently, successful pattern applications require equal attention to (1) the patterns themselves; (2) the process that supports their development and (3) pattern application including user feedback and constant update.

In the future it might become increasingly important to indentify which parts of a pattern require updating. In some cases when patterns are used by a large group the challenge is to discover the needs of the group and to amalgamate all the different feedback. A grassroots approach of allowing each user to suggest candidate patterns in a development environment could therefore be helpful. As an additional benefit the company would be able to see the different solutions that the employees are using and assess the current situation, indentify gaps, as well as plan development actions.

Patterns reside in repositories, content management systems, tools, wikis and other kinds of collaboration platforms. Relationships among patterns as well as with other internal and external information sources are usually established manually by the pattern developers. This is a tedious and often neglected task with little or no automation support. As a result it is not done thoroughly and users are left wondering what else (e.g. other supporting technologies, policies, risks) is relevant to the proposed solution and where the relevant information can be found. While there are tools that are able to automatically find and recommend hyperlinks, such functionality is not sufficiently developed and widely used. It should also be extended towards automatic web service discovery.

Most patterns are described in text supported by code or model fragments. Regardless of the technology used for representation, users have to search, assess suitability, and decide by themselves how to apply the proposed solution. There are contributions that include patterns in development environments, e.g. design patterns in CASE tools such as ModelMaker or the EUREQA approach and tool presented in [17]. But currently this is done only with design patterns addressing IS design problems, similar to the Gang of Four patterns, with software patterns containing reusable code, or with workflow patterns. While this is good starting point, a more explicit connection should be established between various business problems and IT solutions. In the future model driven development tools should be able to connect business problems to patterns and executable components as well as allow users to create and add their own. This would improve traceability and transition between the business requirement elicitation and IS development. In essence, we should be striving towards a modern kind of patterns that are business problem-solution-execution triplets.

5   Outlook on Patterns for Capability Delivery

In the recently started FP7 project CaaS – "Capability as a Service for digital enterprises" patterns are used within capability design and delivery. The ethos of the project is to facilitate development of business solutions requiring customization as the context of delivery changes. The CaaS project aims to facilitate configuration of business services and development of executable software to monitor the fitness of purpose of these services to evolving business contexts and where necessary to adjust these services according to the context. Patterns will be used for delivering context dependent organizational capabilities as specified in the meta-model of the project's approach [18].

Capability is the ability and capacity that enable an enterprise to achieve a business goal in a certain context. It describes the capability of the business that will be designed and delivered. Capability formulates the requirements for the ability of accomplishing a business goal, realized by applying a solution described by a capability delivery pattern. Patterns are reusable solutions for reaching business Goals under specific situational contexts. The context defined for the Capability (Context Set) should match the context in which the Pattern is applicable.

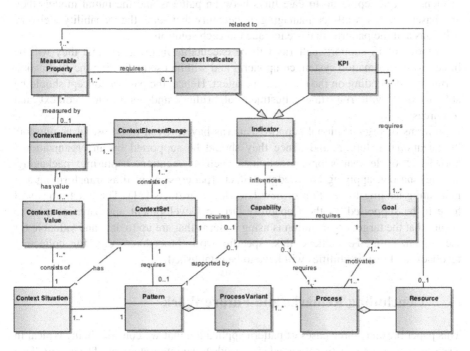

Fig. 4. Capability meta-model [18]

In the CaaS project patterns will represent reusable solutions in terms of business processes, resources, roles and supporting IT components (e.g. code fragments, web service definitions) for delivering a specific type of capability in a given context.

The Context indicators are used to monitor at runtime whether the pattern applied for delivering the capability is valid for the specific context situation. If the pattern is not valid, then the capability delivery should be dynamically adjusted by applying a different pattern, by reconfiguring the existing pattern or by aggregating several patterns into a new pattern. More about the overall vision of Capability Driven Development and the CaaS project is available in [19] and [20].

Concerning the use patterns the following challenges will have to be addressed in terms of model representation, way of modeling, IS support and organizational support.

In terms of model representation: the approach will be model driven and hence patterns will have to be represented in a model form. The relationships between pattern and its application context (represented by context set in the meta-mode) and the solution the pattern proposes (represented by a process variants) will have to be supported by methodological guidelines concerning issues such as efficient ways of modeling context, modeling process variants as part of patterns etc.

In terms of the way of modeling: both dimensions of reuse will have to be supported – pattern discovery and development from existing enterprise models as well as using patterns in constructing solutions for capability delivery. The main challenges are keeping up to date links between patterns and the initial models they are based on, as well as managing traceability between the capability delivery solutions and the patterns that are included in each solution.

In terms of IS support: patterns will be executable in the sense that they will be linked with information system components and will be used adjusting the application at run time depending on the changes in context. Hence, the pattern concept should be able to deal with run time adjustment algorithms and monitoring context and resources.

In terms of organizational support: Patterns have proven to be useful as reusable organizational solutions and hence they should be supported by an organizational knowledge cycle that supports activities such as creation, capturing, packaging, storing, sharing, applying knowledge artifacts (patterns) as well as transforming and innovating leading to creation of new knowledge artifacts [21]. These activities will have to be supported by the Capability Driven Development approach in order to ensure that the target organization is using patterns that are up to date and valuable for the organization. To achieve this, specific work procedures, e.g. for collecting feedback, and responsibilities will have to be established.

6   Concluding Remarks and Future Work

This paper presents three cases of pattern application that we consider being typical in a setting where organizational knowledge needs to be integrated with IT support. To a large extent patterns have been used for improving business and IT alignment by offering means for capturing, documenting and sharing best practices. As the application cases discussed in the paper suggest, patterns have the potential of linking business solutions with IT solutions. The current state of the art in the respect is, however, not offering practicable solutions, especially in cases when business solutions should be tailored according to context changes. To this end a proposal to use the concept of capability has emerged that further extends the use of patterns.

Another area of future work will be related to the different usage scenarios of patterns. Development of patterns on the CaaS project indicated the possibility to distinguish between solution-oriented and design-oriented patterns. Solution-oriented patterns incorporate how to solve a context related problem at runtime, i.e. the degree of freedom in these patterns is reflected in how to combine executable components. This characteristic puts such patterns close to software services, but there is still an important difference: services work as solution elements on their own with defined interfaces and deterministic behavior. Solution-oriented patterns need composition and decision logic at runtime, and hence we needs to know how to compose and configure them. Design-oriented patterns are closer to the "traditional" meaning of software, ontology and workflow patterns: they capture the core structure and elements of a design solution, which needs to be incorporated into a business service design. Examples are parts of processes or variations for defined context settings.

Both pattern types have been identified in CaaS; examples were developed and their differences exposed. However, the connection between the pattern types has to be explored in more detail. Design-time patterns can be further developed and combined at design time to solution-patterns. Such a development process basically is similar to a conventional engineering process. But there also is a potential of using design time patterns to model the decision logic for how solution-patterns have to be combined and configured at runtime. To this end we need to capture the flow of the decision process and part of the logic. Elaborating this connection will be part of the future work.

Furthermore, we will investigate the possibility to use the same pattern representation for both types. On a very general level, we will need the typical "gang-of-four" pattern structure of context, problem, solution and effects. For the problem and solution part we will furthermore have to link both pattern types to business services. Whether or not this can be done with the same mechanisms needs further exploration.

Acknowledgement. This work has been partially supported by the EU-FP7 funded project no: 611351 CaaS - Capability as a Service for Digital Enterprises.

References

1. Alexander, C.: A pattern language. Oxford University Press, New York (1977)
2. Niwe, M., Stirna, J.: Organizational Patterns for B2B Environments –Validation and Comparison. In: Halpin, T., Krogstie, J., Nurcan, S., Proper, E., Schmidt, R., Soffer, P., Ukor, R. (eds.) Enterprise, Business-Process and Information Systems Modeling. LNBIP, vol. 29, pp. 394–406. Springer, Heidelberg (2009)
3. Gamma, E., Helm, R., Johnson, R., Vlissides, J.: Design Patterns: Elements of Reusable Object-Oriented Software Architecture. Addison Wesley, Reading (1995)
4. Fowler, M.: Analysis patterns: Reusable object models. The Addison-Wesley series in object-oriented software engineering. Addison-Wesley, Menlo Park (1997)

5. Hay, D.C.: Data model patterns: Conventions of thought. Dorset House, New York (1995)
6. Fowler, M.: Patterns of enterprise application architecture. The Addison-Wesley signature series, vol. 2. Addison-Wesley, Boston (2003)
7. Buschmann, F., Meunier, R., Rohnert, H., Schmidt, D.C., Henney, K., Sommerlad, P., Stal, M.: Pattern-oriented software architecture. Wiley series in software design patterns. Wiley, New York (2000)
8. Van der Aalst, W.M.P., ter Hofstede, A.H.M., Kiepuszewski, B., Barros, A.P.: Workflow Patterns. Distributed and Parallel Databases 14, 5–51 (2003)
9. Blomqvist, E., Sandkuhl, K.: Patterns in Ontology Engineering: Classification of Ontology Patterns. In: Proc. of ICEIS 2005 (2005)
10. Beck, K.: Smalltalk best practice patterns. Prentice Hall, Upper Saddle River (1997)
11. Rolland, C., Stirna, J., Prekas, N., Loucopoulos, P., Persson, A., Grosz, G.: Evaluating a Pattern Approach as an Aid for the Development of Organisational Knowledge: An Empirical Study. In: Wangler, B., Bergman, L.D. (eds.) CAiSE 2000. LNCS, vol. 1789, pp. 176–191. Springer, Heidelberg (2000)
12. Persson, A., Stirna, J., Aggestam, L.: How to Disseminate Professional Knowledge in Healthcare. Journal of Cases on Information Technology 10(4), 41–64 (2008)
13. Stirna, J., Persson, A.: Anti-patterns as a means of focusing on critical quality aspects in enterprise modeling. In: Halpin, T., Krogstie, J., Nurcan, S., Proper, E., Schmidt, R., Soffer, P., Ukor, R. (eds.) Enterprise, Business-Process and Information Systems Modeling. LNBIP, vol. 29, pp. 407–418. Springer, Heidelberg (2009)
14. Mikelsons, J., Stirna, J., Kalnins, J.R., Kapenieks, A., Kazakovs, M., Vanaga, I., Sinka, A., Persson, A., Kaindl, H.: Trial Application in the Riga City Council, deliverable D6, IST Programme project no. IST-2000-28401, Riga City Council, Riga, Latvia (2002)
15. Sandkuhl, K., Stirna, J.: Evaluation of Task Pattern Use in Web-based Collaborative Engineering. In: Proc. of the 34th EUROMICRO. IEEE (2008) ISBN 978-0-7695-3276-9
16. Malone, E., Leacock, M., Wheeler, C.: Implementing a pattern language in the real world: A Yahoo! case study. Boxes and Arrows (2005), http://boxesandarrows.com/implementing-a-pattern-library-in-the-real-world-a-yahoo-case-study/ (accessed March 28, 2014)
17. Austrem, P.G.: The EUREQA Approach: A Method and Tool for Leveraging Design Patterns in End-User Development, PhD thesis, Univ. of Bergen, Norway (2011)
18. Bērziša, S., Bravos, G., Gonzalez Cardona, T., Czubayko, U., España, S., Grabis, J., Henkel, M., Jokste, L., Kampars, J., Koc, H., Kuhr, J., Llorca, C., Loucopoulos, P., Juanes Pascual, R., Sandkuhl, K., Simic, H., Stirna, J., Zdravkovic, J.: Deliverable 1.4: Requirements specification for CDD, CaaS – Capability as a Service for Digital Enterprises, FP7 project no 611351, Riga Technical University, Latvia (2014)
19. Zdravkovic, J., Stirna, J., Henkel, M., Grabis, J.: Modeling Business Capabilities and Context Dependent Delivery by Cloud Services. In: Salinesi, C., Norrie, M.C., Pastor, Ó. (eds.) CAiSE 2013. LNCS, vol. 7908, pp. 369–383. Springer, Heidelberg (2013)
20. Egido, J.C., González, T., Llorca, R., Grabis, J., Stirna, J., Zdravkovic, J.: Deliverable 1.3: Vision of the CDD methodology, CaaS – Capability as a Service for Digital Enterprises, FP7 project no 611351. Everis, Spain (2013)
21. Persson, A., Stirna, J., Aggestam, L.: How to Disseminate Professional Knowledge in Healthcare – The Case of Skaraborg Hospital 3, 42–64 (2008), Journal of Cases on Information Technology 10 (2008) ISSN: 1548-7717

Low–Cost Eye–Trackers:
Useful for Information Systems Research?*

Stefan Zugal and Jakob Pinggera

University of Innsbruck, Austria
{stefan.zugal,jakob.pinggera}@uibk.ac.at

Abstract. Research investigating cognitive aspects of information systems is often dependent on detail–rich data. Eye–trackers promise to provide respective data, but the associated costs are often beyond the researchers' budget. Recently, eye–trackers have entered the market that promise eye–tracking support at a reasonable price. In this work, we explore whether such eye–trackers are of use for information systems research and explore the accuracy of a low–cost eye–tracker (Gazepoint GP3) in an empirical study. The results show that Gazepoint GP3 is well suited for respective research, given that experimental material acknowledges the limits of the eye–tracker. To foster replication and comparison of results, all data, experimental material as well as the source code developed for this study are made available online.

Keywords: Eye–tracking, eye movement analysis, accuracy of fixations.

1 Introduction

To facilitate the development of information systems, numerous modeling languages, –methods and –tools have been devised over the last decades [1]. Thereby, researchers found that not only the technical perspective—such as correctness and expressiveness—are central requirements, but also the human perspective needs to be taken into account. For instance, in the field of business process management, researchers found that a good understanding of a process model has a measurable impact on the success of a modeling initiative [2]. Likewise, business process vendors and practitioners ranked the usage of process models for understanding business processes as a core benefit [3].

To support humans in their interaction with artifacts created during the development of information systems, e.g., models or source code, various research methods have been followed. For instance, researchers analyzed communication protocols gathered in modeling workshops [4], sought to adapt theories from cognitive psychology [5], investigated think aloud protocols [6] or adopted techniques from eye movement analysis for assessing the comprehension of business process models [7]. In this work, we focus on the role of eye movement analysis, as we think that the adoption of eye movement analysis is still below

---

* This research is supported by Austrian Science Fund (FWF): P26140–N15, P23699–N23.

L. Iliadis, M. Papazoglou, and K. Pohl (Eds.): CAiSE 2014 Workshops, LNBIP 178, pp. 159–170, 2014.

its full potential. In particular, it seems plausible that the costs of eye tracking infrastructure poses a considerable burden for the adoption of eye movement analysis [8].[1] To counteract this problem, efforts have been undertaken for developing eye–trackers at a low price by assembling off–the–shelf components, e.g., [9]. However, it is questionable in how far researchers who are not deeply involved in the peculiarities of assembling hardware are able to set up such an infrastructure on their own. Rather, we see a big potential in low–cost ready–to–use eye–trackers that have entered the market, seeking to compete with the high–priced versions.[2] Particularly in times of shortened research budgets, respective cost–efficient infrastructure seems indispensable.

In this sense, the research question investigated in this study can be defined, as follows: *Are low–cost eye–trackers useful for information systems research? If yes, which limitations apply?* To approach this research question, we bought *Gazepoint GP3*[3] and employed it in an empirical study for assessing its accuracy. Likewise, the contribution of this work is threefold: First, we report on the accuracy of Gazepoint GP3 with respect to the detection of fixations. Second, we use respective data for describing how experimental material, e.g., models, source code or tools, should be designed so that acceptable error rates can be expected. Third, we provide the source code used for this study, thereby providing an infrastructure for evaluating Gazepoint GP3 in different settings. Likewise, the remainder of this paper is structured, as follows. Section 2 introduces background information on eye–tracking. Then, Section 3 describes the experimental design of this study, whereas results are described in Section 4. Finally, Section 5 discusses related work and Section 6 concludes with a summary and an outlook.

2   Eye Movement Analysis

Before describing the experimental design followed in this study, we briefly introduce basic concepts related to eye movement analysis (for a more detailed introduction, see e.g., [10]). The fundamental idea of eye movement analysis is capturing the position a person is currently focusing on. To this end, usually the *pupil center corneal reflection method* [11] is adopted, in which the center of the pupil is computed by assessing the corneal reflection (Purkinje reflection) through infrared light. Thereby, either remote systems (i.e., video and infrared cameras that are affixed to a table) or head–mounted systems (i.e., devices that are fixed on the person's head) are employed [12]. However, only capturing the position a person is looking at is not enough, as it is known that high–resolution visual information input can only occur during so–called *fixations*, i.e., when the person fixates the area of interest on the fovea, the central point of highest visual acuity [13]. These fixations can be detected when the velocity of eye movements

---

[1] High–precision eye–trackers can cost more than several ten–thousand US$, see:
http://www.arringtonresearch.com/prices.html (accessed February 2014).

[2] For instance: http://theeyetribe.com/, http://gazept.com/,
http://mygaze.com/ (accessed February 2014).

[3] http://gazept.com/products/ (accessed February 2014).

is below a certain threshold for a pre-defined duration [14]. Using eye fixations, we can identify areas on the screen the person is focusing attention on [15], e.g., features of the modeling environment or modeling constructs. Due to the central role of fixation for processing visual information, we focus on the accuracy of fixation detection in the following.

3   Experimental Design

The goal of this empirical investigation is to determine whether low–cost eye–trackers provide enough accuracy to be of use for information systems research. As discussed in Section 2, fixations are of central interest, hence next we describe the experimental design followed for investigating the accuracy of fixations.

Experimental Procedure. The procedure followed in this experimental design consists of 5 steps. First, the subject is informed about potential risks involved in participating in the experiment and that all data is collected anonymously. Second, the eye tracker is calibrated by a 9–point calibration, as provided by the Gazepoint GP3 API. Third, the first visual task is presented to the subject, which basically asks the subject to look at specific points at the screen (details are provided in Paragraph *Visual Tasks*). Fourth, as it may be the case that the subject was not entirely focused on the visual task, the task is repeated once more. Finally, each experimental session is concluded by administering a survey about demographical information. To enable replication, the entire experimental material and data is freely available.[4]

Fig. 1. Experimental design

Visual Tasks. The visual tasks administered in this study were designed for measuring accuracy, i.e., computing the difference between the position on the screen the subject looked and the fixations the eye tracker computed. To this end, subjects are asked to look at a specific position for a given time interval. To ensure that subjects were indeed looking at this specific point, we asked to press a key as soon as the subject fixated on the point. As it is then known where the subject looked, fixations can be compared with this position. Technically, we implemented a Java component, which displays a configurable list of points according to the following procedure:

---

[4] The experimental material and data are available at:
   http://bpm.q-e.at/eye-tracking-accuracy

1. Fill the screen with white color
2. For each point in the configured lists of points
   (a) Draw solid black point on the screen (10 * 10 pixel) at given position
   (b) Wait until user presses arbitrary key
   (c) Capture the moment when the user presses the key
   (d) Wait for 500 ms
   (e) Fill the screen with white color

Using this mechanism, we configured 9 points, equally distributed on a grid on the screen. Since the employed eye–tracker is not able to track points outside the screen, we avoided points near the ending of the screen, i.e., the grid started at point (0.25 * width, 0.25 * height) and ended at point (0.75 * width, 0.75 * height). Apparently, subjects require time to locate and fixate on the current point. Hence, we only captured data between the moment when the subject pressed the key and the next 500 ms. The duration in which fixations are collected for analysis, i.e., 500 ms, is a trade–off between the amount of data points that can be collected and the quality of the data. In a longer time window more data can be collected, but at the same time it becomes likelier that the subject gets distracted, and vice versa. The eye–tracker's cameras operate at 60 Hz, likewise 60 points are recorded per second. Thus, 500 ms, resulting in approximately 30 data points per subject seem to be an acceptable trade–off.

Subjects. The population under examination in this study were all persons that may participate in eye–tracking research. The tasks involved in this experimental design does not require special training, rather basic reading skills are sufficient. However, during the preparation of the software displaying the visual tasks, we observed that the eye–tracker could not properly handle the reflections of glasses (no complications could be observed for persons wearing contact lenses). Hence, we exclude persons wearing glasses from our experimental setup.

Experimental Setup. For performing the eye movement analysis, a table mounted eye tracker, i.e., Gazepoint GP3, was used, recording eye movements at a frequency of 60 Hz. The visual tasks were performed on a 20" monitor with a resolution of 1600 * 1200 pixels and a dimension of 40 cm * 30 cm. In addition, we attached a second monitor, on which the eye–tracking software was running, allowing to monitor whether subjects were within the area accessible to the eye–tracker's cameras. The second monitor was positioned away from the main monitor, allowing the subject to fully concentrate on the visual tasks. The subject was seated comfortably in front of the screen in a distance of approximately 65cm (as recommended by the eye–tracker's manual). To minimize undesired fluctuations regarding light, we closed blinds of the office windows.

Response Variable. The interest of this study is to examine the accuracy of an eye–tracker with respect to the detection of fixations. Hence, the response variable of this study is the distance between the point the subject was supposed to look at and the corresponding fixations measured by the eye–tracker, subsequently referred to as *error*. As described in Paragraph *Visual Tasks*, we stored the moment when the subject pressed any key and showed the point for another 500 ms; only data points collected during this time window are used for analysis. For all of the data points falling into this time frame, in turn, the error is computed as the Euclidean distance between the measured fixation and the point displayed. Furthermore, data points are only taken into account when considered to be a valid fixation according to the eye–tracker's internal fixation filter.

Instrumentation and Data Collection. To allow for an efficient collection and analysis of data, we implemented the experimental procedure shown in Fig. 1 as an experimental workflow in Cheetah Experimental Platform (CEP) [16]. In other words, each activity from the experimental procedure was supported by a Java component, which in turn was executed in the order prescribed by the experimental procedure. Thereby, CEP provided ready–to–use components for displaying a consent dialog and administering a survey, whereas eye–tracking related components had to be implemented.

4 Results and Discussion

So far we described the experimental design adopted in this study. In the following, we focus on the execution of the empirical study in Section 4.1, discuss implications in Section 4.2, and present its limitations in Section 4.3. We would like to repeat at this point that all data collected is available on–line.[5]

4.1 Experimental Execution

In the following, we describe the preparation of the experiment, before we turn to the execution of the experiment and subsequently present the collected data.

Experimental Preparation. Preparation for this empirical study included acquiring the eye–tracker, implementing components accessing the eye–tracker's API, configuring the experimental procedure in CEP and acquiring subjects. Since our experimental procedure does not involve any particular skills besides reading, we relied on a convenience sample, i.e., we acquired friends and co–workers at the Department of Computer Science at the University of Innsbruck. As described in Section 3, none of the persons wore glasses during the experiment. However, we included subjects that wore glasses in daily life, but were able to read texts without glasses (these subjects participated without glasses).

Experimental Execution. The eye–tracking sessions were performed in February 2014 at the University of Innsbruck, where 16 subjects participated. However, for one subject the eye–tracker had problems identifying the subject's pupils, so we decided to exclude the data from analysis, leaving 15 data sets for analysis.

---

[5] All data collected in this study is available at:
http://bpm.q-e.at/eye-tracking-accuracy

Due to the nature of eye–tracking, only one subject could participate at a time. In this way, each subject could be welcomed, introduced to the experimental procedure and guided through the eye–tracking session. To reward and motivate subjects, a plot showing all fixations was produced immediately *after* each session, allowing subjects to see how well they performed.

Data Validation. To assess whether the collected data is valid, we plotted the results of each visual task for each subject and inspected the plots for abnormalities. Interestingly, the analysis revealed that for certain subjects the fixations of the visual task that was intended as familiarization were more accurate than for the second visual task. Knowing that subjects usually need a little training to get acquainted with tasks, these results seemed implausible. However, a discussion revealed that certain subjects had remembered where the next dot would appear and did not fully concentrate on the current point, but already moved on to the next point. To compensate for this shortcoming, we compared the results for the first and the second visual task and selected the task showing the *lower median* of error values. We argue that this procedure is acceptable, since it can be assumed that the eye–tracker's accuracy is stable for the *same* task and *same* subject. In other words, fluctuations can be rather attributed to subject–related factors, e.g., familiarization with the task or the discussed anticipation of points, hence selecting the visual task with lowest errors will probably result in selecting the visual task with the least influence of subject–related factors.

Results. Next, we describe the data obtained in this study from three perspectives. First, we look into demographical statistics, second, turn to error quantiles and, third, discuss the results of one subject. A summary of demographical data can be found in Table 1. Subjects were on average 30.67 years old ($SD = 3.27$) and 33.3% female. None of the subjects reported eye diseases or wore glasses. However, 5 subjects used contact lenses during the experiment.

Table 1. Demographical data

Variable	Data
Age	Min: 26, Max: 41, M: 30.67, SD: 3.27
Gender	Female: 5 (33.3%), Male: 10 (66.7%)
Eye diseases	0 (0%)
Glasses during experiment	0 (0%)
Contact lenses during experiment	5 (33.3%)

To give an overview of the collected fixations, we have summarized the error occurred during calibration (ε_{calib}), quantiles describing the error distributions (Q_{95} to Q_{80}) as well as the median of errors. In particular, as shown in Table 2, the average error measured during calibration was 45.20 pixel and quantiles range from 116.38 (Q_{95}) to 58.00 (Q_{80}); the median of errors was 32.20 pixel. All in

Table 2. Results for fixations (in pixel)

Subject	ε_{calib}	Q_{95}	Q_{90}	Q_{85}	Q_{80}	Median
S_1	47.14	59.91	47.30	37.64	31.32	21.00
S_2	62.59	66.22	62.77	59.48	50.45	30.27
S_3	53.19	92.46	87.86	68.18	65.37	44.91
S_4	28.86	46.10	37.95	34.79	32.70	17.03
S_5	43.96	103.62	97.51	58.18	52.35	27.29
S_6	49.67	43.42	38.12	31.40	29.83	19.72
S_7	38.24	96.13	73.82	71.69	70.26	27.78
S_8	74.56	180.50	166.21	146.01	128.23	56.63
S_9	37.74	86.76	84.91	51.43	48.26	34.07
S_{10}	47.74	86.59	66.94	61.55	57.01	34.46
S_{11}	43.23	121.25	117.69	67.78	66.48	33.94
S_{12}	43.48	88.20	76.55	71.87	65.51	33.62
S_{13}	42.85	181.11	178.02	173.00	152.27	116.87
S_{14}	24.02	51.88	50.25	48.26	47.10	35.18
S_{15}	40.65	43.57	41.76	40.31	38.28	21.93
Total	45.20	116.38	84.96	66.73	58.00	32.20

all, 4,122 fixations were captured, of which 3,869 were considered to be valid according to the eye–tracker's fixation filter. Furthermore, it can be observed that fixations seem to be rather homogeneous—a box plot of median values only detected S_8 and S_{13} as outliers.

So far, we have discussed the error distributions measured in pixel. To give an impression what these errors mean with respect to screen size, we have listed the error in mm in Table 3. As described in Section 3, the eye–tracking sessions were performed on a screen with an extent of 1600 * 1200 pixel and a screen size of 40 * 30 cm, i.e., 4 pixels were displayed per mm. In other words, values listed in Table 3 were computed by dividing the pixel–values from Table 2 by factor 4.

For visualizing how these ranges of errors relate to a screen of 1600 * 1200 pixel, we have selected the fixations for a subject with approximately average errors, i.e., subject S_3, and visualized the results in Fig. 2. In particular, the box to the left represents the screen with the 9 points at which S_3 was asked to look at. The green dots, in turn, represent the fixations as obtained through the eye–tracker. To the right, we have selected three regions to show patterns we could observe in the data. Mostly, as shown in the square at top right, fixations were measured in a rather small region, which does not necessarily directly overlap with the point the subject was supposedly looking. Also, as shown in the square in the middle right, fixations may have also been scattered over a larger region. This behavior could particularly be observed for subjects with large errors, e.g., subject S_8. Finally, as shown in the square bottom right, fixations for almost the same location were reported. However, the fixations were not necessarily directly at the location the subject was supposedly looking. We do not want to speculate here about potential reasons for these results, but rather give some visually accessible perspective on the data.

Table 3. Results for fixations (in mm)

Subject	ε_{calib}	Q_{95}	Q_{90}	Q_{85}	Q_{80}	Median
S_1	11.78	14.98	11.82	9.41	7.83	5.25
S_2	15.65	16.55	15.69	14.87	12.61	7.57
S_3	13.30	23.11	21.97	17.05	16.34	11.23
S_4	7.22	11.52	9.49	8.70	8.17	4.26
S_5	10.99	25.90	24.38	14.55	13.09	6.82
S_6	12.42	10.85	9.53	7.85	7.46	4.93
S_7	9.56	24.03	18.46	17.92	17.57	6.95
S_8	18.64	45.12	41.55	36.50	32.06	14.16
S_9	9.44	21.69	21.23	12.86	12.06	8.52
S_{10}	11.94	21.65	16.74	15.39	14.25	8.62
S_{11}	10.81	30.31	29.42	16.94	16.62	8.49
S_{12}	10.87	22.05	19.14	17.97	16.38	8.40
S_{13}	10.71	45.28	44.50	43.25	38.07	29.22
S_{14}	6.00	12.97	12.56	12.06	11.77	8.79
S_{15}	10.16	10.89	10.44	10.08	9.57	5.48
Total	11.30	29.10	21.24	16.68	14.50	8.05

4.2 Discussion

So far we described the data, next we discuss implications with respect to the adoption of low–cost eye–trackers. Basically, certain criteria must be fulfilled so that Gazepoint GP3 can be used in a meaningful way.[6] As described in Section 3, we could not manage to get the eye–tracker working for subjects wearing glasses, since reflections of the glasses were confused with reflections of the eyeball. Also, subjects with small eyes caused significant troubles in identifying pupils. Interestingly, also particularly glossy hair caused problems—in fact, for one subject it was only possible to conduct the session after the subject covered the hair. In addition, direct sunlight complicated the identification of fixations. However, as all of these problems could be identified and resolved during calibration, they presumably did not influence the results of this study. Regarding the accuracy promised by the vendor, the manual specifies an accuracy of 0.5° to 1° *of visual angle*. Assuming that the line of sight, error and screen form a right angle, an error of 1° results approximately in an error of 1.05 cm, or 42 pixels (tan(1) * 60 cm ≈ 1.05 cm). These promises are in line with our findings: As shown in Table 3, the median error for fixations was 8.05 mm.

To finally answer the research question approached in this work, i.e., whether low–cost eye–trackers are useful for information systems research, we discuss whether these accuracies are good enough for identifying where subjects looked. For this purpose, consider the illustration in Fig. 3, showing two objects (A and B) that should be identified in a study, e.g., activities in business process models, source code snippets or parts of a user interface. In particular, the figure

---

[6] We are not aware of any published studies utilizing this particular device.

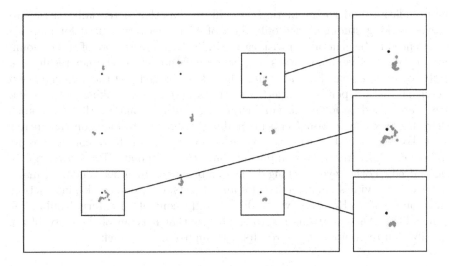

Fig. 2. Fixations measured for subject S_3

shows objects A and B, the distance between the center of A and the center of B ($d(A, B)$) as well as the errors involved in measuring fixations for the position of A (ε_A) and the position of B (ε_B). Conservatively assuming that errors are always directed toward the opposite object, fixations can only be unambiguously assigned to an object if the distance between the objects is smaller than the sum of error, i.e.,

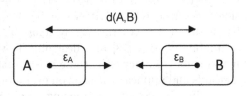

Fig. 3. Distinguishing objects

$d(A, B) < \varepsilon_A + \varepsilon_B$. As listed in Table 2, the median error was 32.20 pixel, i.e., if the difference between 2 objects is less than 64.40, the objects cannot be distinguished anymore. Likewise, when increasing the distance between objects, the probability of properly identifying objects increases. Whether these distances can be achieved in a meaningful way then depends on the specific research question. On the one hand, for instance, studies that investigate reading source code respective distances between source code characters seems infeasible. On the other hand, for instance, when evaluating, the user adoption of recommendations (e.g., [17]), respective distances in a user interface can easily be achieved. Hence, depending on the specific research question, the accuracy of Gazepoint GP3 may or may not be sufficient.

4.3 Limitations

As in every empirical study, the results have to be seen in the light of several limitations. First, the question arises in how for results can be generalized to the population under examination, i.e., all persons that potentially participate in eye–tracking studies. Since only data of 15 subjects was used for analysis, results need to be generalized with care. Similarly, subjects were of rather young age, i.e., on average 30.67 years old, hence it is not clear whether results also apply to older persons. Second, it must be acknowledged that the performance of the visual tasks depends on whether subjects were indeed looking at the points they were asked to focus on. For instance, subjects remarked that they knew where the next point would appear, making it difficult to focus on the current point. By selecting the task with higher accuracy, we sought to compensate for this issue. Third, results are applicable only to Gazepoint GP3 and cannot be generalized to other eye–tracking devices as produced by other vendors. Finally, we tried to provide similar settings for all subjects, e.g., same tasks, instructions and monitor size. However, we could not fully control all external influences, such as light. Also, we would like to emphasize that it is out of the scope of this contribution to compare these results with high–end eye–trackers.

5   Related Work

In this work, we focused on eye–tracking in information systems research, seeing eye–trackers from the perspective of users. However, also on the developers' side vivid research activities can be observed, e.g., investigating the feasibility of self–built eye–tracking systems [9], developing support for eye–tracking on mobile devices [18] and designing new algorithms for the detection of eye movements [19]. However, these works rather focus on the development of new methods and applications than on evaluation the feasibility, as done in this work. Regarding the use of eye–tracking, applications in a variety of domains can be observed. For instance, experiments have been conducted for investigating the understandability of UML models [20] and the interpretation of data models [21]. Similarly, a research agenda for investigating user satisfaction has been proposed in [22]. Other works employed eye–tracking for investigating process model comprehension [7] or for inspecting the way how modelers create process models [23]. However, all these works focus on the direct application of eye movement analysis rather than seeking to examine its usefulness, as done in this work. Even though we focus on eye–tracking, it is clearly not the only promising approach for investigating cognitive aspects in information systems. For instance, think aloud protocols, i.e., the thoughts subjects uttered during an empirical study, may be used to get insights into the cognitive processes involved in working with information systems artifacts [6,24]. Also, researchers have sought to transfer theoretical concepts from other domains, e.g., cognitive psychology, for advancing information systems research [25,26] and to conduct controlled experiments, e.g., [27,28]. It is important to stress that these approaches should be not seen as competing. Rather, best results can be expected by combining two or more paradigms, i.e., through method triangulation [29].

6   Summary and Conclusion

In this work, we set out to examine the accuracy of a low–cost eye–tracker regarding the detection of fixations. In an empirical study, we asked participants to look at specific positions at the screen and recorded the computed fixations. The analysis of errors showed that the median error lies well within the accuracy promised by the vendor. In a next step, we discussed the implications of these findings with respect to the development of experimental material, showing that the eye–tracker is well suited—given that elements at the screen are placed in proper distance. Thus, we conclude that if certain preconditions are fulfilled, e.g., not wearing glasses, appropriate light and covering glossy objects, Gazepoint GP3 appears to be a suitable choice for affordable eye–tracking studies.

Particularly for research that focuses on cognitive aspects, multiple perspectives as well as detail–rich data is indispensable. By providing data about the eye–tracker's accuracy, respective recommendations for developing experimental material and making available the source code involved in this study, we hope to help spreading and establishing eye–tracking for information systems research in general and research on cognitive aspects in particular. Regarding our research, we seek to employ the findings of this study for developing algorithms that automatically detect the modeling element a process modeler is looking at. With respective support, the cognitive processes involved in creating process models could then be investigated in an even more efficient and detailed manner.

References

1. Mylopoulos, J.: Information modeling in the time of the revolution. Information Systems 23, 127–155 (1998)
2. Kock, N., Verville, J., Danesh-Pajou, A., DeLuca, D.: Communication flow orientation in business process modeling and its effect on redesign success: Results from a field study. DSS 46, 562–575 (2009)
3. Indulska, M., Green, P., Recker, J., Rosemann, M.: Business Process Modeling: Perceived Benefits. In: Laender, A.H.F., Castano, S., Dayal, U., Casati, F., de Oliveira, J.P.M. (eds.) ER 2009. LNCS, vol. 5829, pp. 458–471. Springer, Heidelberg (2009)
4. Hadar, I.: When intuition and logic clash: The case of the object-oriented paradigm. Science of Computer Programming 78, 1407–1426 (2013)
5. Zugal, S.: Applying Cognitive Psychology for Improving the Creation, Understanding and Maintenance of Business Process Models. PhD thesis, University of Innsbruck, Department of Computer Science (2013)
6. Haisjackl, C., Zugal, S., Soffer, P., Hadar, I., Reichert, M., Pinggera, J., Weber, B.: Making Sense of Declarative Process Models: Common Strategies and Typical Pitfalls. In: Nurcan, S., Proper, H.A., Soffer, P., Krogstie, J., Schmidt, R., Halpin, T., Bider, I. (eds.) BPMDS 2013 and EMMSAD 2013. LNBIP, vol. 147, pp. 2–17. Springer, Heidelberg (2013)
7. Petrusel, R., Mendling, J.: Eye-tracking the factors of process model comprehension tasks. In: Salinesi, C., Norrie, M.C., Pastor, Ó. (eds.) CAiSE 2013. LNBIP, vol. 7908, pp. 224–239. Springer, Heidelberg (2013)

8. Hennessey, C., Duchowski, A.T.: An open source eye-gaze interface: Expanding the adoption of eye-gaze in everyday applications. In: Proc. ETRA 2010, pp. 81–84 (2010)

9. Li, D., Babcock, J., Parkhurst, D.J.: Openeyes: A low-cost head-mounted eye-tracking solution. In: Proc. ETRA 2012, pp. 95–100 (2006)

10. Duchowski, A.: Eye Tracking Methodology. Springer, Heidelberg (2007)

11. Ohno, T., Mukawa, N., Yoshikawa, A.: Freegaze: A gaze tracking system for everyday gaze interaction. In: Proc. ETRA 2002, pp. 125–132 (2002)

12. Rauthmann, J.F., Seubert, C.T., Sachse, P., Furtner, M.: Eyes as windows to the soul: Gazing behavior is related to personality. Journal of Research in Personality 46, 147–156 (2012)

13. Posner, M.I.: Attention in cognitive neuroscience. In: The Cognitive Neurosciences, pp. 615–624. MIT Press (1995)

14. Jacob, R.J.K., Karn, K.S.: Eye Tracking in Human-Computer Interaction and Usability Research: Ready to Deliver the Promises. In: The Mind's Eye: Cognitive and Applied Aspects of Eye Movement Research, pp. 573–603. Elsevier (2003)

15. Furtner, M., Sachse, P.: The psychology of eye-hand coordination in human computer interaction. In: Proc. HCI 2008, pp. 144–149 (2008)

16. Pinggera, J., Zugal, S., Weber, B.: Investigating the Process of Process Modeling with Cheetah Experimental Platform. In: Proc. ER-POIS 2010, pp. 13–18 (2010)

17. Zangerle, E., Gassler, W., Specht, G.: Recommending#-Tags in Twitter. In: Proc. SASWeb 2011, pp. 67–78 (2011)

18. Dybdal, M.L., Agustin, J.S., Hansen, J.P.: Gaze Input for Mobile Devices by Dwell and Gestures. In: Proc. ETRA 2012, pp. 225–228 (2012)

19. Vidal, M., Bulling, A., Gellersen, H.: Detection of Smooth Pursuits Using Eye Movement Shape Features. In: Proc. ETRA 2012, pp. 177–180 (2012)

20. Cepeda Porras, G., Guéhéneuc, Y.G.: An empirical study on the efficiency of different design pattern representations in uml class diagrams. Empirical Software Engineering 15, 493–522 (2010)

21. Nordbotten, J.C., Crosby, M.E.: The effect of graphic style on data model interpretation. Information Systems Journal 9, 139–155 (1999)

22. Hogrebe, F., Gehrke, N., Nüttgens, M.: Eye Tracking Experiments in Business Process Modeling: Agenda Setting and Proof of Concept. In: Proc. EMISA 2011, pp. 183–188 (2011)

23. Pinggera, J., Furtner, M., Martini, M., Sachse, P., Reiter, K., Zugal, S., Weber, B.: Investigating the Process of Process Modeling with Eye Movement Analysis. In: Proc. ER-BPM 2012, pp. 438–450 (2013)

24. Seeber, I., Maier, R., Weber, B.: Macrocognition in Collaboration: Analyzing Processes of Team Knowledge Building with CoPrA. Group Decision and Negotiation 22, 915–942 (2013)

25. Zugal, S., Pinggera, J., Reijers, H., Reichert, M., Weber, B.: Making the Case for Measuring Mental Effort. In: Proc. EESSMod 2012, pp. 37–42 (2012)

26. Zugal, S., Pinggera, J., Weber, B.: Assessing Process Models with Cognitive Psychology. In: Proc. EMISA 2011, pp. 177–182 (2011)

27. Pinggera, J., Zugal, S., Weber, B., Fahland, D., Weidlich, M., Mendling, J., Reijers, H.: How the Structuring of Domain Knowledge Can Help Casual Process Modelers. In: Proc. ER 2010, pp. 231–237 (2010)

28. Claes, J., et al.: Tying Process Model Quality to the Modeling Process: The Impact of Structuring, Movement, and Speed. In: Barros, A., Gal, A., Kindler, E. (eds.) BPM 2012. LNCS, vol. 7481, pp. 33–48. Springer, Heidelberg (2012)

29. Jick, T.D.: Mixing Qualitative and Quantitative Methods: Triangulation in Action. Administrative Science Quarterly 24, 602–611 (1979)

Supporting BPMN Model Creation
with Routing Patterns

Idan Wolf and Pnina Soffer

Information Systems Department, University of Haifa, A. Hushi 199
Haifa 3498838, Israel
idanwf@gmail.com, spnina@is.haifa.ac.il

Abstract. Business process modelers often struggle with appropriately representing routing situations in a model. In particular, difficulties may be encountered when using BPMN, due to its large number of constructs and the lack of ontological clarity of this language.

The paper proposes routing patterns combined with a decision guidance tool to support BPMN model creation. The use of patterns is proposed based on cognitive considerations, which are explained to provide justification to the proposed support. The set of patterns builds on an existing set of routing behaviors and operationalizes these behaviors by providing their BPMN representations. The effect of this support is tested in a study, whose findings indicate a significant effect on the quality of the produced models. The findings also indicate that the use of the guided routing patterns leads to a longer time required for modeling as compared to unsupported modeling.

Keywords: BPMN, Routing patterns, Process modeling, Empirical study.

1   Introduction

Business process models play an important role in the development of business processes and information systems. The creation of a business process model requires gaining an understanding of the domain and specifying its required behavior using some process modeling language. The resulting model should be syntactically correct (correctly using the modeling language), logically and semantically correct (truthfully representing the behavior of the domain and lacking logical errors such as deadlocks), and understandable to its readers. These quality requirements make process modeling a challenging task.

A particularly challenging task in process modeling is the appropriate construction of routing structures. Routing structures include split nodes, where the thread of control is split into several threads that can be taken alternatively or in parallel, and merge nodes, where several threads are merged into a single one. Empirical evidence show that such structures are associated with difficulties both in model reading (are more difficult to understand [4, 16]) and in model construction (entail modeling errors [8, 9]). Explanations suggested for these difficulties include the existing variety of possible behaviors at these nodes [17], the need to accurately specify decision

L. Iliadis, M. Papazoglou, and K. Pohl (Eds.): CAiSE 2014 Workshops, LNBIP 178, pp. 171–181, 2014.

logic [20], and the fact that as opposed to other process model elements (e.g., activity, resource), routing nodes are not directly observable in a domain but rather abstraction of possible behavior patterns across different process instances.

Routing structures form basic constructs in practically all the process modeling languages, although different languages employ different sets of constructs for this purpose. Business Process Model and Notation (BPMN) [11] is a popular modeling language, and is the current de facto standard process modeling language. BPMN has a strong expressive power (see evaluation in [7]), facilitated by a large set of constructs. However, a large number of constructs might include construct redundancy [22], leading to unclear semantics and entailing a less conclusive modeling decision making [18]. In fact, evaluations of BPMN for ontological clarity have identified such deficiencies [7, 15]. In addition, a study of the actual use of BPMN constructs has indicated that only a relatively small set of constructs are commonly used by modelers and can be considered core constructs, while many other constructs are seldom used [23]. In addition, several studies have criticized BPMN from a perspective of cognitive effectiveness [4,5,6].

BPMN includes seven kinds of gateways (actually specified using 8 symbols), which are constructs directly used for routing, but routing can also be specified using other constructs (flows, events) or combinations of them. This makes the specification of routing in BPMN a considerably challenging part of process modeling.

This paper attempts to support the modeling of routing structures in BPMN. It does so by using a combination of routing design patterns and a decision support sheet. We suggest this combination based on cognitive considerations and evaluate it by an experiment whose subjects are Information Systems students.

The paper is organized as follows. Section 2 provides a background about the cognitive process of modeling, justifying the proposition of patterns to support this process. Section 3 describes the experimental study and its findings, which are discussed in Section 4. Finally, conclusions are given in Section 5.

2   A Cognitive Perspective of Modeling

We consider the construction of a process model which represents a given domain behavior as a problem solving task and the model as the solution. Empirical observations [14] have indicated that process modeling involves three phases: comprehension, when the modeler develops an understanding of the represented domain; modeling, when this understanding is transformed into modeling constructs; and reconciliation, when model elements are reconciled, moved, and renamed, to improve appearance and understandability. These three phases are repeated in iterations, each relating to a chunk of the model. Iterative chunking has been indicated to take place in general problem solving [10], and attributed to working memory limitations. We focus on the comprehension and modeling phases, when the modeler develops domain understanding and maps it into constructs of a modeling language.

According to Newell and Simon [10], when facing a task, the problem solver formulates a mental model of the problem, and uses it to reason about the solution and to apply solution procedures. In process modeling, solution procedures entail mapping the mental model of the domain behavior into a model in the particular modeling language. According to [10] the mental model is affected by the characteristics of the task and the methods used for achieving it. Consequently, for a BPMN modeling task, the mental model might use concepts related to BPMN constructs (e.g., gateway, event), and then the appropriate BPMN constructs (e.g., a specific type of event) should be selected and combined to form a concrete process model.

According to the cognitive schema theory [3], mental models are types of cognitive schemas related to the understanding of a specific situation that serve for solving a current problem. Mental models are constructed by using lower-level cognitive schemas, called memory objects, as building blocks. Memory objects are components of human knowledge stored in long-term memory. The simplest objects are basic concepts, called p-prims; above them are integrated objects that enable people to recognize and classify patterns in the external world so they can respond with appropriate mental or physical actions. A mental model is constructed by mapping memory objects onto components of a currently faced real-world phenomenon, reorganizing and connecting them into a model of the whole situation. A complex memory object can also be an example from past experience, which is retrieved from long term memory and adapted by analogy to the current situation.

The construction of the mental model is highly affected by the available memory objects. According to the cognitive load theory [2], the burden on the limited capacity of working memory can be reduced by using schemas that allow categorizing multiple elements as a single element [12]. When the cognitive schemas used are low level and require further integration to construct a mental model, cognitive load is increased. This might lead to reduced task performance [13].

When the task is to create a BPMN model of complex routing behavior, two main difficulties arise. First, BPMN constructs are basic objects that require effort for combining them into a mental model that fits the current situation. As a result, it is likely that the mental model does not use specific constructs, but generalized and higher-level concepts (e.g., split, event). Second, the selection of a specific combination of constructs to which the mental model should map is difficult due to the construct redundancy of BPMN [7, 15]. This makes the mapping decision inconclusive and difficult [18].

To overcome these two difficulties, we suggest the use of routing patterns. First, the patterns as concepts can form objects at a suitable granularity level for effectively serving as building blocks in a mental model. As such, they help the modeler classify the situation and generalize it. Second, the mapping to specific combinations of BPMN constructs is immediate, as these are specified in the patterns. In addition, the selection of an appropriate pattern for a given situation can be supported by a structured process of alternatives evaluation, which can be guided by a series of designated questions that classify the situation.

3   Empirical Study

The empirical study was aimed at evaluating the use of routing patterns and decision guidance when constructing a BPMN model. The main question was whether the guided use of patterns yields models of a higher syntactic and semantic quality. As a baseline for comparison we addressed the use of individual BPMN constructs, which is the common set of concepts analysts possess. Moreover, while individual constructs can serve as basic memory objects, model examples can be used as composite ones to be used by analogy. We hence decided that the study should compare the guided use of patterns – composite reusable building blocks that can be easily composed at a given situation – with the combination of atomic concepts and relevant examples. While the main question related to the effectiveness of the modeling, we also posed a second question, related to modeling efficiency in terms of the time required.

3.1   Routing Patterns and Decision Support

To address the above questions, we have used the set of routing behaviors which was tested in the study reported by [19]. This set addresses binary split/merge situations, and includes four split types and seven merge types, including types that are not recognized as Workflow Patterns [17]. In the study reported by Soffer et. al [19], training with this set had a positive effect on the formation of mental models, reflected in understanding domain behavior from textual descriptions. This set, however, is abstract and unrelated to a modeling notation. Hence, to make is operational for BPMN modeling, we developed BPMN representations of the behavior types in the set.

The set of routing behaviors, listed in Table 1, relates to binary splits and merges, but can easily be generalized to larger cases. The representation of the types as BPMN routing patterns was developed by one of the researchers and evaluated by the other. When more than one representation was possible, the alternative representations were discussed by both researchers until a preferred option was agreed upon. Finally, all the patterns were evaluated by an independent BPMN expert. An example pattern is presented in Fig. 1.

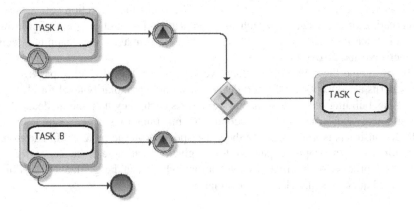

Fig. 1. BPMN routing pattern for immediate continuation with cancellation. When a task is completed (either A or B) it throws a signal event and the process continues with Task C; the signal is caught by the other task (A or B) as an interrupting event, which terminates this task.

Table 1. Set of routing behavior types for binary cases

Type	Description
Splits	
Exclusive (XOR)	Exactly one branch needs to be activated
Parallel (AND)	Both branches need to be activated
Inclusive (OR)	At least one branch needs to be activated
Constrained Or (COR)	A specific branch needs to be activated, the other is optional
Merges	
Immediate continuation	The process continues when the merge is reached. When both branches are active and one reaches the merge – the other proceeds independently.
Immediate continuation with cancellation	The process continues when the merge is reached. When both branches are active and one reaches the merge – the other is stopped.
Immediate continuation with asymmetric cancellation	The process continues when the merge is reached. If one branch arrives first – the other is stopped. If the other branch arrives first – the first one proceeds. In other words – if both branches are active – one always completes and the other completes only if it arrives first.
Immediate continuation with mutual blocking	The process can continue when either branch arrives at merge but is stopped when both arrive together.
Synchronization	The process can continue when both branches have arrived at the merge. When one branch arrives, continuation "waits" for the other.
Asymmetric synchronization	The process can continue only when a specific ("necessary") branch arrives at the merge. If the other branch arrives first, the necessary one must proceed independently since continuation requires it. If the necessary branch arrives first, the other one can still proceed.
Asymmetric synchronization with cancellation	The process can continue only when a specific ("necessary") branch arrives at the merge. If the other branch arrives first, the necessary one must proceed independently since continuation requires it. If the necessary branch arrives first, the other one is stopped.

In addition, to facilitate the selection of an appropriate pattern for a given situation, we have developed a decision tree-like guidance sheet for selecting an appropriate pattern for a given situation, as shown in Fig. 2.

3.2 Settings

The experiment was conducted with 36 Information Systems students attending a course on systems analysis. Throughout the course, the participants had already studied business process modeling using Event-driven Process Chains (EPC), Petri nets and BPMN. The participants had also experienced using the mentioned modeling notations in several projects and realistic case studies.

The students were randomly divided into two separate rooms and groups. To verify that the assignment was indeed random, we conducted an independent-samples T-test on the average homework grades achieved in the course, and found no significant difference between the groups.

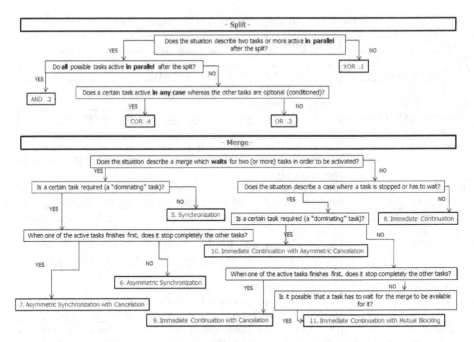

Fig. 2. A decision tree-like guidance for type selection

One group, the "Treatment" group (consisted of 17 participants), was trained with the routing patterns, and then performed the experimental assignment. The "Control" group (consisted of 19 participants) was trained with the precise meaning of individual BPMN constructs, emphasizing event and routing constructs. Both groups were shown illustrative examples; in fact, the same examples were used in the training of both groups. However, for the Treatment group these were examples of the reusable routing patterns, while for the Control group the same examples were presented as illustrating possible combinations of BPMN constructs.

The task included four descriptions of short business process situations that had to be modeled in BPMN. The business process situations focused on the dynamics of routing points in a process (merges and splits) in different domains.

3.3   Procedure

Training: Each group received one hour of training. The treatment group received, first, a short explanation on the concept of reusable patterns in process modeling. Afterwards, each pattern was presented by its business meaning, specification and an example. An example situation was analyzed using the decision support sheet. Yet, it was clarified to the subjects that the use of patterns is not mandatory and they can decide differently.

The training provided to the Control group included a reminder of the elements in BPMN. Since the notation consists of many elements, and in order to keep relevance, the reminder addressed the elements of gateways, flows, and relevant events, discussing semantic differences among them and how they can be combined. The reminder was accompanied by modeling examples, whose form was similar to the cases in the task. Moreover, the examples included the routing patterns. However, the participants were not aware that the examples include reusable patterns.

Printout: At the beginning of both training sessions, printouts were handed to the participants in both groups so they could write notes during the training and also as a reference during the task. The Treatment group received a printout consisting of: a list of BPMN elements, the BPMN routing patterns, and the decision sheet. The control group received a printout consisting of a list of BPMN elements.

Task Performance: The task was performed right after the training. No time limit was set. When the students completed the task they submitted their work; the submission time was recorded for every student. As an incentive for good performance, a bonus of 3 points to the total course grade was promised to the five best performing students in each one of the groups.

Task Materials: The task materials included four situation descriptions that had to be modeled in BPMN. In total, the participants had to compose 10 routing structures in their task models (5 splits and 5 merges). The situations were selected to include routing behaviors which cannot be represented by single constructs, and correspond to our routing patterns. Table 2 presents the task cases and their corresponding routing patterns.

Table 2. Task cases and corresponding patterns

Case	Splits	Merges
1	AND, AND	Immediate continuation with cancellation; Synchronization
2	AND	Asymmetric Synchronization
3	AND	Immediate continuation with mutual blocking
4	COR	Asymmetric synchronization with cancellation

In order to avoid a learning curve effect, we created four different versions of the assignment. Each version had a different order of the cases, so participants received different versions of the assignment.

3.4   Measurement and Hypotheses

The dependent variables were the performance score for the modeling assignment and the time taken to complete the assignment. We hypothesized a difference between the Treatment group and the Control group in these two variables. Accordingly:

H_{1a}: The performance scores for subjects in the Treatment group will be different than those of subjects in the Control group.
H_{1b}: The times for performing the task for subjects in the Treatment group will be different than those of subjects in the Control group.

As shown in Table 2, the four cases included 10 routing structures. Each case was scored based on the following scheme:

- 0 points were given for mostly inappropriate representation, syntactically and semantically.
- 1 point was given for partially appropriate representation.
- 2 points were given for fully appropriate representation.

The grading was done separately by the two researchers and discussed in cases of disagreement until consensus was reached. The time taken to complete the assignment was measured in minutes and recorded upon submission of the assignment.

3.5   Analysis and Findings

The results obtained for performance scores as well as time are presented in Table 3. To test whether the observed differences between the groups' results are statistically significant, we have used an independent sample T-test for both variables, after verifying that they were Normally distributed.

Table 3. Results: performance score and time

Variables / Groups		N	Min	Max	Mean	Std. Deviation	Sig.
Performance score	Control	19	10	18	14.47	2.653	0.007*
	Treatment	17	12	20	16.71	2.544	
Task time (minutes)	Control	19	22	50	34.95	8.423	0.000*
	Treatment	17	34	66	49.18	10.513	

As both tests yielded significant results (see p values in Table 3), we can make the following conclusions. Considering the performance scores hypothesis, H_{1a} can be accepted. Furthermore, the difference in the performance scores is significantly in favor of the Treatment group, thus our conclusion is that the guided use of the routing patterns has a positive effect on the quality of the model. Considering the task times hypothesis, H_{1b} can be accepted. Furthermore, the task performance times are significantly higher for the Treatment group, indicating that the guided pattern-based modeling process is longer than when they are not used. This can be concluded for a novice population, like the participants of the study.

4   Discussion

The findings of the reported study indicate that a guided use of routing patterns can yield BPMN models of higher semantic and syntactic quality than a modeling process that does not use such patterns. The study compared a treatment group, using a set of patterns and a decision-support sheet, with a control group that served as a proxy to the "ordinary" modeling process – using the constructs of the modeling language and some experience-based examples. While the use of individual BPMN constructs as basic concepts is rather straightforward, the use of examples requires careful attention for several reasons.

First, the use of worked examples as a learning approach has been extensively studied (e.g., [1]) and found effective for strengthening problem solving capabilities with a focus on structural aspects. This seems to be in contrast to our findings. However, the example-based learning approach devotes much attention to how the examples are presented to the learner. In particular, it is stressed that examples should be presented in the context of problem classification. In our study, such context existed for the treatment group and not for the control group. Following this, the use of examples by the control group is not in line with the example-based educational approach and is not expected to yield similar learning effects.

Second, the immediacy and short period of time between seeing the example and performing the task is important when interpreting the results of the study. According to [21] events that occurred recently are easier to recall, and this might bias the judgment of their appropriateness as a basis for decisions at the current situation. In our study it is likely that having recently seen relevant examples made it easy for the subjects to recall and use them. Indeed, many of the models created by the control group attempted to adapt these examples to the given situations. As a result, the scores of the control group were generally high, although still significantly lower than those of the treatment group. It is plausible to believe that a longer delay between the training and the task performance would have made the relevant examples harder to recall, and result in models that are less similar to the examples in the control group. Accordingly, the difference in the scores of the control and the treatment group might have been larger. Furthermore, an interesting experimental setting for future research would introduce other, less relevant, examples during the time between the training and the task performance. These might then be easier to recall than the previously given examples, creating bias and reducing the quality of the produced models.

Another interesting finding is the difference in performance time between the groups. It appears that while supporting a systematic and effective modeling process, our guided patterns slowed this process significantly. This is not surprising, since a structured cognitive process that evaluates alternatives and selects an appropriate one should take longer than a quick retrieval and adaptation of an example. Furthermore, the longer time can also be explained by the fact that in our case the subjects were using printed material (i.e., "paper objects" rather than memory objects). Going over this material took time and slowed the modeling process.

It should be noted that while the reported study addressed modeling in BPMN, the set of routing behavior has served as abstract concepts in the study reported in [19], detached from any modeling language, and compared against a subset of the workflow patterns 17]. No decision-support sheet was used there, and yet the mere training with this set of conceptual routing behaviors was found to support domain understanding. This encourages the development of similar patterns for other modeling languages as well (subject to their expressive power limitations).

Also note that we did not ask the subjects about their perceptions regarding usefulness of the patterns, ease of use, and mental effort required for performing the task. These can be addressed in future studies.

5   Conclusion

Empirical evidence accumulated over time indicates that business process modelers often struggle with appropriately representing routing situations. In particular, difficulties may be encountered when using BPMN, due to its large number of constructs, the numerous possible combinations of these constructs, and the lack of ontological clarity of this language.

The paper proposes routing patterns combined with a decision guidance tool to support BPMN model creation. Cognitive considerations justify our prediction that the guided use of patterns would constitute an appropriate modeling support. These relate to the formation of a mental problem representation, where the patterns can serve for classifying the situation, and to immediately transforming the mental model into BPMN. The set of patterns builds on an existing set of routing behaviors and operationalizes these behaviors by providing their BPMN representations.

We have conducted an empirical study to evaluate the effect of the proposed support on modeling routing situations in BPMN. The results of the study indicate that the proposed support significantly improves the quality of the models, but increases the modeling time. These findings imply a potential contribution of embedding similar routing patterns and decision guidance into modeling tools that are used in practice.

However, the experiment used novice subjects in a learning environment, and its findings are limited to similar settings. Furthermore, additional and deeper understanding is still required, especially with respect to repeated application of this modeling support over time. Questions such as what would be the prolonged effect of providing such modeling support, would the respective decision criteria be internalized and become automatically used by modelers or abandoned with time are still unanswered. These should still be addressed by future research.

References

1. Atkinson, R.K., Derry, S.J., Renkl, A., Wortham, D.: Learning from examples: Instructional principles from the worked examples research. Review of Educational Research 70(2), 181–214 (2000)
2. Chandler, P., Sweller, J.: Cognitive load theory and the format of instruction. Cognition and Instruction 8, 293–332 (1991)
3. Derry, S.D.: Cognitive Schema Theory in the Constructivist Debate. Educational Psychologist 31(3/4), 163–174 (1996)
4. Figl, K., Mendling, J., Strembeck, M., Recker, J.: On the Cognitive Effectiveness of Routing Symbols in Process Modeling Languages. In: Abramowicz, W., Tolksdorf, R. (eds.) BIS 2010. LNBIP, vol. 47, pp. 230–241. Springer, Heidelberg (2010)
5. Figl, K., Recker, J., Mendling, J.: A study on the effects of routing symbol design on process model comprehension. Decision Support Systems 54(2), 1104–1118 (2013)
6. Genon, N., Heymans, P., Amyot, D.: Analysing the Cognitive Effectiveness of the BPMN 2.0 Visual Notation. In: Malloy, B., Staab, S., van den Brand, M. (eds.) SLE 2010. LNCS, vol. 6563, pp. 377–396. Springer, Heidelberg (2011)

7. Recker, J.C., Indulska, M., Rosemann, M., Green, P.: How good is BPMN really? Insights from theory and practice. In: 14th European Conference on Information Systems (2006)

8. Mendling, J., Moser, M., Neumann, G., Verbeek, H.M.W., van Dongen, B.F., van der Aalst, W.M.P.: Faulty EPCs in the SAP Reference Model. In: Dustdar, S., Fiadeiro, J.L., Sheth, A.P. (eds.) BPM 2006. LNCS, vol. 4102, pp. 451–457. Springer, Heidelberg (2006)

9. Mendling, J., Verbeek, H.M.W., Dongen van, B.F., Aalst van der, W.M.P., Neumann, G.: Detection and Prediction of Errors in EPCs of the SAP Reference Model. Data and Knowledge Engineering (64), 312–329 (2008)

10. Newell, A., Simon, H.: Human Problem Solving. Prentice Hall, Englewood Cliffs (1972)

11. OMG. Business Process Model and Notation (BPMN) version 2.0. OMG (2011), http://www.omg.org/spec/BPMN/2.0:

12. Paas, F., Tuovinen, J.E., Tabbers, H., Gerven, P.W.M.V.: Cognitive Load Measurement as a Means to Advance Cognitive Load Theory. Educational Psychologist 38(1), 63–71 (2003)

13. Paas, F.A., Renkl, J.: Cognitive Load Theory: Instructional Implications of the Interaction between Information Structures and Cognitive Architecture. Instructional Science 32, 1–8 (2004)

14. Pinggera, J., Soffer, P., Fahland, D., Weidlich, M., Zugal, S., Weber, B., Mendling, J.: Styles in business process modeling: an exploration and a model. Software & Systems Modeling, 1–26 (2013)

15. Recker, J., Rosemann, M., Green, P., Indulska, M.: Do ontological deficiencies in modeling grammars matter? MIS Quarterly 35(1), 57–79 (2011)

16. Reijers, H.A., Mendling, J.: A Study into the Factors that Influence the Understandability of Business Process Models. IEEE Transactions on Systems, Man, And Cybernetics – Part A 41(3), 449–462 (2011)

17. Russell, N.C., ter Hofstede, A.H.M., Aalst van der, W.M.P., Mulyar, N.: Workflow Control-Flow Patterns: A Revised View, BPM Center Report BPM-06-22, BPMcenter.org (2006)

18. Soffer, P., Hadar, I.: Applying Ontology-Based Rules to Conceptual Modeling: A Reflection on Modeling Decision Making. European Journal of Information Systems 16(4), 599–611 (2007)

19. Soffer, P., Kaner, M., Wand, Y.: Towards Understanding the Process of Process Modeling: Theoretical and Empirical Considerations. In: Daniel, F., Barkaoui, K., Dustdar, S. (eds.) BPM Workshops 2011, Part I. LNBIP, vol. 99, pp. 357–369. Springer, Heidelberg (2012)

20. Soffer, P., Wand, Y., Kaner, M.: Semantic analysis of flow patterns in business process modeling. In: Alonso, G., Dadam, P., Rosemann, M. (eds.) BPM 2007. LNCS, vol. 4714, pp. 400–407. Springer, Heidelberg (2007)

21. Tversky, A., Kahneman, D.: Judgment under uncertainty: Heuristics and biases. Science 185(4157), 1124–1131 (1974)

22. Wand, Y., Weber, R.: On the Ontological Expressiveness of Information Systems Analysis and Design Grammars. J. of Information Systems (3), 217–237 (1993)

23. Muehlen, M.z., Recker, J.: How much language is enough? Theoretical and practical use of the business process modeling notation. In: Bellahsène, Z., Léonard, M. (eds.) CAiSE 2008. LNCS, vol. 5074, pp. 465–479. Springer, Heidelberg (2008)

Coupling Elements of a Framework for Cognitive Matchmaking with Enterprise Models

Sietse Overbeek

Institute for Computer Science and Business Information Systems,
University of Duisburg-Essen, Reckhammerweg 2, D-45141 Essen, Germany, EU
Sietse.Overbeek@uni-due.de

Abstract. Actors working in knowledge intensive organizations have
to cope with an increased cognitive load by increasing complexity of
knowledge intensive tasks that these actors have to fulfill. This is caused
by developments such as: Globalization, growing product and service
complexity, customers that become more and more powerful, outsourcing, and inter-organizational alliances that cause organizations to grow
more rapidly. Excessive cognitive load negatively influences the quality of
knowledge intensive task fulfillment. It is discussed how elements from
a cognitive matchmaking framework can be coupled with an example
enterprise model to partly provide a solution for avoiding cognitive load
of actors in becoming too excessive. This exercise enables to achieve a
better understanding of the cognitive fit of actor types and knowledge
intensive task types they have to fulfill.

Keywords: cognitive matchmaking, DSML, enterprise modelling,
knowledge intensive tasks, MEMO.

1 Introduction

Organizational value includes both financial and intellectual capital [20]. Financial capital represents the book value of the organization and includes the value
of its financial and physical assets [10]. On the contrary, intellectual capital
consists of assets created through intellectual activities ranging from acquiring
new knowledge (learning) and inventions leading to the creation of valuable relationships [20]. Organizations that derive their *raison d'être* to a large extent
from intellectual capital can be referred to as *knowledge intensive organizations*.
Actors working in these organizations perform knowledge intensive tasks, which
are tasks for which acquisition, application, or testing of knowledge is necessary
in order to successfully fulfill the task [15]. However, the complexity of these
knowledge intensive tasks increases, which is a result of, for example, organizational growth, increased globalization, growing product complexity, an increasing customer power, outsourcing, shorter product life cycles and return flows,
and inter-organizational alliances [12,19]. Actors that are responsible to fulfill
knowledge intensive tasks in organizations may experience an increased cognitive load if task complexity increases [21]. Cognitive load, increased by growing

L. Iliadis, M. Papazoglou, and K. Pohl (Eds.): CAiSE 2014 Workshops, LNBIP 178, pp. 182–193, 2014.
© Springer International Publishing Switzerland 2014

task complexity, can influence the frequency of errors by affecting the strength of procedural and sensory cues [2,17]. Eventually, the quality of fulfilled tasks may be negatively influenced.

A cognitive matchmaker system has been developed in earlier work [14,15], which matches cognitive characteristics supplied by types of actors and cognitive characteristics required to fulfill types of knowledge intensive tasks. The resulting matches can then be used to achieve a better fit between actors and tasks which is assumed to positively affect the quality of task fulfillment. A cognitive characteristic is considered to be a specific cognitive part of the cognitive system that is possessed by an actor which enables an actor to think, learn, or make decisions [1,18]. For example, the *volition* characteristic is concerned with an actor's willpower to fulfill some knowledge intensive task [11]. The aforementioned cognitive matchmaker system is based on a formal framework for cognitive matchmaking [15], which is briefly summarized as follows. An actor of a certain type is characterized by means of the cognitive characteristics that it supplies at a certain level and a task type is characterized by the characteristics it requires at a certain level. Each individual characteristic is matched based on the supply and demand levels. Subsequently, weigh values can be provided to stress that some characteristic match result is considered more important than another one. Finally, these weighed characteristic matches are summated and then normalized to determine a single suitability match result. This shows how suitable an actor type is to perform a knowledge intensive task type.

In this paper, elements from the cognitive matchmaking framework are combined with the method for multi-perspective enterprise modelling (MEMO) [8]. MEMO guides the creation and application of enterprise models. "An enterprise model comprises conceptual models of software systems, e.g., object or component models, that are integrated with conceptual models of the surrounding action systems, e.g., business process models or strategy models" [8]. An action system is considered to be: "A system of interrelated actions that reflect the corresponding actors' intentions and abilities, organizational goals and guidelines, contextual threats and opportunities, as well as mutual expectations" [7, p. 42]. Elements from the cognitive matchmaking framework could also have been combined with a different enterprise modeling approach. However, approaches such as MEMO are multi-perspective in that they provide different groups of stakeholders with specific abstractions and views on their areas of concern within an enterprise. Therefore, this enables to relate cognitive elements to a variety of different abstractions and views of an enterprise. MEMO includes the meta modeling language MEMO-MML, with which an extensible set of domain-specific modelling languages (DSMLs) can be specified. In concrete, this means that a meta meta modelling language serves to develop new modelling languages. A DSML includes a meta model which specifies the abstract syntax and semantics of the domain-specific language. Eventually, models can be created by instantiating this meta model. A goal modelling language called MEMO-GoalML and a business process modelling language called MEMO-OrgML are used to design goal models respectively business process models for specific domains.

The (MEMO-)GoalML and (MEMO-)OrgML are two examples of DSMLs. The concrete syntax of OrgML includes graphical symbols that enable to specify which tasks are part of a (sub) process. The concept of a task is pivotal to couple an enterprise model with elements of the aforementioned cognitive matchmaking framework. As processes can be further differentiated into tasks by means of the OrgML language, an OrgML business process model is studied as those kinds of enterprise models are particularly suited to combine with cognitive elements. Based on knowledge gained by studying how these models can be combined with cognitive elements, further research in this area includes how to combine other enterprise models with cognitive elements, such as: Organizational structures, goal models, and models illustrating organizational decision processes.

This paper is structured as follows. First of all, an overview of related work is presented in section 2. In section 3, the coupling of an enterprise model with cognitive elements is illustrated by means of an OrgML business process model of an order management process which includes a sub process that is further differentiated into tasks. It is discussed how key elements of the cognitive matchmaking framework can be coupled with such an enterprise model. The resulting benefits of this exercise are discussed in section 4. Finally, section 5 presents the conclusions and ideas for future research.

2   Related Work

The existing body of literature reveals that other approaches exist that are oriented towards relating cognitive aspects with (enterprise) modelling languages. The approach presented in [9] is oriented towards organizational change and how organizational change processes can be modelled. The discussed approach to model these processes incorporates cognitive aspects in the form of mental states of those actors involved in the change. An expressive language is introduced called the meta Temporal Trace Language. With this language, it is, for example, possible to express the changing (belief) states of actors involved in a changing organization and new roles that are taken up by actors. Explicit cognitive characteristics are not related to actors, as cognitive aspects are considered to be the expressed internal (belief) states of actors. Another difference is that in [9] a new modelling language is developed to describe organizational change processes which takes cognitive aspects of actors into account, while in this paper the orientation is towards coupling existing enterprise modelling languages with elements from cognitive matchmaking.

In [3], an approach called structured process modeling is introduced which encourages modelers to work on a few elements of a process model at the same time. The argument is that when modelers work on elements in parallel when designing a business process model less working memory capacity is required than when working on several parts of the model simultaneously. In summary, structured process modeling is argued to be a breadth-first modelling approach for the modelling of business processes that can cause process model quality to increase. It can be concluded that the research in [3] focuses on preventing the overloading of the working memory by offering modelers a modeling style that takes the cognitive aspects of the processing capabilities of the human brain into account. Compared to our research, we do not suggest a new modeling style to reduce cognitive load of process modelers, however, we focus on reducing cognitive load of actors that fulfill knowledge intensive tasks in general by using enterprise models enriched with cognitive aspects as an instrument to improve the understanding what types of tasks should be allocated to what types of actors in order to achieve a cognitive match. Therefore, this research could be seen as complementary to our approach.

The work of [16] provides insights in cognitive aspects of novice process designers and it is stipulated that task performance is best when the mental representation of a problem matches that of the 'cognitive design vehicle', for example, the process model that is used to solve the problem at hand. Furthermore, their plans for future work include considerations on how well modelling languages fit to mental representations of the processes being designed, and the effect on the performance of the process design task. Analogously to our research, it could be stated that the mental representation of the (knowledge intensive) task at hand would then need to match the types of design tools that an actor has at its disposal in order to achieve better task performance. As we are trying to understand how to improve the match between an actor/task-combination, the approach by [16] can also be seen as complementary to reduce cognitive load and increase task performance by taking a different solution strategy into account.

3   Illustrating the Coupling of an Enterprise Model with Cognitive Elements

Figure 1 shows an OrgML business process model of an order management process as part of a fictitious company that sells printers [6, p. 92]. The product line ranges from low budget printers that are sold at less than €100 a piece to high performance printers with a price tag of €5.000 and more. The figure shows start and stop events, as well as events that indicate a state change in the process. There are six sub processes shown, which are in this case semi-automated processes as they are performed by humans with the support of a computer. The model also includes four branches. For example, at the right end of the 'check credibility' sub process a branching symbol is shown indicating that a rule-based decision is made by a human after completing a sub process. Furthermore, a merger symbol is shown that combines two alternative paths of execution into one common path and an AND- and OR-synchronizer is shown. The process starts when an order is received of a customer that wants to order one or more printers. After receiving the order, the credibility of the customer is checked. Dependent of this outcome, a subsequent path is chosen. In case the credibility is in order, both the 'check availability' and 'check delivery' sub processes can be executed in parallel. Finally, the order is denied or accepted, based on the resulting events. It is shown that the 'check delivery' sub process has been differentiated into three tasks, which are part of the rectangle that is connected

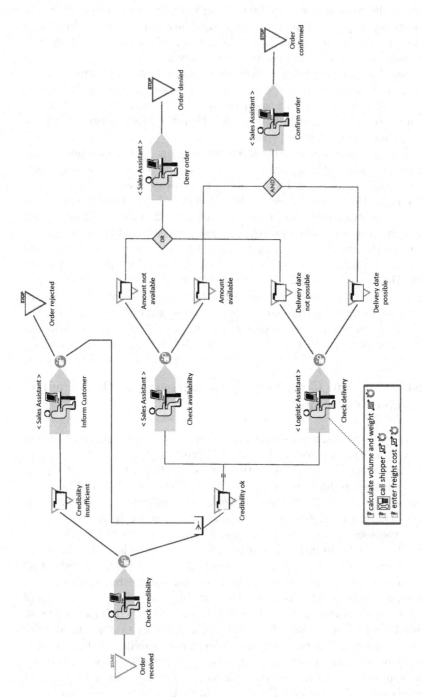

Fig. 1. OrgML model of an order management process, based on [6, p. 92]

with a dashed line to this sub process. The names of the three tasks are given, as well as a used medium, the complexity of the tasks and temporal aspects are taken into account. In this case, it is illustrated that the task 'calculate volume and weight' is of a medium complexity and that the other two tasks are of a low complexity. The temporal duration to complete a task is the same for all three tasks, which is 'medium'. It is illustrated that a telephone is required as a medium to complete the task 'call shipper'. It can also be seen that the 'check delivery' sub process itself is carried out by a logistics assistant.

The 'check delivery' sub process provides an opportunity to determine possibilities to couple the business process model description with elements of the cognitive matchmaking framework, as it includes a differentiation into tasks and includes a description of the actor that is responsible to fulfill this sub process. The cognitive matchmaking framework includes descriptions of cognitive actor settings [15], that indicate on an abstract level which cognitive characteristics are supplied by which type of actor. Five different abstract actor types have been provided based on a classification of knowledge worker types [4] and on cognitive literature [5,11], each characterized by a cognitive actor setting. More specific actor types such as, for example, the logistics assistant in the case of the order management process can be abstracted to such an abstract actor type. As a consequence, this indicates which basic cognitive characteristics are supplied by the logistics assistant. Two of the five abstract actor types as part of the cognitive matchmaking framework are the *expert* and *collaborator* types [15]. When a logistics assistant conducts the 'call shipper' task, he would fit the description of a collaborator type of actor. An actor of this type always possesses the *volition, causability,* and *improvability* characteristics.

A collaborator has the ability to exert an influence on state changes of knowledge involved during task fulfillment. A collaborator is also able to improve its own cognitive abilities during task fulfillment. However, a collaborator does not have complete awareness of all required knowledge to fulfill a task instance and requires others for task completion. The volition characteristic has already been explained in section 1. Causability expresses that an actor has the ability to exert an influence on state changes of knowledge involved during task fulfillment. When the logistics assistant processes acquired knowledge from the shipper and documents this in the context of the order management system, he causes knowledge that is implicitly present in his head to be made explicit [13]. This means that the logistics assistant causes knowledge to change from one type to another. During fulfillment of the 'call shipper' task as part of the 'check delivery' sub process, the logistics assistant might have improved his own cognitive abilities. This is indicated by the improvability characteristic. When a logistics assistant conducts the 'calculate volume and weight' and 'enter freight cost' tasks, he would fit the description of an expert type of actor. Next to the characteristics possessed by a collaborator, an expert type of actor also possesses the *sentience* and *independency* characteristics. Sentience expresses that an actor has awareness of required knowledge to fulfill some task. In this case, a logistics assistant is considered to be an expert when it comes to calculating volumes and weights of shipments and when entering freight costs and that he is aware of which knowledge is needed for the task. Independency indicates that an expert is fully able to fulfill a task on his own.

Next to cognitive actor settings, the cognitive matchmaking framework also includes cognitive task settings. These task settings clarify which cognitive characteristics are in any case demanded by the various task types independent of the actor that fulfills the task. Possible knowledge intensive tasks that can be fulfilled can be abstracted to three types [15], which includes the *acquisition* task type, the *synthesis* task type, and the *testing* task type. The acquisition type is related with the acquisition of knowledge. The 'call shipper' task is considered to be a task of this abstract type, as knowledge related to freight costs has to be acquired from shippers to fulfill this task. The synthesis type is related with the actual utilization of acquired knowledge. The other two tasks as part of the sub process 'check delivery' are tasks of this type. Knowledge has to be utilized in order to calculate the volume and weight of a shipment and to determine the freight cost. The testing task type is related with the identification and application of knowledge in practice inducing an improvement of the specific knowledge applied. For example, a student who failed an exam studies a teacher's feedback on his exam. Then, a re-examination attempt follows to improve his previously acquired and utilized knowledge. The three tasks as part of the sub process do not seem to fit the description of the testing task type.

The cognitive characteristics that are demanded by the acquisition task type are *satisfaction* and *relevance* [15]. The satisfaction characteristic is related with a knowledge need during task fulfillment and the eventual disappearance of that need. When the logistics assistant calls a shipper to understand what a shipment may cost and how these costs are calculated, the logistics assistant's need for this knowledge may have substantially been decreased. Relevance is concerned with whether or not knowledge acquired is deemed appropriate during task fulfillment. This is the case if the logistics assistant is able to acquire the necessary knowledge by calling the shipper. In this case, the logistics assistant is able to determine the total freight cost. The cognitive characteristics that are demanded by the synthesis task type are *applicability* and *correctness* [15]. The applicability characteristic expresses to what extent knowledge is applicable in a task. When calculating the volume and weight of a shipment, the logistics assistant applies previously acquired knowledge. When knowledge is applied it should meet its requirements. This is indicated by the correctness characteristic. When completing the 'enter freight cost' task, for example, the logistics assistant should enter the correct amount in the order management system. Table 1 summarizes the abstraction of the specific actor and task types to the aforementioned abstract actor and task types. It also shows the cognitive characteristics that characterize a combination of an actor type and task type from a cognitive point of view. At this point it is understood which cognitive characteristics are considered to be important for task fulfillment after abstracting the specific actor and task types that are part of the 'check delivery' sub process to abstract types that are part of a cognitive matchmaking framework [15]. From this point

Table 1. Actor type and task type abstraction

Specific actor type	Abstract actor type	Specific task type	Abstract task type	Cognitive characteristics
Logistics assistant	Expert	Calculate volume and weight	Synthesis	Volition Sentience Causability Improvability Independency Applicability Correctness
Logistics assistant	Collaborator	Call shipper	Acquisition	Volition Causability Improvability Satisfaction Relevance
Logistics assistant	Expert	Enter freight cost	Synthesis	Volition Sentience Causability Improvability Independency Applicability Correctness

onwards, it is perfectly possible to apply the remaining steps of the cognitive matchmaking framework as mentioned in section 1 as well, however, for that purpose it is needed to determine the levels on which characteristics are supplied and demanded in an actor/task-combination and weigh values need to be determined to underline which characteristics are most respectively less important in calculating a match. How and in what ways the actor type and task type abstraction could be advantageous for task performance is discussed next.

4 Benefits of Coupling Enterprise Models with Cognitive Aspects

Understanding which cognitive characteristics are of importance for the fulfillment of a certain task as part of a process can prove to be beneficial for stakeholders such as a process owner, personnel of the human resource (HR) department, and most certainly also the actor performing knowledge intensive tasks himself. Possible benefits of coupling enterprise models with cognitive aspects are described from three viewpoints, which are: A 'design time' viewpoint, a 'runtime' viewpoint, and a 'post-mortem' viewpoint. (1) Based on the abstraction shown in table 1, a process owner or HR employee can determine at *design time* that a logistics assistant responsible for fulfilling the 'check delivery' sub process should be sufficiently capable of supplying a specific set of cognitive characteristics to successfully complete the tasks as part of the sub process. In case of the 'call shipper' task, this implies the actor should: Manifest enough willpower to fulfill this task (volition), should be able to process different types of knowledge (causability), improve his own cognitive abilities through conducting the task (improvability), should be able to acquire knowledge from the shipper such that the task can be fulfilled (satisfaction), and all knowledge acquired should be relevant for the task at hand (relevance). Such an exercise can be performed for each type of task that a logistics assistant in the company should be able to conduct, which raises awareness whether an actor is ready and fully capable to conduct the tasks as part of his work profile or whether more training or education is needed. It is also beneficial for process owners or an HR department to determine what a cognitive profile of in this case a logistics assistant should look like in order to be a successful logistics assistant for the company. An HR department might even adapt their recruitment policy accordingly.

(2) During the execution of a process, problems might occur at *runtime*, i.e., during task fulfillment. Knowing which cognitive characteristics are required to be supplied for which task can prove to be beneficial in finding an adequate solution from a cognitive point of view. I.e., when it is determined by means of runtime analysis that the satisfaction characteristic is not adequately supplied by some actor that performs an acquisition task, the solution to improve task performance might be found in making sure to solve the problem that the actor is unable to diminish his knowledge need in the context of the problematic task. (3) From a *post-mortem* point of view, the performance of a business process can be analyzed retrospectively. It can be analyzed for which tasks the performance has been adequate and for which tasks the performance was problematic. For those tasks that were problematic it can then be determined whether demanded characteristics have been adequately supplied. For example, for an acquisition task type it can be analyzed whether the knowledge that has been acquired by an actor was satisfactory and relevant in order to fulfill the task. This kind of analysis also provides insights for which tasks some actor needs to improve certain cognitive abilities or perhaps needs to learn how to supply other characteristics that were previously not supplied by that actor.

Besides studying an enterprise model coupled with cognitive aspects from these three viewpoints, it makes sense to look more closely at the graphical notation of the enterprise model itself. I.e., in the context of this paper an OrgML business process model also provides graphical information that can be used for determining what type of task is part of a sub process and what type of actor would probably be suitable for performing the task. Especially, the symbols that indicate the complexity and expected duration of a task provide additional information which is beneficial in determining what actor type should be allocated to the task. For example, the most complex tasks should be fulfilled by experts and by knowing which cognitive characteristics should be supplied by expert actor types it becomes transparent what should be expected from actors that perform such complex tasks from a cognitive point of view. The temporal duration symbol as part of an OrgML model can be used to express that tasks do not require a lot of time to fulfill, however, it can also be expressed that tasks require a lot of time to fulfill. The temporal factor might have an effect on an actor's ability to supply cognitive characteristics as well. For example, it is interesting to know whether a 'long' temporal duration has an effect on supplying the volition characteristic. I.e., an actor might become less motivated if a task consumes a lot of his working time. On the other hand, low task complexity and a short temporal duration might also affect supplying the volition characteristic, for example, when an actor becomes overqualified for such a task.

5   Conclusions and Future Research

Actors working in knowledge intensive organizations deal with increasing cognitive load due to an increase in the complexity of the knowledge intensive tasks they have to fulfill. This growth in the complexity of those tasks is caused by developments such as: Growing product and service complexity, customers that become more and more powerful, globalization, outsourcing, and inter-organizational alliances that also cause organizations to grow more rapidly. Knowledge intensive organizations largely depend on their intellectual capital in order to exist. In this paper, a part of a possible solution has been presented to provide support for actors struggling to cope with their cognitive load. By building on existing research, we have combined elements from a framework for cognitive matchmaking with elements from enterprise modelling. An example enterprise model in the form of a business process model that shows an order management process of a company selling printers serves as an illustration to determine which elements in such an enterprise model are pivotal for the coupling with cognitive aspects. The business process model has been modelled with a language for organizational modelling called OrgML, that is part of the method for multi-perspective enterprise modelling (MEMO). MEMO includes an extensible set of domain-specific modelling languages, that are suitable to design and, subsequently, interrelate these designs of different parts of an enterprise.

As it is possible to differentiate (sub) processes into tasks by means of the OrgML, it is shown how this differentiation into tasks serves as a pivot point to couple with the key elements from the cognitive matchmaking framework. This framework includes abstract cognitive actor and task settings. The cognitive actor settings reflect what kinds of actors in knowledge intensive organizations are characterized by the cognitive characteristics they can offer. The cognitive task settings reflect which cognitive characteristics are required by which types of knowledge intensive tasks. By means of these elements, it is possible to reason about which total set of cognitive characteristics are required to be supplied in an actor/task-combination in order to fulfill a task. Several benefits of coupling an enterprise model with cognitive elements have been discussed. Among those benefits it is mentioned that the coupling raises awareness whether an actor is ready and fully capable to conduct tasks as part of his work profile or whether more training or education is needed. Also, knowing which cognitive characteristics are required to be supplied for which task can prove to be beneficial in finding an adequate solution from a cognitive point of view when problems occur during task fulfillment. For those tasks that were problematic it can then be determined whether demanded cognitive characteristics have been adequately supplied. Finally, it is also discussed that the graphical information provided by an OrgML business process model which reveal the complexity and temporal duration of a certain task can be used for determining what type of actor would probably be suitable for performing the task. For example, very complex tasks should be handled by experts and by knowing which cognitive characteristics should be supplied by expert actor types it becomes transparent what should be expected from actors that perform very complex tasks.

As has been mentioned in the introduction 1, future research will be oriented towards studying how other enterprise models than business process models can be combined with cognitive elements. Furthermore, we want to get a better understanding of which types of tasks are candidates for (partial) automation based on cognitive characteristics or capabilities that are demanded to fulfill such a task. In contemporary knowledge intensive organizations there are task types that are already fully automated, there are task types that are typically performed by humans with the support of computers and there are also types of tasks that are not automated at all. An example of a task that is hard to automate is a task that includes complex communication, for instance, when a consultant has to explain to a customer why a particular decision is a better choice than another possible decision in a given context. Especially in the context of those task types it is interesting to understand how computers can provide support in task fulfillment by understanding the capabilities that a computer should offer. The graphical notation of OrgML already enables to differentiate between a manual process, a computer-supported process, and a fully automated process. Using the task-oriented symbols to specify which tasks should be fulfilled as part of a process it is then possible to understand which kind of specific tasks are still non-automated. This way, an enterprise model can be used for analyzing which types of tasks are candidates for automation. Another question that we would like to see answered as part of future research is related to processes that are semi-automated and non-automated. More understanding is needed to know how and what kind of support can be provided in case a choice has to be made which type of actor is suitable to fulfill a semi- or non-automated task. Subsequently, more knowledge should be gained when it comes to determining the criteria with which it is possible to select an actor type over another actor type to perform some task type. From a cognitive point of view, it is then important to understand which cognitive characteristics can be offered by which actor type and for which task types these characteristics are of utmost importance.

References

1. Anderson, J.: Rules of the mind. Lawrence Erlbaum Associates, Hillsdale (1993)
2. Back, J., Blandford, A., Curzon, P.: Slip errors and cue salience. In: Brinkman, W.P., Ham, D.H., Wong, W. (eds.) ECCE 2007: Proceedings of the 14th European Conference on Cognitive Ergonomics, London, UK, EU, pp. 221–224. ACM Press, New York (2007)
3. Claes, J., Gailly, F., Poels, G.: Cognitive aspects of structured process modeling. In: Franch, X., Soffer, P. (eds.) CAiSE Workshops 2013. LNBIP, vol. 148, pp. 168–173. Springer, Heidelberg (2013)
4. Davenport, T.: Thinking for a Living – How to get Better Performances and Results from Knowledge Workers. Harvard Business School Press, Boston (2005)

5. Dowty, D.: Thematic proto-roles and argument selection. Language 67(3), 547–619 (1991)
6. Frank, U.: Memo organisation modelling language (2): Focus on business processes. ICB Research Report 49. Institute for Computer Science and Business Information Systems, University of Duisburg-Essen, Essen, Germany, EU (2011)
7. Frank, U.: Multi-perspective enterprise modelling: Background and terminological foundation. ICB Research Report 46. Institute for Computer Science and Business Information Systems, University of Duisburg-Essen, Essen, Germany, EU (2011)
8. Frank, U.: Multi-perspective enterprise modeling: Foundational concepts, prospects and future research challenges. Software and Systems Modeling (in press)
9. Hoogendoorn, M., Jonker, C., Schut, M., Treur, J.: Modeling centralized organization of organizational change. Computational and Mathematical Organization Theory 13(2), 147–184 (2007)
10. Joia, L.: Measuring intangible corporate assets. Journal of Intellectual Capital 1(1), 68–84 (2000)
11. Kako, E.: Thematic role properties of subjects and objects. Cognition 101(1), 1–42 (2006)
12. Mohamed, M.: The triad of paradigms in globalization, ICT, and knowledge management interplay. VINE: The journal of Information and knowledge Management Systems 37(2), 100–122 (2007)
13. Nonaka, I., Takeuchi, H.: The Knowledge Creating Company. Oxford University Press, New York (1995)
14. Overbeek, S.J., van Bommel, P., Proper, H.A.: Information systems engineering supported by cognitive matchmaking. In: Bellahsène, Z., Léonard, M. (eds.) CAiSE 2008. LNCS, vol. 5074, pp. 495–509. Springer, Heidelberg (2008)
15. Overbeek, S.J., van Bommel, P., Proper, H.A.: Matching cognitive characteristics of actors and tasks in information systems engineering. Knowledge-Based Systems 21(8), 764–785 (2008)
16. Recker, J., Safrudin, N., Rosemann, M.: How novices design business processes. Information Systems 37(6), 557–573 (2012)
17. Rukšėnas, R., Back, J., Curzon, P., Blandford, A.: Formal modelling of salience and cognitive load. Electronic Notes in Theoretical Computer Science 208, 57–75 (2008)
18. Smith, E.: Mental representations and memory. In: Gilbert, D., Fiske, S., Lindzey, G. (eds.) The Handbook of Social psychology, 4th edn., pp. 391–445. McGraw-Hill, New York (1998)
19. Staab, S., Studer, R., Schnurr, H., Sure, Y.: Knowledge processes and ontologies. IEEE Intelligent Systems 16(1), 26–34 (2001)
20. Tai, W.S., Chen, C.T.: A new evaluation model for intellectual capital based on computing with linguistic variable. Expert Systems with Applications 36(2), 3483–3488 (2009)
21. Weir, C., Nebeker, J., Bret, L., Campo, R., Drews, F., LeBar, B.: A cognitive task analysis of information management strategies in a computerized provider order entry environment. Journal of the American Medical Informatics Association 14(1), 65–75 (2007)

Investigating Differences between Graphical and Textual Declarative Process Models*

Cornelia Haisjackl and Stefan Zugal

University of Innsbruck, Austria
{cornelia.haisjackl,stefan.zugal}@uibk.ac.at

Abstract. Declarative approaches to business process modeling are regarded as well suited for highly volatile environments, as they enable a high degree of flexibility. However, problems in understanding declarative process models often impede their adoption. Particularly, a study revealed that aspects that are present in both imperative and declarative process modeling languages at a graphical level—while having different semantics—cause considerable troubles. In this work we investigate whether a notation that does not contain graphical lookalikes, i.e., a textual notation, can help to avoid this problem. Even though a textual representation does not suffer from lookalikes, in our empirical study it performed worse in terms of error rate, duration and mental effort, as the textual representation forces the reader to mentally merge the textual information. Likewise, subjects themselves expressed that the graphical representation is easier to understand.

Keywords: Declarative Process Models, Empirical Research, Mindshift Learning Theory.

1 Introduction

In the context of analyzing and designing information systems, the positive influence of conceptual modeling on understanding and communication has been documented [1]. For example, *business process models* (*process models* for short) have been employed in the context of process–aware information systems, service–oriented architectures and web services [2]. Recently, *declarative approaches* have received increasing attention due to their flexibility with respect to modeling and execution of processes [3]. While imperative process models specify exactly *how* things must be done, declarative models focus on the logic that governs the interplay of process actions by describing activities that may be performed as well as constraints prohibiting undesired behavior. Existing research has addressed technical issues of declarative process models, such as maintainability [4], verification [5] and execution [6]. Understandability concerns of declarative models, on the contrary, have been considered only to a limited extent. So far, a study

---

* This research is supported by Austrian Science Fund (FWF): P26140–N15, P23699–N23

L. Iliadis, M. Papazoglou, and K. Pohl (Eds.): CAiSE 2014 Workshops, LNBIP 178, pp. 194–206, 2014.
© Springer International Publishing Switzerland 2014

was conducted focusing on common strategies and typical pitfalls when system analysts make sense of declarative process models [7]. The study revealed that aspects that are present in both imperative and declarative process modeling languages at a graphical level—while having different semantics—cause considerable troubles. To understand these findings, we would like to refer to the theory of *Mindshift Learning* [8]. This theory postulates that, when learning new modeling languages, concepts that are similar, but still show subtle differences, are most difficult to learn. In this work, we investigate whether mindshift learning indeed imposes a burden on understanding declarative process models by conducting an empirical study, trying to avoid mindshift learning by using a declarative process modeling notation based on text. We handed out graphical and textual declarative process models to subjects and asked them to perform sense–making tasks. Results of this study indicate that the graphical representation is advantageous because it gives rise to fewer errors, shorter durations, and less mental effort. Therefore, even though it might be recommendable to avoid representing declarative models in a way similar to imperative models, a pure textual representation does not seem to be the right solution.

The remainder of the paper is structured as follows. Sect. 2 gives background information. Then, Sect. 3 describes the setup of the empirical investigation, whereas Sect. 4 deals with its execution and presents the results. Finally, related work is presented in Sect. 5, and Sect. 6 concludes the paper.

2   Backgrounds

Next, we present background information on declarative models (Sect. 2.1) and present the concept of mental effort as a measure for understanding (Sect. 2.2).

2.1   Declarative Process Models

Declarative approaches to business process modeling have received increasing interest, as they promise to provide a high degree of flexibility [5]. Instead of describing how a process must be executed, declarative models focus on the logic that governs the interplay of activities. For this purpose, declarative process models specify *activities* that may be performed as well as *constraints* prohibiting undesired behavior. Constraints found in literature may be divided into existence constraints, relation constraints and negation constraints [9]. *Existence constraints* specify how often an activity must be executed for one particular process instance (e.g., *exactly*, cf. Fig. 1). In turn, *relation constraints* restrict the ordering of activities (e.g., *response*, cf. Fig. 1). Finally, *negation constraints* define negative relations between activities (e.g., *neg_coexistence*, cf. Fig. 1).

A *trace* is defined as a *completed* process instance [3]. It can have two different states: either it satisfies all constraints of the process model (*valid*, also referred to as *satisfied*), or the trace violates constraints in the process model (*invalid*, also referred to as *violated*). A *minimal trace* is defined as a valid trace with a minimum number of activities. A *sub–trace*, in turn, can be in three different states: First, a sub–trace can be *valid* (the sub–trace satisfies all constraints of the process model). Second, it can be *temporarily violated* (the sub–trace does not satisfy all constraints of the process model, but there is an affix or suffix that could be added to the sub–trace such that all constraints are satisfied), or third, *invalid* (the sub–trace violates constraints in the process model and no affix or suffix can be added to the sub–trace to satisfy all constraints).

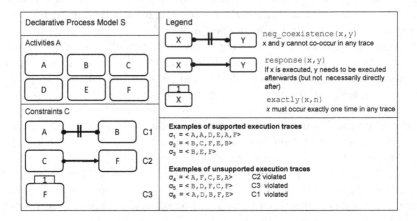

Fig. 1. Example of a declarative process model [3]

An example of a declarative process model S, using Declare (formerly known as ConDec) [5], is shown in Fig. 1. S consists of 6 activities A to F and 3 constraints. The *neg_coexistence* constraint (C1) forbids that A and B co-occur in the same trace. In turn, the *response* constraint (C2) requires that every execution of C must be followed by one of F before the process instance may complete. Finally, the *exactly* constraint (C3) states that F must be executed exactly once per process instance. For instance, trace σ_1=<A,A,D,E,A,F> satisfies all constraints (C1–C3), i.e., these are valid traces, whereas, e.g., trace σ_6 is invalid as it violates C1. Trace σ_7=<F> is the minimal trace since there exists no other valid trace comprising a lower number of activities.

Declarative Process Model S textual				
Activities A		**Constraints C**	**Mapping Activities - Constraints**	
A B C		C1: neg_coexistence(A,B)	A: C1	D: -
D E F		C2: response(C,F)	B: C1	E: -
		C3: exactly(F,1)	C: C2	F: C2, C3

Fig. 2. Example of a textual declarative process model

In the empirical investigation we try to avoid mindshift learning by using a declarative process modeling notation based on text. Fig. 2 shows the textual representation of the declarative process model S (cf. Fig. 1). The textual representation consists of three parts. First, a list of activities (activities A to F). Second, a list of constraints (C1 to C3). Third, an activity–constraint mapping list, to support subjects when looking up all constraints that are related to a specific activity (e.g., F is related to constraints C2 and C3).

2.2   Mental Effort

To investigate the sense–making of declarative process models, it seems necessary to also take into account the humans cognitive system—in particular *working memory*, which is responsible for maintaining and manipulating a *limited* amount of information for goal–directed behavior, such as the interpretation of a declarative process model (cf. [10]). The amount of working memory currently used is thereby referred to as *mental effort* [11]. Research indicates that a high mental effort increases the probability of errors, especially when the working memory capacity is exceeded [12]. In the context of conceptual models, [13] argues that higher mental effort is in general associated with lower understanding of models. Various techniques exist for assessing mental effort, including pupillometry, heart–rate variability and rating scales [11]. Especially rating scales, i.e., self–rating mental effort, has been shown to reliably measure mental effort and is thus widely adopted [11]. Furthermore, this kind of measurement can be easily applied, e.g., by using 7–point rating scales. In the context of conceptual modeling, it was argued that mental effort should be considered as an additional measure of understanding together with error rates and duration [13].

3   Defining and Planning the Empirical Investigation

To investigate whether mindshift learning indeed imposes a burden on understanding declarative process models we conduct an empirical investigation.

Research Question. Goal of this empirical investigation is to avoid difficulties because of mindshift learning due to similarities between imperative and declarative modeling notations. Therefore, we investigate how system analysts answer several tasks about declarative process models, once with a graphical model representation (with presence of mindshift learning) and once with a textual model representation (with absence of mindshift learning). In particular, we are interested in differences between graphical and textual model representations regarding errors, duration and mental effort. Therefore, our research questions can be stated as follows:

Research Question $RQ_{1.1}$ *What are the differences between a graphical and textual representation regarding error rates?*
Research Question $RQ_{1.2}$ *What are the differences between a graphical and textual representation regarding duration?*
Research Question $RQ_{1.3}$ *What are the differences between a graphical and textual representation regarding mental effort?*

With our last research question, we take a broader perspective and ask subjects directly for advantages and disadvantages for each representation as well as personal suggestions for improving the understandability of declarative process models.

Research Question RQ_2 *What are advantages of each representation and what are potential improvements for the understandability of declarative process models?*

Subjects. To ensure that obtained results are not influenced by unfamiliarity with declarative process modeling, subjects need to be sufficiently trained. Even though we do not require experts, subjects should have at least a moderate understanding of declarative processes' principles.

Objects. The process models (P_1 and P_2) used in this investigation originate from a previous study (cf. [7]) and describe real–world business processes. Since we were interested in the influence of differences regarding the process models' representation, we created a second variant of each process model describing the exact same process, but with a textual representation. The variants for P_1 are illustrated in Fig. 3. For the graphical models we use the declarative process modeling language Declare [5], where activities are represented as boxes and constraints as lines or arcs. The textual models are described in Sect. 2.1.[1]

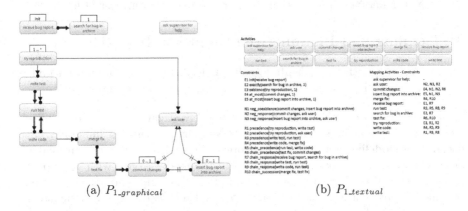

(a) $P_{1\_graphical}$ (b) $P_{1\_textual}$

Fig. 3. Graphical and textual variant of P_1

The models vary regarding the number of activities (between 12 and 24), number of constraints (between 18 and 25) and degree of interconnectivity of constraints, i.e., models consist of 3 to 6 components (cf. [7]). The process models are based on two different domains describing bug fixing in a software company

---

[1] The empirical investigation's material can be downloaded from:
http://bpm.q-e.at/GraphicalTextualDPM

and a worker's duties at an electronic company. Both models contain constraints of all three types, i.e., existence, relation and negation constraints.

Design. Fig. 4 shows the overall design of the empirical investigation: First, subjects are *randomly* assigned to two groups of similar size. Regardless of the group assignment, demographical data is collected and subjects obtain introductory assignments. To support subjects, sheets briefly summarizing the constraints' semantics are provided, which can be used throughout the investigation. Then, each subject works on one graphical and one textual process model. Group 1 starts with the graphical representation of P_1, while Group 2 works on the textual representation of the same model. A session is concluded by a discussion with the subject to help reflecting on the investigation and providing us with feedback. For each process model, a series of questions is asked (cf. Fig. 4b): First, subjects are asked to describe what the goal of the process model is, allowing subjects to familiarize with the model. Second, we seek to assess whether subjects understand the process model by asking 3 questions regarding traces in declarative process models: naming the minimal trace, naming 2 valid traces and naming 2 invalid traces (cf. Sect. 2.1). Further, a series of questions is designed based on the findings of [7] to investigate hidden dependencies, pairs of constraints, combinations of constraints and existence constraints. Third, we ask the subjects about their opinion on advantages and disadvantages of each model representation, what parts are most challenging and if they have any suggestions to make the model easier to read/understand.

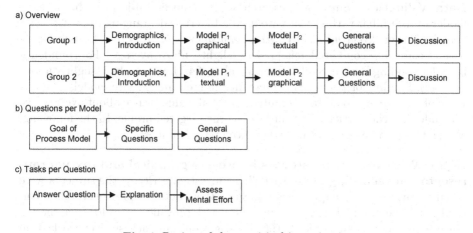

Fig. 4. Design of the empirical investigation

For each question, a three–step procedure is followed, cf. Fig. 4 c). First, the subject is asked to answer the question either by *True*, *False* or *Don't Know*. Second, the subject has to fill in an explanation field, where it should be reasoned why the specific answer was given. Third, the subject is asked to assess the expended mental effort. To this end, a 7–point rating scale is used, which is known to reliably measure mental effort [11].

Instrumentation. For the operationalization of this setup, we relied on Cheetah Experimental Platform (CEP) [14]. CEP guided the subjects through the sessions, starting with an initial questionnaire, two questionnaires about declarative process models (one represented graphically and one textually), a concluding questionnaire and a feedback questionnaire. Data was collected automatically, ensuring that each session, the collected demographic data was stored as a separate case of the empirical investigation.

4   Execution and Results

So far we described the experimental setup, next we briefly describe its execution as well as the results.

Execution. The empirical investigation was conducted in December 2013 at the University of Innsbruck in the course of a weekly lecture on business processes and workflows; all in all 9 students participated. To prepare the students, a lecture on declarative process models was held one week before the empirical investigation. In addition, students had to work on several modeling assignments using declarative processes before the investigation took place. Immediately before the sessions, a short lecture revisiting the most important concepts of declarative process models and the setup was held. The rest of the session was guided by CEP's experimental workflow engine [14], as described in Sect. 3.

Data Validation. Since our research setup requires subjects to be at least moderately familiar with Declare, we used a Likert scale, ranging from *"Strongly agree" (7)* over *"Neutral" (4)* to *"Strongly disagree" (1)* to screen for familiarity with Declare. The computed mean is 4.11 (slightly above average). For confidence in understanding Declare models a mean value of 4.11 was reached (slightly above average). Finally, for perceived competence in creating Declare models, a mean value of 4 (average) could be computed. Since all values range about average, we conclude that the participating subjects fit the targeted profile. In the following, we use the gathered data to investigate the research questions.

$RQ_{1.1}$**: What are the differences between a graphical and textual representation regarding error rates?** To investigate $RQ_{1.1}$, the subjects were asked to answer specific questions (cf. Sect. 3) As detailed previously, they had to identify one minimal trace, 2 valid traces and 2 invalid traces for each model. Since 9 subjects participated in the investigation and each subject worked on two process models, 18 answers were collected regarding the minimal trace (9 for each model). Further, 36 for valid traces (18 for each model) and 36 invalid traces (18 for each model) were collected. Additionally, we asked subjects 2 questions regarding 4 categories for each model. As described in Sect. 3, the categories are hidden dependencies, pairs of constraints, combinations of constraints and existence constraints. Therefore, there are 9 subjects, 8 questions per model, 2 models, resulting in 144 answers. Table 1 shows the distribution of answers: Overall, subjects gave 179 out of 234 correct answers (76.50%).

Table 1. Percentage of correct answers

Category	Graphical			Textual		
	P_1	P_2	Both	P_1	P_2	Both
Traces	80%	80%	80%	92%	60%	78%
Hidden Dependencies	100%	90%	94%	90%	75%	83%
Pairs of Constraints	75%	60%	67%	70%	63%	67%
Combination of Constraints	63%	90%	78%	70%	50%	61%
Existence Constraints	63%	90%	78%	70%	75%	72%
Overall	77%	82%	79%	82%	63%	74%

As mentioned in Sec. 3, we asked subjects to give us an explanation for each answer. We used these explanations for identifying and classifying reasons for errors. Table 2 gives an overview of the data analysis: Overall, 55 answers were incorrect (23.50%).

Table 2. Error analysis

Category	Graphical	Textual	Both
Subtrace definition	8	7	15
Overlooked model elements	4	6	10
Unknown	5	5	10
Constraint definition	3	6	9
Lacking modeling knowledge	3	2	5
Hidden dependency	1	3	4
Problem with setup	0	2	2

All in all, we could identify 7 categories why subjects failed to give a correct answer. Considering the most commonly reason for errors, 15 times subjects answered incorrectly because they had problems with the definition of a sub–trace (cf. Sect. 2.1). Ten times a wrong answer was given due to overlooked model elements, i.e., activities or constraints. Additionally 10 times we were not able to categorize the error, because either the subject did not enter an explanation or the explanation was not sufficient. Nine times the subjects answered incorrectly due to problems with constraint definitions, e.g., confusing two constraints with each other. Five errors were caused by lack of modeling knowledge. Four times a wrong answer was given due to hidden dependencies. Two times we identified that an error was made because of a problem with the setup, i.e., we asked for two valid traces, but the subjects just entered one.

Overall, 31 out of 55 error are due to problems with the setup (either direct problems with setup or indirect, i.e., lack of knowledge or troubles with definitions) and 10 unknown. The 14 remaining errors were made because of overlooking model elements when combining constraints, or hidden dependencies (cf. [7]).

Discussion. In general, we observed that subjects make less errors when the model is represented graphically. As previous findings [7] indicate that subjects have considerable problems making sense of graphically represented pairs of constraints, we expected that subjects would give fewer wrong answers using the textual representation. However, our findings indicate that there is no difference between textual or graphical representation in this category. It seems that having the disadvantage of mindshift learning is still less challenging for subjects than the extraction of information from text, i.e., information that needs to be computed in the human mind [15].

$RQ_{1.2}$: **What are the differences between a graphical and textual representation regarding duration?** To target this research question, we investigated how long it took subjects to answer all specific questions (c.f., Section 3). Table 3 shows the duration in minutes for the 11 questions per model.

Table 3. Duration in minutes

	Minimum	Maximum	Mean
P_1 graphical representation	17	41	28
P_1 textual representation	23	55	37
P_2 graphical representation	10	20	15
P_2 textual representation	19	30	24

Discussion. The findings obtained in $RQ_{1.2}$ indicate that answering questions about a graphically represented model needs less time than for a textual model. In particular, the disadvantage of mindshift learning is not only less challenging for subjects than the extraction of information from text (c.f., $RQ_{1.1}$), but it also needs less time.

$RQ_{1.3}$: **What are the differences between a graphical and textual representation regarding mental effort?** When investigating the sense–making of declarative process models, it seems desirable to have measures that allow researchers to assess in how far proposed concepts support the human mind in interpreting declarative process models. As described in Sect. 2.2, the measurement of mental effort seems to be promising, as it presumably allows assessing subtle changes with respect to understandability [13]. To this end, we computed the average mental effort for each question. Table 4 shows the mental effort for the specific questions per model mentioned in Sect. 3 (11 questions per model).

Discussion. The empirical investigation indicates that answering questions to a graphically represented model requires a higher mental effort than for a textual one. To understand these findings, we would like to refer to the *Split–Attention Effect* [16]. This effect occurs when information from different sources has to be integrated and is known to increase mental effort. In our case, when studying

Table 4. Mental effort

	Minimum	Maximum	Mean
P_1 graphical representation	3.09	4	3.68
P_1 textual representation	3.36	6	4.47
P_2 graphical representation	3.45	4.73	3.96
P_2 textual representation	4.27	4.82	4.48

a textually represented model that consists of three separate lists (activities, constraints and an activity–constraint mapping), the subject has to keep parts of one list in working memory while searching for the matching parts in other lists. Thereby, two basic effects are distinguished. First, the reader has to switch attention between different information sources, e.g., constraint and mapping lists. Second, the reader has to integrate different information sources. These two phenomena in combination are then known to increase mental effort and are referred to as split-attention effect.

RQ_2: What are advantages of each representation and what are potential improvements for the understandability of declarative process models? The goal of RQ_2 is to complement findings obtained so far with opinions from students, i.e., subjective measures. In particular, after all specific questions were answered, we additionally asked general questions for each model. To analyze answers, we identified and classified issues, which—according to the subjects—influence the sense–making of declarative business process models. All in all, we could find 5 factors that subjects considered to be harmful for the sense–making of declarative process models (cf. Table 5). Three subjects mentioned that the pairs of constraints posed a considerable challenge for the sense–making (cf. [7]). In addition, 3 subjects explicitly mentioned that they experienced problems with the high number of constraints and resulting dependencies (combination of constraints). One subject explained that he had problems due to too many activities. Another one mentioned that he was challenged making sense of P_2 because there were too many components. Also, 6 subjects perceived the textual representation as a negative influence.

Table 5. Why do you think the model was (not) difficult to understand?

Category	Factor	Subjects	Influence
Constraints	Pairs of constraints	3	–
	Combination of constraints	3	–
	Number of activities	1	–
	Number of components	1	–
Other	Representation	5	–

Regarding advantages or disadvantages of each representation, 6 subjects mentioned that the graphical representation was easier to grasp. One subject answered that the graphical representation is also unclear sometimes due to pairs of constraints (cf. [7]). One subject praised the good overview of the constraints at the textual representation. Overall, the subjects had a better perception of the graphical representation, which might also be concerned with the shorter duration and lower mental effort (cf. $RQ_{1.2}$ and $RQ_{1.3}$). Also, subjects made propositions how to make declarative process models easier to understand. In particular, 7 subjects proposed to only use the graphical representation. In addition, one subject indicated that paired constraints should be simplified. Unsurprisingly, suggestions for the improvement of declarative process models are closely connected to respective problems (cf. Table 5). In general, it can be observed that the basic building blocks of declarative process models—activities and constraints—are rather unproblematic. However, the combination of constraints and in particular pairs of constraints, in turn, pose considerable challenges. In this sense, for instance, approaches providing computer–based support for the interpretation of constraints seem promising [17].

Limitations. Our work has the following limitations. First, the number of subjects in the empirical investigation is relatively low (9 subjects), hampering the only of descriptive nature result's generalization. Second, even though process models used in this investigation vary in the number of activities, number of constraints and representation, it remains unclear whether results are applicable to declarative process models in general, e.g., more complex models. Third, all subjects are students, further limiting the generalization of results. Finally, most errors were due to problems with the setup of the investigation (cf. Table 2).

5 Related Work

In this work, we investigated the *understanding* of graphical and textual declarative process models. More generally, factors of conceptual model comprehension were investigated in [18], and the understandability of imperative process models was investigated in [2]. Comparisons of graphical and textual notations were examined from different angles. For instance, the interpretation of business process descriptions in BPMN (graphical notation) and in an alternative text notation (based on written use-cases) was investigated in [19]. More generally, [20] provides an overview of relative strengthes and weaknesses of textual versus flowchart notations. For this investigation, we have focused on the declarative modeling language Declare. Recently, also Dynamic Condition Response (DCR) graphs [21] have gained increasing interest. Unlike Declare, DCR graphs focus on a set of core constraints instead of allowing for the specification of arbitrary constraints. However, so far, contributions related to DCR graphs have rather focused on technical aspects, such as technical feasibility and expressiveness, while understandability was not approached yet.

6   Summary and Outlook

Declarative approaches to business process modeling have recently attracted interest, as they provide a high degree of flexibility [5]. However, the increase in flexibility comes at the cost of understandability and hence might result in maintainability problems of respective process models [5]. The presented empirical investigation presents differences between graphical and textual represented declarative business process models. The results indicate that the graphical representation is advantageous in terms of errors, duration and mental effort. In addition, subjects themselves expressed that the graphical representation is easier to understand. As indicated in [7], it might be recommendable to avoid representing declarative models in a way similar to imperative models, especially when semantic differ considerably (cf. Mindshift Learning theory [8]). However, a pure textual representation does not seem to be the right solution. To accomplish our goal of a better understandability of declarative process models, further investigations are needed. Particularly, replications utilizing an adapted hybrid representation seem to be appropriate means for additional empirical tests.

References

1. Mylopoulos, J.: Information modeling in the time of the revolution. Information Systems 23, 127–155 (1998)
2. Reijers, H.A., Mendling, J.: A Study into the Factors that Influence the Understandability of Business Process Models. IEEE Transactions on Systems, Man and Cybernetics, Part A 41, 449–462 (2011)
3. Reichert, M., Weber, B.: Enabling Flexibility in Process-Aware Information Systems: Challenges, Methods, Technologies. Springer, Heidelberg (2012)
4. Zugal, S., Pinggera, J., Weber, B.: The impact of testcases on the maintainability of declarative process models. In: Halpin, T., Nurcan, S., Krogstie, J., Soffer, P., Proper, E., Schmidt, R., Bider, I. (eds.) BPMDS 2011 and EMMSAD 2011. LNBIP, vol. 81, pp. 163–177. Springer, Heidelberg (2011)
5. Pesic, M.: Constraint-Based Workflow Management Systems: Shifting Control to Users. PhD thesis, TU Eindhoven (2008)
6. Barba, I., Weber, B., Valle, C.D., Ramírez, A.J.: User Recommendations for the Optimized Execution of Business Processes. Data & Knowledge Engineering 86, 61–84 (2013)
7. Haisjackl, C., Zugal, S., Soffer, P., Hadar, I., Reichert, M., Pinggera, J., Weber, B.: Making Sense of Declarative Process Models: Common Strategies and Typical Pitfalls. In: Nurcan, S., Proper, H.A., Soffer, P., Krogstie, J., Schmidt, R., Halpin, T., Bider, I. (eds.) BPMDS 2013 and EMMSAD 2013. LNBIP, vol. 147, pp. 2–17. Springer, Heidelberg (2013)
8. Armstrong, D.J., Hardgrave, B.C.: Understanding Mindshift Learning: The Transition to Object-Oriented Development. MIS Quarterly 31, 453–474 (2007)
9. van der Aalst, W.M.P., Pesic, M.: Decserflow: Towards a truly declarative service flow language. In: Bravetti, M., Núñez, M., Zavattaro, G. (eds.) WS-FM 2006. LNCS, vol. 4184, pp. 1–23. Springer, Heidelberg (2006)
10. Baddeley, A.: Working Memory: Theories, Models, and Controversies. Annual Review of Psychology 63, 1–29 (2012)

11. Paas, F., Renkl, A., Sweller, J.: Cognitive Load Theory and Instructional Design: Recent Developments. Educational Psychologist 38, 1–4 (2003)
12. Sweller, J.: Cognitive load during problem solving: Effects on learning. Cognitive Science 12, 257–285 (1988)
13. Zugal, S., Pinggera, J., Reijers, H., Reichert, M., Weber, B.: Making the Case for Measuring Mental Effort. In: Proc. EESSMod 2012, pp. 37–42 (2012)
14. Pinggera, J., Zugal, S., Weber, B.: Investigating the process of process modeling with cheetah experimental platform. In: Proc. ER-POIS 2010, pp. 13–18 (2010)
15. Scaife, M., Rogers, Y.: External cognition: How do graphical representations work? International Journal on Human-Computer Studies 45, 185–213 (1996)
16. Kalyuga, S., Ayres, P., Chandler, P., Sweller, J.: The Expertise Reversal Effect. Educational Psychologist 38, 23–31 (2003)
17. Zugal, S., Pinggera, J., Weber, B.: Creating Declarative Process Models Using Test Driven Modeling Suite. In: Nurcan, S. (ed.) CAiSE Forum 2011. LNBIP, vol. 107, pp. 16–32. Springer, Heidelberg (2012)
18. Mendling, J., Strembeck, M., Recker, J.: Factors of process model comprehension— Findings from a series of experiments. Decision Support Systems 53, 195–206 (2012)
19. Ottensooser, A., Fekete, A., Reijers, H.A., Mendling, J., Menictas, C.: Making sense of business process descriptions: An experimental comparison of graphical and textual notations. Journal of Systems and Software 85, 596–606 (2012)
20. Whitley., K.: Visual programming languages and the empirical evidence for and against. J. Vis. Lang. Comput. 8, 109–142 (1997)
21. Hildebrandt, T.T., Mukkamala, R.R.: Declarative Event-Based Workflow as Distributed Dynamic Condition Response Graphs. In: Proc. PLACES 2010, pp. 59–73 (2010)

Reducing Technical Debt: Using Persuasive Technology for Encouraging Software Developers to Document Code

(Position Paper)

Yulia Shmerlin[1], Doron Kliger[2], and Hayim Makabee[3]

[1] Information Systems Department, University of Haifa, Haifa, Israel
[2] Economics Department, University of Haifa, Haifa, Israel
[3] Yahoo! Research Labs, Haifa, Israel
yshmerlin@is.haifa.ac.il, kliger@econ.haifa.ac.il,
makabee@yahoo-inc.com

Abstract. Technical debt is a metaphor for the gap between the current state of a software system and its hypothesized 'ideal' state. One of the significant and under-investigated elements of technical debt is documentation debt, which may occur when code is created without supporting internal documentation, such as code comments. Studies have shown that outdated or lacking documentation is a considerable contributor to increased costs of software systems maintenance. The importance of comments is often overlooked by software developers, resulting in a notably slower growth rate of comments compared to the growth rate of code in software projects. This research aims to explore and better understand developers' reluctance to document code, and accordingly to propose efficient ways of using persuasive technology to encourage programmers to document their code. The results may assist software practitioners and project managers to control and reduce documentation debt.

Keywords: technical debt, documentation debt, documentation, software maintenance, persuasive technology, FBM Model.

1 Introduction

Traditionally, the evolution of software development methods and tools has focused on improving the quality of software systems. The most obvious quality attribute is correctness: the ability of a software system to satisfy its requirements. Correctness is a functional quality attribute, since it relates to the functions performed by the system.

However, software systems should also have several desirable non-functional quality attributes, such as maintainability, extensibility and reusability[3]. These attributes relate to the way a system has been implemented, i.e., to the complexity of the relationships among the modules that compose the system, independently of its correctness. Hence a system is *maintainable* if it may be easily changed, *extensible* if it is easy to add new features and *reusable* if its modules may be easily adopted in new applications.

L. Iliadis, M. Papazoglou, and K. Pohl (Eds.): CAiSE 2014 Workshops, LNBIP 178, pp. 207–212, 2014.

Recently, the metaphor of technical debt has been widely used to describe the gap, both in functionality and quality, between "the current state of a software system and a hypothesized 'ideal' state, in which the system is optimally successful in a particular environment" [4]. One form of technical debt is internal documentation debt [20], i.e., inappropriate, insufficient or non-existing internal documentation. Low-quality documentation is known to affect negatively quality attributes such as maintainability [18][16].

Previous works have identified some of the reasons for poor documentation in software systems. For example, many developers are under-motivated to document, since they perceive writing internal documentation as a secondary task, as opposed to writing the code itself [4]. Moreover, some software development approaches promote the idea that good code should be self-explanatory [17], and therefore comments are not always necessary.

Our goal is to address these and other causes for low-quality documentation, and propose practical solutions that may be adopted to improve this situation. In particular, we believe that a combination of a persuasive technology approach with advanced tool support may transform the nature of internal documentation tasks, in such ways that software developers will choose to adopt them. This paper describes practical experiments that we plan to conduct in order to examine if and how developers can be encouraged to improve documentation and thus reduce documentation debt.

2   Problem Background and Description

Technical debt can be seen as a compromise between a project's different dimensions, for example, a strict deadline and the number of bugs in the released software product. "Shipping first time code is like going into debt. A little debt speeds development so long as it is paid back promptly with a rewrite" [5]. Technical debt is defined as the gap between the current and the ideal states of a software system [1]. This suggests that known defects, unimplemented features and outdated documentation are all considered aspects of debt. Despite the increasing interest in technical debt among both academics and practitioners, this metaphor still lacks a more rigorous and specific definition. Tom et al. [20] identified different elements of technical debt, such as code debt, architecture debt, infrastructure debt, and documentation debt. Devising ways to reduce the latter is the focus of the current study.

Documentation quality has a direct effect on software maintenance. Software maintenance usually refers to the activities carried out after the development completion, and is the most expensive part in the lifecycle of modern software systems [1]. Maintenance includes a broad spectrum of activities, such as error correction, enhancements of capabilities, deletion of obsolete capabilities and optimization. In order to perform these activities effectively, correct and up-to-date technical documentation is required. Outdated or lacking documentation increases the maintenance costs [18].

Yet, currently, lack of proper documentation during development and release of software systems is prevalent [6]. According to Pfleeger [16] 40%- 60% of the maintenance time is spent on studying the software prior to modification because of the lack of appropriate documentation. Additional studies have shown that source code comments are the most important artifact to understand a system to be maintained [7] and that inline comments can greatly assist in the maintenance work of software engineers [14]. Programs with appropriate documentation were found to be considerably more understandable than those without documentation comments [21].

Despite the importance of documentation, there is evidence in the literature that source code and comments do not evolve in the same rate. Fluri et al. [9] found that newly added code is rarely commented; not all code is commented equally (e.g., the frequency of comments for method calls is much lower than for method declarations); and 97% of comment changes are done in the same revision as the associated source code change. The code evolves in a significantly higher rate than its comments and, as software evolves, it is common for comments and source code to be out-of-sync [13]. In summary, while software engineers may understand the importance of documentation [7], the code is not documented enough in practice [9], [13].

There may be several explanations for this phenomenon. One of the reasons is that documenting is not considered a creative activity, and many engineers prefer solving algorithmic problems instead of writing documentation [4]. Another reason is that many programmers assume that good code is self-explanatory, justifying the lack of documentation [17]. Additionally, since practitioners often work under very strict deadlines, it is easy to leave the documentation behind. Besides, sometimes not documenting can increase job security[8], because it helps programmers to keep an advantage over others and, thus, ensures demand for their services .Finally, the reason may lay in human perception, since software students do not fully understand the need for proper documentation [2].

Recently, several works investigated the investment of companies using agile methods in documentation. The agile manifesto states that direct communication is more valuable than internal documentation [12]. A study of the role of documentation in agile development teams showed that while over 50% of developers find documentation important, or even very important, too little documentation is available in their projects [19].

In conclusion, regardless of the development method used, documentation plays an important role in software products development. Proper documentation drives a more efficient and effective software maintenance and evolution, requiring lower cost and effort. Therefore, it is important to find ways to improve the quantity and quality of comments. To this end, we must find efficient techniques to encourage developers to document their code, thus improving the readability and reducing maintenance time and cost. The objective of this study is to investigate the current state of documentation, and specifically the reasons for developers' reluctance to comment code, and propose a technique to encourage them to document their code, thus decreasing the costs induced by technical debt.

3   Solution Approach

In order to overcome developers' reluctance to document code, we plan to apply the persuasive technology approach. Persuasive technology is an interactive computer technology, which is designed with the goal of reinforcing, changing or shaping people's attitudes or behavior [10]. When a persuasive system is used for reinforcement purpose, the desired outcome of its use would be to make the users' current behavior more resistant to change. When using the system for changing purposes, the expectation is that the users will alter their attitude or behavior due to the interaction with the system. Finally, when using the system for shaping purposes, successful outcome would be creating a behavior pattern for a specific situation, which did not exist prior to using the system [15].

When designing a persuasive system, it is important to take into consideration the desired influence of the system on its users, since different techniques should be used depending on the desired outcome [15]. In our context, as discussed in the previous section, while programmers are often aware of the importance of documentation, this is not reflected in their behavior.

In order to produce a successful persuasive design, it is important to understand which factors influence behavior. Fogg [10] introduced the Fogg Behavior Model (FBM) for analysis and design of persuasive technologies, which provides a systematic way of studying the factors behind behavior changes. The model implies that behavior depends on the following three factors: motivation, ability, and triggers, each of which has several subcomponents. The motivation factor consists of three core motivators, each of which having two sides: pleasure vs. pain, hope vs. fear and social acceptance vs. rejection. The ability factor represents the simplicity of performing the targeted behavior, and its six subcomponents are time, money, physical effort, brain cycles, social deviance, and non-routine. Finally, the triggers refer to prompts, cues, calls to action, etc. The purpose of a trigger is to signal to the user that the moment for performing the behavior has come. An additional concept of the FBM model is the behavior activation threshold. For a trigger to evoke the desired behavior, a person has to be above that threshold, in a high enough level of motivation and ability.

It should be noted that most of the people are in moderate levels of ability and motivation and effective persuasive system should raise motivation, ability, or both, as well as provide a trigger for the desired behavior. An additional implication of the FBM model is that there exists a trade-off between motivation and ability of performing the behavior, so if we influence at least one factor of this equation, the desired behavior might be triggered [10]. This model has direct implications to our research, since our aim is to propose a system, which will increase performance in the code documentation task, as well as provide a proper trigger in an appropriate time for this behavior to take place.

4   Research Plan and Method

The objectives of our study are to identify the reasons and challenges that impede developers' motivation to document code, and to propose a utility for encouraging documentation and facilitating proper documentation. For this purpose, we will perform two studies: (1) a think-aloud protocol for examining program maintenance tasks performance, and (2) an experiment to assess triggers for documentation.

In the first study we plan to conduct individual think-aloud sessions with about 15 students in their last year of IS undergraduate studies. Each subject will perform a maintenance task, namely, add functionality, to code written and documented by another student. The purpose is to gain a deeper understanding of the cognitive process a software programmer faces when maintaining code, and specifically while trying to understand the existing code. We will observe to what extent the subject relies on the code documentation during this process, and what are the important features in code comments that help understand existing code.

The objective of the second study is to check whether the use of an existing documentation-triggering tool (CheckStyle:[1] a plug-in for Eclipse IDE) improves documentation. The subjects of this experiment will be first year IS student in a Java course. The students will be divided into three groups: treatment group A will receive the plug-in to activate a module, which will remind them to add comments to the code as they develop it. Treatment group B will receive the same treatment as well as a social motivation – publishing their documentation level status among their peers. The control group will receive the same plug-in with a different module enabled (not related to code commenting). Our hypotheses are as follows:

- H0a: Group A's documentation level will be similar to that of the control group.
- H1a: Group A's documentation level will be higher than that of the control group.
- H0b: Group B's documentation level will be similar to that of Group A.
- H1b: Group B's documentation level will be higher than that of Group A.

The results will be calculated using documentation metrics. In addition, following the experiment, we plan to collect qualitative data via questionnaires with open-ended questions, in order to gain a deeper understanding about the triggers and motivators from the students' perspectives.

Based on the results obtained in these two studies, and additional external validation with professionals from industry, we intend to create a utility, using persuasive technology principles, for encouraging and motivating developers to document their code with proper and contributing comments. The proposed utility will be evaluated and validated with professional software developers.

References

[1] Brown, N., Cai, Y., Guo, Y., Kazman, R., Kim, M., Kruchten, P., Zazworka, N.: Managing technical debt in software-reliant systems. In: Proceedings of the FSE/SDP Workshop on Future of Software Reengineering Research, pp. 47–52. ACM (2010)
[2] Burge, J.: Exploiting multiplicity to teach reliability and maintainability in a capstone project. In: 20th IEEE Conference on Software Engineering Education and Training, CSEET 2007, pp. 29–36 (2007)
[3] Chung, L., do Prado Leite, J.C.S.: On non-functional requirements in software engineering. In: Borgida, A.T., Chaudhri, V.K., Giorgini, P., Yu, E.S. (eds.) Mylopoulos Festschrift. LNCS, vol. 5600, pp. 363–379. Springer, Heidelberg (2009)
[4] Clear, T.: Documentation and agile methods: striking a balance. ACM SIGCSE Bulletin 35(2), 12–13 (2003)
[5] Cunningham, W.: The WyCash portfolio management system. ACM SIGPLAN OOPS Messenger 4(2), 29–30 (1992)

---

[1] http://eclipse-cs.sourceforge.net/

[6] Daich, G.T.: Document Diseases and Software Malpractice. CrossTalk (2002)

[7] De Souza, S.C.B., Anquetil, N., de Oliveira, K.M.: A study of the documentation essential to software maintenance. In: Proceedings of the 23rd Annual Int. Conference on Design of Communication: Documenting and Designing for Pervasive Information, pp. 68–75. ACM (2005)

[8] Drevik, S.: How to comment code. Embedded Systems Programming 9, 58–65 (1996)

[9] Fluri, B., Wursch, M., Gall, H.C.: Do code and comments co-evolve? on the relation between source code and comment changes. In: IEEE 14th Working Conference on Reverse Engineering, WCRE 2007, pp. 70–79 (2002)

[10] Fogg, B.J.: Persuasive technology: Using computers to change what we think and do. Morgan Kaufmann Publishers, Elsevier Science (2003)

[11] Fogg, B.J.: A behavior model for persuasive design. In: Proceedings of the 4th ACM Int. Conference on Persuasive Technology (2009)

[12] Highsmith, J., Fowler, M.: The agile manifesto. Software Development Magazine 9(8), 29–30 (2006)

[13] Jiang, Z.M., Hassan, A.E.: Examining the evolution of code comments in PostgreSQL. In: Proceedings of the 2006 ACM Int. Workshop on Mining Software Repositories, pp. 179–180 (2006)

[14] Lethbridge, T.C., Singer, J., Forward, A.: How software engineers use

[15] Oinas-Kukkonen, H., Harjumaa, M.: A systematic framework for designing and evaluating persuasive systems. In: Oinas-Kukkonen, H., Hasle, P., Harjumaa, M., Segerståhl, K., Øhrstrøm, P. (eds.) PERSUASIVE 2008. LNCS, vol. 5033, pp. 164–176. Springer, Heidelberg (2008)

[16] Pfleeger, S.L.: Software Engineering: Theory and Practice, 2nd edn. Prentice-Hall (2001)

[17] Parnas, D.L.: Software aging. In: Proceedings of the 16th Int. Conference on Software Engineering, pp. 279–287. IEEE Computer Society Press (1994)

[18] Shull, F.: Perfectionists in a world of finite resources. IEEE Software 28(2), 4–6 (2011)

[19] Stettina, C.J., Heijstek, W.: Necessary and neglected? an empirical study of internal documentation in agile software development teams. In: Proceedings of the 29th ACM Int. Conference on Design of Communication, pp. 159–166. ACM (2011)

[20] Tom, E., Aurum, A., Vidgen, R.: An exploration of technical debt. Journal of Systems and Software, 1498–1516 (2013)

[21] Woodfield, S.N., Dunsmore, H.E., Shen, V.Y.: The effect of modulari-zation and comments on program comprehension. In: Proceedings of the 5th Int. Conference on Software Engineering, pp. 215–223. IEEE Press (1981)

Conceptual Understanding of Conceptual Modeling Concepts: A Longitudinal Study among Students Learning to Model

Dirk van der Linden[1,2,3], Henderik A. Proper[1,2,3],
and Stijn J.B.A. Hoppenbrouwers[4,2,3]

[1] Public Research Centre Henri Tudor, Luxembourg, Luxembourg
{dirk.vanderlinden,erik.proper}@tudor.lu
[2] Radboud University Nijmegen, Nijmegen, The Netherlands
[3] EE-Team, Luxembourg, Luxembourg
[4] HAN University of Applied Sciences, Arnhem, The Netherlands
stijn.hoppenbrouwers@han.nl

Abstract. We discuss our investigation into the conceptual understanding that students have of common concepts used for conceptual modeling (e.g., actors, processes, goals). We studied if and how those understandings may change over time during a student's progress through their academic curriculum. To do so, we performed a longitudinal study with a group of students starting computing and information science studies at Radboud University Nijmegen. We followed them from the beginning of their studies as they learned new theories, techniques, and languages for modeling. We focused on investigating whether their conceptual understandings changed as they became acquainted with new languages and techniques, and whether there were correlations between the introduction of such educational stimuli and changes in their conceptual understanding. We discuss the seeming lack of connection between these stimuli and such changes, and reflect on what this means for the training of people in conceptual modeling.

Keywords: conceptual modeling, conceptual understanding, longitudinal study, learning modeling, training of students, semantic differential.

1 Introduction

We are interested in understanding whether students develop specific conceptualizations or conceptual prejudices when it comes to conceptual modeling concepts. As most academic programs are focused on training well-rounded people who can orient them in new conceptual environments, we could assume that the point is not to steer people into specific, narrow interpretations (i.e., conceptualizations that strongly bias people into accepting one kind of thing as correct), but instead to focus on opening their minds to many different, equally valid, viewpoints from which they can analyze multiple situations (i.e., to steer them in a direction where their conceptualizations allow for many possible correct things). Concretely, we will treat the following research questions in this paper:

L. Iliadis, M. Papazoglou, and K. Pohl (Eds.): CAiSE 2014 Workshops, LNBIP 178, pp. 213–218, 2014.
© Springer International Publishing Switzerland 2014

1. Do the conceptualizations students have of modeling concepts become more refined or nuanced as they progress through their studies?
   – If there is such a change, is it of a discrete or continuous nature?
   – If there is such a change, is it one-directional or reversible?
2. Is there a correlation between the educational stimuli students receive and the possible change in their conceptualizations of modeling concepts?
   – Do conceptualizations follow the semantics of a specific language?

2   Method

Materials: The concepts we look at are ACTORS, EVENTS, GOALS, PROCESSES, RESOURCES, RESTRICTIONS and RESULTS. The different semantic dimensions we investigate are whether they are believed to naturally occur, are intentional or unintentional in nature, are a logical necessity or not, physically exist or not, and if they are vague or not. They will be respectively referred to as *natural, human, composed, intentional, necessary, material* and *vague*. Combinations of these features can be used to characterize a given concept, for example a resource typically being a non-human, material thing. These concepts and dimensions result from previous research we reported on in [1].

Participants: We initially gathered students in the very first session at the beginning of their studies, at which 46 students enrolled to participate. Of these, 19 actually participated in the first phase. Over the course of our study, several students either stopped responding (without specific reason given), stopped because they changed their study program, or because they dropped out entirely. At the final measurement, 9 people participated, however, because one of them had not participated in an earlier phase we were forced to reduce the total set down to 8 complete measurements of the total timespan. All participated voluntarily and received no compensation for their participation.

Procedure: We adapted the basic technique of developing a semantic differential (taking into account the quality criteria set out by [4]) which we have detailed in earlier work [2]. The selection of study participants, concepts and semantic dimensions to investigate and materials needed for them have already been done, as detailed in the materials above. For each semantic dimension we wanted to investigate we selected a set of 5 adjectives from an earlier pilot study, which ensured a significant reaction for that dimension [4]. We then constructed a differential with a page for each concept in which we included (1) a priming task to ensure participants responded in the context of conceptual modeling, (2) a differential in which each of the adjectives were presented to each participant in a random order, and they were asked to rate them on a 5 point Likert scale. We started the study at the beginning of the students' studies, and from then on, at the end of each semester, students received an email inviting them to the semantic differential, where they were also asked to detail what courses they had followed, and what new languages or techniques they were introduced to.

Processing: The resulting data from the semantic differential was processed to calculate an average score for each concept-dimension combination based on the individual adjectives used to describe that dimensions. From this we constructed a vector for each concept, which contained scores ranging from 2.0 to −2.0, describing for each dimension how it relates to that concept. We considered scores ≥ 1.0 as positive judgments, and scores ≤ -1.0 as negative judgments. Other scores were considered as neutral. These judgments were then used to calculate a percentage wise breakdown of the amount of different polarities (i.e., negative or positive connotations) found for each concept.

3   Results and Discussion

A visualization of the concept-dimension scores is given in Fig. 1. It shows the averaged results for each concept-dimension combination for each phase, with error bars showing the range of individual results. The polarities we calculated which show the relative amount of positive, neutral and negative responses to each concept-dimension combination are shown in Table 1, with some potentially interesting ones detailed in Table 2. Due to the amount of people that dropped out during the study, we cannot guarantee a strong external validity. This might have been prevented by including multiple, parallel groups of students (originating from different universities). However, this would lead to a strong heterogeneity of the results because different academic institutes and programs focus on different aspects. Whether those results could be first combined in order to create a larger coherent set of data is debatable as well. Nonetheless, the results here are still a thorough examination of specific individuals, and can be used to reason about the effects found in them, and to what degree measurement of their conceptual understanding is a feasible, and useful endeavor.

We can answer our primary research question by looking at both Fig. 1 and Table 1. In Fig. 1 we see that there is not an obvious shift for any of the concepts or individual concept-dimension combinations to a particular understanding. For this to happen, the bars should either gradually or suddenly switch from ranging to one of the extremes to the other, or stay neutral in the middle. However, as we can see over time the general pattern of all the results stays similar to a sine wave, not having any of its constituents change too much. The semantic dimensions natural, human, and vague stay mostly negative for most concepts, while the dimensions composed, necessary, intentional stay positive. The dimension material is the one dimension in which we clearly see both positive and negative polarities for different concepts, although these particular concept-dimension combinations still do not seem to change much over time. Table 1 verifies this lack of systematic change. Here we also see that, while there are subtle variations from phase to phase in the relative amount of negative, neutral, and positive responses, there does not seem to be a significant gradual change increasing or decreasing over time for any of them. However, some specific concept-dimension combinations, do seem to have gradual shifts in one direction, which are documented in Table 2.

Thus, our first subquestion becomes irrelevant. However, the second subquestion is still interesting to look at, as the data do show that there are sometimes shifts for specific concept-dimension combinations where the polarity changes,

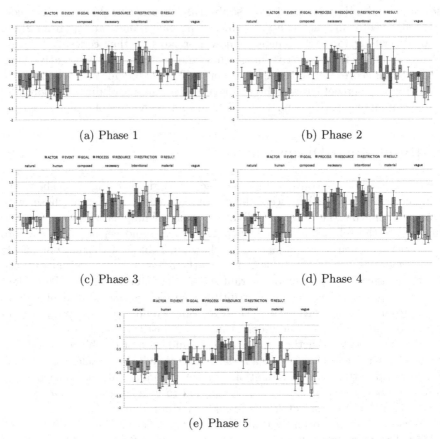

(a) Phase 1   (b) Phase 2

(c) Phase 3   (d) Phase 4

(e) Phase 5

Fig. 1. Visualization of the average concept-dimension scores and individual variations for each phase of the longitudinal study

and reverses again over the course of our study. While this might also be attributed to individual or contextual factors, it can hint at the flexibility of the students in their conceptual understandings while focusing on a specific way of thinking and working (e.g., because in one semester they work in a different paradigm than the others). Our second main question, and its related subquestion can be answered by also taking into account the educational stimuli students received (details omitted due to space constraints). There do not seem to be specific systematic shifts that can be correlated with educational stimuli, nor do they seem to be systematically widening or refining to fit a specific way of thinking that could be attributed to them. Given that students used several languages and techniques almost from the beginning of their studies until the final measurement, one could have expected to see some kind of development towards fitting those ways of thinking. However, given the lack of specific shifts into particular conceptual understandings discussed for question 1, this seems unlikely as well. There were some specific concept-dimension combinations that

Table 1. Average polarities over all concept-dimension responses for each phase of the longitudinal study. Polarity scores of individual concept-dimension combinations are excluded due to space constraints, but are available upon request.

polarity	actor	event	goal	process	resource	restriction	result
			phase 1				
neg	26%	31%	31%	27%	21%	30%	20%
neu	53%	57%	46%	43%	47%	51%	54%
pos	21%	11%	23%	30%	31%	19%	26%
			phase 2				
neg	10%	30%	26%	20%	17%	26%	27%
neu	63%	57%	46%	63%	56%	51%	49%
pos	27%	13%	29%	17%	27%	23%	24%
			phase 3				
neg	7%	36%	31%	24%	24%	30%	26%
neu	57%	56%	41%	53%	46%	49%	49%
pos	36%	9%	27%	23%	30%	21%	26%
			phase 4				
neg	10%	37%	30%	30%	20%	29%	29%
neu	60%	49%	37%	37%	49%	44%	36%
pos	30%	14%	33%	33%	31%	27%	36%
			phase 5				
neg	17%	33%	31%	29%	24%	33%	24%
neu	59%	59%	39%	51%	44%	46%	47%
pos	24%	9%	30%	20%	31%	21%	29%

did show a development towards a specific conceptual understanding. Some are shown in Table 2. These patterns all show an example of a different polarity gaining or losing ground, which translates into the willingness of a specific person accepting or rejecting a particular thing as being a good example of that modeling concepts. When we see that someone has a much stronger negative view on a particular thing (e.g.., the humanity of results), it becomes obvious that during modeling sessions those views might come to the foreground. Finding such specific strong polarized concept-dimension combinations could thus be a useful aid in steering modeling discussions.

Given that much training is done with a specific purpose, it is disheartening to see such a seemingly chaotic development of the conceptual understandings we measured, and a lack of correlation to the educational stimuli. However, given other recent studies into the way people learn modeling languages, this might not be entirely unexpected. In a study [3] on how well people understood different process modeling languages without formally being taught them, Recker and Dreiling showed that once someone had mastered or knew one particular language, the threshold to go to a different, similar one was very low They concluded that it seemed not useful for an IT-oriented curriculum to teach students multiple languages just for the sake of doing so, as they would likely be able to master them on their own when needed to. Given this understanding, one could perhaps infer that such continued educational stimuli (e.g., additional languages

Table 2. Some interesting shifts of conceptual understanding in the results of the average (i.e., all participants) polarity scores

polarity	p1	p2	p3	p4	p5	primary trend
		humanity of results				
neg	60%	60%	80%	70%	80%	
neu	40%	40%	20%	30%	20%	stronger negation
pos	0%	0%	0%	0%	0%	
		necessity of results				
neg	0%	10%	10%	0%	0%	
neu	50%	40%	30%	30%	30%	stronger acceptance
pos	50%	50%	60%	70%	70%	
		vagueness of actor				
neg	60%	20%	40%	50%	50%	
neu	40%	80%	60%	50%	50%	slight decrease in negation
pos	0%	0%	0%	0%	0%	
		naturality of actor				
neg	40%	0%	0%	10%	20%	
neu	50%	70%	80%	90%	70%	increase in neutrality
pos	10%	30%	20%	0%	10%	

and techniques) should not necessarily be expected to have significant effect on the cognitive make-up of a student, which would include their basic conceptual understandings of the concepts used in those languages and techniques. Instead, such programs could perhaps focus more on exposing students to radically different languages and techniques, which have such different conceptual basis that they would learn a new way of looking at things.

Acknowledgements. This work has been partially sponsored by the *Fonds National de la Recherche Luxembourg* (www.fnr.lu), via the PEARL programme.

References

1. van der Linden, D.J.T., Hoppenbrouwers, S.J.B.A., Lartseva, A., Proper, H.A(E.): Towards an investigation of the conceptual landscape of enterprise architecture. In: Halpin, T., Nurcan, S., Krogstie, J., Soffer, P., Proper, E., Schmidt, R., Bider, I. (eds.) BPMDS 2011 and EMMSAD 2011. LNBIP, vol. 81, pp. 526–535. Springer, Heidelberg (2011)
2. van der Linden, D., Hoppenbrouwers, S., Lartseva, A., Molnar, W.: Beyond terminologies: Using psychometrics to validate shared ontologies. Applied Ontology 7, 471–487 (2012)
3. Recker, J.C., Dreiling, A.: Does it matter which process modelling language we teach or use? An experimental study on understanding process modelling languages without formal education. In: 18th Australasian Conference on Information Systems, Toowoomba, Australia, pp. 356–366 (2007)
4. Verhagen, T., Meents, S.: A framework for developing semantic differentials in is research: Assessing the meaning of electronic marketplace quality (EMQ). Serie Research Memoranda 0016. VU University Amsterdam, Faculty of Economics, Business Administration and Econometrics (2007)

What Do Software Architects Think They (Should) Do?

Research in Progress

Sofia Sherman and Naomi Unkelos-Shpigel

Information Systems Department, University of Haifa
Carmel Mountain 31905, Haifa, Israel
{shermans,naomiu}@is.haifa.ac.il

Abstract. Software architecture is an integral part of software development, and has become more complex, with the transition from traditional to agile development methods. Hence, the architect's tasks in the software development project must be well defined. Though there was some amount of empirical research addressing architects` perceptions, most of the research in the area of software architecture addressed this topic theoretically. Perception, being a part of, and having an effect on, cognitive processes and decision making, is explored in this research in order to gain a deeper understanding of what tasks architects find to be included in their role and responsibility. Thus far, 8 in-depth interviews were conducted in various hi-tech firms, followed by distributing an on-line questionnaire, with the response of 12 architects. The obtained results demonstrate several differences between the role of the architect, as defined in literature, and the way architects perceive their role.

Keywords: Software architecture, cognition, perceptions.

1   Introduction

In a managerial meetings regarding software development process, in which the first author participated, which took place in a large, global IT service provider, an unexpected question regarding the role of the software architect was raised. From that moment on and during almost the entire meeting, all participants discussed this question. At the end of this meeting there was no answer but rather more questions: 'What is software architecture?' and 'What is the role of the software architect?'

As software architecture becomes more complicated, the role of the architect emerges to be one of the most challenging and wide in responsibilities within any software development project. In academic literature, the software architect is defined, for example, as "*responsible for the design and technological decisions in the software development process*" [1]. However, in practice, the definition of the role of the architects and the scope of their responsibility is diverse. Ameller et al. [2] refer to the situation where firms often do not have a designated job for architects, or have practitioners labeled as "architect", who among other engineering tasks, also practice architectural tasks.

L. Iliadis, M. Papazoglou, and K. Pohl (Eds.): CAiSE 2014 Workshops, LNBIP 178, pp. 219–225, 2014.
© Springer International Publishing Switzerland 2014

Recently, the difference between the definition of the architect's role in literature and in practice was discussed in the context of handling NFR (non-functional requirements) within the architect's practice [2], and the difference between the way academia and industry perceive the architect's role[3]; however, most discussions did not present empirical evidence. Additional theoretical research included an effort to understand the role of the architects, considering their communication with other stakeholders in the firm (such as marketing, management, developers, etc.) and outside of the firm (customers) [4]. Recent research regarding the role of the architect in the product development process has shown that an architect is a central figure in the development process, serving as the main stakeholder responsible for developing the deployment architecture solution (ibid).

The objective of our research is to define the role of the architect based on two perspectives: 1. Definition of the role of software architect in the literature (what architect is expected to do) and 2. What software architects really do and think they should do. This objective can contribute to understanding the difference between the traditional role of the architect, defined in literature, and the tasks architects actually perform, and the tasks they believe the should perform, in industry. Understanding the precise needs of industry and accordingly defining the architecture role responsibilities and required skills, will ultimately lead to better architectural work.

The objective of preliminary study presented in this paper is to investigate of software architects perceptions regarding their role. Accordingly, our research question is: How do software architects perceive their role?

In this paper we present preliminary results of an ongoing study that included interviews and open ended questionnaires for eliciting architects' perceptions. In the next section, a brief literature review summarizes literature regarding the definition of the role of the architects and their responsibilities. Section 3 presents research settings and outcomes. Section 4 summarizes this study, its limitation and future steps.

2   The Role of the Software Architect

2.1   Role Definition

When defining the role of the architect, two major aspects need to be taken into account: the technological aspects and the soft – cognitive and social – aspects. Hofstader [8] examines the role of the architect from a technological point of view: "*The role of the IT architect is to solve a problem by defining a system that can be implemented using technology. Good architects define systems by applying abstract knowledge and proven methods to a set of technologies with the goal of creating an extendible and maintainable solution.*" ([8], p. 2). Based on this definition, Hofstader lists four key skills, which a good architect must possess: domain knowledge, conceptual thinking, technical acumen and understanding of the patterns. Ameller et al. [2] also refer to technological aspects of software architecture; they interviewed 13 software architects and compared their description of addressing nonfunctional requirements (NFR) with the description found in literature. Based on their findings, they emphasize the centrality of NFR in the work of the architect. Similarly, McBride [1] presents a definition of the architect's role and skills, referring mostly to managing functional and non-functional requirements, but also to non-technical skills such as communication with stakeholders and leadership.

Berenbach [3] researched the difference between the perception of novices and professionals practicing solution architectural work. He proposed several guidelines for teaching undergraduates the fundamental skills required when practicing architecture, focusing mostly on soft skills. Kruchten [7] further divided the definition of the architect's role to soft aspects, classifying several types of architects, according to their daily work and communication with other stakeholders in and outside the firm. This study suggests an interesting definition to the architect's tasks: a good balance is 50:25:25, where 50% of the time is dedicated to design, 25% is dedicated to getting input relevant for the solution, and 25% is dedicated to providing information to other stakeholders, i.e. the customer. In addition, Kruchten defined two types of architects – "Golden plate" architects, who dedicate 60% of the time is to design, 20% to input and only 10% to outgoing communication, and "Ivory tower" architects – who dedicate 70% of the time to design and the rest to communication.

2.2 Responsibilities

Looking at the literature about architecture tasks and responsibilities, we found a variety of tasks, which we classified to the following three main categories (1)

Table 1. Tasks of the software architect

Tasks	Sub-tasks
Development team oriented	Effective communication [1][6]
	Stakeholder education [1][6]
	Detailed planning of the architecture [1][2][3][7][10]
	Provide a common language for communication [4]
	Communication with stakeholders - consulting with, guiding, reviewing[1][3][7]
	Translating the architecture to all stakeholders [1][3][6]
	Requirements planning [2][10]
Solution/ technology oriented	Separation of the system into logical layers [1]
	Interface definition [1]
	System level design [1][10]
	Modular solution creation [7]
	Logical level design [1]
Costumer/ requirements oriented	Monitoring requirements elicitation, requirements identification and validation [1][2][6]
	Elicitation of additional information from the customer [1][7]
	Elicitation and implementation of non-functional requirements [2] [7]
	Requirements and product capabilities documentation [2][4]
	Business level compatibility check[6][7]

Solution/technology oriented tasks – characterized by the technological aspects of architecture development; (2) Development team oriented task – characterized by different kinds of communication between the architect and the development team; (3) Client/requirement oriented tasks – involving communication with customer and requirements elicitation. Table 1 presents this summary.

3   Empirical Study

3.1   Method and Settings

The main objective of this ongoing study was to identify software architects perceptions regarding the role of the architect. We used qualitative research methods and tools, which are appropriate when trying to learn a phenomenon and identify its characteristics, rather than corroborating predetermined hypothesis[5].

At the first stage of this study we interviewed eight architects from four different firms. The objective of the interviews was to capture the architects' perceptions of their role and responsibilities. The data obtained in the pilot interviews provided some preliminary understanding about architects' perceptions and practices, and helped focus the next steps of the study.

In the second stage of this study, based on the findings of the interviews, a questionnaire, composed of open-ended questions, was developed and distributed among architects in additional firms. The questionnaire was aimed at achieving a preliminary identification of software architects' perceptions regarding their role, responsibilities and required skills. The questionnaire included background questions about the architects' experience and expertise, as well as questions about their daily tasks and their importance in the architect's work.

So far, we received back 12 appropriately completed responses from architects, from 10 different firms. The data collected underwent a qualitative inductive analysis by two coders, in which categories gradually emerged [5]. When applying grounded theory approach, consideration of literature is allowed for guiding data analysis [5,9]. In this research, we compared the data to the categories found above based on literature review, and found common ground as well as emerging categories. Analysis and Findings.

In this section we present categories of tasks that emerged during data analysis, including brief examples of relevant quotations from interviews and questionnaires.

Development team oriented tasks: This category includes statements relating the architects' interaction with the development team, including different aspects such as: brainstorming "...brainstorming with the team to find out a technical solution to a particular business problem", mentoring "...support the development and infrastructure teams".

Answering the question what additional tasks should be part of their job description, the architects emphasized the importance of serving as part of the development team, and superficially supporting and leading it: " I think an architect should be a very good team player and should possess good leadership skills so that he can lead *people through examples,"* and to the architect as an educator*: "The software architect should also be partially responsible for providing general education for software engineering teams, i.e., from time to time he can give "lectures" (or workshops) on specific software development skills. This task is a natural extension of the responsibility of the software architect."*

Solution/technology oriented tasks: All 17 architects referred to the technical part of their responsibility, such as design tasks: *"design and maintain IT solutions; write documents."* Architects also reported researching technologies and solution construction as their responsibilities: *"... to explore new technologies"* or *"...integration of existing architecture into the new one."*

An interesting issue of whether to include coding as an architectural task was raised in the interviews and questionnaires. Five architects stated that coding is part of their job; one of them mentioned that implementation should, however, be out of scope of the architect's role; and one of the architects stated an opposite point of view: *"I think many would view feature implementation as outside the role of an architect, but I think it is vital that architects keep their hands on the code to continually evaluate the architecture's effectiveness."*

In addition, some architects found tasks such as developing software infrastructure, requirements handling and research out of the scope of the architect's role: *"Architecture must be more based on coordinating and designing than on the researching of new technologies."*

Customer/requirement oriented tasks: This category refers to tasks that include communication with the customer (or with marketing, as customer representatives). Communication with the customer reported by the architects included two main aspects: (1) requirements elicitation: *"[An architect] works with customers on understanding the systems engineering workflows and needs and introduces capabilities"; "Gathering requirements from marketing,"* and (2) Analysis of the solution according to customer's needs: *"Scoping of the problem or the business need of the client with good analytical skills."*

Only few (4 out of 17) architects referred to this type of tasks. None of the other architects mentioned this type of tasks as part of the architect's job description, and in one case this task was explicitly mentioned as out of scope. This is in contrast with the view reflected in the papers we reviewed, where the relationship with the customer is considered an important part of the architect's role [2, 3, 7].

Development process oriented tasks: This new category includes tasks related to establishing development process: *"[My responsibility as an architect includes] applying the organizational development processes (Agile), while collaborating with other R&D teams, external partners and customers.",* and architecture review process within the teams: *"We developed internal architecture review process that helps us to create higher quality architecture."*

4   Conclusion

In recent years, software architects are expected to be leaders in the firm in general, beyond their development teams, promoting new approaches and ideas.

In this research, we discovered several differences between the tasks of the architects, as described in table 1, and the perception of the architects of their tasks. As described in chapter 3, architects perceive themselves as part of the development team and product oriented (which is in line with the literature). However, they do not perceive themselves as oriented to communication with other stakeholders in the firm. Another finding regards their attitude towards knowledge sharing with other stakeholders. Some research covered knowledge management in software architecture [12], but it did not stand out in our literature review and questionnaires. In the interviews, architects repeatedly referred to the lack of appropriate tools for knowledge management as a motivation for them to serve as a knowledge authority and as "translators" in order to make sure that the client's requirements are reflect in the solution.

Several limitation of this study are to be considered. In this study we collected data from a small sample of architects, and did not include other stakeholders involved in the architecture process. In the next step of this research we plan to further expand the sample by including additional architects as well as other stakeholders (developers, team leaders, product managers, etc.) that may contribute to the understanding of different aspects of the role of software architect. Since this is a preliminary research, further research and validation is needed in order to have generalizable results.

Understanding the architects' perceptions of their role and responsibilities will help bridge the cognitive gap between the traditional definitions of the role of software architect and the tasks architects actually perform, and believe they should perform, in industry. Understanding the precise needs of industry, and accordingly defining the architect role, responsibilities, and required skills, would ultimately contribute to more effective development processes and the establishment of the role of software architects within them. It also may contribute to the education of future software architects in academia and industry. We believe that further research is required in order to obtain a more detailed view of the actual tasks of the architects, and plan to extend our preliminary research. Having a good understanding of the actual tasks of the architects, would assist firms when hiring architects to better describe the job requirements, and novice architects to have a more precise perception of their role.

References

[1] McBride, M.R.: The software architect. Comm. of the ACM 50(5), 75–81 (2007)
[2] Ameller, D., Ayala, C., Cabot, J., Franch, X.: How do software architects consider non-functional requirements: An exploratory study. In: 2012 20th IEEE International Requirements Engineering Conference (RE) 2012, pp. 41–50. IEEE (September 2012)
[3] Berenbach, B.: The other skills of the software architect. In: Proceedings of the first International Workshop on Leadership and Management in Software Architecture. ACM (2008)

[4] Unkelos-Shpigel, N., Hadar, I.: Using boundary objects as a basis for ICT: The case of deployment architecture. In: Proceedings of the Pre-ICIS 2013, SIG-Organizational Systems Research Association (OSRA) Workshop, Milan, Italy (December 15, 2013)

[5] Strauss, A., Corbin, J.: Grounded Theory Methodology: An Overview. In: Denzin, N.K., Lincoln, Y.S. (eds.) Handbook of Qualitative Research. Sage, Thousand Oaks (1994)

[6] Hoorn, J.F., Farenhorst, R., Lago, P., Van Vliet, H.: The lonesome architect. Journal of Systems and Software 84(9), 1424–1435 (2011)

[7] Kruchten, P.: What do software architects really do? Journal of Systems and Software 81(12), 2413–2416 (2008)

[8] Hofstader, J.: We Don't Need No Architects! The Arch Journal 15, 2–7 (2008)

[9] Suddaby, R.: From the editors: What grounded theory is not. Academy of Management Journal 49(4), 633–642 (2006)

[10] Abrahamsson, P., Babar, M.A., Kruchten, P.: Agility and architecture: Can they coexist? IEEE Software 27(2), 16–22 (2010)

[11] Sherman, S., Hadar, I., Levy, M.: Enhancing Software Architecture Review Process via Knowledge Management. In: Proceedings of the Sixteenth Americas Conference on Informhation Systems, Lima, Peru (2010)

Towards Semantic Collective Awareness Platforms for Business Innovation

Fabrizio Smith[1], Emanuele Storti[2], and Francesco Taglino[1]

[1] Istituto di Analisi dei Sistemi ed Informatica "A. Ruberti", CNR,
Viale Manzoni 30, 00185 Roma, Italy
{fabrizio.smith,taglino}@iasi.cnr.it
[2] Dipartimento di Ingegneria dell'Informazione, Università Politecnica delle Marche,
Via Brecce Bianche, 60131 Ancona, Italy
e.storti@univpm.it

Abstract. Innovation represents the main driver for enterprises to evolve, and very often to survive in the globalized market. In the last decades, innovation in enterprise contexts has seen the introduction of new paradigms leveraging the so-called collective intelligence. Such paradigms have gained momentum thanks to the diffusion of the Internet, and the Web 2.0 in particular, and many supporting platforms have been developed. A critical aspect here regards the availability of tools able to manage the knowledge flow across the whole innovation lifecycle (problem awareness, idea generation, solution implementation), overcoming the fragmentation and heterogeneity of the informative resources of the involved players. With this respect, we propose a Semantics-based Collective Awareness Platform for supporting business innovation activities, in which semantic facilities are provided for a smarter knowledge acquisition and sharing, as well as for supporting solutions to complex problems.

Keywords: Collective Awareness Platform, Semantic Technologies, Innovation.

1 Introduction

In the last decades, business models for supporting innovation have been characterized by new paradigms such as Open Innovation [1], Crowd-sourcing [2], and Peer Production [3]. All these paradigms exploit the so-called *collective intelligence*, "a form of *universally distributed intelligence*, constantly enhanced, coordinated in real time, and resulting in the effective mobilization of skills" [4]. The envisioned benefit is that the participation of a large group of people can produce, in many cases, results that are better than what could be made by any individual member of the group.

The above paradigms have been showing their potentiality mainly thanks to the diffusion of the Internet, which makes possible the interaction and the establishment of connections among geographically dispersed people, potentially all over the world. Nowadays, many examples of software platforms implementing such paradigms are available (see Related Work section). At the same time, many corporate initiatives have been launched with the aim of tapping externally developed intellectual property

L. Iliadis, M. Papazoglou, and K. Pohl (Eds.): CAiSE 2014 Workshops, LNBIP 178, pp. 226–237, 2014.

to accelerate internal innovation (e.g., P&G Connect + Develop, IBM Innovation Jam). To further witness the momentum of such platforms, it is worthy to underline the Horizon 2020 initiative on Collective Awareness Platforms for Sustainability and Social Innovation (CAPS) [5]. CAPS are ICT systems leveraging the emerging network effect by combining: open online social media (e.g., Facebook, and Youtube), distributed knowledge creation (e.g., Wikipedia), and data from real environments (e.g., Internet of Things applications), in order to create awareness of problems and possible solutions requesting collective efforts.

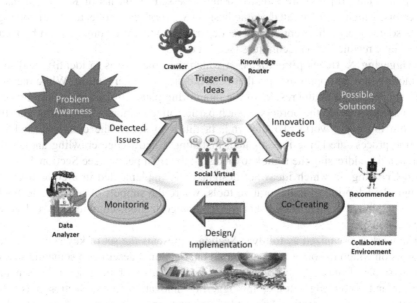

Fig. 1. A semantically enhanced enterprise innovation lifecycle

The objective of this paper is to exploit the results achieved in the BIVEE[1] project, in order to set the basis for a Semantics-based Collective Awareness Platform for supporting the development of innovation initiatives in an enterprise context, with a particular focus on Virtual Enterprises (VEs). Awareness implies the enactment of activities requiring intense collaboration, communication and interaction, as well as the integration of data coming from different sources (e.g., physical and social sensors), and ultimately a high level of knowledge sharing among the involved autonomous actors. Efficient access to knowledge resources is however hindered by interoperability issues coming from fragmentation and heterogeneity of the involved players, their data, information and knowledge resources. In order to address the

[1] BIVEE Project (Business Innovation in Virtual Enterprise Environments) is co-funded by the European Commission under the "Seventh Framework Programme" (2007-2013), contract n° FP7-ICT-285746. The authors wish to acknowledge the Commission for its support and all the BIVEE project partners for their contribution in the development of various ideas and concepts presented in this paper.

above challenging problems, we propose an approach based on semantic technologies to make available to users the support of smart tools and services. Here, semantic technologies can support collective knowledge systems for *i)* enriching user-generated content with structured data, in order to enhance the exploitation of knowledge originated through virtual social interactions, and *ii)* enabling interoperability across applications, in order to facilitate the integration of information. The platform covers the following three main phases (see Fig. 1).

Monitoring and Evaluating, where VE activities (production processes and innovation-oriented projects) are monitored and assessed by means of Key Performance Indicators, which are computed on the basis of *sensors' data* collected from heterogeneous sources (e.g., different enterprise departments) that are homogenized by means of semantic reconciliation techniques (see Section 3).

Triggering & Developing Ideas, in which the objective is to identify, and focus on, those issues and opportunities that need a disruptive intervention. While the main input is constituted by the results of the monitoring phase, it is also crucial observing what happens outside the borders of each participating company, in order to get stimuli from the outer world. To this end, facilities to solicit the creativity and idea creation process are being investigated, including a knowledge crawling and routing approach for addressing the right knowledge to the right people (see Section 4).

Co-Creating, in which ideas are designed and implemented in a collective way, through the adoption of collaborative tools, where the support of semantic technologies is exploited for enhancing knowledge categorization, combination and access (see Section 5).

The work is organized as follows: Section 2 presents the set of key semantic technologies on which the other tools are based on; Section 3 describes a semantic support to analyse data from real environments; Section 4 deals with the role of the Semantic Crawler and Knowledge Router in triggering innovation ideas; Section 5 is about semantics in a collaborative knowledge creation process; Section 6 reports about works on how computers can help in triggering creativity, and on collective intelligence platforms. Finally Section 7, reports about conclusions and future works.

2   Key Enabling Semantic Technologies

Within the BIVEE project, a semantic infrastructure, namely Production and Innovation Knowledge Repository (PIKR) [6], has been conceived to support semantics-enabled knowledge management along the different steps of an innovation venture. While the BIVEE Platform, through its *front-end*, provides several tools (such as whiteboards, serious games, and rewarding mechanisms) to foster social interactions and collaborative activities for supporting open innovation tasks, the PIKR enables knowledge sharing among the different tools, smart access to, and organization of such a knowledge, as well as interoperability among the VE members. The proposed infrastructure provides the following baseline services.

Collaborative Knowledge Engineering. The collaborative framework discussed in [7] aims at supporting the building of domain ontologies shared and agreed within the participant organizations. An iterative and incremental process, supported by a software platform built upon a semantic wiki, allows a community of practice, including knowledge engineers, domain experts, and ontology stakeholders to cooperate for: (i) producing conceptual models and reaching a consensus on their suitability with respect to the application domain at hand; (ii) guaranteeing a formal encoding into a computational ontology. Depending on the particular requirements at hand, the output can be a full-fledged axiomatic theory (encoded as an OWL ontology), or a rich semantic network (according to SKOS standard).

Ontology Based Informative Resource Representation. The PIKR is organized as a federation of reference ontologies, which are primarily used to semantically enrich any kind of tangible and intangible artefact in the scope of a given VE. In particular, the ontologies are partitioned into Knowledge Resource Ontologies, which are independent of any application domain and provide the means for the representation of the main knowledge resources (e.g., members' profiles/competencies, business processes, reports, performance indicators), and Domain Specific Ontologies providing the semantics of a specific business scenario.

Semantic Access and Processing of Knowledge. The PIKR exposes a set of services that exploit the ontology-based knowledge representation, in order to provide advanced semantic facilities for data harmonization, search and retrieval, and verification of business rules. Among them, a similarity engine, implementing the *SemSim* method [8], enables (i) concept-driven search service, (ii) recommendation of contents to users, by matching users' profiles with annotated resources, (iii) correlation of knowledge fragments based on their semantic affinity. Basically, *SemSim* is aimed at finding those digital resources, out of a repository, that best match a user request, where both, resources and user request, are described by a set of concepts (*Ontology-based Feature Vector - OFV*) from a Reference Ontology [8].

3   Semantic Analysis of Data from Real Environments

Data is a crucial asset in innovation management to gain a better understanding of the environment (both internal and external) and to support decision making. In particular, the awareness of the existence of open problems and inefficiencies is one of the major forces driving innovation. For such reasons, data monitoring and analysis is a distinguished feature of a Collective Awareness Platform, as it involves the capability to collect and share objective measures addressing user activities.

Such measurements usually refer to the notion of Key Performance Indicators (KPI) and are used to monitor performances of specific activities, to recognize criticalities and inefficiencies, and to predict future trends. KPIs can refer to indicators measuring time and cost during production activities, but they can also monitor innovation-related aspects, for instance the number of new ideas generated during a project or the ratio of such ideas that have been actually developed.

In collaborative environments, consolidating performance data from different enterprises into a coherent system is a key aspect to compare indicators and enable more advanced analysis over the whole platform. However, especially in highly distributed environments, the autonomy of each enterprise leads to a high level of heterogeneity due to the adoption of different languages, models and technologies for data representation and storage, naming conventions and standards, levels of granularity (e.g., indicators measured each week or each month). Therefore, moving from heterogeneous data captured by sensors, and belonging to distributed partners, to the identification of open problems is a challenging process. In fact, it requires proper solutions for supporting data *interpretation*, which involves gathering and reconciliation of data and schemas, information retrieval and discovery to support data *analysis*, and ultimately human expertise and collaboration for the *understanding* of results and recognition of open issues (Fig. 2).

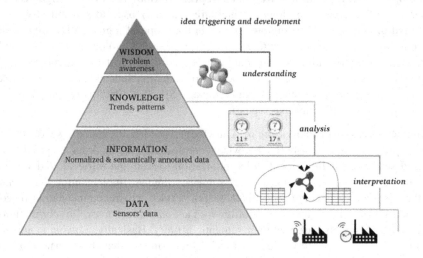

Fig. 2. DIKW model for Problem Awareness

Semantic technologies can leverage data integration by providing a common shared conceptualization of the domain the sources refer to. To this aim, in the BIVEE project, a KPI ontology and a set of reasoning functionalities have been developed [9], as part of the PIKR. The ontology serves as a global conceptual model, providing formal definition of indicators and their properties, including the mathematical formula describing how to compute a compound indicator starting from other KPIs. Data coming from every enterprise can then be annotated through ontological concepts, easing in this way the process of identification and reconciliation of heterogeneous data, schemas and formulas. Specific functions aimed to reason on mathematical formulas of KPIs are capable to manipulate formulas and to detect identities, equivalences and incoherencies among indicators, in order to guarantee consistency of the repositories. Once data have been normalized and semantically annotated, users can express queries in terms of the global conceptual model with the aim to extract KPI values.

Rewriting mechanisms are capable to transform a query in order to dynamically adapt it to the dimensional schemas of the underlying repositories, providing users with aggregated results. In this way, the query mechanisms allow to gain, instead of the access to a single dataset, a more comprehensive view over the data. This enables the development of a dashboard including a set of advanced functionalities for KPI monitoring and analysis. Among them, tools to monitor the evaluation of trends with respect to a certain indicator, functions for benchmarking and reporting, and for performance comparisons among enterprises.

Detection of the pitfalls and inefficiencies in shared processes cannot be a fully automated task, as it deeply involves expertise and background knowledge from domain users. However, the functionalities described above support users in understanding the current situation and recognizing critical issues. Moreover, these also allow to assess whether an implemented innovative solution is capable to overcome the recognized issues and outperform the previous situation.

4   Triggering Creativity through Knowledge Routing

Innovations, in any organization, can only come from the people, and not from the systems. The first spark that triggers an innovation has not yet found effective support: there are no automatic established ICT methods and tools specifically focused on this starting discontinuity, while they can support most of the other stages of the process of innovation. The implicit assumption commonly shared in many projects is: the main ingredient for supporting the creation process is the availability of existing knowledge, which needs to be adequately proposed to (human) designers.

The main challenge here is to exploit a wide corpus of knowledge, e.g., a corporate document repository or potentially the whole Web, taking advantage of the searching speed of bots, to propose contents able to foster creative thinking and problem solving. Even if the cognitive mechanisms are not yet completely understood, there have been many studies relevant to thinking techniques that have been proven to favour creativity. The use of metaphors and lateral thinking [10] is an example of recognized enabler of creativity, by bridging different conceptual domains. A general characteristic of these techniques is the recommendation of avoiding usual thinking paths, habitual mind frames, which is facilitated by putting oneself in unusual physical settings, or introducing absurd concepts, and the like.

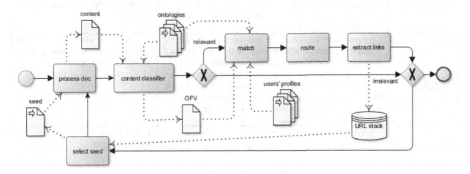

Fig. 3. Crawling and Routing Scheme

In what follows, it is assumed to have availability of semantic descriptions of users' profiles, in the form of a collection of OFVs, representing topics of interests to the user (e.g., an *open issue* identified by monitoring the production reality, or a *subject* occurring frequently in discussions authored by the user). Then a crawling system should be devoted to the exploration of knowledge units (e.g., documents) available within or outside the VE boundaries, identifying for each resource an OFV from the available domain ontologies (possibly through an automatic ontology-based document classifier whenever an annotation is not available) to characterize its content at best. In this way, annotated resources are semantically analysed and matched with user profiles to enable smart routing of knowledge fragments to VE participants. During the BIVEE project, an approach based on a pipeline of semantic services implementing the scheme outlined in Fig. 3 [11] has been proposed.

The Crawler starts from an input seed, corresponding to a documental resource r (e.g., a Web page) that is downloaded and parsed. The main textual content is then processed in order to retrieve (or automatically generate) the associated semantic annotation, as the OFV f_r. A document is considered relevant on the basis of the percentage of the keywords contained in the text that refer to concepts defined in some available ontology. If the article has been judged relevant, r is characterized accordingly to two metrics (in the following, we assume a four-level graduated rate scale **D, C, B, A**): (i) the relevance of r with respect to a given domain ontology o_i, i.e., the percentage $\delta(f_r, o_i)$ of elements in f_r belonging to o_i; (ii) the relevance of r with respect to the profile p_u of user u, i.e., the semantic similarity $SemSim(f_r, p_u)$. The semantic routing, after the calculation of the aforementioned metrics, notifies a knowledge resource r, potentially relevant to a user u, according to the routing criteria described in Table 1. Finally, whether the resource has been judged relevant, the related links are added to the URL stack, in order to select a new seed and start the next iteration.

Table 1. Exemplary Routing Criteria

	$SemSim(f_r, p_u) = C$	$SemSim(f_r, p_u) \geq B$
$\delta(f_r, o_i) \geq B$ $\delta(p_u, o_i) \geq B$	r is barely relevant to the user **but** is focused on a *single domain* relevant to the user.	r is focused on a *single domain* relevant to the user, **and** is relevant with respect to the interests of the user
$\delta(f_r, o_i) \geq C$ $\delta(f_r, o_k) \geq C$	r is barely relevant to the user **but** is *cross domain*; in this case we expect that the different members of the VE which are notified with r can open discussions and ultimately start joint activities.	r is relevant with respect to the interests of the user **and** is cross domain.
$\delta(f_r, o_i) = C$ $\forall k \neq i.$ $\delta(f_r, o_k) < C$	r is barely relevant to the user, **but** it deals with a *lateral domain*; the first condition ensures that the analysed document can be of interest to the user, while the second constraint ensures that the analysed document deals with other topics in a considerable measure, being at the same time somehow connected to the VE interests; in this case we expect that the notification of r can trigger *lateral thinking* mechanisms.	r is relevant with respect to the interests of the user **and** it deals with a lateral domain.
–	–	r is relevant with respect to the user's interests

5   Semantics-Based Collaborative Knowledge Creation

From a technological point of view, open approaches to innovation have gained momentum thanks to the Internet expansion, the advent of the Web 2.0, and Social Media platforms. Such platforms have increased the opportunity to establish communication, collaborations and co-operations. Many general purposes social networks have been set up (e.g., Facebook, Twitter), as well as many very focused initiatives (see Section 6). Interactions mediated by social software platforms generate a huge amount of contents, carrying a significant amount of knowledge potentially relevant. However, all this knowledge is often hard to exploit, since the informative content in the interest of a user can be easily lost in complex social interactions, and the exploitation of such solutions, as groupware infrastructures at the enterprise level, is mined as well by the fragmentation and lack of structure of the available information.

The whole BIVEE Platform has been conceived by collecting and analysing the requirements coming from the two end user organizations (LOCCIONI and AIDIMA) that are involved in the project. The analysis of the collected requirements has brought to the design of a set of functionalities and tools to be implemented, and aimed to facilitate open participation, support crowd-sourcing, and stimulate collaboration:

-   An open virtual space (Shared Whiteboard) where open calls can be published and ideas can be collected, shared, discussed, and evaluated by the largest number of people. Pricing and rewarding mechanisms are provided as well, to incentive the participation of people.
-   Collaborative tools for: (i) editing documents during the running of an innovation project; (ii) allowing people to provide input, comments, and suggestions to any shared resource.
-   A virtual *observatory,* to keep under control what happens outside the boundaries of a given enterprise, in terms of innovation initiatives and innovation trends.

The application of ontology-based techniques to support the above components has been largely investigated during the project, and in this frame a leading role of semantic technologies with respect to the following key facilities is envisioned.

Knowledge Classification. The organization of documental resources in terms of reference ontologies enables advanced knowledge management techniques. The adopted baseline infrastructure (Section 2) heavily relies on ontologies to represent structured information. However, also mechanisms to handle unstructured textual information have to be provided to group and classify documents and posts according to topics in the scope of the VE. In [12] we applied in this context a (semi-) automatic classification procedure, where the textual content is analysed according to a weighted term frequency approach. The classifier is driven by a collection of *training models*, where each concept has an associated set of weighted terms (*features*), obtained by analysing its natural language description, the relations in which it is involved, and the concepts it specializes. For the classification of the textual content, a set of chunks (i.e., *key noun phrases*) is automatically extracted from it, by applying statistical techniques. Then, the document's relevance, with respect to the domain ontologies, is assessed by matching the concepts' *features* against the extracted chunks. The output is constituted by an OFV that enables further semantic processing techniques.

Knowledge Retrieval. A crucial requirements often raised in highly dynamic, collaborative environments regards the need for mechanisms to search over past initiatives and share contents in order to learn from previous experiences, reuse achieved outcomes, and avoid repeating mistakes. Indeed, once a user proposes a new idea through the platform, she/he is interested in assessing if similar issues have been addressed in the past, and collecting knowledge resources related to these previous initiatives as useful material for a further development of the proposed idea. Relying on the *SemSim* similarity reasoner (see Section 2), a semantic search engine has been developed, where search criteria are expressed as an OFV. Users are thus provided with a keyword-based search service, or, as an alternative, focused search requests can be automatically formulated by selecting a given resource (e.g., a post) and using the associated feature vector as input of the query to find related knowledge resources.

Knowledge Combination. The collaborative platform should provide mechanisms to support a group of users working on a particular issue by suggesting automatically related knowledge items (technical solutions, patents and so on), possibly crossing the boundaries of their respective enterprise repositories. In particular, when a new idea is posted into the system, the platform should assess if similar issues have been addressed in the past, collect knowledge resources related to these previous initiatives, and finally identify related innovation seeds to put involved people in contact. The semantic facilities discussed so far can be applied to the analysis of user generated contents, including their indexing, aimed at computing and storing in advance the clusters of semantically related items it belongs to. This functionality can be then exploited to semantically correlate pieces of collective knowledge to available informative resources, for enhancing the information consumption of users during collaborative tasks.

6   Related Works

This section reports about existing initiatives related to challenging issues addressed by this paper. The objective of this section is to report about those research areas, focusing on semantics-based solutions, it is worthy to invest further research.

Triggering Creativity. *Brainstorming*, *Mind-Mapping*, and *Lateral Thinking* are example of techniques, rooted in cognitive sciences, to facilitate creativity. However, research efforts have been done on computational models implementing brain processes involved in creative thinking. *Computational creativity* [13] is the Artificial Intelligence subfield aimed at building and working with computational systems exhibiting a creative behavior to generate artifacts and ideas. The Syzygy surfer [14] is a creative search engine, which combines analogies and the ambiguity of natural language, with the precision of semantic web technologies, to yield novel, but non-random, results. [15] refers to the *Obscure Features Hypothesis* innovation theory, by proposing the adoption of *AhaNets*, semantic networks where common and *obscure* features of connected entities are modeled. *Bisociation* [16], proposed by Koestler, is a general process for combining two unrelated ideas or thoughts into a new idea. PERCEPTION [17] is a computational model, based on concept properties to compare similar concepts to blend two distinct concepts to solicit creativity. [18] investigates on graph-based representations of entities and concepts, and the application of a personalized PageRank algorithm, to infer semantic similarity, and novel associations as part of a creative process.

Knowledge Creation in a Collaborative Environment. Historically, Douglas Engelbart, referred to as the *Father of Groupware*, is considered the pioneer of computer supported collaborative work. In 1968, in his demonstration referred to as the *Mother of All Demos* [19], he presented the NLS integrated system, which included computer-supported real-time collaboration features. However, only in the early 1990s the first groupware commercial products, whose major representative was probably Lotus Notes, began delivering up to their promises. Finally, in the 2000s, with the advent of the Web 2.0, Wiki-based platforms and Social Networks, platforms leveraging collective intelligence, have gained momentum. Different purposes characterize existing platforms: *civic engagement*, to support collective actions that address issues of public concern, such as mobility, e-democracy; *collective knowledge*, to develop knowledge assets or information resources from a distributed pool of contributors, e.g., *Wikipedia; crowdfunding*, to promote financial contributions from online investors. More focused on supporting innovation initiatives: *collective creativity platforms*, which are creative talent pools to design and develop original art, media or content, e.g., *OpenIDEO* (openideo.com); *open innovation platforms*, which use sources outside of the entity or group to generate, develop and implement ideas, e.g., *Quirky* (www.quirky.com).

Basically, collective knowledge systems are expected to be supported by semantic technologies into two main ways: augmenting user-contribution with structured data; enabling interoperability across applications, and facilitate access to knowledge. The former is currently supported by several automatic annotation techniques, see, e.g., a recent survey in [20]. A complementary aspect is to enable people to add structured data, to increase the value of the annotation. The challenge here is to provide services that give personal and social value to the individual in return, e.g., by involving games [21]. About the latter: [22] presents an architecture, which makes use of ontologies and rules to enable interoperability among heterogeneous collaborative tools; [23] supports collective intelligence by encouraging people to collaboratively express ideas regarding a complex issue, by means of ontology-based solutions to enhance searching and browsing as well as to facilitate users editing.

7   Conclusions and Future Works

In this paper, we recapped some of the achievements of the BIVEE project, envisioning their adoption in a platform oriented to the exploitation of collective and distributed knowledge in order to create awareness and problem solving capabilities in the context of enterprise innovation. While the methods and technologies proposed during the project constitute a valuable baseline towards the development of a CAP able to impact on complex real-world scenarios, several challenges have still to be faced, addressing both technological and organizational aspects. In the following, three challenges that are considered paramount for future works are outlined.

Challenge 1. *Being structured but not rigid.* The overall framework should be able to integrate automatic support and human efforts, guiding knowledge workers in order to correctly interpret and exploit the available information. However, while a structured methodology is needed to bring original ideas into commercial solutions, a prescriptive approach can seriously hamper creative thinking. A critical aspect is related to the interpretation of data derived from the monitoring phase to identify *issues* to be addressed through *innovative* solutions rather than undertaking typical production improvement or process reengineering efforts. Supporting the identification of the *discontinuities* that may possibly lead to radical innovations constitutes a very interesting and challenging open issue.

Challenge 2. *Being a lot, but not too many.* The success of innovation ventures may be positively influenced by the collaboration of a large number of actors, which contribute with their different skills and background. Indeed, an enterprise may often strive for competences not available within its borders. However, relying on the *wisdom of crowd* may be worth only for particular tasks[2]. Instruments are needed to dynamically select proper borders, depending on the scenario at hand, for setting-up *innovation teams* that cover the needed competences and guarantee appropriate levels of mutual trust and motivation.

Challenge 3. *Being open. but not exposed.* To embrace an open innovation perspective, both inbound and outbound processes need to be fostered. This requires a continuous harvesting of data for decision making, and at the same time mechanisms to publish data related to each individual enterprise. The enforcement of the Open Data philosophy appears a viable approach for achieving a sustainable and flexible framework for large scale observation and information sharing, which can guarantee at the same time adequate access control and privacy levels. Further work will investigate strategies to integrate in the platform open dataset, with a particular focus on the Linked Data [25] paradigm. This aspect may enhance the global awareness on a certain topic, serving as contextual information to better understand a given phenomenon. For instance, both internal production indicators and a public dataset reporting market analysis results should be interrelated, to discover whether a decrease in sales volume of a given product in a certain place can be explained by a more general market trend.

References

1. Chesbrough, H.W.: Open Innovation: The New Imperative for Creating and Profiting from Technology. Harvard Business Press (2003)
2. Howe, J.: The Rise of Crowdsourcing. Wired Magazine 14 (2006)
3. Benkler, Y.: The Wealth of Networks: How Social Production Transforms Markets and Freedom. Yale University Press (2006)
4. Levy, P., Bononno, R.: Collective Intelligence: Mankind's Emerging World in Cyberspace. Perseus Books (1997)
5. Sestini, F.: Collective Awareness Platforms: Engines for Sustainability and Ethics. IEEE Technology and Society Magazine 31(4), 54–62 (2012)

---

[2] In [24] the impact of different kinds of open innovation partners is analyzed. Internal employees result to be the most valuable source. Regarding external partners, customers, universities, suppliers and the final consumers are all rated higher in importance than average. By contrast, competitors and communities (restricted or unrestricted) are rated as lowest in importance.

6. Diamantini, C., Potena, D., Proietti, M., Smith, F., Storti, E., Taglino, F.: A Semantic Framework for Knowledge Management in Virtual Innovation Factories. International Journal of Information System Modeling and Design 4(4), 70–92 (2013)
7. Ludovici, V., Smith, F., Taglino, F.: Collaborative Ontology Building in Virtual Innovation Factories. In: Proc. of Int. Conf. on Collaboration Technologies and Systems 2013, pp. 443–450. IEEE (2013)
8. Formica, A., Missikoff, M., Pourabbas, E., Taglino, F.: Semantic Search for Matching User Requests with Profiled Enterprises. Computers in Industry 64(3), 191–202 (2013)
9. Diamantini, C., Potena, D., Storti, E.: A Logic-based Formalization of KPIs for Virtual Enterprises. In: Franch, X., Soffer, P. (eds.) CAiSE Workshops 2013. LNBIP, vol. 148, pp. 274–285. Springer, Heidelberg (2013)
10. De Bono, E.: The Use of Lateral Thinking. Intl. Center for Creative Thinking (1967)
11. Taglino, F., Smith, F.: Triggering Creativity through Semantic Cross-domain Web Crawling and Routing. In: Proc. of Int. Conf. on Collaboration Technologies and Systems 2014. IEEE (to appear, 2014)
12. Smith, F., Taglino, F.: Semantics-based Social Media for Collaborative Open Innovation. In: Proc. of Int. Conf. on Collaboration Technologies and Systems 2014. IEEE (to appear, 2014)
13. Colton, S., Wiggins, G.A.: Computational Creativity: The Final Frontier? In: Proc. of the 20th European Conference on Artificial Intelligence. 242, pp. 21–26. IOS Press (2012)
14. Handler, J., Hugill, A.: The syzygy surfer (Ab)using the Semantic Web to Inspire Creativity. Int. J. Creative Computing 1(1), 20–34 (2013)
15. McCaffrey, T., Spector, L.: Innovation is Built on the Obscure: Innovation-enhancing Software for Uncovering the Obscure. In: Proc. of 8th ACM Conf. on Creativity and Cognition, pp. 371–372. ACM (2011)
16. Koestler, A.: The Act of Creation, Hutchinson, London (1964)
17. De Smedt, T.: Modeling Creativity: Case Studies in Python. Univ. Press Antwerp (2013)
18. Chang, C.Y., Clark, S., Harrington, S.B.: Getting Creative with Semantic Similarity. In: Proc. of the 7th Int. Conf. on Semantic Computing, pp. 330–333. IEEE (2013)
19. Engelbart, D., English, B.: A Research Center for Augmenting Human Intellect. In: Proc. of the 1968 Fall Joint Computer Conference (1968)
20. Bontcheva, K., Rout, D.: Making Sense of Social Media Streams through Semantics: A Survey. Semantic Web Journal (2012)
21. von Ahn, L.: Games with a Purpose. IEEE Computer Magazine 39(6), 92–94 (2006)
22. Martinez Carreras, M.A., Marın Pérez, J.M., Bernabé, J.B., Alcaraz Calero, J.M., Gomez Skarmeta, A.F.: Towards A Semantic-Aware Collaborative Working Environment. Computing and Informatics 30, 7–30 (2011)
23. Maleewong, K., Anutariya, C., Wuwongse, V.: SAM: Semantic Argumentation Based Model for Collaborative Knowledge Creation and Sharing System. In: Nguyen, N.T., Kowalczyk, R., Chen, S.-M. (eds.) ICCCI 2009. LNCS (LNAI), vol. 5796, pp. 75–86. Springer, Heidelberg (2009)
24. Chesbrough, H.W., Brunswicker, S.: Managing Open Innovation in Large Firms. Survey Report, Fraunhofer IAO (2013), http://openinnovation.berkeley.edu/managing-open-innovation-survey-report.pdf
25. Bizer, C., Heath, T., Berners-Lee, T.: Linked Data - The Story So Far. International Journal on Semantic Web and Information Systems 5(3), 1–22 (2009)

Leveraging User Inspiration with Microblogging-Driven Exploratory Search

Maria Taramigkou[1], Fotis Paraskevopoulos[1], Efthimios Bothos[1],
Dimitris Apostolou[2], and Gregoris Mentzas[1]

[1] National Technical University of Athens, Greece
[2] University of Piraeus, Greece
{martar,fotisp,mpthim,dapost,gmentzas}@mail.ntua.gr

Abstract. In creative tasks, the user expects to acquire holistic information, to explore the space of available information and to come up with diverse views before converging to a solution for the creative task. We hypothesize that the implicit use of social chatter in information seeking activities can enhance the potential for novel, diverse and unexpected encounters which can in turn inspire users. We present an interactive exploratory search tool that combines diversification of content and sources with a user interface design that visualises cues from the social chatter generated with microblogging services such as Twitter and lets users interactively explore the available information space. A task-based user study comparing our system to a query-based baseline indicates that our system significantly improves inspirational discoveries by providing access to more interesting, novel and unexpected information.

Keywords: Exploratory search, inspirational systems.

1 Introduction

Creativity is the process of generating new ideas and concepts or making connections between ideas into producing new ones, which previously did not exist [1]. Among the most important enablers of creativity is the capability to be inspired. Inspiration requires among others an environment that offers space for exploration, cognitive stimuli and accessibility to information resources [2]. Our work is based on the observation that social recommendations through e.g., social media feeds, already provide an everyday inspirational channel to people. Many users already use social media such as Twitter for exchanging links to web pages that are of interest to them. Such links, although not necessarily relevant to an explicitly expressed need, have the potential to inspire.

We aim to examine how to extract inspirational cues from social chatter and use them to assist users in finding inspirational information during creative tasks. To do so, we follow the approach of funnelling social chatter into an information seeking service that enables users to indirectly consume streams of information, not by reading them explicitly, but by utilizing information embedded in them in order to expand

L. Iliadis, M. Papazoglou, and K. Pohl (Eds.): CAiSE 2014 Workshops, LNBIP 178, pp. 238–249, 2014.

their search queries. Social chatter may contain valuable information that can inspire, though it is difficult for the user to process each nugget of information manually. Moreover, the inspiration potential of each informational resource may increase if combined with other cues and used to enhance a targeted search initiated by the user. For example, [3] showed that focusing search on the referrals of the users' friends can return highly serendipitous results, albeit with lower relevance to the query.

We formulate the following research questions: (1) How to extract and present to the user cues from the social chatter in order to stimulate the user's ability to identify and combine important aspects pertaining her search quest? (2) How to use social media information to form novel search paths for exploring available search spaces? (3) How to boost diversity of content, media and resources in order to enhance the ability to discover serendipitous resources with high inspiration potential? The paper proceeds as follows. Section 2 presents previous work related to our research questions. Section 3 provides the overview of our approach, which is instantiated in a tool called CRUISE, whereas Section 4 shows how the tool is used with a walkthrough scenario. Section 5 describes the detailed design of the building blocks of our tool. The results of a pilot study and a focused experiment which were used to evaluate our tool are presented in Section 6. Finally, we conclude in Section 7 with our main findings and suggestions for further research.

2   Related Work

We distinguish three areas which are related to our three research questions: information extraction from social media, interactive information exploration and diversity-aware search.

Tweetspiration is a search application which displays filtered tweet results through a word cloud visualization [4]. Bernstein et al. [5] proposed a Topic Based Browsing interface for the categorization of tweets and guided exploration using NLP in order to produce a list of nouns as a representative of each tweet, which is then used by the system to perform queries over an external search engine. SLANT [3] is a tool that automatically mines a user's email and Twitter feeds and populates four personalized search indices that are used to augment regular web search. In [6], users browse in order to explore popular bookmarks, browse other people's collections and find people with specific expertise. Chen et al. [7] provide interesting URL recommendations from Twitter by combining popular tweets and the notion of followees of the followees.

Contrary to typical information retrieval systems that direct users to specific information resources, interactive information exploration systems are designed to reveal latent, alternative directions in the information space in order to enable user orientation and engagement [8], [9]. To this end, researchers have proposed a variety of techniques involving rich user interface support with learning algorithms to assist users to comprehend the results and the existing information space [10], and visualizing and summarizing the resulting information to enable faster relevance judgment of the quality of the information returned by the search engine [11]. Głowacka et al. [12] developed an interactive information retrieval system that combines Reinforcement

Learning techniques along with a user interface design that allows active engagement of users in directing the search. Devendorf et al. [13] proposed a novel interactive interface for guided exploration through topics visualization over a large corpus. TweetMotif [14] extracts a set of topics from Twitter in order to provide a faceted search interface. Finally, several works have focused on the exploration of image and other rich media resources, see e.g. [15].

Diversity-aware search systems [16] have been proposed to cope with the uncertainty of query ambiguity [17], aiming at revealing multiple aspects of a query. Related approaches focus on reducing information redundancy comparing the documents of the result set with each other [18] while others consider documents independent from each other and compare their relevance to each aspect of a query providing results proportionally to their probability to belong to each query aspect [19]. In order to diversify the set of the documents displayed by their exploratory search application, Glowaca et al. [12] sample the results retrieved by the search engine using the Dirichlet Sampling Algorithm. Content metadata have been used to diversify based on categorical distance by making use of the Open Directory Project Taxonomy [19]. xQuAD [20] models an ambiguous query as a set of sub-queries and computes the relevance of search results comparing them not to each other, but to each sub-query instead. The OptSelect algorithm [21] identifies the different intents that appear in the query refinements of most users' query sessions and calculates the probability distributions in order to ensure that they are covered proportionally to the associated probabilities. The Max-Min algorithm [22] maximizes the minimum relevance (to the topic) and dissimilarity (between two results) of the selected set, whereas the Max-Sum algorithm maximizes the sum of relevance and dissimilarity of the selected set.

3   Creative User Centric Inspirational Search

We developed CReative User centric Inspirational SEarch (CRUISE) with the main objective to support search for inspirational resources during creative tasks. The tool couples techniques inspired from social search with information visualization and diversification. In this section we briefly describe how the tool interface design addresses our three research questions.

Extracting and visualizing cues: CRUISE utilises information from Twitter to support users explore available search spaces. The exploration starts with the users entering a set of terms as an initial entry point to their exploration. The tool uses the exploration terms and queries Twitter for the most recent popular tweets. Then it constructs a word cloud of high frequency terms found in recent popular tweets. Unlike existing trending topic interfaces like Twitter's trending topics, CRUISE identifies emerging terms even if only a single user on Twitter tweets about it. Moreover, CRUISE offers the ability of injecting into the word cloud terms which are derived from tweets by specific users or hashtag streams which are relevant to a particular context or scenario. Terms derived from their tweets are promoted and presented alongside terms derived from the Twitter stream and are represented in a different colour so that the user can discern between them.

Exploring the search space: Users can browse through available search spaces by making multiple selections of terms appearing on the word cloud. This interaction results in new terms appearing on the cloud as well as a new set of resources presented to the user. Using a slider, the user is able to adjust the depth of the search space, which is directly related to the terms' popularity; they can drill down into the word cloud to reveal terms, previously hidden due to their low frequency in relation to other terms.

Querying external search engines and diversifying results: Whilst exploring the word cloud, users are able to add any of the terms into their 'search path'. Search paths function as queries to external information sources which may be public such as Bing, Flickr or Google scholar or private information found in a company's intranet, such as portals, intranets, etc. Users are presented with diversified results and are provided with the capability to restrict their search paths by selecting more terms from the cloud or relaxing them by removing terms.

4   Walkthrough

We present a simple example which explains the functionality of the tool and the interaction design that accompanies an exploratory search task. Consider a concept developer working with a food company as a client. The developer aims at investigating future challenges of the food industry and coming up with new product concepts addressing them. The developer starts an exploration using the query 'food company'.

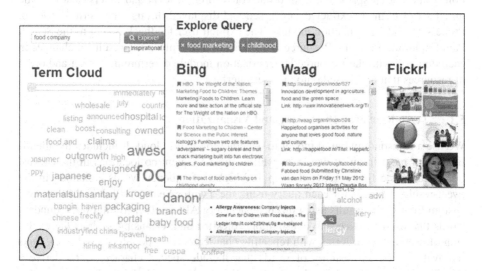

Fig. 1. CRUISE funnels social chatter into an information seeking service that enables users to indirectly consume streams of information– not by reading them explicitly, but by utilizing information embedded in them in order to expand their search directions

A word cloud is created with terms that are extracted from the most popular tweets relevant to the query. Terms such as 'allergy', 'baby-food', 'toxic over-eating' appear in the word cloud (Figure 1.A). The concept developer goes through these terms to see how they are related to children. She finds tweets about 'Bio-tech industries that slip propaganda into school text-books' and also tweets about the 'relation of food marketing to children obesity, referring to the influence of the industry on the nutritional behaviour of children. She continues by clicking on the terms 'food marketing' and 'childhood' (Figure 1.B). This initiates a new search to the available search spaces, having as a query the triplet {food marketing childhood}. She skims the results and she observes a Bing result about 'the impact of food advertising to childhood obesity', which decides to bookmark. A result coming from her company site ('Waag' in Figure 1.B) on 'injecting fun in food' reminds her of a workshop she attended one year ago, where, together with clients, they created fabbed food with the use of 3D printing. (With 3D printing one can print food in the desired shape and flavour) She finds the idea new and interesting and she is inspired to start investigating the idea further; she continues using CRUISE over a new iteration, making a focus-shift with the goal to investigate how 3D printing for child food can affect children's nutritional behaviour.

5   Tool Design

There are three main building blocks associated with the three research foci: one is responsible for the extraction of cues from the social chatter, another one for exploration of the search space and a third one for results retrieval and diversification. The initial set of terms is extracted, processed and displayed through the Term Retrieval, Processing and Visualization module. The explicit user feedback is sent to the Search Path Exploration and the Resource Diversification modules. The result set changes in each iteration with the Resource Diversification module determining the set and order of resources that are passed onto the user interface.

5.1   Term Retrieval, Processing and Visualization

We use a folksonomy based model to generate the word cloud. It includes the identification of most frequent words, as well as most frequent co-locations in the corpus. Specifically, we first retrieve the top 100 highest frequency words contained in the tweet-results returned for each query using the Twitter Search API. We then apply a custom filter to the results using lucene.apache.org API in order to filter out redundant words that exist in tweets. We also apply rules for data cleansing such as the exclusion of usernames, of terms with repeating characters (i.e. 'boooh', 'loool' etc), links removal as well as cleaning of words that include special characters. To derive a weighting for the words, we adapt the typical formula of TF-IDF which is

$$tfidf(t, c, N) = tf(t, c) * idf(t, N) \tag{1}$$

by considering $tf(t,c)$ as being the number of times t the word c appears in the results, not in every tweet, because words typically appear just once or twice in the 140 characters of tweets. Term frequency is multiplied by $idf(t, N) = \log \frac{N}{dft}$, where N the total number of tweets and *dft* the number of tweets the word appears in. Note that we could have just used as weighting factor the number of times a word appears in the results but by applying IDF we strike a balance between the few frequent words, which typically dominate in the results set, and less frequent words which neverthe-less should be visible in the cloud because they may reveal interesting cues. Next, we generate bigrams, which typically are n-grams for n=2 (for example, a sentence such as 'Leave me now.' would result in tokenized strings like 'Leave me', 'me now'). The key idea behind is to capture words that co-occur more than once in the "corpus of documents" and avoid splitting and scattering them around the cloud. This way, we enable users to foster associations between words, which may in turn instigate further explorations.

N-grams generation pseudocode

```
T=set of tweets (t) in the index
n=minGram
N=maxGram
NGrams{} → Ø // hash to store ngrams and their numberofoccurrences
for tᵢ in T do
  words[] ← Split(tᵢ)
    for i=n to N do
      for j = 0 to length(words) – i do
  ngram = ''
          for k = j to i do
  ngram = Concat(ngram, words[k])
          end for
          if ngram in NGrams
NGrams[ngram] += 1
          Else
NGrams[ngram] = 1
        end for
      end for
    end for
RemoveSingleOccurences(NGrams) //removes ngarms that occur only once
NgramFilter(NGrams) //filters ngrams according to regular expressions
  returnNGrams
```

Fig. 2. N-grams algorithm implementation

The pseudo-code listed in Figure 2 describes the algorithm for the extraction of n-grams. The algorithm loops over each tweet that belongs to the initial result set, splits the words contained in the tweet and then generates n-grams by concatenating consecutive words. In our case, minGram and maxGram are set to the value of two because we are looking to get only bi-grams. In case, e.g., we feed the method with minGram=2 and maxGram=3, then we would get bi-grams and 3-grams. The Re-moveSingleOccurences method continues with checking the frequency of n-grams eliminating those that occur only once in the corpus. Finally, the method NgramFilter is called in order to filter and clean the n-grams as also happened in the case of single terms. If one term of the n-gram is unacceptable due to filtering rules then the n-gram is eliminated from the list, too.

5.2   Search Path Exploration

Hovering over terms appearing in the cloud displays a preview of the tweets that include the term (see Figure 1.A). This enables users to see how the term relates to the initial query. We enable end users to interact with the words not only by exploring what people post but also by using them to form search paths. Selecting (or deselecting) terms gives users the capability to form (or modify) search paths which are used as queries to the available search spaces. We utilize the APIs of public search engines such as Bing as well as custom search engines for querying private spaces. The tool provides immediate feedback to the user by refreshing the screen with results from search spaces and allows for further interactions by modifying search paths. With this, we aim to enable users to recognize or create associations between cues and information that may lead to serendipitous discoveries.

5.3   Resource Diversification

Diversity examined from several aspects [16] can be a supporter of serendipitous encounters. In CRUISE, we have exploited this principle and attempted to inject visual and content diversity by including several sources of information such as Twitter, Bing and Flickr. Considering that a) the user capability to diverge is mostly based on her perception that the environment and the pieces of information are diverse and b) the typical user checks the top ten to fifteen results before proceeding to the reformulation of her query, we apply post processing to the search engines results: We diversify the results using an algorithm that re-ranks results with a goal to reveal content that is related to all the possible aspects of the query in the top ten results. For this purpose, we use the canonical version of Maximal Marginal Relevance (MMR) framework [18]:

$$MMR = Arg\ max_{D_i \in \mathcal{R} \setminus S}[\lambda Sim(D_i, Q) - (1 - \lambda)\max_{D_j \in S} Sim(D_i, D_j)] \qquad (2)$$

where $Sim(\text{Di}, \text{Q})$ is the similarity of the document with respect to the query Q, and $Sim(\text{Di}, \text{Dj})$ is the similarity between the current document and a document in previous ranks and λ is a parameter that optimizes a linear combination of the criteria of relevance and diversity. When $\lambda = 1$ then the standard relevance-ranked list is produced, whereas when $\lambda = 0$ a maximal-diversity list of documents is generated We consider as document the snippet of each Bing result, title for Flickr and web-page content for the case of company's portal results.

Since we rely on public search APIs and hence cannot be aware of the actual similarity scores of the results with respect to the query, we compute them by exploiting the documents' positions in the list as follows [23]:

$$Sim(Di, Q) = \frac{N - Pos(Di)}{N} \qquad (3)$$

Where $Pos(\text{Di})$ is the position of document d in the query result list returned by the search engine and N is the size of the list. The document ranked first gets a value of $Sim(\text{Di}, \text{Q}) = 1$ while the last one gets a value of $Sim(\text{Di}, \text{Q}) = 1/N$.

In order to compute the similarity between the documents in the result set R we use cosine similarity:

$$Sim(\text{Di}, \text{Dj}) = \cos(\theta) = \frac{Di\,Dj}{||Di||\,||Dj||} \tag{4}$$

where θ is the angle between the vectors of documents. We use the Vector Space Model (VSM) to represent each document as a vector, the components of which represent the importance of a term using TF-IDF metrics, given a bag of words that derive from the documents in R. For the lexicographic analysis (tokenization, stop words removal and stemming) of the documents in R, we use the Apache Lucene Standard analyser.

MMR Implementation

Input: S = set of documents (D) returned by the search engine, Q=query
Output: Final Ranked list = re-ranked documents
FinalRank{} → Ø
Temp{} → Ø // List that holds the candidate documents
for the next rank
forD_i in S do
Calculate TF*IDF vector
Calculate Sim(D_i, Q)
end for
while $|FinalRank|<|S|$ **do**
    ford_i in S **do**
            for $d_j$in *FinalRank*do
Score$_i$← Similarity(D_i, D_j)
            end for
Score$_i$← 0,1*Sim(D_i, Q) – 0,9* Score$_i$
Temp ← {d_i, Score$_i$}
    end for
maxScoreDoc← Call FindMaxScore(Temp)
FinalRank{ } ← {maxScoreDoc}
end while
returnFinalRank

Fig. 3. Diversification algorithm implementation

Figure 3 shows in more detail the implementation of MMR in CRUISE. The algorithm starts with the representation of each document as a vector of all words included in the index and the calculation of the similarity of each document with the query. It then proceeds with applying MMR that starts by placing the first document in the final list of documents, which will be the diversified bucket of documents. It iterates through the remaining documents and for each one calculates the MMR score summing its similarities with each of the documents that are already in the final bucket. The document with the maximum Maximal Marginal Relevance will occupy the place of the next element in the final bucket of documents. The process continues until all documents are placed in the bucket.

6   Evaluation

We conducted a pilot study and a focused experiment to evaluate our tool[1]. A team of professional concept developers from the Waag[2] Society institute for art, science and technology, have performed search tasks with the purpose of getting inspired in the context of their actual work assignments. Once the participants completed the tasks, they filled a questionnaire to provide their subjective usability and perceived usefulness assessment. To this end, we adapted the standard System Usability Scale [24] and the ResQue evaluation framework [25]. Moreover, we employed a think-aloud methodology and recorded qualitative user comments to gain additional insights.

In addition to the pilot study, we ran a laboratory study in order to evaluate the specific research objectives of CRUISE and whether CRUISE is subjectively better for leveraging inspiration than standard query-based interfaces. Thus, the baseline system was a typical query–based retrieval system, which used neither social chatter-based term extraction and visualization, nor search path exploration and resource diversification. The search spaces and search engines were the same in both systems. In the baseline, users could express their information need only through typing queries and the results were presented as a list of resources.

We recruited 20 CS researchers from our university to participate in the laboratory study. Their task was to formulate an outline for a short-term research proposal, e.g., a diploma thesis, in cloud computing. We limited the time available to complete the task to 15 minutes to make sure that the participants were actively searching during the experiment and had equal time to complete the task. Half of the participants performed the task using CRUISE and the other half using the baseline system. Participants were asked to evaluate the top 10 results of each exploration for novelty (whether a given resource was showing a new aspect), interestingness (whether this resource is interesting yet neither relevant nor directly related) and unexpectedness (whether this resource was relevant to the assignment yet not directly related and not expected to be found).

After the completion of the experiment we asked two professors to assess the quality of the thesis outlines based on the perceived relatedness to cloud computing research and their originality. Moreover, professors provided feedback on the theses fluency which refers how detailed theses were. We hypothesized that users who had access to inspiring resources would be able to formulate their ideas better.

In the pilot study, the overall impression from the concept developers' comments was positive. One developer stated that CRUISE provides a solid basis for "a very powerful inspiration tool". Many commented that with CRUISE they could "reach inspiring information from search engines and the company's portal faster", nevertheless a messy arrangement of sources and additional media types would be more inspiring for "visual people" as concept developers are. Another noted that "those red-coloured words that appeared to be really interesting" referring to the terms that came from design platforms that concept developers followed in Twitter and which were fed to CRUISE. Another developer suggested that the user should get feedback about

---

[1] Please visit http://imu.ntua.gr/software/ cruise for a url pointing to CRUISE
[2] http://waag.org

the origin of the related tweet. The diversity of sources was appreciated because they "didn't always get common results in the top ranks". However, the cloud formation by exploiting just one social source was considered very restricting in terms of the variety of viewpoints they could get.

Table 1. Overview of the average, standard deviation and mode for our post pilot study questionnaire based on a five point Likert scale from 1, strongly disagree to 5, strongly agree

Aspect	Mean	Std	Mode
Quality of Results (Novel, Interesting, Ser/pitous, Diverse)	4.2	0.8	4
Interaction Adequacy (to express, revise needs)	4	0.7	4
Interface Adequacy (attractive, adequate layout)	4	0.7	4
Perceived Ease of Use (familiarity with the tool)	4.8	0.4	5
Perceived Usefulness (supported in exploring)	4.7	0.5	5
Control/Transparency (control to express preferences)	4.2	0.6	4
Attitudes (confidence of getting inspired)	4.8	0.4	5
Behavioral Intention (use again, tell my friends)	4.8	0.4	5

The quantitative results from the post laboratory study (see also Table 1) favoured CRUISE in terms of its adequacy to support users into expressing their needs (m=5 std=0.7) and getting familiar with it (m=4.7 std=0.4). With respect to quality of content, the users tended to agree that CRUISE offers valuable, novel and unexpected content (m=4.2 std=0.8) with strong confidence that it could inspire them (m=4.7 std=0.4). Data logged from the interactions with CRUISE and baseline system including details of the articles displayed, terms displayed by the system, manipulated terms, queries typed by the participants and user ratings of results revealed that with CRUISE users performed more queries (m=1.8) than using the baseline (m=1.14). The difference was statistically significant ($p < 0.05$). Moreover, with CRUISE users found more unexpected and valuable results than in the baseline (see Table 2).

Table 2. Overview of the ratings of results for CRUISE and baseline

Type of results	Mean per session
Novel	Cruise: 0.23 Baseline: 0.2
Valuable	Cruise: 0.20 Baseline: 0.15
Unexpected	Cruise: 0.26 Baseline: 0.061

Considering the professors' assessment of the creative outcomes, we ascertained that our approach had some effect with respect to fluency (p-value: 0.05 and quality (p-value: 0.01) (See Table 3) which indicates that users who had access to resources with CRUISE were able to formulate their ideas better than those who didn't. A possible explanation for this finding could be that with CRUISE users could access diverse resources and could identify content of better quality than in the baseline. Moreover, CRUISE guides users towards more targeted searches that may help into finding novel ideas.

Table 3. Analysis of research thesis proposals

	CRUISE	Baseline
Fluency mean	3.8	2.7
Fluency STD	1.4	0.9
Quality mean	3.8	2.4
Quality STD	0.6	1.2

7 Conclusions

We presented an interactive, exploratory search system that combines diversity of content and information sources with a novel user interface design to allow the social chatter generated with micro-blogging services such as Twitter to actively help users in exploring the information space. Users can direct their search by manipulating terms extracted from online chatter and formulate new search paths. A task-based user study comparing our system to a query-based baseline indicated that our system improves inspirational discoveries by providing access to more interesting, novel and unexpected information. Our results are encouraging, providing evidence that the implicit use of social chatter in information seeking activities can enhance the potential for novel, diverse and serendipitous encounters which can in turn inspire users. We plan to conduct further empirical studies to understand the effect of each of our three research constituents and to enhance CRUISE with social and team-oriented features that will e.g., allow team members to view relevant searches of colleagues, as well as with user profiling capabilities that will enable personalization of user interaction by taking into account the user social network.

Acknowledgement. This work has been partly funded by the European Commission through IST Project COLLAGE "Creativity in learning through Social Computing and Game Mechanics in the Enterprise", Grant agreement no: 318536.

References

1. Amabile, T.M.: Creativity and innovation in organizations, pp. 1–15. Harvard Business School (1996)
2. Woodman, R.W., Sawyer, J.E., Griffin, R.W.: Toward a theory of organizational creativity. Academy of Management Review, 293–321 (1993)
3. Nagpal, A., Hangal, S., Joyee, R.R., Lam, M.S.: Friends, romans, countrymen: lend me your URLs. using social chatter to personalize web search. In: Proc. CSCW 2012, pp. 461–470. ACM Press (2012)
4. Herring, S.R., Poon, C.M., Balasi, G.A., Bailey, B.P.: TweetSpiration: leveraging social media for design inspiration. In: Proc. CHI 2011, pp. 2311–2316. ACM Press (2011)
5. Bernstein, M.S., Suh, B., Hong, L., Chen, J., Kairam, S., Chi, E.H.: Eddi: Interactive topic-based browsing of social status streams. In: Proc. UIST 2010, pp. 303–312. ACM Press (2010)
6. Millen, D., Yang, M., Whittaker, S., Feinberg, J.: Social bookmarking and exploratory search. In: Proc. ECSCW 2007, pp. 21–40 (2007)

7. Chen, J., Nairn, R., Nelson, L., Bernstein, M., Chi, E.: Short and tweet: Experiments on recommending content from information streams. In: Proc. CHI 2010, pp. 1185–1194. ACM Press (2010)

8. Marchionini, G.: Exploratory search: From finding to understanding. Communications of the ACM 49(4), 41–46 (2006)

9. Teevan, J., Alvarado, C., Ackerman, M.S., Karger, D.R.: The perfect search engine is not enough: A study of orienteering behavior in directed search. In: Proc. of SIGCHI 2004, pp. 415–422 (2004)

10. Baldonado, M., Winograd, T.: Sensemaker: An information-exploration interface supporting the contextual evolution of a user's interests. In: Proc. SIGCHI 1997, pp. 11–18 (1997)

11. Havre, S., Hetzler, E., Perrine, K., Jurrus, E., Miller, N.: Interactive visualization of multiple query results. In: Proc. IEEE Symposium on Information Visualization 2001, p. 105 (2001)

12. Glowacka, D., Ruotsalo, T., Konuyshkova, K., Kaski, S., Jacucci, G.: Directing exploratory search: Reinforcement learning from user interactions with keywords. In: Proc. IUI 2013, pp. 117–128. ACM Press (2013)

13. Devendorf, L., O'Donovan, J., Hollerer, T.: TopicLens: An Interactive Recommender System based on Topical and Social Connections. In: Proc. RecSys 2012, p. 41 (2012)

14. O'Connor, B., Krieger, M., Ahn, D.: TweetMotif: Exploratory Search and Topic Summarization for Twitter. In: Proc. ICWSM (2010)

15. Waitelonis, J., Sack, H.: Towards exploratory video search using linked data. Multimedia Tools and Applications 59(2), 645–672 (2012)

16. Denecke, K.: Diversity-Aware Search: New Possibilities and Challenges for Web Search. Library and Information Science 4, 139–162 (2012)

17. Vallet, D., Castells, P.: Personalized diversification of search results. In: Proc. SIGIR 2012, pp. 841–850. ACM Press (2012)

18. Carbonell, J., Goldstein, J.: The use of MMR, diversity-based reranking for reordering documents and producing summaries. In: Proc. SIGIR 1998, pp. 335–336. ACM Press (1998)

19. Agrawal, R., Gollapudi, S., Halverson, A., Ieong, S.: Diversifying search results. In: Proc. WSDM 2009, pp. 5–14. ACM Press (2009)

20. Santos, R.L., Macdonald, C., Ounis, I.: Exploiting query reformulations for web search result diversification. In: Proc. WWW 2010, pp. 881–890. ACM Press (2010)

21. Capannini, G., Nardini, F.M., Perego, R., Silvestri, F.: Efficient diversification of web search results. VLDB Endowment 4(7), 451–459 (2011)

22. Gollapudi, S., Sharma, A.: An axiomatic approach for result diversification. In: Proc. WWW 2009, pp. 381–390. ACM Press (2009)

23. Bordogna, G., Campi, A., Psaila, G., Ronchi, S.: Disambiguated query suggestions and personalized content-similarity and novelty ranking of clustered results to optimize web searches. Information Processing & Management 48(3), 419–437 (2012)

24. Brooke, J.: Susa quick and dirty usability scale. Usability Evaluation in Industry 189, 194 (1996)

25. Pu, P., Chen, L., Hu, R.: A user-centric evaluation framework for recommender systems. In: Proc. RecSys 2011, pp. 157–164 (2011)

System Architecture of the BIVEE Platform for Innovation and Production Improvement

Mauro Isaja

Engineering Ingegneria Informatica SpA, Rome, Italy
mauro.isaja@eng.it

Abstract. The BIVEE acronym stands for Business Innovation and Virtual Enterprise Environment. The ICT outcome of the BIVEE Project is the BIVEE System: an integrated solution enabling business innovation in virtual factories and enterprises. In line with the Future Internet vision, the BIVEE System is delivered as a set of modular applications deployed on top of a commodity, cloud-ready service platform, This service platform, named *BIVEE Platform*, provides a base layer of data, knowledge, services and capabilities. This paper briefly describes the BIVEE Platform, from both the conceptual and the technical point of view.

Keywords: BIVEE, Innovation, Virtual Enterpise, Platform, Future Internet, FInES, FI-PPP, ISU, Generic Enabler, Knowledge Base, Ontology, KPI.

1   Introduction

Quoting from the BIVEE Project's Description of Work document: *"Business Innovation is the most promising exit strategy for European manufacturing industry to recover from the current economic crisis… The BIVEE Project aims to develop a conceptual reference framework, a novel management method and a service-oriented ICT platform … to enable Business Innovation in Virtual Factories and Enterprises"* [1]. This paper briefly describes, from both the conceptual and the technical point of view, the service-oriented ICT platform proposed by BIVEE.

The BIVEE Project focuses on two areas: **value production space** and **innovation space**. Value production space is where all activities related to the core business take place, and where business models and processes are designed, deployed, monitored and adjusted over time. At the same time, to counter the natural tendency of models and processes to become obsolete in a rapidly changing scenario, continuous open innovation is promoted and fostered in its own separate – but tightly connected – space. There is a continuous information flow between these two spaces, in both directions: value production feeds innovation with new challenges, innovation feeds value production with new ideas.

Each BIVEE space is covered by a dedicated application, targeted at end users: the Mission Control Room (**MCR**) tackles value production [4], while innovation is addressed by the Virtual Innovation Factory (**VIF**) [5]. Both rely on a common, shared platform providing both with a base layer of data, knowledge, services and capabilities. The fully integrated solution – the two **BIVEE Applications** plus the **BIVEE Platform** – is collectively known as the **BIVEE System**.

L. Iliadis, M. Papazoglou, and K. Pohl (Eds.): CAiSE 2014 Workshops, LNBIP 178, pp. 250–255, 2014.
© Springer International Publishing Switzerland 2014

The FInES Cluster Research Roadmap envisions a 2020 Internet-based universal business environment, where a common, available and affordable service infrastructure, based on the concepts of Interoperability Service Utility (ISU), will set the playing field for innovation [2].

This infrastructure is seen as a commodity: basically, it results from the aggregation of several generic, stable and well understood building blocks – implemented by commodity software – into a feature-rich, integrated, universally-available environment where the new generation of Future Internet applications can be developed and deployed.

The BIVEE System can be considered as a small-scale experimentation of the Future Internet vision. The BIVEE acronym stands for Business Innovation and Virtual Enterprise Environment, and is well-representative of the underlying architecture: the specific Business Innovation goal is targeted by BIVEE Applications, which run on top of a Virtual Enterprise Environment represented (and serviced) by the more generic BIVEE Platform. Actually, the BIVEE Platform aims at being the first prototype of a "commoditized", Future Internet-ready platform for enterprise ecosystem.

2   The BIVEE System Reference Architecture

The block diagram in Fig. 1 illustrates, from a logical perspective, the reference architecture of the BIVEE System, and the relationship existing between the BIVEE

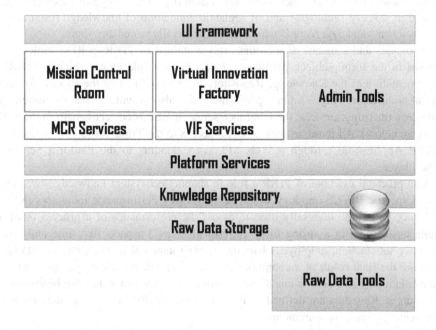

Fig. 1. BIVEE System reference architecture: the logical layers

Platform and the two BIVEE Applications. It also shows the composite structure of the Platform: three layers of foundation – Raw Data, Knowledge and Services – plus platform-specific capabilities such as a User Interface Framework and some Administrative Tools. Raw Data Tools, while an integral part of the Platform, are depicted as a separate element due to their substantially different technology.

3   The BIVEE Platform

In a handful of words, the scope of the BIVEE Platform can be defined as "enterprise ecosystem interoperability". To achieve this goal, the Platform needs to address some basic requirements [8]. From a top-level point of view, these can be categorized as **Sharing of knowledge, Harmonization of data, Unified access, Federated security**. Quite obviously, such a wide range of functionality cannot be successfully implemented by a monolithic architecture. The BIVEE Platform is actually a collaboration of Modules, which are designed as self-contained components. Modules can be deployed on separate nodes of the network, to achieve a distributed BIVEE System. The following sections will describe the two main Modules, PIKR and RDH, in some detail.

3.1   Production and Innovation Knowledge Repository (PIKR)

The PIKR Module is a multi-tier application implementing a knowledge base, and enabling knowledge sharing across the ecosystem [6]. Knowledge in PIKR is materialized as a set of ontologies and of semantic annotation of knowledge resources – i.e., documents and data records which can be physically stored anywhere.

Ontologies and semantic annotations are maintained by PIKR as RDF triples (assertions in the form: subject, predicate, object) in its Triple Store, which is PIKR's implementation of the Knowledge Repository layer as defined by the BIVEE System logical architecture (Fig. 1). On top of this, PIKR also provides semantic reasoning and query rewriting services, the latter as a semantic-enhanced access path to the KPI data (see below). All these, as well as direct access to the Triple Store, are exposed to BIVEE Applications through a Web API, corresponding to the Platform Services logical layer.

As a practical example of PIKR's role in shaping ecosystem knowledge, we consider a specific BIVEE ontology which describes Key Performance Indicators (KPI): *KPIOnto*. KPIs are universally used to assess the performance of a process or of a whole business, with a strong focus on critical ("key") aspects like time and cost, customer satisfaction, employees happiness, environmental respect, etc. In BIVEE, KPIs are the final result of a complex data gathering and processing pipeline, where the mediation of KPIOnto is mandatory in order to collate raw data from heterogeneous sources. Raw data are defined as Process Indicator (PI) Facts – i.e., data records representing atomic measurements.

As with other PIKR ontologies (here we can mention *DocOnto* for document-like resources, and *ProcOnto* targeted at business processes, KPIOnto comes off-the-shelf as basic set of classes, and is meant to be extended by the user to suit her own ecosystem needs. Extensions are in the form of new sub-classes and class instances. E.g., KPI definitions are instances of the Indicator ontology class, while KPI properties are sub-classes of the Dimension class. Once complete, KPIOnto represents a standardized, machine-readable model of the real world from which raw data originates: using this model, it is then possible to achieve a unified view of PI Facts, regardless of their original source and structure.

3.2   Raw Data Handler (RDH)

The RDH Module addresses the need of collecting heterogeneous KPI raw data – PI Facts – from ecosystem members, and make it available and understandable to consumer applications. The most relevant feature of RDH is its integration with the PIKR, which defines the KPIOnto ontology for the semantic enhancement of raw data (see also the Production and Innovation Knowledge Repository section above).

In the RDH context, the Raw Data Storage logical layer of the reference architecture (Fig. 1) is implemented by the RDH-DS sub-module. Facts are kept in *normalized* form – i.e., in a form that is highly compatible with the logical structure modelled by KPIOnto. The main value of data normalization is that application queries, which are expressed in terms defined by KPIOnto, can be automatically translated into equivalent RDH queries, which will perform very fast. By virtue of this mechanism, facts can be collected from heterogeneous sources - typically Enterprise IT systems belonging to different organizations - and still be presented and analyzed in a homogeneous way. This ontology-driven approach to data interoperability is commonly called *semantic lifting* [7].

RDH-DS is implemented as a SQL database, with a specific data schema in which Facts are stored. This schema is auto-generated, and continuously kept in-sync, using KPIOnto as a blueprint. Basically, KPIOnto classes derived from the Dimension class are translated into domain tables following a set of rules (Fig. 2), and are populated with records corresponding to concrete instances; each Indicator instance becomes a fact table by its own, connected with the relevant domains. The resulting schema is described in the RDH-DS Catalogue, and from there entities can be easily mapped back to KPIOnto concepts.

The collection of PI Facts follows a de-centralized approach: each data contributor – typically an enterprise – designs, deploys and runs its own set of ETL batch procedures which *E*xtract data from ICT systems, *T*ransform them in normalized form, and finally *L*oad them on the BIVEE Platform. To support this strategy, the BIVEE Platform provides the Raw Data Tools layer (Fig. 1), implemented by the RDH-ETL sub-module. This is a desktop application for the assisted development of executable programs capable of feeding RDH-DS with normalized PI Facts. The loading of PI Facts is accomplished by a Platform Service (Fig. 1), which in the RDH context is implemented by the RDH-WS sub-module.

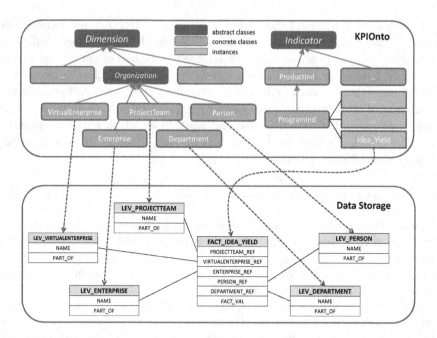

Fig. 2. Example of how KPIOnto concepts are mapped to RDBMS tables

4   Conclusions

The BIVEE System, as composed by the two BIVEE Applications – MCR and VIF – and by the BIVEE Platform, is currently under active experimentation.

At the end of the BIVEE Project (December 2014), a cloud-based instance of the complete BIVEE System will be deployed, as a proof-of-concept demonstrator of BIVEE's results. This instance will actually provide a Future Internet environment as well: the BIVEE Platform as an enabling infrastructure for enterprise ecosystems, on which to build domain-specific extensions and/or applications. The BIVEE Platform captures and implements the low-level, cross-domain requirements of such enterprise ecosystem environments, and translates them into the Raw Data, Knowledge and Services layers of its reference architecture. We believe that such architecture is well suited for Future Internet applications in the Business Innovation usage area, and we expect that it may evolve into – or at least significantly contribute to – a Future Internet commodity infrastructure.

Acknowledgement. This work has been partly funded by the European Commission through the FoF-ICT Project BIVEE (No. 285746). The author wishes to acknowledge the Commission and all the BIVEE project partners for their contribution.

References

1. The BIVEE Consortium: Grant Agreement for Collaborative Project #285746, Annex I - "Description of Work", pp. 53–55 (2011)
2. The FInES Cluster: FInES Research Roadmap Final Report (2010),
   http://www.fines-cluster.eu/jm/Documents/Download-document/
   2-FInES-Cluster-2010-Research-Roadmap.html
3. Rossi, A., Knoke, B., Efendioglu, N., Woitsch, R.: Specification of Business Innovation Reference Framework. Technical report D2.2, BIVEE Project (2012)
4. Woitsch, R.: Hybrid Modelling with ADOxx: Virtual Enterprise Interoperability using Meta Models. In: Franch, X., Soffer, P. (eds.) CAiSE Workshops 2013. LNBIP, vol. 148, pp. 298–303. Springer, Heidelberg (2013)
5. Calle, F., Perea, C.: BIVEE Virtual Innovation Factory. In: Proceedings of NGEBIS Workshop at CAISE Conference, Valencia, Spain, June 18. CEUR Workshop Proceedings, vol. 1006, pp. 18–23 (2013) ISSN 1613-0073
6. Diamantini, C., Potena, D., Proietti, M., Smith, F., Storti, E., Taglino, F.: A Semantic Framework for Knowledge Management in Virtual Innovation Factories. International Journal of Information System Modeling and Design (IJISMD) 4(4), 70–92 (2013)
7. Kehrer, T., Kelter, U., Taentzer, G.: A rule-based approach to the semantic lifting of model differences in the context of model versioning. In: Proceedings of the 2011 26th IEEE/ACM International Conference on Automated Software Engineering, pp. 163–172. IEEE Computer Society (2011)
8. Cristalli, C., Piersantelli, M., Sinaci., A., Basar, V., Gigante, F., León, V., Crespí, P.: Definition of BIVEE Pilot Application Validation Cases, r2.0. Technical report D7.12, BIVEE Project (2013)

Cooperative Decision Making in Virtual Enterprises

Nesat Efendioglu, Vedran Hrgovcic, Ronald Quirchmayr, and Robert Woitsch

BOC Asset Management, Operngasse 20b,
1040 Vienna, Austria
firstname.lastname@boc-eu.com

Abstract. Virtual enterprises provide an environment where flexible production and corresponding service delivery is cooperatively and efficiently carried out by involved stakeholders focused on utilizing their core competences. This unarguably promising approach raises many challenges – in this paper we focus on two. First we investigate how hybrid modelling approach can be applied to design amalgamated meta models covering artefacts required by the stakeholders within such a distributed environment – e.g. to design a distributed value chain. Second we propose how insights from other domains such as eHealth can be applied to solve the cooperative decision making challenge – e.g. fundamental due to having more than one process owner. We elaborate on three possible realization scenarios and select one to investigate how the previously designed meta model has to be extended to apply the proposed solution.

Keywords: Cooperative Decision Making, Meta-models, Conceptual Model, Conceptual Integration, Virtual Enterprise.

1 Introduction

In the conjunction with activities concerned with raising the flexibility level of small to medium enterprises by shifting production towards distributed networks (e.g. Virtual Enterprises) [3] a set of enterprise interoperability related challenges [9] can be identified. These challenges include: (1) description of such complex and distributed systems; (2) interoperability between enterprises comprising such systems and their monitoring; (3) based on the dynamic changes of short-term objectives/preferences the dynamic re-arrangement; (4) finding cooperative consensus about long and short-term objectives. They impose the necessity to provide tools and methods capable of conceptualizing the distributed networks [11] and enabling collaboration of involved stakeholders on the appropriate level of detail to allow efficient management of such networks. According to authors in [11] the application scenario for such tools and corresponding methods is identified as a requirement at the design phase of Virtual Enterprises. The design phase consists of several tasks: integrating organizational aspects of each stakeholder, selecting appropriate services, skills and tools, etc. Given the assumption that each involved stakeholder is likely to utilize a different description language and different modelling procedures for specific enterprise interoperability dimensions – as introduced in [9] – during the design phase, the reduction of the complexity on the virtual enterprise level, becomes indispensable.

L. Iliadis, M. Papazoglou, and K. Pohl (Eds.): CAiSE 2014 Workshops, LNBIP 178, pp. 256–267, 2014.
© Springer International Publishing Switzerland 2014

As elaborated in [2], [13] and practically applied and evaluated the in EU-projects: BIVEE[1], ComVantage[7] and e-SAVE [14], hybrid modelling represents an appropriate approach in order to overcome the aforementioned challenges by using meta-modelling platforms such as ADOxx [12]. Such meta-modelling platforms are capable of supporting dynamic adaptation of the conceptual base structure typically found in distributed networks.

This paper proposes a set of realization scenarios and integration of a cooperative decision making mechanisms into a modelling language based on the hybrid modelling approach. This enables cooperative design of distributed networks based on automatically calculated consensus by considering individual preferences of each involved stakeholder. In order to ensure completeness, we summarized the hybrid modelling approach as solution toward specific enterprise interoperability challenges in section two, also we revisit the Virtual Production Space (VPS) Modelling Language realized in [1] following the hybrid modelling approach.. In section three we present cooperative decision mechanism in virtual enterprises and in section four we investigate and formalize relevant meta model parts of the VPS Modelling Language, where mechanisms, such as cooperative decision making can be integrated and then we elaborate on three possible realization scenarios and present one implemented sample. Section five finalizes the paper with a conclusion and outlook on future work.

2   Hybrid Modelling as Enterprise Interoperability Solution

The conceptual models are knowledge representation of real world, where each observes relevant part of the real world. Hybrid modelling is an approach that aims to create one holistic conceptual model, therefore aiming to merge several meta models in order to enable merging of different viewpoints of the real world [2]. In order to apply the approach in the first step all relevant meta models (within a specified Virtual Enterprise) are differentiated and classified according to (1) their domain, (2) the level of technical granularity , (3) the degree of formalization and (4) the cultural dependencies of the applying community.

The second step is the composition of the meta models – so called meta model merging. According to [2] we distinguish between meta model merging techniques: (1) loose integration of meta models, (2) strong integration of meta models and (3) hybrid integration of meta models. Additionally in [15] we may find the meta model merging patterns that may range from loosely coupled to fix coupled meta models. While loose coupling is very flexible, fixed coupling enables the realization of additional functionality.

An important task for the integration is the correct formalization of the meta models – Generic Meta Modelling Specification Framework (GMMSF) based on [17] is one prominent sample. The FDMM (A Formalism for Describing ADOxx® Meta Models and Models) [5] which follows the GMMSF proposes a formalization approach for meta models realized on the ADOxx®. In the following paragraphs a brief introduction to simplified version of FDMM is provided as it is used to formalize the Value Production Space Modelling Language presented in the next sub-section. As specified in [5] the FDMM defines a meta-model of modelling language as a tuple:

$$\text{MM: } <\text{MT}, \preccurlyeq, \text{domain}, \text{range}, \text{card}> \qquad (1)$$

where MT is a set of Model Types:

$$\text{MT: } \{\text{MT}_1, \text{MT}_2, \dots, \text{MT}_n\} \qquad (2)$$

and where each MTi is defined as a tuple:

$$\text{MT}_i\text{: } <O^T_i, D^T_i, A_i> \qquad (3)$$

MT_i consists of O^T_i, which represent a set of object types, D^T_i, which represents a set of data types, and A_i, which represents set of attributes. The relation $\preccurlyeq$ defines an ordering on the set of object types O^T. It can be used to express inheritance of classes defined in MT (e.g. $o^T_A \preccurlyeq o^T_B$ means o^T_A is a subtype of the object type o^T_B).

The domain function is used to map the set of attributes A to a specific set of objects OT.

$$\text{domain: } \mathbf{A} \rightarrow \mathcal{P}\left(\cup_j \mathbf{O}^T_j\right) \qquad (4)$$

The range function is used to map an attribute to the set of all pairs of object types and model types:

$$\text{range: } \mathbf{A} \rightarrow \mathcal{P}(\cup_j (\mathbf{O}^T_j \times \{\mathbf{MT}_j\}) \cup \mathbf{D}^T \cup \mathbf{MT}) \qquad (5)$$

The card function maps attributes and object types to a set of integers – e.g. to define cardinality of relation classes.

$$\text{card: } \boldsymbol{O}^T \times \mathbf{A} \rightarrow \mathcal{P}(\mathbb{N} \times (\mathbb{N} \cup \{\infty\})) \qquad (6)$$

In the next sub-section we revisit VPS Modelling Language, and we apply the FDMM notation to formalize it.

2.1   Value Production Space Modelling Language

The EU research project BIVEE [18] introduces the notion of a Value Production Space (VPS), which considers the different viewpoints of involved stakeholders in order to enable management of the virtual enterprise by a collaborative means [1]. The VPS modelling stack – identifying and orchestrating the different meta models within VPS Modelling Language- is depicted in Fig. 1. It identifies relevant meta models applied to describe the Virtual Enterprise from VPS point of view (for details on state-of-the-art analysis and specification of VPS Modelling Language see [1]). The meta models within VPS modelling stacks include:

(1) Value Production Space Chart, which represents geographical scope models and value flow models based on e3 value methodology [19], (2) Product, which defines products, their components, as and their sub-components,(3) Process, which represents processes in phases and levels comparable to SCOR (Supply Chain Operations Reference Model)[20], (4) Network, which represents organizational structures and roles within the network of the participating enterprises in the distributed network), (5) Key Performance Indicator (KPI), which enables conceptualization of

relevant parts of the concrete instances of the production processes, (6) IT-System Pool, which describes relevant IT-systems where user interaction or computation is significant to the designed processes, (7) Artefact Pool, which represents a reference pool to the relevant documents and (8) Semantic Transit Model, which is used to enable semantic lifting of the VPS Modelling Language (for more details on semantic lifting see [11]).

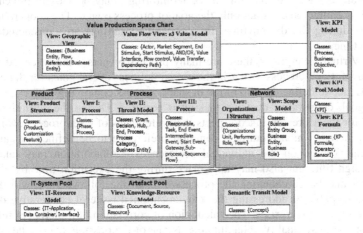

Fig. 1. VPS Meta-model (simplified excerpt)

Having defined VPS Modelling Language and corresponding requirements imposed by the enterprise interoperability within Virtual Enterprise a challenging application scenario is to define objectives of a business process. This is challenging due to fact that it involves a large number of stakeholders, hence requiring a collaborative definition of objectives of the business process. In this context, a question on "How to collect preferences from multiple stakeholders and calculate joint preferences" arises. We provide an answer to this question in section four by introducing possible realization scenarios and by presenting an implemented solution. These scenarios are adapted from eHealth domain, which has the similar challenges like VE in context of decision making. In the eHealth domain, different actors, such as patient, medical doctors with different proficiency, family and professional caregivers, administrative personnel, etc, are involved in the decision making process, similar to heterogeneous stakeholders involved in the processes executed within Virtual Enterprises. Starting from this in the next section we elaborate on the challenges related with cooperative decision making in Virtual Enterprises.

3   Cooperative Decision Making in Virtual Enterprises

Distributed networks such as Virtual Enterprises bring new challenges and enforce adaptations to the "Decision Making" process. We can identify a subset of relevant challenges for the decision making context by comparing the situation within a single enterprise with requirements to complete such an activity in a conglomerate of separate entities usually found in Virtual Enterprises.

In the single enterprise dimension there exists one process owner, responsible for defining the goals of the delegated business process. Given that complexity of the business process may be high, depending on the specifics of the scenario and relevant aspects like IT-systems, knowledge resources, the question "what shall be monitored and what are the KPIs to be utilized for monitoring" may be loosely linked to the process, it is enough to consider only the goal of process owner. The cooperation may take place during the design time, the cooperative settings are considered during execution time.

In the Virtual Enterprises, there are many process owners – the so-called process owner crowd. Each process owner in the crowd defines several goals for the business process. Hence to define the aim of the business process complying with each process owner's goal, cooperative decision making is required. During the definition of the "best-fit" for the aforementioned aspects the preferences of each process owner need to be considered, which requires a common preference to be defined or calculated automatically based on the individual preferences. Collaboration may take place during design time but also may take place during the execution time by changing preferences and hence changing the process aim. In the following we will define a mechanism capable of addressing the abovementioned issue of cooperative decision making in Virtual Enterprises. The calculation of correlation of preferences related to criteria such as cost, quality, reliability etc. is one of the possible approaches in order to find a common preference.

In the next paragraphs we describe an approach on how to generate a set of correlated preference values depending on two sets of values provided by two different process owners. Thereby the correlation takes both sets of preference values equally into account. Correlation values are normalized, i.e. between zero and one. High positively agreeing preference values yield a high correlation value. The case that one process owner sets a positive preference value and the other one sets a negative value results in a low correlation value. The same is true if both define negative values. In the following we describe the details of this approach.

Given process owners in a Virtual Enterprise can be represented with object type $o_{ProcessOwner}^{T}$ And given two process owners having N number of preferences represented with the object type

$$ProcessOwner, \ Preference, \ CorrelationVector \in OMTT \qquad (7)$$

$$A, B \in \ ProcessOwner, \ pAi, pBi \in Preference \qquad (8)$$

$$domain(Preference) = \{ProcessOwner\} \qquad (9)$$

$$card \ (ProcessOwner, Preference) = \{1, n\} \qquad (10)$$

Each preference has a weight assigned with a value from predefined range of values represented by $Weight_i$ where $Weight_i \in A_{MT}$

$$domain \ (Weight_i) = \{Preference\}, \qquad (11)$$

$$range \ (Weight_i) = \{Enumeration_{weight}\} \qquad (12)$$

$$card\ (Preference, Weight_i) = \{1,1\} \tag{13}$$

$$Enumeration_{weight} = \{-w_i, -w_i + 1, \ldots, -1, (0), 1, \ldots, w_i - 1, w_i\} \quad, \quad with \ w_i \in$$
$$\mathbb{N} \ (i = 1, 2, \ldots, N) \tag{14}$$

The weighting of preferences results in two preference vectors, one for each process owner:

$$P_A = (p_A^1, p_A^2, \ldots, p_A^N) \quad and \quad P_B = (p_B^1, p_B^2 \ldots, p_B^N). \tag{15}$$

In order to calculate correlation between A and B's preferences we define a vector

$$CorrelationVector_{AB} = (c_{AB}^1, c_{AB}^2, \ldots, c_{AB}^N) \ given\ by$$

$$c_{AB}^i = \begin{cases} \frac{1}{2} + \frac{(-1)P_A^i P_B^i}{2m_i^2} & if\ P_A^i < 0\ and\ P_B^i < 0 \\ \frac{1}{2} + \frac{P_A^i P_B^i}{2m_i^2} & else. \end{cases} \tag{16}$$

Due to the above scaling, $c^i \in [0,1]$.

Example. Let $N = 2$,

$$Enumerationweight1=-1, 1 \sim "no","yes" \tag{17}$$

$$Enumertation_{weight2} = \{-3, -2, -1, 0, 1, 2, 3\} \sim \{"verylow", \ldots ,"very\ high"\} \tag{18}$$

$$p_A^1 = 2 \sim"high"p_A^2 = -1 \sim"no", pB1=3 \sim"very\ high", \ p_B^2 = -1 \sim"no" \tag{19}$$

$$CorrelationVector_{AB} \approx (0.83, 0.00) \sim ("high", "no"). \tag{20}$$

Processes are annotated with thresholds for preference values: lower and upper bounds. A process is selected by the mechanism, if all preference values of the correlation vector are within the corresponding lower and upper bound: Let

$$([L_{Process}^1, U_{Process}^1], [L_{Process}^2, U_{Process}^2], \ldots, [L_{Process}^N, U_{Process}^N]) \tag{21}$$

be the vector of thresholds for Process with $L_{Process}^i$ being lower bounds and $U_{Process}^i$ being upper bounds $(i = 1, \ldots, N)$. Then Process is selected, if $c_{AB}^i \in [L_{Process}^i, U_{Process}^i]$ for all $i \in \{1, \ldots, N\}$.

4   Realization of Cooperative Decision Making

In order to enable cooperative decision making in hybrid modelling,-as mentioned before- we have investigated approaches utilized in the EU-project eHealthMonitor[8]. Following the results of the project we propose integration of the so-called "Cooperative Attribute" concept in the meta-model of a VPS Modelling Language following the hybrid modelling approach. The "Cooperative Attribute" enables users to enter their own preferences for the criteria (such as technology, trust, localization, cost, time, reliability, quality, and environment) and contains correlation vectors.

With regard to adapt these scenarios, we need to identify the appropriate meta-model part in VPS Modelling Language and required concepts in order to plug-in cooperative decision mechanism into the VPS Modelling Language. For that concern we investigated applicability of the e3 Value Model Type, Product Structure Model Type and Thread Model Type as possible candidates. In order to test the applicability the first step is the formalization by applying FDMM on the object type level.

Model Type: e3 Value Model; e3 Value Model is utilized to provide detailed view of interactions between production units, such as information or material flow [1]. Object Types of e3 Value Model:

O^T_{E3}: {Actor, Market Segment, Value Interface, Flow control, Value Transfer, End Stimulus, Start Stimulus, AND/OR, Dependency path, Referenced Business Entity, Referenced Concept}

Since investigation focuses on object type level, formalization of attributes and data types are not included in the paper.

Model Type: Product Structure: Product structure models are utilized, to model product structure conceptually [1]. Object Types of Product Structure Model:

O^T_{PSM}: {Product, Customization Feature, Includes, Referenced thread model}

Model Type: Thread Model; Thread model is utilized to conceptualize the actual supply chain for a specific product configuration. It is based on a set of processes where the flow of material or information indicates the sequence of execution [1]. Object Types of Thread Model:

O^T_{TM}: {Business Entity, Process, Process Category, Start, End, Decision, Hub, Assigned Processes, Described by, Enabled by, Flow, KPI Cockpit, Planed by, Responsible}

In order to integrate a "Cooperative Attribute" into candidate model types of VPS Modelling Language we need to extend it. This is possible using any of the following extension scenarios (ES);

ES 1: Integration into Model Type: e³Value Model;

As we defined in section 3 $Actor \in O^T_{E3}$, $Actor \equiv ProcessOwner$,

$$domain(Preference) = \{Actor\}$$

$$domain\ CorrelationVector = \{CooperativeAttribute\} \tag{22}$$

$$CooperativeAttribute \in O^T_{E3} \tag{23}$$

$$domain\ (CorrelationVector) = \{CooperativeAttribute\} \tag{24}$$

$$domain\ (CooperativeAttribute) = \{MT_{E3}\} \tag{25}$$

ES 2: Integration into Model Type: Thread Model;

$$Business\ Entity \in OTMT,\ Business\ Entity \equiv ProcessOwner \tag{26}$$

$$domain(Preference) = \{Business\ Entity\} \tag{27}$$

$$CooperativeAttribute \in O_{TM}^{T} \tag{28}$$

$$domain\ (CorrelationVector) = \{CooperativeAttribute\} \tag{29}$$

$$domain\ (CooperativeAttribute) = \{Process\} \tag{30}$$

ES3: Integration into Model Type: Product Structure Model; Although in this model type there is no concepts semantically equivalent with ProcessOwner –since the preferences on criteria are related with customization feature of product we can integrate *CooperativeAttribute* as following;

As we defined in section 4 *Customization Feature* $\in O_{PSM}^{T}$, add new object type Actor in the model type

$$Actor \in O_{PSM}^{T},\ Actor \equiv ProcessOwner,\ CooperativeAttribute \in O_{PSM}^{T} \tag{31}$$

$$domain\ (CorrelationVector) = \{CooperativeAttribute\} \tag{32}$$

$$domain\ (CooperativeAttribute) = \{Customization\ Feature\} \tag{33}$$

We propose to integrate lower- and upper-bound $L_{Process}^{i}, U_{Process}^{i}$ into the model type: Process Model as following; $L_{Process}^{i}, U_{Process}^{i} \in A_{PrcM}$, and assign these attributes to the model type itself;

$$domain\ \left(L_{Process}^{i}, U_{Process}^{i}\right) = \{MT_{PrcM}\} \tag{34}$$

Moreover we propose an additional model type so-called "Preference Pool Model", which contains preference objects for each criterion

$$MT_{PrfM}: < O_{PrfM}^{T}, A_{PrfM}, D_{PrfM}^{T} > \tag{35}$$

$$O_{PrfM}^{T}: \{Preference, Criteria, InterrefReferencedCriteria\} \tag{36}$$

$$A_{PrfM}: \{PreferenceName, CriteriaName, Weight_{i}\ \} \tag{37}$$

$$D_{PrfM}^{T}: \{String, Enummeration_{weight}\} \tag{38}$$

$$domain\ (PreferenceName, Weight_{i}\ ) = \{Preference\} \tag{39}$$

$$range\ (PreferenceName) = \{String\} \tag{40}$$

$$range\ (Weight_{i}\ ) = \{Enummeration_{weight}\} \tag{41}$$

There exist three realization scenarios to realize the "Cooperative Attribute". As a sample we took model type "Product Structure Model" from the candidate model types as sample to demonstrate the realization of the CooperativeAttribute

Given that *domain (CooperativeAttribute) = {Customization Feature}*

- **RS1:** "Cooperative Attribute" as type of Expression: In this scenario the values of the *CooperativeAttribute*are calculated via expressions, which reacts to changes of preferences of any user and re-calculates correlations automatically.

$$range\ (CooperativeAttribute) = \{Expression\}$$
$$card\ (CooperativeAttribute, CustomizationFeature) = \{1,1\} \qquad (42)$$

- **RS2:** "Cooperative Attribute" is self is an Attribute Type

$$CooperativeAttribute\ \in D_{PSM}^{T} \qquad (43)$$

- **RS3:** Preferences are taken and correlation among them are calculated by script and saved in the "Cooperative Attribute". In this scenario the values of the cooperative attribute calculated via execution of a script, which considers preference of two users for selected dimensions.

$$range\ (CooperativeAttribute) = \{Record\}$$
$$card\ (CooperativeAttribute, CustomizationFeature) = \{1,1\} \qquad (44)$$

- A solution based on RS3 has been implemented within the project eHealthMonitor [8] and has been reviewed and approved by external experts during the project review.

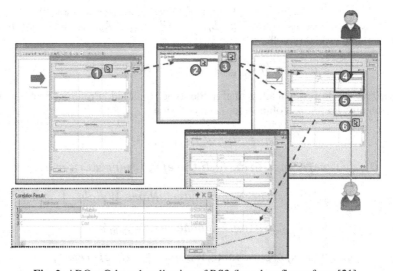

Fig. 2. ADOxx® based realization of RS3 (based on figure from [21]

Fig. 2 depicts implemented solution within the project eHealthMonitor. In the first step by execution of an ADOscript (for details see [6]), relevant criteria are selected and set, so that both users can define their preferences. In following step two users may enter their preferences for each of the selected criteria. Finally by execution of an ADOscript (as shown in the code snippet below), pairs of preferences entered by two different users are retrieved. For each preference pair the corresponding correlation is calculated and saved in the attribute "CooperativeAttribute" for further processing such as selection of concrete business process. Relevant part of the ADOscript code is presented below (to see realization discussion please refer to [21]).

"...

PROCEDURE GET_PREFERENCE_VALUES intproc_objid:integer
pref_attrid:integer answers: reference
{

...

FOR i from:0 to:(n_numberof_pref_space-1)
{

...

CC "Core"   GET_ATTR_VAL objid:(n_rec_pref_rowid)
attrname:("Preference")
CC "Core"   GET_ATTR_VAL objid:(n_rec_pref_rowid)
attrname:("Weight") as-string
SETL s_temp_weight:(val)

...

PROCEDURE CALCULATE_CORRELATION a_answers_1_array: array
a_answers_2_array: array max_w_1:integer max_w_2:integer
a_prefandcorranddim_array: reference
{

...

FOR i from:0 to:((n_questions_count-1))
{

...

SET a_product_s_array[i]:
((((1/2)+(flg*co*(n_weight_1*n_weight_2)))))

...

}..."

5   Conclusion and Outlook

This paper followed two goals. First goal was to identify the challenges that arise
when moving away from single to multi and virtual enterprises. Second, starting from
identified challenges, to evaluate and select the prominent ones and to apply the proposed solution. These challenges included the necessity to establish a common means
of understanding between the involved stakeholders and their enterprises. To achieve
this we have applied the hybrid modelling approach to structure and design the amalgamated VPS Modelling Language– covering the full cycle of production and delivery in virtual enterprises – building on top of the vast literature and practical research
performed in the BIVEE project. And second to address the challenge of cooperative
decision making – raising from the one-to-many process owners transition we (1)
formalized both the VPS Modelling Language and the proposed extensions using
FDMM, and (2) performed a research on appropriate solutions in other domains. The
identified solution – in the eHealth domain - was then evaluated in the eHealthMonitor project and accepted by experts in an EC review and it's applicability within
Virtual Enterprises has been elaborated with the experts from the BIVEE project.

Open research questions include the adaptation of the VPS meta model to include extensions needed to efficiently use and apply the introduced consensus mechanism and it's testing, evaluation and approval in the real life test cases with end users in the BIVEE project.

Acknowledgement. This work has been partly supported by the European Commission co-funded projects BIVEE (www.bivee.eu) under contract FP7-285746 and eHealthMonitor (www.ehealthmonitor.eu), under contract FP7-287509.

References

1. Woitsch, R., Efendioglu, N., Knoke, B., Verdu, J.H.: State of the Art and Mission Control Room Specification, BIVEE Project Delivaerable D3.1,
   http://wordpress.bivee.eu/wp-con-tent/uploads/2013/07/
   D3.1_State_of_the_Art_and_Mission_Control_v1.1_pub.pdf
   (accessed February 17, 2012)
2. Woitsch, R.: Hybrid Modeling: An Instrument for Conceptual Interoperability. In: Revolutionizing Enterprise Interoperability Through Scientific Foundations, pp. 97–118. IGI Global (2014)
3. Fraunhofer IAO, Industrie 4.0, http://www.iao.fraunhofer.de/lang-de/
   geschaeftsfelder/unternehmensentwicklung-und-
   arbeitsgestaltung/1009-industrie-40.html (accessed, February 17, 2014)
4. FInES Cluster, FInES Research Roadmap, http://cordis.europa.eu/fp7/ict/
   enet/documents/fines-researchroadmap-final-report.pdf (accessed February 17, 2010)
5. Fill, H.-G., Redmond, T., Karagiannis, D.: FDMM: A Formalism for Describing ADOxx Meta Models and Models. In: ICEIS (2012)
6. ADOxx.org, http://www.adoxx.org (accessed February 28, 2014)
7. Karagiannis, D., Buchmann, R., Burzynski, P., Brakmic, J.: Specification of Modelling Method Including Conceptualisation Outline. ComVantage Project Deliverable D3.1.1 (2012)
8. Hrgovcic, V., Efendioglu, N., Woitsch, R., Quirchmayr, R., Popescu, S.: Mobile and Community aspects of the eHealthMonitor Knowledge Space. eHealth Monitor Project Deliverable D3.3 (2013)
9. Popplewell, K., Lampathaki, F., Koussouris, S., Mouzakitis, S., Charalabidis, Y., Goncalves, R., Agostinho, C. (2012) EISB State of Play Report, Deliverable D2.1 ENSEMBLE, http://www.fines-cluster.eu/fines/jm/Publications/
   Download-document/339-ENSEMBLE_D2.1_EISB_State_of_Play_
   Report-v2.00.html (retrieved June 24, 2013)
10. Karagiannis, D., Hrgovcic, V., Woitsch, R.: Model driven design for e-applications: The meta model approach. IEEE iiWAS (2011)
11. Hrgovcic, V., Karagiannis, D., Woitsch, R.: Conceptual Modeling of the Organisational Aspects for Distributed Applications: The Semantic Lifting Approach. In: COMPSACW. IEEE (2013)
12. ADOxx.org, Homepage, http://www.adoxx.org/live/home (accessed February 21, 2014)

13. Woitsch, R.: Hybrid Modelling with ADOxx: Virtual Enterprise Interoperability Using Meta Models. In: Franch, X., Soffer, P. (eds.) CAiSE Workshops 2013. LNBIP, vol. 148, pp. 298–303. Springer, Heidelberg (2013)

14. Utz, W., Hrgovcic, V., Woitsch, R., Pramatari, K., Tarantilis, C., Zachariadis, M., Zampou, E.: Operations and Supply Chain Management Tools Description – Initial Version. e-SAVE Project Deliveralbe D3.1 (2013)

15. Kühn, H.: Methodenintegration im Business Engineering, PhD Thesis (2004)

16. PlugIT, Overview of Modelling Languages, http://plug-it.org/plugITwiki/index.php5/Main_Page (accessed February 21, 2014)

17. Karagiannis, D., Kühn, H.: Metamodelling Platforms. In: Bauknecht, K., Tjoa, A.M., Quirchmayr, G. (eds.) EC-Web 2002. LNCS, vol. 2455, p. 182. Springer, Heidelberg (2002)

18. BIVEE EU Project, http://bivee.eu/ (accessed February 21, 2014)

19. e3Value, e3Value Methodology:Exploring innovative e-business ideas, http://e3value.few.vu.nl/e3family/e3value/ (accessed February 21, 2014)

20. Supply Chain Council, SCOR, https://supply-chain.org/scor (accessed February 21, 2014)

21. Adoxx.org, Cooperative Attribute Scripted, http://www.adoxx.org/live/faq/-/message_boards/message/87135 (accessed March 25, 2014)

A Methodology for the Set-Up of a Virtual Innovation Factory Platform

Cristina Cristalli and Daniela Isidori

Loccioni Group Research for Innovation Department, Ancona, Italy
{c.cristalli,d.isidori}@loccioni.com

Abstract. BIVEE project will enhance a new point of view on the latest generation methods and on the industrial systems oriented to promoting and managing innovation. A new ICT platform able to manage the innovation process has been developed and installed in one of the end-user of BIVEE project. During the validation and comparison activities, end users and related stakeholders are called to provide feedbacks regarding any issues detected in the BIVEE Platform. Based on these feedbacks, a series of actions has been implemented on the BIVEE Platform. In this context the support of technical partners in order to map the requirements of the actual architecture of BIVEE is a fundamental aspect. This paper will present the set up procedure needed in order to test the effectiveness of BIVEE proposed approach.

Keywords: BIVEE, Innovation Space, Open Innovation, Virtual Enterprise, SME, KPIs, end users.

1   Introduction

The BIVEE Environment aims at deploying advanced methods for boosting creativity and innovation with an open innovation approach, for supporting their lean implementation and for monitoring the concrete outcomes, managing the innovation ventures in a collaborative networked industrial setting.

The Open Innovation approach written by Henry Chesbrough, who is considered the father of this model, in *Open Innovation: The new Imperative for creating and profiting from technology* [1] "is the use of purposive inflows and outflows of knowledge to accelerate internal innovation, and expand the markets for external use of innovation, respectively. This paradigm assumes that firms can and should use external ideas as well as internal ideas, and internal and external paths to market, as they look to advance their technology". Open Innovation implies to access to distributed knowledge. New value is created from a new innovation environment, composed by people inside and outside the company. It is a way to accelerate innovation, and it can give the capabilities to improve velocity (Time to Market reduction), direction, and new business paths.

An important aspect is to establish a methodology to quantify Open Innovation level. There are a lot of existing works in the literature that try to define the concept

L. Iliadis, M. Papazoglou, and K. Pohl (Eds.): CAiSE 2014 Workshops, LNBIP 178, pp. 268–273, 2014.

of Open Innovation but also several discussions and methods that suggest the development of the open innovation measure based on a diverse set of activities [2] [3]. For example, the degree of openness through the number and type of partners and the phases of the innovation process [4]. Rangus K, et al. [2] define the tendency for open innovation as "the firm's predisposition to perform open innovation activities, such as external participation, inward Intellectual Property (IP) licensing, external networking, outsourcing of R&D, customer involvement, employee involvement, venturing, and outward IP licensing". These aspects could become Key Performance Indicators (KPIs) for the measuring of Open innovation level of an enterprise.

The members of a Virtual Enterprise (VE) in a Business Ecosystem (BE), working on Open Innovation activities, require a continuous interaction because they have the intent to share common resources to do business together. Therefore the management of the VE, i.e. business partners moved from the ecosystem to a VE, removal of an enterprise from a VE, contact details for BE members, is a key aspect and it is handled through the BIVEE environment. [5].

For this reason the introduction of a platform able to manage the ideas and to follow their development is needed. BIVEE addresses the full lifecycle of the 'inventive enterprise' that spans from creativity and idea generation to engineering of new businesses, to continuous production improvement. The BIVEE platform is based on a *Mission Control Room* (MCR), for monitoring of Virtual Enterprises value production activities, of a *Virtual Innovation Factory* (VIF), for continuous innovation production and of an *Advanced knowledge repository* (PIKR). At the same time, BIVEE will provide means for measuring the success of any process improvement or innovation venture (Raw Data Handler, RDH) [6, 7].

Through the tool called VIF users proposes their idea, updates their proposal and lists other idea submissions. These submissions can have technical materials attached. Feedback mechanisms such as comments or likes are very useful. Validation shows itself in every domain in different levels. A validation mechanism, before the idea proposals, is published and this is conducted through a domain expert. Domain expert has an important role because he should call for ideas for pulling innovation and he should evaluate the inserted issues in order to eliminate irrelevant ideas.

The most important requirements related to open innovation tool are: Manage Virtual Enterprise, Collaboration, Partner Search, Invitations, Meeting management, Discovery Mechanism, Idea Management, Idea Approval, Idea Analysis, Idea Rejection, Monitoring Tool, Notification [8].

The BIVEE environment will be tested involving end users with two radically different pilot applications, addressing a spectrum of cases that involve different degrees of innovation activities. As end-users of the project, Loccioni and Aidima are involved in the definition of the pilot application scenarios for mapping the requirements of the pilot applications to the actual architecture of BIVEE. Two monitoring campaigns have been defined and will be carried out in order to verify its implementation.

During the Second Measuring Campaign (SMC) the validation of the two pilot applications follow a quantitative and comparative analysis for observing BIVEE impact. The introduction of full platform in end-user settings allows measuring the same set of KPIs measured during First Measuring Campaign (FMC). During the SMC Loccioni, as end users, and its related stakeholders are called to provide feedbacks regarding any issues detected with the implementation of the VIF. In this context the support of technical partners for specifying the requirements of the actual architecture of BIVEE is a fundamental aspect.

2   Innovation Knowledge Flow, Storage and Monitoring with BIVEE Platform

The proposed innovation flow is organized in 4 (partially overlapping) parts that we refer to as *waves* [5] that evolve over time and their produced achievements are reported in a sequence of documents that follows a consistent logic. For each wave several groups of documents and a set of dependencies among documents are proposed. The 4 waves are: Creativity, Feasibility, Prototyping, and Engineering. Creativity starts with an innovation idea or a problem to be solved, described by a number of preliminary documents and with the creation of an innovation team. Feasibility defines impact and includes a refined planning to justify the required investment. Prototyping involves the first implementation of the initial ideas, achieving a first full scale working model that is tested and analyzed to verify the actual performance and characteristics. Engineering aims at producing the specification of the final version of the new product ready for the market, and the corresponding production process [5]. The full innovation flow from end user perspective is shown in Fig. 1.

The SMC will observe the relevant aspects related to innovation projects management of Loccioni Group, and to KPIs collection connected to innovative potential of a team or of a single project.

3   Virtual Innovation Factory (VIF) Platform

Before starting SMC, as end users, we collaborate with technical partner in order to detect technical problems, fixing bugs, and to indicate the "expected usefulness" of the platform components and functionality setup.

The VIF functionality [9] that we are testing during the preparation phase are:

•   Personal Dashboard, where one can check all the personal notification, personal information about profile, and use the calendar.

•   Ideas Dashboard where it is possible to insert a new idea specifying: which is the issue, the title, the description, some tags, document in attachment and cover, comments, which are the members that I can choose inserting the name or directly the skills connected to the idea, the visibility choosing between Virtual Enterprise (VE), Business Ecosystem (BE), or Public (PU). Then, the end user can choose if one want to submit the idea to a domain expert that can evaluate posted idea and launch an innovation project or simply save the idea in the draft panel, sharing it only with selected members.

- Innovation project panel shows the posted ideas submitted to domain experts and the launched innovation projects. When an Innovation project is selected, it is possible to enter in the specific project page where we can set the calendar, the Gantt and the project member, we can submit the document, insert comments and check the project status.
- Observatory panel that allows to select the sources that could come from social network, Semantic Web crawler, BIVEE organization dimensions ad Virtual enterprise, business ecosystem and world web.
- Collaboration panel and chat tool. with Meeting rooms or forum and chat
- VIF Admin tool to check, create and modify user list and related information, and VE.

Several internal tests are conducted in order to understand the idea visibility. When we create the idea in the draft panel one should share the idea wizard only with selected members, while, when one submits an idea he should share it with domain experts with specific competencies in the field of research of the proposed idea that should evaluate if the idea is good to start an innovation project.

Domain expert role is a very delicate aspect. In fact the crucial argument of discussion is related to the choice of domain expert. Should be chosen by the idea owner or there is a list of domain experts that could evaluate the idea? In this case when one can launch an innovation project? When just one expert gives a positive feedback or are there a minimum number of positive evaluations? In any case the idea should be attached to a specific domain because the choice of domain experts may be more accurate. We need to fix a deadline for this evaluation because usually, the time elapsed between posted idea and creativity wave start, from our point of view, needs to be very short. With respect to VE management, once the idea is inserted, we would like to decide with whom to collaborate in a VE in order to carry on the innovation project, considering the list of members chosen for their skills or for their degree and the list of selected comments related to the idea. The comments are not inserted only from chosen members but it should depend on the visibility that was set (VE, BE, PU). So we can choose, for example to collaborate with a "BIVEE user" that proposed a valid solution for an idea. For these reasons we should create a VE related to the single innovation project and we should set the visibility of the posted idea choosing from Loccioni BE, from other BEs or from a list of VEs.

There should be a sort of "moderator or administrator" that can check all the aspect related to proper right in order to accept an idea, the reliability of user profile.

Finally this innovation administrator should coordinates the evaluation of the ideas by domain experts, establishing reviewer, deadline,...In fact, who choice how "to take in charge" the evaluation of an idea? This evaluation should be obtained very quickly so this couldn't be obtained only through a spontaneous candidacy of a domain expert but should be pushed by an administrator.

4   KPI Selection and BIVEE Platform

One of the most important aspects in BIVEE is to monitor and determine the current condition of an enterprise through values of a set of variables called Key Performance Indicators (KPIs).

Starting from a list of around 40 KPIs used in the FMC, we proceeded with the definition of the formula for these KPIs [7].

For example the KPI related to cost is equal to

$$\text{Cost KPI} = \text{material} + \text{labour} + \text{other} \tag{1}$$

Moreover the original list of KPI are repeated for each wave that are in turn split in 3 or 4 activities for each wave. So the number of KPIs increases from 41 to 126 (Fig. 1a).

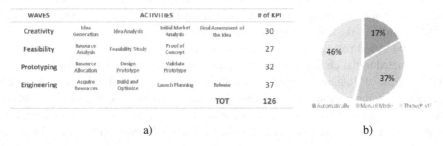

WAVES	ACTIVITIES				# of KPI
Creativity	Idea Generation	Idea Analysis	Initial Market Analysis	Final Assessment of the Idea	30
Feasibility	Resource Analysis	Feasibility Study	Proof of Concept		27
Prototyping	Resource Allocation	Design Prototype	Validate Prototype		32
Engineering	Acquire Resources	Build and Optimize	Launch Planning	Release	37
				TOT	126

Automatically   Manual Mode   Through VIF

a)   b)

Fig. 1. a) Total number of KPIs; b) types of KPIs collection

After these steps we identified from the list of KPIs which of them could be collected automatically, which of them in a manual mode, and very important, which KPIs could be extracted directly from data inserted in the VIF. As we can observe from Fig. 1b there is a relevant number of KPIs that could be extracted by VIF or manually while there is a low number of KPIs obtained automatically updating these data from Loccioni's database. Moreover, KPIs could be automatically downloaded from database only from the feasibility wave because the work order related to a single project in created only from the feasibility study in Loccioni. In fact, for example, all the cost related to the creativity wave are usually downloaded in a work order related to a particular competency. Then KPIs collected from VIF are useful because: we can't introduce KPI related to creativity wave automatically; we can monitor the whole procedure of innovation potential followed by Loccioni Group because the application scenario is not related only to a single project.

The BIVEE Platform prototype [10] is composed by a Monitoring Platform that includes the Raw Data Handler (RDH) component and the Data Storage, the Service Platform and BIVEE Portal that includes the front-end to the BIVEE Platform and components. At the moment, through BIVEE Portal in the monitoring Platform, we are collecting manually or automatically the KPIs related to the projects monitored.

5   Conclusions

For the adoption and implementation of a VIF platform able to manage the innovation management the preparation phase was a decisive step, absolutely not negligible. From end user point of view some internal procedures have to be re-organized in order to understand if the new methodologies introduced by BIVEE platform will improve innovation project management. First of all we had to re-organize the way to create an internal "work order" and how to automatize some operations that before were done manually. The implementation was not a simple and short procedure, but meetings and formal steps should be organized before the complete adoption of the VIF that will be completed with the SMC.

Acknowledgements. BIVEE Project (Business Innovation in Virtual Enterprise Environments) is co-funded by the European Commission under the "Seventh Framework Programme" (2007-2013), contract n° FP7-ICT-285746. The authors wish to acknowledge the Commission for its support and all the BIVEE project partners for their contribution in the development of various ideas and concepts presented in this paper.

References

1. Chesbrough, H.W.: The Era of Open Innovation. Sloan Management Review 44(3), 35–41 (2003)
2. Rangus, K., Drnovšek, M., Di Minin, A.: Proclivity for Open Innovation: Construct Conceptualization and empirical validation. ACAD MANAGE Proceeding, Academy of Management Journal (2013)
3. Schroll, A., Mild, A.: Open innovation modes and the role of internal R&D: An empirical study on open innovation adoption in Europe. European Journal of Innovation Management 14(4), 475–495 (2011)
4. Lazzarotti, V., Manzini, R., Pellegrini, L.: Open innovation models adopted in practice: An extensive study in Italy. Measuring Business Excellence 14(4), 11–23 (2010)
5. De Panfilis, S., Missikoff, M.: A Knowledge-centric Approach to Virtual Enterprise Innovation. In: NGEBIS 2012, pp. 1-10 (2012)
6. BIVEE Deliverable D2.2 – Specification of business innovation reference frameworks (in the context of the VEMF),
   http://wordpress.bivee.eu/resources/publications/
7. BIVEE Deliverable D6.12 – Analysis of User Requirements,
   http://wordpress.bivee.eu/resources/publications/
8. BIVEE Deliverable 2.1 – State of the Art about the Collection and Discussion of Requirements for Systemic Business Innovation and Definition of KPIs,
   http://wordpress.bivee.eu/resources/publications/
9. BIVEE Deliverable D4.21 – Virtual Innovation Factory prototype (v1.0),
   http://wordpress.bivee.eu/resources/publications/
10. BIVEE Deliverable D6.32 – BIVEE Environment Prototype (v2.0),
   http://wordpress.bivee.eu/resources/publications/

Data Mart Reconciliation
in Virtual Innovation Factories*

Claudia Diamantini, Domenico Potena, and Emanuele Storti

Dipartimento di Ingegneria dell'Informazione
Università Politecnica delle Marche
via Brecce Bianche, 60131 Ancona, Italy
{c.diamantini,d.potena,e.storti}@univpm.it

Abstract. The present paper deals with the problem of collaboration at strategic level in innovation-oriented Virtual Enterprises. The problem is taken from the perspective of sharing a special kind of data, Key Performance Indicators, that are measures adopted to monitor the achievement of certain strategic goals. We discuss the main conflicts that can arise in measures coming from autonomous enterprises, adopting the conceptual multidimensional cube model. Then we propose a novel semantic model to deal with conflicts related to the structure of a measure, that arise when the "same" KPI is calculated in different ways by different enterprises. Finally, conflict reconciliation strategies enabled by the semantic model are discussed.

Keywords: semantic reconciliation, data mart integration, data warehouse, Key Performance Indicators, Virtual Innovation Factories.

1 Introduction

In an Open Innovation scenario [1] enterprises pool their experiences and resources in order to leverage their innovation potential, and to optimize innovation costs. In other words, a Virtual Enterprise (VE) is established, namely a (temporary) network of independent organizations that collaborate in order to achieve a common goal. In particular, they form a Virtual Innovation Factory (VIF), aimed at the production of innovation [2]. It is a dynamic environment where enterprises enter and leave over time according to their interest for shared innovation projects, and is characterized by openness, autonomy and distribution of partners as well as heterogeneity and distribution of resources. From an information system point of view, a VIF should implement all the kinds of processes of a traditional enterprise, from (innovation) production processes, to management and strategic control. Innovation management is the focus of the present paper: although innovation is largely perceived as a matter of creativity,

---

* This work has been partly funded by the European Commission through the ICT Project BIVEE: Business Innovation and Virtual Enterprise Environment (No. FoF-ICT-2011.7.3-285746).

L. Iliadis, M. Papazoglou, and K. Pohl (Eds.): CAiSE 2014 Workshops, LNBIP 178, pp. 274–285, 2014.

a systematic monitoring and control of the actions performed during an innovation project is necessary to transform a great idea into a new successful product, and to guarantee efficiency and effectiveness to the whole process. In the EU Project BIVEE[1] a reference framework has been developed, that includes the definition of a set of innovation Key Performance Indicators (KPIs). KPIs are a kind of performance measurement, that allow to assess the achievement of certain strategic goals, like the percentage of defective products, the level of customer satisfaction or, in the context of innovation, the number of new ideas produced. In order for a VIF to work properly, partners should agree on the set of KPIs to use and share data for their assessment. The sharing of KPIs demonstrates itself particularly challenging due to a number of heterogeneities that can arise. They will be discussed in this paper in the context of Data Marts, i.e. computer systems for KPI management and decision support, implementing the conceptual multidimensional cube model.

The key element of a Data Mart schema is the fact, i.e. a particular goal to be monitored (e.g. productivity). A Fact schema includes a set of measures, allowing to assess the goal under different perspectives (for instance, productivity can be measured by monitoring the total number of produced ideas, their revenue, the average number of ideas per employee). Measures correspond in fact to the notion of KPI. Each measure is analysed along a set of dimensions, discrete attributes, usually arranged in hierarchies, specifying a way to aggregate and segment the analysis. For the number of new ideas produced, relevant dimensions are time (e.g. monthly trend), product lines, organization.

In the Literature, as shown in Section 2, much work is devoted to the problem of reconciliation of heterogeneities that can arise when trying to integrate Data Marts from autonomous enterprises. Among them, they mainly address conflicts due to different naming or unit of measure conventions, structure and definition of the dimensional hierarchies. In this paper we deal with reconciliation at measure level considering heterogeneities related to the structure of a measure, intended as the formula used to calculate the KPI, as discussed in Section 3.

The approach, described in Section 4, relies on the definition of a semantic multidimensional model serving as a shared global model on which every element belonging to a fact schema in the Data Marts (i.e. measure and dimensions) is mapped. The main novelty of such a model is that it includes both a conceptual definition of KPIs and the mathematical representation of their formulas. Although the full conceptual specification of KPIs and their formulas in real-world scenarios is a demanding task and may require a significant effort, the experience gained within the BIVEE project suggests that such an approach is particularly stable and robust, as the model requires only minor and incremental changes once it has been developed. On the top of the model a set of logic-based functionalities are defined, capable to effectively ease Data Mart integration by supporting strategies for conflicts reconciliation based on formula manipulation, shown in Section 5 together with a case-study. Finally, Section 6 ends the paper and proposes extensions to this work.

---

[1] http://bivee.eu

2   Related Work

Although the increasing interest in collaboration and networking in business environments, there is a general lack of work on KPIs reconciliation, especially in distributed and collaborative contexts. Most of the proposals in the Literature about integration of independent Data Marts has dealt with the resolution of conflicts about reconciliation of heterogeneous dimensions (e.g., [3,4]), while only few specifically focused on conflicts about measures (e.g. [4], that proposes an XML-based approach). Recently, due to the explosive growth of distributed applications, semantic technologies have gained more and more interest both as a global conceptualization useful to support the definition of semantic mappings between the local sources and the global ontology, and then to ease reconciliation and integration of Data Marts (e.g. [5]) However, to the best of our knowledge, the only attempt to deal with design and interoperability issues related to the compound nature of indicators is in [6], where mappings between measures include the description of the formula linking them. However, KPI formulas are purely syntactic and no reasoning is enabled.

For what concerns formal definition of indicators, several approaches to semantic modeling have been proposed (see [7] for a survey). However, almost all of them are specifically targeted to support more advanced monitoring (e.g. [8]) or analysis (e.g., [8,9]) within the context of business processes, and hence focusing only on the operational levels with little or no regard to strategic and managerial perspectives, or to innovation KPIs. To the best of our knowledge, the only work dealing with the explicit representation of KPI formulas is by Barone et al. [8], in which indicators are formally represented and arranged in hierarchies, with the aim to exploit run-time monitoring and what-if analysis of business processes.

3   Typologies of Conflicts

Integration of heterogeneous Data Marts from autonomous enterprises is a particularly challenging task due to the multidimensional and aggregate nature of the information. Heterogeneities lead to a large number of possible conflicts when semantically related elements (facts, dimensions and measures) are characterized by different properties. In the following, to support the discussion about the specific typologies of conflict, we refer to a case study that will be used as an illustrative example through the paper. Following the BIVEE framework, we consider a scenario in which two enterprises, to establish a Virtual Enterprise, agree on a set of KPIs to use and share data they have at disposal. These data are the KPIs they usually adopt within the boundaries of the enterprise to monitor and assess how they are innovating. Figures 1 and 2 show the Data Marts used by the enterprise A (hereafter DM_A) and enterprise B (DM_B) to manage innovation projects.

Two Data Marts are characterized by conflicts between facts if they are conceived to analyse the same phenomenon in different ways. Usual fact conflicts

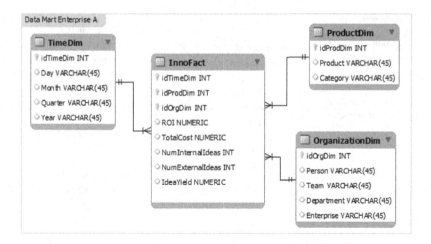

Fig. 1. Innovation Data Mart of the Enterprise A

occur when Data Marts refer to different representation models (e.g., star schema vs. snowflake). An *inconsistent fact schema* occurs when two semantically related Data Marts describe the same fact through different set of measures [10], like in the case study. This problem is similar to a structure conflict in database integration, where the same concept is described using two different structures.

As regards dimensions, a *dimension naming conflict* occurs when two Data Marts have different names for the same dimensional element (member, level or dimension). In our example, ProductDim in DM_A and ProjectDim in DM_B refer to the same dimension, and Team and Group in the OrganizationDim to the same level. A *dimension schema conflict* occurs when Data Marts have different dimensions or different hierarchies for the same dimension; for instance, the hierarchy of OrganizationDim is Person $\rightarrow$ Team $\rightarrow$ Department $\rightarrow$ Enterprise in DM_A and Person $\rightarrow$ Group $\rightarrow$ Enterprise in DM_B. Finally, there is a *dimension member conflict* when two semantically related levels differ in members. This kind of conflict can not be recognized by just observing the Data Mart schema, and values of dimensional tables must be considered. In our example, since the two SMEs are autonomous, it is very likely that there are no common members, apart those for the time dimension, until the two SMEs begin to develop projects together.

Measure conflicts occur when semantically related measures of the two Data Marts differ in name (*measure naming conflict*), formulas (*inconsistent formula*), values (*inconsistent measures*) and units (*measure scaling conflict*). In order to detect these conflicts, it is necessary to rely on an expressive representation model capable to deepen the meaning of the reported indicators. In our case study the enterprises provide also the description of metrics used in DMs, as given in the glossaries of Table 1 and Table 2. We observe measure naming conflicts, since TotalCost in DM_A and to TotalInnoCosts in DM_B refer to the same indicator, but they have different names: this is a case of *synonymy*. The use of IdeaYield

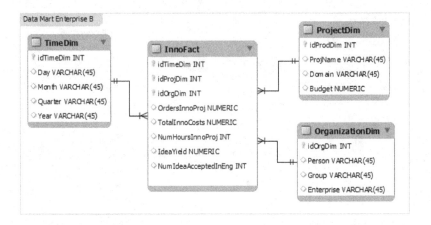

Fig. 2. Innovation Data Mart of the Enterprise B

Table 1. Measure glossary of DM_A

Data Mart A (DM_A)	
KPI	**Description**
ROI	Return on investment related to innovation projects, that is the ratio between value of received orders related to products designed in innovation projects and costs of innovation projects
TotalCost	The sum of materials costs, personnel costs and other costs related to innovation projects
NumInternalIdeas	Number of ideas generated from enterprise's employees
NumExternalIdeas	Number of idea generated from the external stakeholders
IdeaYield	The ratio of proposed ideas that have been developed

leads to another measure naming conflict, namely a *homonymy*. In this case, the two measures share the same name, but from the description one understands a variation in the way they are computed, which makes de-facto the two measures semantically different.

It is noteworthy that it is hard to recognize homonymies relying only on the textual description provided by enterprises, which by nature is ambiguous and not formalized. Indicators `TotalCost` and `TotalInnoCosts` give origin also to an inconsistent formula, since they refer to the same metric about the *total cost of an innovation project*, but their description suggests a different way to compute it. In the DM_A the total cost of innovation is given as the sum of different kinds of cost, while in DM_B the formula is given as the sum of costs of each wave. Since the cost of a wave can be divided in turn in material, personnel and other costs, the two formulas are equivalent and corresponding measures point to the same metric. Also, in this situation it is not easy to recognize the conflict from textual description, and further details about formulas used to compute the indicators

Table 2. Measure glossary of DM_B

Data Mart B (DM_B)	
KPI	**Description**
OrdersInnoProj	Sum of total margin of orders related to innovation projects
TotalInnoCosts	All costs involved in the whole innovation life-cycle (from creativity to engineering)
NumHoursInnoProj	Number of hours for innovation projects
IdeaYield	Ratio between ideas proposed and ideas that have been accepted for the Engineering wave, and then will be further developed
NumIdeaAcceptedInEng	The number of idea accepted for the Engineering wave

are required. Furthermore, it is noteworthy that **IdeaYield** measures do not lead to an inconsistent formula: the two measures refer to semantically non-related indicators. We have to emphasize that values provided in the Data Marts can not be used to identify measure conflicts; since the enterprises are different, the sets of dimensional members on which indicators are computed have almost empty intersection. For the same reason, we do not expect any inconsistent measures conflict in this case study; in fact, this kind of conflict occurs when two semantically related measures, having same name and same formula, take different values on common members. Finally, to simplify the discussion, we assume that there are no measure scaling conflicts in our example.

Given that the two DMs have only one indicator in common (i.e. the total cost of innovation project), more information is of course needed to monitor and assess the innovation projects that have been carried out and will be developed together. For instance, the two SMEs may decide that it is useful to observe also the *TotalOrdersRelatedInnovationProjects*, namely the value of orders for products/services that have been developed as outcome of an innovation project, and the *IdeasProposed*, that is the total number of ideas that have been proposed for a given common project. The former KPI is available only in DM_A (i.e. **OrdersInnoProj**), while the latter is in no Data Mart. Hence, in order to obtain these KPIs, each enterprise should involve their own IT Managers, providing them the new requirements and waiting for the new implementation of the Data Mart. Such a process is time-consuming and constitutes a barrier to the formation of a new VIF or to the entry of new enterprises in an existing VIF. Furthermore, we have to emphasize that Data Marts store historical data obtained over time by querying transactional databases, which by nature maintain current data. Therefore, often it is not possible to obtain values of additional KPIs related to past projects, hence producing sparse Data Marts.

4   Semantic Multidimensional Model

In this work, in order to provide support to integration of heterogeneous Data Marts, we extend the multidimensional model with semantic annotations, by mapping every element in a Data Mart with a corresponding concept of an ontology called KPIOnto. Such an ontology is devoted to formally specify and disambiguate the meaning of both measures and dimensions and the relations among them. In our context every fact table contains a set of measures related to KPIs whose semantics is formalized into KPIOnto as instances of the class Indicator. The class Indicator arranges KPIs in classes according to the Value Reference Model (VRM) taxonomy [11]. Indicators can be either atomic or compound: while the former is obtained as direct aggregation of transactional data, the latter is a structured datum built by combining several indicators of lower level, that are its dependencies. An indicator is fully described only if both its shared meaning, structure and dependencies are made explicit. For this reason, in our model for each compound indicator a *Formula* must be defined, i.e. an algebraic expression describing how to compute it from its dependencies. For instance, $IdeaYield = \dfrac{NumIdeaAcceptedInEng}{IdeasProposed}$.

In multidimensional models, every dimension is structured into a hierarchy of levels (e.g., the time dimension has Year, Semester, Month, Day, Week as levels), where each level represents a different way of grouping elements of the dimension [12], namely members (e.g., "2013" and "2014" are members of the level "Year" for the dimension "Time"). Resorting to the approach proposed in [13], the dimensions along which an indicator is measured (e.g., process, organization, time) are modeled as classes, where levels are their subclasses. A hierarchy among members is defined through a part-of relation, that links a member of a level to one belonging to an upper level (e.g., "June 2014", member of "Month" is part-of "2014", member of "Year").

For the implementation of the conceptual model introduced herein we make use of various knowledge representation formalisms and languages. In particular, we refer to OWL2-RL for the representation of descriptive information about indicators, whereas a more sophisticated representation language is needed for the encoding of mathematical definitions of KPIs. To this aim, we rely to MathML [14] and OpenMath [15], that are mathematical standards for describing both syntax and semantics of formulas in a machine-readable fashion. On the top of these languages, in order to define KPI reasoning functionalities as a support to integration and analysis, we need to represent both OWL2-RL axioms and MathML formulas in a common logic-based layer. To this end, we refer to the first-order logic and define the functionalities in logic programming (LP), to which both languages have a simple translation preserving expressiveness and (sub)polynomial complexity in reasoning.

Hence, KPI reasoning functionalities are implemented as Prolog predicates, and include basic functions for formula manipulation, capable to simplify and solve an equation, and more specific functions to support integration and advanced analysis. The support to the integration is mainly based on functions for checking inconsistencies among independent definitions of indicators and for the reconciliation of indicators provided by different enterprises. For what concerns analysis, the proposed ontological model enables usual OLAP operations over indicators, namely *roll-up*, that has a direct correspondence with the part-of relationship, and *drill-down*. Moreover, the ontological description of formulas and dimensions enables a generic method for exploring multidimensional data by moving from one level of detail to the next, namely an *extended drill-down*. This operator generalizes the definition of drill-down, allowing to decompose the value of a KPI both descending the hierarchy of a dimension (from the value about "2013" to values about "January 2013", ..., "December 2013") and extracting the values of components of its mathematical formula (from "IdeaYield" to "NumIdeaAcceptedInEng" and "IdeasProposed").

In addition, further predicates are devoted to provide specific support for Virtual Enterprise setup. Such functions are developed to support enterprises in understanding how a certain indicator can be measured by using other indicators already available in the ontology, exploiting inference and algebraic manipulations over the set of formulas. We refer the interested reader to [2] for more details on KPIOnto and to [16] for more details on reasoning functionalities.

5 Conflict Reconciliation

By exploiting the semantic model described in previous section, several conflicts can be easily solved once the semantic annotation of the Data Marts has been performed. Annotation is usually done by means of manual/automatic techniques well studied in the Literature [17], that for lack of space are not discussed here. For what concerns *naming conflicts*, two elements from different Data Marts linking to the same ontological concept are considered synonymous. As concerns *dimension schema conflict*, the joint use of part-of relations between levels' members and the semantic annotation of Data Mart elements, as exemplified in Figure 3, allows us to derive common hierarchies and, hence, to resolve the conflict. As an example, consider the conflict due to the `OrganizationDim` dimension of our case study:

- since members of both level `Team` in DM_A and level `Group` in DM_B point to the same class in the ontology, the two levels are equivalent;
- since instances of the *Team* class in the ontology are part-of instances of *Department* class, which in turn are linked by the same relation with instances of *Enterprise* class, and being part-of transitive, we derive that instances of *Team* are part-of instances of *Enterprise*.

As a consequence, the `OrganizationDim` hierarchy of DM_A is contained in the one of DM_B. Hence, the hierarchy `Person` → `Team` → `Enterprise` is shared by the two DMs, and can be used to perform drill-across queries over both DMs.

A specific goal of this work is to address *measure conflicts* that occur when two measures are associated to different formulas. Differently from other proposals in the Literature, given the explicit formal representation of mathematical formulas of KPIs, our semantic model allows to automatically recognize:

- homonymies, avoiding to handle in the same way two measures with the same name that are semantically not equivalent;
- inconsistencies among formulas.

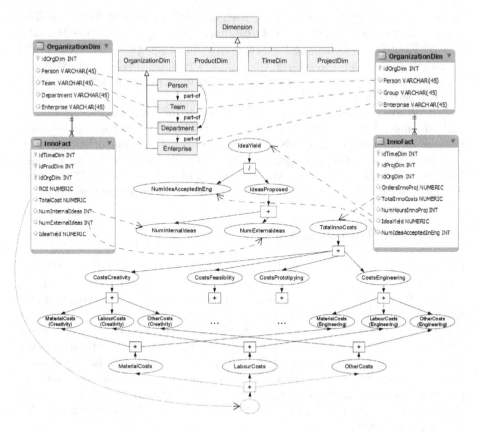

Fig. 3. Mappings between elements in DMs and corresponding concepts in KPIOnto

With respect to the first case, in the example of Section 3 an homonymy occurs between the two measures `IdeaYield`. As a matter of fact, in the DM_A the measure is computed by the formula $IdeaYield_A = \dfrac{IdeasDeveloped}{IdeasProposed}$, while for the DM_B the formula is $IdeaYield_B = \dfrac{NumIdeaAcceptedInEng}{IdeasProposed}$.

Since all instances of class Indicator are declared to be different from each other[2], *IdeasDeveloped* and *NumIdeaAcceptedInEng* denote different indicators in the ontology, and as a consequence *IdeaYield$_A$* and *IdeaYield$_B$* are different as well. Therefore, having the same name but different meanings, the two measures IdeaYields in the DMs are homonyms. As regards the second case of measure conflicts, according to their descriptions in Tables 1 and 2 the two measures

---

[2] In KPIOnto this condition is implemented through the DifferentIndividuals axiom of OWL2, that axiomatises the Unique Name Assumption.

`TotalCost` and `TotalInnoCosts` have the same meaning. However, an inconsistency can be identified between their formulas:

DM$_A$: $TotalCost = MaterialsCosts + LabourCosts + OtherCosts$
DM$_B$: $TotalInnoCosts = CostsCreativity + CostsFeasibility + CostsPrototyping + CostsEngineering$

By using formulas in the ontology we have that `MaterialsCosts` is the sum of costs related to materials of the four phases of an innovation project[3], and the same holds true for `LabourCosts` and `OtherCosts` (see Figure 3). Furthermore, costs of each phase is given as the sum of costs of materials, labour and other for the given phase. As a consequence, it is straightforward to derive that the formulas for `TotalCost` and `TotalInnoCosts`, although syntactically different, are mathematically equivalent. Hence, the two measures can be mapped to the same indicator in the ontology.

The proposed semantic model allows to extract also information that is not explicitly provided by schemas of DMs. Besides the application to the problem of integration of heterogeneous Data Marts, this approach can be also applied to the execution of drill-across queries. In both cases the output is a new view over the whole data warehouse: while a new integrated Data Mart can be considered a materialized view, a drill-across generates a virtual view. To provide an example, a drill-across query can be used to extract the value of orders related to innovation projects (i.e. *TotalOrdersRelatedInnovationProjects*), which is directly provided only by one enterprise, or the number of ideas proposed (i.e. *IdeasProposed*), that is not given in any Data Mart. In the following, we discuss this second example, as it is more general.

Let us assume that the two SMEs are working on a joint innovation project called P. During the collaboration the two enterprise have continued to collect KPIs as represented in DM$_A$ and DM$_B$, without altering their policies for data sharing and their information systems. At VIF level, SMEs want to analyse the values of *IdeasProposed* for the whole project P and for each `Month`, without providing further details about organization (i.e. at maximum level of the `OrganizationDim`). In order to simplify the description, we introduce the following notation for a multidimensional query MQ:

$$MQ = < \{I, L, M, \sigma, S\} >$$

where I is the set $\{i_1, \ldots, i_n\}$ of requested KPIs, L is the set $\{l_1, \ldots, l_m\}$ of requested levels, M the set $\{m1, \ldots, m_m\}$ of members on which to filter, σ is an optional boolean filtering condition, and S is the source Data Mart. While M works on members, the filter σ defines a condition on other elements of the DM: both descriptive attributes of dimensional schema (e.g. *Budget>50K*) and values of measures (e.g. *NumInternalIdeas<NumExternalIdeas*). Hence, the previous query at VIF level becomes:

$$MQ = <\{IdeasProposed\}, \{Product, Month\}, \{Product='P'\}, TRUE, VIF>$$

---

[3] In BIVEE they are named Creativity, Feasibility, Prototyping, Engineering.

In order to answer the query, we proceed as follows:

1. From the ontology, we obtain that the aggregation function of *IdeasProposed* is *SUM* along all dimensions. Hence, given the additivity of the measure, the query can be rewritten as follows:
   $MQ = MQ_A + MQ_B$, where:
   MQ_A =<{IdeasProposed},{Product,Month},{Product='P'},TRUE,DM_A>
   MQ_B =<{IdeasProposed},{Product,Month},{Product='P'},TRUE,DM_B>

2. From the formula of *IdeasProposed* in the ontology (see also Figure 3), MQ_A becomes:
   MQ_A =< {$NumInternalIdeas + NumExternalIdeas$},{Product, Month}, {Product='P'},TRUE,DM_A>

3. By using reasoning services, we infer a new formula for *IdeasProposed*, which is built on measures provided in DM_B, and allow us to rewrite MQ_B:
   MQ_B =< {$\dfrac{NumIdeaAcceptedInEng}{IdeaYield}$},{Product,Month},
   {Product='P'},TRUE,DM_B>

6 Conclusion

In this paper we discussed a preliminary work on an ontology-based approach for supporting the reconciliation of heterogeneous Data Marts in the context of Virtual Innovation Factories, in which collaborating partners share some data in order to achieve a common innovation project. We analysed the various types of conflicts occurring in Data Mart integration, and presented a strategy for reconciliation of conflicts related to measures, that in our context refer to KPIs measuring parameters of an innovation projects. Unlike other solutions in the Literature, the usage of a semantic description of KPIs and their formulas, together with the reasoning functionalities, allows to recognize both homonymies among measures, and algebraic equivalences/inconsistencies among formulas.

Although the approach described herein is focused on reconciliation, it can be extended with the aim to recognize also similarities among indicators that have different but structurally similar formulas, e.g. $X * Y$ and $X * Y + c$. Further investigation will also be devoted to consider other typologies of conflicts that may occur among indicators with the same formula but with different descriptive properties. For instance, the conflict related to different sets of dimensions for the same indicator can be reconciliated by aggregating at the highest level those dimensions that are not in common.

Within the BIVEE project, 356 KPIs (of which 281 compound and 75 atomic) have been represented so far according to the model described in this paper. The evaluation of complexity and completeness issues of the reasoning functionalities in this real-world context will be topic of future work.

References

1. Chesbrough, H.: Open Innovation: The New Imperative for Creating and Profiting from Technology. Harvard Business Press, Boston (2003)
2. Diamantini, C., Potena, D., Proietti, M., Smith, F., Storti, E., Taglino, F.: A semantic framework for knowledge management in virtual innovation factories. Int. J. Inf. Syst. Model. Des. 4, 70–92 (2013)
3. Torlone, R.: Two approaches to the integration of heterogeneous data warehouses. Distrib. Parallel Databases 23, 69–97 (2008)
4. Tseng, F.S., Chen, C.W.: Integrating heterogeneous data warehouses using XML technologies. J. Inf. Sci. 31, 209–229 (2005)
5. Niemi, T., Toivonen, S., Niinimki, M., Nummenmaa, J.: Ontologies with semantic web/grid in data integration for OLAP. Int. J. Semantic Web Inf. Syst. 3, 25–49 (2007)
6. Golfarelli, M., Mandreoli, F., Penzo, W., Rizzi, S., Turricchia, E.: OLAP query reformulation in peer-to-peer data warehousing. Information Systems 37, 393–411 (2012)
7. del Río-Ortega, A., Resinas, M., Cabanillas, C., Ruiz-Cortés, A.: On the definition and design-time analysis of process performance indicators. Information Systems 38, 470–490 (2013)
8. Barone, D., Jiang, L., Amyot, D., Mylopoulos, J.: Reasoning with key performance indicators. In: Johannesson, P., Krogstie, J., Opdahl, A.L. (eds.) PoEM 2011. LNBIP, vol. 92, pp. 82–96. Springer, Heidelberg (2011)
9. del-Río-Ortega, A., Resinas, M., Ruiz-Cortés, A.: Defining process performance indicators: An ontological approach. In: Meersman, R., Dillon, T.S., Herrero, P. (eds.) OTM 2010, Part I. LNCS, vol. 6426, pp. 555–572. Springer, Heidelberg (2010)
10. Diamantini, C., Potena, D.: Data mart integration at measure level. In: De Marco, M., Te'eni, D., Albano, V., Za, S. (eds.) Information Systems: Crossroads for Organization, Management, Accounting and Engineering, pp. 123–131. Physica-Verlag HD (2012)
11. Value-Chain Group: Value reference model (VRM), http://www.value-chain.org/en/cms/1960
12. Kimball, R., Ross, M.: The Data Warehouse Toolkit: The Complete Guide to Dimensional Modeling, 2nd edn. John Wiley & Sons, Inc., New York (2002)
13. Neumayr, B., Schrefl, M.: Multi-level conceptual modeling and OWL. In: Heuser, C.A., Pernul, G. (eds.) ER 2009 Workshops. LNCS, vol. 5833, pp. 189–199. Springer, Heidelberg (2009)
14. Ausbrooks, R., Carlisle, S.B.D., Chavchanidze, G., Dalmas, S., Devitt, S., Diaz, A., Dooley, S., Hunter, R., Ion, P., Kohlhase, M.: et al.: Mathematical markup language (MathML) version 3.0. w3c working draft of 24. September 2009 World Wide Web Consortium (2009)
15. Buswell, S., Caprotti, O., Carlisle, D.P., Dewar, M.C., Gaetano, M., Kohlhase, M.: The open math standard. Technical report, version 2.0. The Open Math Society (2004), http://www.openmath.org/standard/om20
16. Diamantini, C., Potena, D., Storti, E.: A logic-based formalization of KPIs for virtual enterprises. In: Franch, X., Soffer, P. (eds.) CAiSE Workshops 2013. LNBIP, vol. 148, pp. 274–285. Springer, Heidelberg (2013)
17. Doan, A., Halevy, A.Y.: Semantic-integration research in the database community. AI Mag. 26, 83–94 (2005)

Requirements Refinement and Exploration of Architecture for Security and Other NFRs

Takao Okubo[1], Nobukazu Yoshioka[2], and Haruhiko Kaiya[3]

[1] Institute of Information Security, 2-14-1 Tsuruyamachi,
Kanagawa-ku, Yokohama, Japan
[2] National Institute of Informatics, 2-1-2 Hitotsubashi, Chiyoda-ku, Tokyo, Japan
[3] Kanagawa University, 2946 Tsuchiya, Hiratsuka-shi, Kanagawa-ken, Japan

Abstract. Earlier software architecture design is essential particularly when it comes to security concerns, since security risks, requirements and architectures are all closely interrelated and interacting. We have proposed the security driven twin peaks method with a mutual refinement of the requirements, and architectures. However, there are multiple alternatives to an architecture design for initial requirements, and their choices depend on non-functional requirements (NFRs), such as security, performance, and costs which have a big impact on the quality of the software. We propose a new method called TPM-SA2 to avoid any back-track in refinement. Each architectural alternative in TPM-SA2 is refined so that it aligns with the requirements. For each refinement, the requirements can be updated vice versa. TPM-SA2 enables us to predict the impacts on the NFRs by each candidate for the architecture, and choose the most appropriate one with respect to the impact. As a result, we can define the requirements and architectures, and estimated the development costs earlier than ever.

1 Introduction

Security requirements analyses are often caught in a dilemma. Although precise and comprehensive threat analysis needs architectural design in detail, it is hard to obtain decomposed architectural design specification in the early requirement analysis stage. The pure water fall model of software development is not enough, so that we need to elaborate on the security requirements and the architecture simultaneously. The twin peaks model [12] is a promising alternative for such development styles involved in security requirements analysis.

In addition, it is also difficult to simultaneously consider several kinds of non-functional requirements for selecting an appropriate software architecture. There is a trade-off among different non-functional requirements, e.g., security may affect the performance and usability, and the performance is generally related to the scalability. We need to find suitable architectures to meet such non-functional requirements with priority.

We have proposed a concept of security oriented twin peaks model, called the Twin Peaks Model application for Security Analysis (TPM-SA) [14].

L. Iliadis, M. Papazoglou, and K. Pohl (Eds.): CAiSE 2014 Workshops, LNBIP 178, pp. 286–298, 2014.
© Springer International Publishing Switzerland 2014

Although we evaluated our method using some examples in our previous work, the evaluation revealed the following practical issues:

1. The boundary between the requirements and the design is unclear;
2. Although there are generally two or more architectural alternatives, it is hard to select the best architecture without conducting a detailed design analysis;
3. There is no criterion for evaluating the architectural alternatives; and
4. We need a method for considering other non-functional requirements such as the performance requirements.

Thus we proposed a new requirements analysis method called TPM-SA2 (Twin-Peaks Model application for Security Analysis, Square) [15]. We can analyze two or more non-functional requirements and the architecture with a twin peaks model using this method. We can, then, select the best architecture based on an estimation of the impact on the non-functional requirements. In other words, our major contributions are an elicitation process for two or more requirements, and the evaluation framework for the architectural alternatives from the multi-requirements points of views.

In this paper we do detailed analysis and evaluation of our TPM-SA2 with an example of software on a geolocation service.

This paper is organized as follows. Section 2 discusses techniques including our previous work. Section 3 describes our new method based on the Twin Peaks model, and Section 4 illustrates an example to which we applied our method. Section 5 discusses the results from using our method, and Section 6 reviews the related works. Finally, we summarize the paper and discuss our future work.

2   Related Work

This section describes related works on analysis of security requirements and architecture. At first, we introduce our recemt work called TPM-SA, and then compare with other works.

2.1   TPM-SA: Twin Peaks Model for Security Analysis

We proposed mutual refinement process between security requirements and architecture called TPM-SA [14]. TPM-SA is based on the Twin Peaks Model (TPM) [12].

The TPM-SA offers a developing framework for two-level structures for adopting TPM for the security. The first level defines the entire process in the form of a spiral that achieves mutual and stepwise refinement of the security requirements and architecture. The second level defines each cycle of the spiral that requires the detailed steps for the security analysis. The term "architecture" in this paper includes the system structure, software structure, design specifications, infrastructure, middleware, and the programming language.

The security requirements (countermeasure) and the architecture are refined in the spiral flow stages with the iteration of the security analysis and design. This process is assumed to be conducted after the functional requirements have been elicited. Therefore, the inputs for this process are the functional requirements. In the first cycle of the spiral, the functional requirements are the inputs. The first refinement level of the architecture can be assumed from the functional requirements. A security analysis is conducted with the help of the assumed architectural information. It helps in imagining the architecture-specific assets and attacks. As a result, the security requirements are outputs at the first refinement level. In the subsequent cycles, the security requirements that were outputs in the previous cycle are the inputs, and then more refined security requirements and architectures are the outputs. The main motivation of the "refinement" in the TPM-SA is to add some new requirements by taking the architecture into considerations, and adding a new architecture from these requirements. This is the essential difference between the original TPM and Security Twin Peaks [5]. Their refinement mainly focuses on decomposing the already identified goals and requirements, and does not focus on adding new elements.

For the steps in each cycle of the spiral, we classified the artifacts into two groups, "Requirements" and "Architecture". We also classified assets into two groups: Architecture-independent Assets (AIA) and Architecture-specific Assets (ASA).

2.2   Other Works

We use the following criteria for comparing the methods that contribute to simultaneously refining security requirements and architecture.

(C1). A method that enables us to update the requirements and architecture simultaneously.

(C2). A method that can be performed step by step based on the architectural decisions.

(C3). A method that enables us to comprehensively find the security requirements based on the analysis of the architecture independent assets (AIA) in addition to the architecture specific assets (ASA).

(C4). A method that enables us to maintain the traceability among the assets, threats, and countermeasures.

(C5). A method that enables us to analyze multiple quality requirements such as the usability, reliability, and security.

(C6). A method that helps us to decide when we may stop refining the requirements and architecture in the early stages of system development, i.e., the requirements definition stage.

(C7). A method that enables us to find and compare several alternatives for refining the requirements and architecture.

Table 1. Comparison of methods based on criteria

method \ criteria	(C1)	(C2)	(C3)	(C4)	(C5)	(C6)	(C7)
TPM-SA2	√	√	√	√	√	√	√
TMP-SA	√	√	√	√			
GORA				√	√		
KB				√	√		
EXP			√				
PATTERN				√			
SQUARE		√		√			
STP	√	√		√			
LISA	√						
ATAM		√		√			

The acronyms in Table 1 denote the following methods.

- TPM-SA2: Method proposed in this paper.
- TMP-SA: Previous version of our method for refining simultaneously the security requirements and architecture [14].
- GORA: Goal-oriented requirements analysis [8] [9] [11] [18].
- KB: Knowledge based approaches [17] [6].
- EXP: Exploring exceptions [9] [4].
- PATTERN: Pattern-based approaches [2] [3].
- SQUARE: System Quality Requirements Engineering [10].
- STP: Security twin peaks model [5].
- LISA: Integration of requirements and design decisions using architectural representation [19].
- ATAM: Architecture Tradeoff Analysis Method [1] [7].

As listed in Table 1, TPM-SA2 is developed to meet the fifth, sixth and seventh criteria above.

3   Revised TPM-SA: TPM-SA2

We have proposed a security driven refinement method for the requirements and architecture that enables for the early and appropriate architecture selection from multiple alternatives [15]. The reason why we mainly focused on security is that it has greater, more unintended and unavoidable impacts on the software. Most of the other NFRs like the usability and performance are predictable, and if some problems are found in the later stage they may be acceptable. However, most of the security problems found in the later stages are critical and force the stakeholders to remedy them.

3.1   Steps in TPM-SA2

TPM-SA2 lets the developers predict the refined requirements and architectural designs in the first refinement level. It also lets them estimate the impact on the

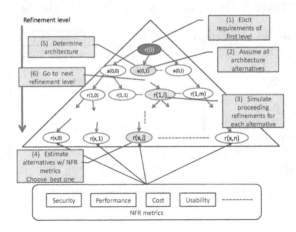

Fig. 1. Prediction Process in TPM-SA2

NFRs for each alternative. This step provides a solution to the criteria (expressly (C5)-(C7)) mentioned in Section 2.2; a reduction of redundant backtracking in refinements and the consideration of other NFRs.

for (C5). With TPM-SA2 analysts can estimate multiple NFRs for each designs.
for (C6). TPM-SA2 provides analysts rough estimate of NFR impacts for each architecture at the requirements analysis stage.
for(C7). With TPM-SA2 analysts can compare the architecture choices with estimating the NFRs impacts.

The inputs and outputs of TPM-SA2 are as follows:

- Inputs: functional requirements and non-functional requirements (NFRs). The NFRs consist of the quality requirements, design and architectural constraints.
- Outputs: refined requirements and intended architecture.

Figure 1 indicates the process for predicting in the architecture assumption steps of TPM-SA2. The process can provide analysts a rough estimate of the effect of architectural choices on security, NFRs and costs in advance.

Step 1). Obtain the requirements from the first refinement level 0 ($r(0)$). The inputs above are these requirements.
Step 2). Assume the architectural alternatives $a(0,0)$, $a(0,1)$,.. $a(0,n)$ which meet $r(0)$. Steps 1) and 2) are the preparation steps of the prediction process.
Step 3). Apply the mutual refinement in TPM-SA to each alternative. TMP-SA is explained in 2.1. Since each alternative can cause refinement and/or modification of $r(0,0)$, each alternative is related to different requirements.

Step 4). Evaluate each architectural alternative in the final level x with respect to the NFRs for the requirements corresponding to the alternative. The evaluation criteria such as the metrics should be prepared for each NFR. Choose the best one after the evaluation. The developer will follow the branch path that contains the leaf with the best NFR value in the following refinement steps.

Step 5). Determine the architecture that includes the best leaf chosen in Step 4) within its branch path.

Each path from $r(0)$ to $r(x, i)$ in Figure 1 corresponds to the mutual refinement of the requirements and architectural alternative. Our previous method TPM-SA [14] can be used for this refinement.

3.2   Prioritizing Alternatives with Respect to NFRs

As to the steps in Section 3.1, several different architectural alternatives are obtained. For each architectural alternative, initial requirements are respectively refined and/or updated. We then prioritize these alternatives with respect to the NFRs specified in the initial version of the requirements. If we cannot prioritize the alternatives with respect to one NFR, we have to continue the refinement of the architecture and requirements according to the steps in Section 3.1. We may stop the refinement when we can perform the prioritization.

Since each NFR has different criteria for the prioritization, we first prioritize the alternatives with respect to each NFR. The experts for each NFR have to provide its criteria. For example, a criterion about the learnability can be defined based on the expected scenarios for system usage, and the characteristics of an architecture that partially provides the effects to such scenarios. The usability experts have to give such criterion based on their expertise. When this method is applied to the improvement of existing systems and the costs for the development is crucial, we can use the impact analysis [13] as a criterion for the costs. A prioritization with respect to a NFR normally differs from a prioritization with respect to another. For example, architecture X is preferred to architecture Y with respect to the usability. However, Y is preferred to X with respect to the performance.

If a NFR is more important than the others, we can simply use its criteria for prioritizing the architectural alternatives. If several NFRs are important, we have to combine the results of their prioritizations so that we can simultaneously take them into account. We can use AHP technique [16] for the combination of several different prioritizations.

4   Illustrative Example: Geolocation Service

In this section we illustrate the application of TPM-SA2 to a system to clarify how it works and how effective it is.

4.1 First-Level Requirements

We focus on a context-aware system that provides services to users according to their context, e.g., geolocation. Some examples of the services are recommending good restaurants that are close to users or finding vacant car parks. The first-level requirements for the system are as follows:

- Functional requirements (FRs)
  - F1: Users can search the services provided according to the location and time, and several services are recommended.
  - F2: Users can rank the recommended services according to their preferences.
  - F3: Users can rank the services according to the current trend.
  - F4: Users can select some of the services.
- Non-functional requirements (NFRs)
  - Q1: The entire FRs must be securely performed. (security)
  - Q2: The entire FRs must be quickly performed. (performance)
  - Q3: The development costs of entire FRs should be low. (cost)
  - Q4: The system will be in operation as soon as possible. (time of delivery)
  - Q5: Users can easily use the FRs. (usability)

Even for the first-level requirements above, there are several assets to be threatened as follows:

- A1: Recommended services.
- A2: Ranking based on personal preferences, time and location.
- A3: Ranking based on the trend.
- A4: Chosen services.

These assets can be regarded as architecture-independent assets (AIAs) in TPM-SA. However, privacy information such as the person's name, age, and gender are not always an asset based on the first-level requirements because the traceability between the person and his/her private information is not always required in these requirements. They are actually candidates for the architecture-specific assets (ASAs) because some architectural types involve them in the refined requirements.

4.2 Exploring Alternatives

By the threat analysis for the first-level requirements, the following threats can be identified.

- Tampering of the service choices
- Tampering of the service ranking information
- Tampering of the services that a user selected

On the other hand, there are two major choices at architecture level 0 for the first-level requirements.

Table 2. Architectural alternatives

level 0	1	2	3
mobile	anonymous (a1)		
	user identification	by user ID, password	rich client (a2)
			cloud (a3)
		by terminal id	rich client (a4)
			cloud (a5)
ubiquitous	setting new terminals and sensors	anonymous (a6)	
		user identification	by id cards, passwords (a7)
			by biometrics (a8)
	using existing terminals (such as vending machines)	anonymous (a9)	

1. Mobile devices and their network infrastructure Many people today have their own smartphones, which provide a powerful functionality for storing data, communicating with servers, identifying the current location and time, and so on. Most of the requirements can be mainly implemented on the smartphones using various sensors.
2. Ubiquitous infrastructure like in Oulu city[1] In contrast to the mobile devices infrastructures, public devices are pre-located all over the city within this infrastructure. The users thus do not have to bring their own devices, but can use the system based on the requirements above. In this case, most of the requirements are implemented on the servers.

The requirements may need to be modified, added, or even deleted according to the architectural choice. Architectural designs may also be affected by the change in requirements. For example, the first requirements do not require the identification of the users. However, some architecture such as smartphones might bring about new requirements for user identification because they are closely linked to their owners and their personal information. If the architectural alternatives containing user identification and authorization ((a2)-(a5)) are chosen, the software has to be able to protect the new assets: the user credentials and privacy data. The following threats arise according to the assets.

- The leakage of the users' private sensor data such as the time and geolocation
- The leakage of the selected services that might cause a violation of the users' privacy

Therefore, most cost is needed for implementing the protection of these assets in the alternatives because of the potential threats. More cost is needed for the authentication with user IDs and passwords ((a2), (a3)), while authentication based on a terminal id needs less cost ((a4), (a5)), but contains higher security risks.

---

[1] http://www.ubioulu.fi/en/home

There are other architectural choices: rich client type ((a2), (a4)) or server type (a3), (a5)). The former mainly needs implementation on clients systems, and the latter mainly on servers. Although the rich client type usually provides better usability than the server type, it brings about other assets from the client environments and other protection costs as well.

4.3   TMP-SA in an Alternative

Since each alternative is derived based on the TMP-SA, we will explain how to concretely derive one alternative. We focus on alternative (a3) in Table 2 because it is threatened more often than the others.

Based on the infrastructure for mobile devices, the location information becomes ASA because it could be tampered with while being sent. We don't have to worry about the time because the system will have its own clock. In addition, the communication paths also become ASA because all the information is sent and received via wireless communications. As a result, we find the following ASAs at level 0 in the mobile infrastructure listed in Table 2.

- A5: Location information
- A6: Communication paths

To protect these new assets, we need the following functional and non-functional security requirements as countermeasures.

- F5: Location will be identified.
- F6: Devices will communicate with the system.
- Q6: F5 will be accurately achieved.
- Q7: F6 will be achieved in integrity.

User identification is useful for F2 because the users' preferences can be registered in advance. It is also useful for F3 because the system can accurately identify the trend. Without the user identification, some malicious users may intentionally and repeatedly select some specific services to make them more popular than the facts. The following asset is thus added at level 1 (a3) in Table 2.

- A7: User identification

Of course, others must not reuse A7. Based on this asset, the following requirements are elicited.

- F7: The system will accept the user identification, and authorize the user.
- Q8: F7 is confidentially achieved.

In the same way, the following assets and requirements are identified and elicited at level 2 (a3).

- A7': Issuable user identification.
- F8: The system will issue the user identification.
- Q9: F8 will be identifiably achieved.

Table 3. Criteria weight

security	0.140
performance	0.047
usability	0.196
cost / time of delivery	0.616

Table 4. Estimation results using AHP

id	security	performance	usability	cost / time of delivery	total
(a1)	0.0617	0.0245	0.0075	0.2553	0.3491
(a2)	0.0122	0.0101	0.0400	0.0523	0.1146
(a3)	0.0457	0.0026	0.0115	0.0761	0.1359
(a4)	0.0048	0.0081	0.1076	0.0630	0.1835
(a5)	0.0159	0.0022	0.0294	0.1694	0.2169

Finally, we have the following at level 3 (a3).

- A8: Personal preferences registered in advance.
- F8: Personal preferences will be registered and updated.
- Q10: F8 will be achieved in integrity.

We have three assets, four functional requirements and five non-functional requirements in addition to the first-level requirements. In the other alternatives listed in Table 2, some of them do not have to be taken into account. For example, A7', F8, and Q9 are out of the scope in (a4) and (a5) because the terminal ID cannot be issued by the system.

4.4 Prioritization

With our prediction method, nine architectural alternatives listed in Table 2 can be assumed. We prioritized the NFRs based on an assumption of a certain development project in which the priority order is the cost, security, usability and performance. Then, we estimated the alternatives (a1)-(a9) using analytic hierarchy process (AHP) [16]. AHP is a method for decision making based on mathematics and psychology. With AHP, analysts determine weights for every decisions and its factors. The criteria weights computed are listed in Table 3.

We eliminated (a6)-(a9) because they require the social ubiquitous infrastructure, which the system cannot solve by itself. The evaluation results for the other five alternatives is described in Table 4. Unless the system needs the user identification, (a1) is the most appropriate decision. If it requires user identification, (a4) is the best choice.

5   Discussion

As shown in Section 4, one of the advantages of TPM-SA2 is that the developers can estimate and compare the impact of multiple architectural alternatives and decide on the best one in the very early levels of refinement. Another advantage over TPM-SA is that with TPM-SA2 developers consider not only the security but also other NFRs such as the performance, cost, and usability. As the "security" column of Table 4 indicates, if the developers evaluate only the security using TPM-SA, the second order of priority is (a3). But it may not meet other NFRs such as the cost. With TPM-SA2, the second order is (a5) using evaluation of multiple NFRs according to the stakeholders' preference.

Our TPM-SA with prediction has some drawbacks. One of them is that the prediction step in the first level is heavy and time-consuming since it requires the traversal of all the branches through all the refinement levels. However, the following information might reduce the deeper traversal from some nodes.

- Past estimation results
  This knowledge is particularly useful for the enhancement of existing software. If there is an architectural design that is the same as that that the design developers are assuming through the prediction process, and the NFR values have already been estimated, and the developers can use these values instead of proceeding into the deeper levels.
- NFR patterns
  Patterns that contain sets of NFR values related to certain architectural designs are also useful. If the assumed architectural alternative matches one of the NFR patterns, the developers can use the values of the pattern such as the past estimation results.

6   Conclusion

We proposed a new method called TPM-SA2 that elicits non-functional requirements and an architecture based on the Twin Peaks Model. In detail, we at first specify the concerns about not only the security requirements but also the other non-functional requirements with the architectural alternatives. We can, then, select the best architecture based on estimation of the impact on the non-functional requirements. TPM-SA2 enables us to explore the non-functional requirements step by step to make adequate architectural decisions from the multi-non-functional requirements' points of view. We applied our method to an application to evaluate it. The results of the evaluations illustrated that our method is especially effective for the iterative development.

Our future work includes developing a tool that supports our methods. Since TPM-SA2 uses domain knowledge concerning the non-functional requirements and expected architectural decisions, such issues can be automatically aligned with the currently elicited security requirements using the domain ontology. Mining architecture patterns which can help estimating security and costs and pruning, is also the future work In addition, non-functional requirements elicitation process can be automatically managed according to the obstacles. The non-functional requirements sometimes conflict with other kinds of non-functional requirements. Therefore, we have to improve our TPM-SA2 to detect such conflicts to resolve them (semi-)automatically. We also need to apply TPM-SA2 to realistic projects to clarity its advantages and limitations.

References

1. Bass, L., Clements, P., Kazman, R.: Software Architecture in Practice, 2nd edn. Addison-Wesley (2003)
2. Fernandez, E.B.: Security patterns and secure systems design. In: Bondavalli, A., Brasileiro, F., Rajsbaum, S. (eds.) LADC 2007. LNCS, vol. 4746, pp. 233–234. Springer, Heidelberg (2007)
3. Ferraz, F.S., Assad, R.E., de Lemos Meira, S.R.: Relating security requirements and design patterns: Reducing security requirements implementation impacts with design patterns. In: ICSEA, pp. 9–14 (2009)
4. Guo, Z., Zeckzer, D., Liggesmeyer, P., Mackel, O.: Identification of security-safety requirements for the outdoor robot ravon using safety analysis techniques. In: International Conference on Software Engineering Advances, pp. 508–513 (2010)
5. Heyman, T., Yskout, K., Scandariato, R., Schmidt, H., Yu, Y.: The security twin peaks. In: Erlingsson, Ú., Wieringa, R., Zannone, N. (eds.) ESSoS 2011. LNCS, vol. 6542, pp. 167–180. Springer, Heidelberg (2011)
6. Houmb, S.H., Islam, S., Knauss, E., Jürjens, J., Schneider, K.: Eliciting security requirements and tracing them to design: An integration of common criteria, heuristics, and umlsec. Requir. Eng. 15(1), 63–93 (2010)
7. Kazman, R., Klein, M.H., Barbacci, M., Longstaff, T.A., Lipson, H.F., Carrière, S.J.: The architecture tradeoff analysis method. In: ICECCS, pp. 68–78 (1998)
8. van Lamsweerde, A.: Elaborating security requirements by construction of intentional anti-models. In: ICSE, pp. 148–157 (2004)
9. Liu, L., Yu, E.S.K., Mylopoulos, J.: Secure-i*: Engineering secure software systems through social analysis. Int. J. Software and Informatics 3(1), 89–120 (2009)
10. Mead, N.R., Hough, E., Stehney, T.: Security quality requirements engineering (square) methodology. Tech. Rep. CMU/SEI-2005-TR-009, Software Engineering Institute, Carnegie Mellon University (2005)
11. Mouratidis, H., Giorgini, P.: Secure tropos: A security-oriented extension of the tropos methodology. International Journal of Software Engineering and Knowledge Engineering 17(2), 285–309 (2007)
12. Nuseibeh, B.: Weaving together requirements and architectures. IEEE Computer 34(3), 115–117 (2001)
13. Okubo, T., Kaiya, H., Yoshioka, N.: Analyzing impacts on software enhancement caused by security design alternatives with patterns. IJSSE 3(1), 37–61 (2012)
14. Okubo, T., Kaiya, H., Yoshioka, N.: Mutual refinement of security requirements and architecture using twin peaks model. In: COMPSAC Workshops, pp. 367–372 (2012)
15. Okubo, T., Yoshioka, N., Kaiya, H.: Security driven requirements refinement and exploration of architecture with multiple nfr points of view. In: IEEE International Symposium on High Assurance on Software Engineering (HASE) (to be appeared, 2014)

16. Saaty, T.L.: The analytic hierarchy process: planning, priority setting, resource allocation, 2nd edn. RWS, Pittsburgh (1990)
17. Saeki, M., Kaiya, H.: Security requirements elicitation using method weaving and common criteria. In: MoDELS Workshops, pp. 185–196 (2008)
18. Tanabe, D., Uno, K., Akemine, K., Yoshikawa, T., Kaiya, H., Saeki, M.: Supporting requirements change management in goal oriented analysis. In: RE, pp. 3–12 (2008)
19. Weinreich, R., Buchgeher, G.: Integrating requirements and design decisions in architecture representation. In: Babar, M.A., Gorton, I. (eds.) ECSA 2010. LNCS, vol. 6285, pp. 86–101. Springer, Heidelberg (2010)

Cloud Forensics Solutions: A Review

Stavros Simou[1], Christos Kalloniatis[1], Evangelia Kavakli[1], and Stefanos Gritzalis[2]

[1] Cultural Informatics Laboratory, Department of Cultural Technology and Communication,
University of the Aegean, University Hill, GR 81100 Mytilene, Greece
`{SSimou,chkallon}@aegean.gr, kavakli@ct.aegean.gr`
[2] Information and Communication Systems Security Laboratory,
Department of Information and Communications Systems Engineering,
University of the Aegean, GR 83200, Samos, Greece
`sgritz@aegean.gr`

Abstract. Cloud computing technology attracted many Internet users and organizations the past few years and has become one of the hottest topics in IT. However, due to the newly appeared threats and challenges arisen in cloud computing, current methodologies and techniques are not designed for assisting the respective forensic processes in cloud environments. Challenges and issues introduced, require new solutions in cloud forensics. To date, the research conducted in this area concerns mostly the identification of the major challenges in cloud forensics. This paper focuses on the identification of the available technical solutions addressed in the respective literature that have an applicability on cloud computing. Furthermore it matches the identified solutions with the respective challenges already mentioned in the respective literature. Specifically, it summarizes the methods and the proposed solutions used to conduct an investigation, in comparison to the respective cloud challenges and finally it highlights the open problems in the area of cloud forensics.

Keywords: Cloud Computing, Cloud Forensics, Cloud Forensics Challenges, Cloud Forensics Solutions, Review.

1   Introduction

In recent years, the traditional computer technology has been transformed into new forms of services dictated by Internet changes. Cloud computing has dominated our world giving a different perspective and new horizons opened to companies and organizations with virtualized services providing, mostly, flexibility, elasticity and on-demand service. Complimentary to the above, the cost reduction along with the benefit of eliminating training and maintenance made cloud very popular. However, the development of this new technology attracted a number of people to carry out criminal activities leaving almost no evidence behind.

Due to the distributed and virtualized environment, cloud forensics is facing a great deal of challenges in comparison to traditional forensics. The ability to conduct a proper cloud forensic investigation depends on the methods and tools used to acquire digital evidence. Unfortunately, current methods and tools do not meet the standards

L. Iliadis, M. Papazoglou, and K. Pohl (Eds.): CAiSE 2014 Workshops, LNBIP 178, pp. 299–309, 2014.
© Springer International Publishing Switzerland 2014

on cloud computing [1], [2], [3], [4]. Many authors have dealt with these challenges and proposed new solutions and frameworks to overcome the problems.

Within this work, we summarize the challenges and issues raised in cloud computing environments regarding the cloud forensics process. We, then, explore the cloud forensic solutions addressed to the challenges and a summary of these findings is presented based on a detailed literature review. Specifically the paper is organized as follows. In section 2 a table summarizing the challenges identified in cloud forensics is presented. Section 3 presents the current cloud forensic solutions addressed based on the identified challenges. Finally, section 4 concludes the paper by presenting a categorization of the results and raises future research issues derived from this review.

Since cloud forensics is a newly developed research area our main and primary fo-cus was to conduct a thorough analysis of the respective literature in order to present an analytic review of the existing solutions regarding the challenges in the respective field. It is not in the scope of this paper to cover the quality of the audit control. The starting point of the review was some certain scientific papers on cloud forensic issues and we broadened our review to the related work referenced. After studying these papers our review broadened to less related academic reports and papers from the field of cloud computing.

2   Cloud Forensic Challenges

Although cloud computing has been introduced and used in the market enough years, the cloud forensics is still at its infancy. There are still many open issues and challenges to be explored. Past years many researchers have tried to identify the challenges and the work produced by some of them is accurate and well documented. The cloud forensics challenges identified from the review conducted in the respective area can be categorized into identification stage, preservation and collection stage, examination and analysis stage, and presentation stage. Table 1 summarizes the challenges identified in the three service models [5]:

Table 1. Cloud Forensics Challenges

Cloud Forensic Challenges / Stage	Applicable to		
	IaaS	PaaS	SaaS
Identification			
Access to evidence in logs	partly	√	√
Physical inaccessibility	√	√	√
Volatile data	√	X	X
Client side identification	√	X	√
Dependence on CSP - Trust	√	√	√
Service Level Agreement (SLA)	√	√	√
Preservation - Collection			
Integrity and stability	√	√	√
Privacy	X	√	√

Table 1. (*Continued.*)

Time synchronization	√	√	√
Internal Staffing	√	√	√
Chain of custody	√	√	√
Imaging	X	√	√
Bandwidth limitation	√	X	X
Multi-jurisdiction - collaboration	√	√	√
Multi-tenancy	√	√	√
Examination – Analysis			
Lack of forensic tools	√	√	√
Volume of data	X	√	√
Encryption	√	√	√
Reconstruction	√	√	√
Unification of log formats	√	√	√
Identity	√	√	√
Presentation			
Complexity of testimony	√	√	√
Documentation	√	√	√
Uncategorised			
Compliance issues	√	√	√

Some may consider that certain of the above challenges are not part of the cloud forensics process/stage as they regard them input to the forensic process itself. Still, most of the researchers identified in the review [1], [2], [3], [4], argue that all of the challenges referred in Table 1 must be considered as challenges.

3   Current Solutions

After summarizing the cloud forensics challenges this section presents all possible solutions addressing clarified challenges, identified from an analytical review conducted in the respective area. In the following section identified solutions are presented categorized per challenge.

3.1   Access to Evidence in Logs

This challenge is the most important one in cloud forensics and is referred from every researcher that deals with the respective field. Many of them have come up with solutions such as Sang [6], who proposed a log-based model which can help to reduce the complexity of forensic for non-repudiation of behaviors on cloud. He proposes that we should keep another log locally and synchronously, so we can use it to check the activities on SaaS cloud without the CSP's interference. The local log module will use information such as unique id and timestamp on the log record locally. HASH code will be also used to detect modification on the log files. In PaaS, the CSPs should supply a log module on PaaS to the third-party in order to create a customized log module, for both of the consumer side and the cloud side.

In PaaS, since the customers have full control on their application over a prepared API, system states and specific application logs can be extracted. Birk et al. [1] proposed a logging mechanism which automatically sign and encrypt the log information before its transfer to a central logging server under the control of the customer. This mechanism will prevent potential eavesdroppers from being able to view and alter log data information on the way to the logging server.

Solving the cloud logging problems Marty [7] proposed a log management architecture that involves three steps: enable logging on all infrastructure components to collect logs from, setup and configure log transport and finally tune log sources to make sure we get the right type of logs and the right details collected. He states that every log entry should log what happened, when it happened, who triggered the event and why it happened. According to this, the minimum fields need to be present in every log record are: Timestamp, Application, User, Session ID, Severity, Reason and Categorization. He also recommends an application on how log entries should be structured. At the end an application logging infrastructure at SaaS company was implemented using application components such as Django, JavaScript, Apache, MySQL, Operating system and Java Backend. Zawoad et al. [2] mentioned that although the advantages to this approach are several, the specific work does not provide any solution about logging network usage, file metadata, process usage and many other evidence, which are important for forensic investigation in IaaS and PaaS.

Damshenas et al. [8] suggested a solution in PaaS, to prepare an API to extract relevant status data of the system, limited by the data related to the client only. In SaaS, depends on the interface, he proposed to implement the feature to check the basic logs and status of the client's usage. The above features should provide read-only access only and demands for specific log and system status manager running as a cloud service.

According to Zafarullah et al. [9] logging standards should be developed, which ensure generation and retention of logs and a log management system that collects and correlates logs. A cloud computing environment was setup using Eucalyptus. Using Snort, Syslog and Log Analyzer (e.g. Sawmill) Eucalyptus behavior was monitored and all internal and external interaction of Eucalyptus was logged. Observing the log entries were generated by the Eucalyptus, not only the attacker's IP address was recorded, but also details on number of http requests along with timestamps, http requests/responses and fingerprinted attacker's OS & web browser were provided.

3.2   Volatile Data

To overcome the problem of volatile data, live investigation has been used as an alternative approach to dead acquisition. Grispos et al. [3] mentioned that the specific approach enables investigators to gather data that might otherwise be lost if a computer is powered down. On the other side it may increase the amount of information an investigator is able to extract. To address this challenge, Damshenas et al. [8]

proposed the cost to be globalized between CSPs to offer persistent storage device for client's data.

To prevent loss of volatile data, Birk et al. [1] suggested frequent data synchronization between the VM and the persistent storage or a non-cloud based storage. According to Zawoad et al. [2] this solution does not provide any guideline about the procedure and he proposed two possible ways of continuous synchronization. CSPs can provide a continuous synchronization API to customers and CSPs can integrate the synchronization mechanism with every VM and preserve the data within their infrastructure.

3.3   Multi-jurisdiction – Distribution – Collaboration

New regulations have to be developed in order to solve the cross border legislation issue. Biggs et al. [10] proposed an international legislation that will police the internet and cloud computing specifically. Global unity must be established so the investigations on cloud environment to be fast and successful. Grispos et al. [3] suggested that a partial solution to different jurisdictions could be the CSPs to have trained and qualified personnel to perform forensic investigations when needed. According to Ruan et al. [4] and Sibiya et al. [11] international laws should be developed to secure that forensic activities will not breach any laws or regulations under any jurisdiction.

3.4   Client Side Identification

To identify evidence on client's side, Damshenas et al. [8] suggested designing and implementing an application to log all potential evidence on the client's machine. However, they did not provide any methodology about the application and the procedure.

3.5   Dependence on CSP - Trust

In cloud environments, customers have to depend completely on the CSPs, which affect the trust relationship between them. The lack of transparency and trust between CSP's and customers is an issue that Haeberlen [12] was dealt with the accountable cloud. He suggested a basic primitive called AUDIT that an accountable cloud could provide. The idea is that the cloud, records its actions in a tamper evident log, customers can audit the log and check for faults and finally they can use log to construct evidence that a fault has (or not) occurred. When an auditor detects a fault, it can obtain evidence of the fault that can be verified independently by a third party. A TrustCloud framework proposed by Ko et al. [13], which consists of five layers of accountability: System, Data, Workflow, Policies, Laws & Regulations layers. To increase accountability detective approaches used rather than preventive.

Nurmi et al. [14] presented Eucalyptus, an open-source software framework for cloud computing that implements IaaS, which is the answer to the trust relationship between CSPs and customers. A model showing the layers of trust has been introduced by Dykstra et al. [15]. In IaaS, six layers have been established and more layers would have added in the other two cloud models. Each layer requires a different amount of confidence. The further down the stack, the less cumulative trust is required.

3.6   Service Level Agreement

SLAs should include important terms regarding cloud forensic investigations. According to Ruan et al. [4] SLAs should include: Service provided, techniques supported, access granted by the CSP to the customer, trust boundaries, roles and responsibilities between the CSP and the cloud customer, security issues in a multi-jurisdictional environment in terms of legal regulations, confidentiality of customer data, and privacy policies and security issues in a multi-tenant environment in terms of legal regulations, confidentiality of customer data and privacy policies. A well-written SLA between CSP and customer should include the client's privacy policies Damshenas et al. [8].

Biggs et al. [10] proposed SLA's to be robust in order to be effective in combating cybercrime. For example illegal activities such as DDOS etc. should test cloud vendors' systems and procedures and return useful feedback to assist forensic procedures. To overcome the SLA's issue with different and multiple relationships Birk et al. [1] suggested a trusted third-party to audit the security measures provided by the CSP. Finally SLAs' violation is another problem in which Haeberlen [12] proposed the trusted timestamping. Timing information must be added to a tamper-evident log in order to detect the violations.

3.7   Integrity and Stability – Privacy and Multi-Tenancy

To validate the integrity of the evidence Zawoad et al. [2] suggested a digital signature on the collected evidence should be generated and then the signature should be checked. Hegarty et al. [16] developed and implemented a distributed signature detection framework that enables forensic analysis of storage platforms. Based on the meta-data driven data storage model and provenance integrity, in SaaS, Shi et al. [17] presented a multi-tenancy model where the data storage security issue should be mapped as a series of integrity issues of data chunks. To ensure the primitiveness and integrity of the evidence Yan [18] proposed a new cybercrime forensic framework to image the relative records and files absolutely.

Juels et al. [19] explored proofs of retrievability (PORs) in which a prover (i.e. back-up service) can produce a concise proof that a verifier (client) can retrieve a file in its entirety. PORs method and cryptographic techniques can help users to ensure the privacy and integrity of files they retrieve. To preserve the integrity of the data Birk et al. [1] proposed the Trusted Platform Module (TPM) to assure the integrity of a platform. This standard allows a secure storage and detects changes to previous configurations. Damshenas et al. [8] suggested all the issues concerning clients' privacy data should be included in an SLA contract.

3.8   Time Synchronization – Reconstruction

To solve the time zones' problem Damshenas et al. [8] suggested a specific time system (i.e. GMT) to be used on all entities of the cloud, as it brings the benefit of having a logical time pattern. In IaaS, the VM time is under the client's control meaning that all date and times used in logs and other records should be converted to the specific time system.

3.9   Internal Staffing

It is hard to find the right people to work as a team in order to be involved in a cloud investigation. Ruan et al. [4] proposed a solution that involves internal staffing, CSP-customer collaboration and external assistance with specific roles. Individuals of the team must be trained on, law regulations, new methodologies, specialized tools and techniques. According to Chen et al. [20] an investigator should possess the abilities of professional forensics skills such programming, networking etc., co-operating, communicating and negotiating with CSPs and understanding laws and regulations.

3.10   Chain of Custody

Grispos et al. [3] suggested trained and qualified personnel in forensic investigations should be hired by CSPs. When an investigation arises the personnel should begin the chain of custody process which will be passed onto the investigation party. According to Ruan et al. [4] organizational policies and legally binded SLAs need to be written, in which, communications and collaborations regarding forensic activities through the chain of CSPs and customers dependencies should be clearly stated.

3.11   Imaging

To overcome the issue of acquiring forensic image Damshenas et al. [8] proposed to generate a track record of all clients' activities Later on, to generate a forensic image of specific clients all it requires is to check the track record of the client and then copy bit-by-bit stream of all the area the client has accessed to.

3.12   Forensic Tools

Most of the researchers acknowledge that tools need to be developed to identify, collect and analyze forensic data. Juels et al. [19] developed Proofs Of Retrievability (PORs) tool for semi-trusted online archives which guarantees the privacy and the integrity of files. In IaaS, Dykstra et al. [15] recommended the appropriate forensic tool for acquiring cloud-based data is the management plane. This is a web-based point and click interface to manage and monitor the infrastructure. They concluded that it offers the most attractive balance of speed and control with trust option. EnCase and Accessdata FTK tools were also used to acquire evidence and the results were successful, but authors do not recommend them because too much trust is required. Recently, Dykstra et al. [21] designed and implemented a management plane forensic toolkit in a private instantiation of the OpenStack cloud platform (IaaS), which is called Forensic Open-Stack Tools (FROST) – It consists of three new forensic tools and it provides trustworthy forensic acquisition of virtual disks, API logs, and guest firewall logs.

3.13   Volume of Data

A solution to the challenge is to use the public clouds to store the evidence but this method arise new issues from a legal and technical perspective Grispos et al. [3]. The other solution is the adoption of triaging techniques. New methods should be developed to allow only partial recovery of data and they should be according to accepted forensic principles.

3.14 Complexity of Testimony

Wolthusen [22] suggested of using interactive presentation and virtualization environments which allow the exploration of data sets in such a way that a focus on relevant data is possible without engendering the risk of leading questions and investigations.

3.15 Documentation

The documentation of the investigation according to Wolthusen [22] must be presented in a way pointing: possible gaps in the data sets, uncertainties about the semantics and interpretation of data and the limitations of the collection mechanisms alongside the actual data.

3.16 Compliance Issues

According to Birk et al. [1] recommended customers should check their compliance requirements and CSPs services to find out which CSP matches customers' needs. On the other hand CSP should offer as much transparency as possible. Finally a Third Party Auditor could be used acting as a trustee between the customer and the CSP.

4   Discussion

Cloud computing undeniable offers various benefits to the users. However, there are plenty of issues that need to be resolved in order to conduct a proper investigation regarding cloud forensics. In the previous section, we have mentioned several solutions addressed to the challenges proposed by researchers. The problem is that most of them have not been tested in real conditions (i.e. only recently, Dykstra implemented FROST, the first dedicated collection of forensic tools). The above mentioned findings regarding the available solutions for every identified cloud forensics challenge are summarized in table 2. This table summarizes the cloud forensic challenges identified from the review conducted in the respective area and all the researchers' proposed solutions addressed to challenges.

As we can see in table 2 there are some challenges missing and some have been combined with others. This is due to the absence of a solution for a respective challenge or that a solution can satisfy more than one challenge. Even though, forensic investigation in cloud environments has moved forward the past years, there are still open issues to explore. Dependence on CSP is still required in various issues, such as access to log files and trust relationship. Most of the problems rely on the CSPs' point of view. Absence of international standards and regulations cannot establish the global unity which can help to cross the boundaries in multi-jurisdiction and collaboration challenge.

Table 2. Cloud Forensics Solutions

Cloud Forensic Challenges	Solution	Related Work
Access to evidence in logs	Log-based model	[6]
	Logging mechanism	[1]
	Log management architecture	[7]
	Status data extraction and checking	[8]
	Eucalyptus framework	[9]
Volatile data	Live investigation	[3]
	Cost globalization between CSPs	[8]
	Data synchronization	[1]
	Continous synchronization API	[2]
Multi-jurisdiction - collaboration	International legislations and global unity	[10]
	Trained and qualified personnel	[3]
	International laws	[4]
		[11]
Client side identification	Log application	[8]
Dependence on CSP - Trust	Accountable cloud	[12]
	TrustCloud framework	[13]
	Eucalyptus framework	[14]
	Layers of trust model	[15]
Service Level Agreement (SLA)	Well and clear-written terms	[8]
		[4]
	Robust SLAs	[10]
	External auditors	[1]
	Trusted timestamping	[12]
Integrity & stability - Privacy & multi-tenancy	Digital signature	[2]
	Distributed signature detection framework	[16]
	Multi-tenancy model	[17]
	Cybercrime forensic framework	[18]
	Proofs Of Retrievability (PORs)	[19]
	Trusted Platform Module	[1]
	SLA contracts	[8]
Time synchronization - Reconstruction	Unified/specific time system	[8]
Internal Staffing	Team collaboration with wide range of skills	[4]
		[20]
Chain of custody	Trained and qualified personnel	[3]
	Organizational policies and SLAs	[4]

Table 2. (*Continued.*)

Imaging	Track record generator	[8]
	Proofs Of Retrievability (PORs)	[19]
Lack of forensic tools	Management plane	[15]
	Forensic Open-Stack Tools (FROST)	[21]
Volume of data	Public cloud storage	[3]
	Triaging techniques	
Complexity of testimony	Interactive presentation	[22]
Documentation	Targeted/pointed presentation	[22]
Compliance issues	Survey	[1]
	Transparency	
	Third Party Auditor (TPA)	

Unification of log formats is another issue which needs to be solved. All the evidence need to be presented in a court of law in such a way that the jury could understand the complexity of the non-standard data sets. Depending on the volume of data, bandwidth limitation is another issue that needs to be solved, when the time, is a crucial factor to an ongoing investigation. The identity of the user who has been engaged in a criminal act is also an unanswered case.

References

1. Dominik, B., Wegener, C.: Technical issues of forensic investigations in cloud computing environments. In: IEEE Sixth International Workshop on Systematic Approaches to Digital Forensic Engineering (SADFE) 2011. IEEE (2011)
2. Shams, Z., Hasan, R.: Cloud Forensics: A Meta-Study of Challenges, Approaches, and Open Problems. arXiv preprint arXiv:1302.6312 (2013)
3. George, G., Storer, T., Glisson, W.B.: Calm Before the Storm: The Challenges of Cloud. Emerging Digital Forensics Applications for Crime Detection, Prevention, and Security, p. 211 (2013)
4. Ruan, K., Carthy, J., Kechadi, T., Crosbie, M.: Cloud forensics: An overview. Advances in Digital Forensics 7, 35–49 (2011)
5. Simou, S., Kalloniatis, C., Kavakli, E., Gritzalis, S.: Cloud Forensics: Identifying the Major Issues and Challenges. In: Jarke, M., Mylopoulos, J., Quix, C. (eds.) CAiSE 2014 26th International Conference on Advanced Information Systems Engineering. LNCS, Springer, Heidelberg (June 2014)
6. Ting, S.: A Log Based Approach to Make Digital Forensics Easier on Cloud Computing. In: 2013 Third International Conference on Intelligent System Design and Engineering Applications (ISDEA). IEEE (2013)
7. Marty, R.: Cloud application logging for forensics. In: Proceedings of the 2011 ACM Symposium on Applied Computing. ACM (2011)
8. Mohsen, D., Dehghantanha, A., Mahmoud, R., Shamsuddin, S.B.: Forensics investigation challenges in cloud computing environments. In: 2012 International Conference on Cyber Security, Cyber Warfare and Digital Forensic (CyberSec). IEEE (2012)

9. Zafarullah, Z.,Anwar, F., Anwar, Z.: Digital forensics for eucalyptus. In: Frontiers of Information Technology (FIT). IEEE (2011)

10. Biggs, S., Vidalis, S.: Cloud computing: The impact on digital forensic investigations. In: International Conference for Internet Technology and Secured Transactions, ICITST 2009. IEEE (2009)

11. George, S., Venter, H.S., Fogwill, T.: Digital forensic framework for a cloud environment (2012)

12. Haeberlen, A.: A case for the accountable cloud. ACM SIGOPS Operating Systems Review 44(2), 52–57 (2010)

13. Ko, R.K., et al.: TrustCloud: A framework for accountability and trust in cloud computing. In: 2011 IEEE World Congress on Services (SERVICES). IEEE (2011)

14. Nurmi, D., et al.: The eucalyptus open-source cloud-computing system. In: 9th IEEE/ACM International Symposium on Cluster Computing and the Grid, CCGRID 2009. IEEE (2009)

15. Dykstra, J., Sherman, A.T.: Acquiring forensic evidence from infrastructure-as-a-service cloud computing: Exploring and evaluating tools, trust, and techniques. Digital Investigation 9, S90–S98 (2012)

16. Hegarty, R., et al.: Forensic analysis of distributed data in a service oriented computing platform. In: Proceedings of the 10th Annual Postgraduate Symposium on the Convergence of Telecommunications, Networking & Broadcasting, PG Net (2009)

17. Shi, Y., Zhang, K., Li, Q.: A new data integrity verification mechanism for SaaS. In: Wang, F.L., Gong, Z., Luo, X., Lei, J. (eds.) WISM 2010. LNCS, vol. 6318, pp. 236–243. Springer, Heidelberg (2010)

18. Yan, C.: Cybercrime forensic system in cloud computing. In: 2011 International Conference on Image Analysis and Signal Processing (IASP). IEEE (2011)

19. Juels, A., Kaliski Jr., B.S.: PORs: Proofs of retrievability for large files. In: Proceedings of the 14th ACM Conference on Computer and Communications Security. ACM (2007)

20. Chen, G., Du, Y., Qin, P., Du, J.: Suggestions to digital forensics in Cloud computing ERA. In: 2012 3rd IEEE International Conference on Network Infrastructure and Digital Content (IC-NIDC). IEEE (2012)

21. Dykstra, J., Sherman, A.T.: Design and implementation of FROST: Digital forensic tools for the OpenStack cloud computing platform. Digital Investigation 10, S87-S95 (2013)

22. Wolthusen, S.D.: Overcast: Forensic discovery in cloud environments. In: Fifth International Conference on IT Security Incident Management and IT Forensics, IMF 2009. IEEE (2009)

Resolving Policy Conflicts - Integrating Policies from Multiple Authors

Kaniz Fatema[1] and David Chadwick[2]

[1] Irish Center for Cloud Computing & Commerce, University College Cork, Ireland
k.fatema@cs.ucc.ie
[2] University of Kent, Canterbury, Kent, UK
D.W.Chadwick@kent.ac.uk

Abstract. In this paper we show that the static conflict resolution strategy of XACML is not always sufficient to satisfy the policy needs of an organisation where multiple parties provide their own individual policies. Different conflict resolution strategies are often required for different situations. Thus combining one or more sets of policies into a single XACML 'super policy' that is evaluated by a single policy decision point (PDP), cannot always provide the correct authorisation decision, due to the static conflict resolution algorithms that have to be built in. We therefore propose a dynamic conflict resolution strategy that chooses different conflict resolution algorithms based on the authorisation request context. The proposed system receives individual and independent policies, as well as conflict resolution rules, from different policy authors, but instead of combining these into one super policy with static conflict resolution rules, each policy is evaluated separately and the conflicts among their authorisation decisions is dynamically resolved using the conflict resolution algorithm that best matches the authorisation decision request. It further combines the obligations of independent policies returning similar decisions which XACML can't do while keeping each author's policy intact.

Keywords: Dynamic policy conflict resolution, XACML, authorization system, multiple policy authors.

1 Introduction

Attempts to protect the privacy of personal data by including policies from the data subject in an access control system are not new [1-3]. These works mainly focus on how to have policies from the data subject and how to enforce them. One issue that is often ignored is that multiple parties may have policies that contribute to the overall decision of whether personal data can be accessed or not. These parties include: the legal authority, the issuer of the data, the subject of the data and as well as the controller (who is currently holding and controlling the flow of the data processing). A strategy that combines all these policies into a single 'super' policy may not work for all situations. In this paper we give such an example. We propose a dynamic

L. Iliadis, M. Papazoglou, and K. Pohl (Eds.): CAiSE 2014 Workshops, LNBIP 178, pp. 310–321, 2014.
© Springer International Publishing Switzerland 2014

conflict resolution strategy that integrates the decisions of the policy decision point(s) (PDPs) evaluating the polices provided by the various parties.

Using XACML [4, 5], due to its static policy / policy set combining algorithm, it is very hard to integrate policies from multiple parties in a dynamic way, in order to always obtain the correct authorisation decision. Our proposed model allows different policy authorities to provide their individual, independent polices and it will integrate the decisions returned by their PDPs in a dynamic way, according to the authorisation decision request.

2   Use Case

By way of a use case scenario, we consider a university which awards degrees and scholarships and maintains a profile for each student/alumnus containing various personal data such as degree certificates, transcripts, and awarded scholarships. For personal data like degree certificates and transcripts, the university may want to deny access to anyone unless the data subject (i.e. the alumnus) has specifically granted access to the requestor in her policy (for example, she can authorise a potential employer to access her degree certificate). For the scholarship awards, the university may want to publish these on its web site for marketing purposes, unless the data subject (i.e. the student) has specifically requested that the public be denied access to it. Since scholarships are usually regarded as an achievement by students most of them will usually like to be honoured in this way, (and the university might also make it a condition of the scholarship that the award can be published except in exceptional circumstances). In the degree certificate case the conflict resolution rule will be grant overrides, since the issuer's (i.e. the university's) policy denies access but the subject's policy may override this with a grant decision. In the scholarship case, the conflict resolution rule will be deny overrides, since the issuer's policy grants access but the subject's policy may deny access. It is not possible to combine into a single policy set the issuer's policy for both resources with a subject's policy for both resources since two different conflict resolution rules are required, whilst XACML only allows one conflict resolution rule to be applied to a set of policies. In order to implement this scenario in a single XACML "super" policy, both the subject's and issuer's policies would need to be dissected into their separate rules for each resource and then combined together per resource with separate conflict resolution rules per resource. Depending upon the number of types and subtypes of resource covered in any policy, this splitting and merging could get very complex. Furthermore it might be envisaged that different conflict resolution rules are needed for different actions or subjects on the same resource, which would make the splitting even more complex. We conclude that in a single organisation, there may be the need for various policy conflict resolution strategies which are not possible to satisfy with one static XACML policy, without sacrificing the integrity of the individual policies provided by the different authors. We therefore propose a solution where each author's policy remains intact and is evaluated as is, but the conflicts between policies are dynamically resolved based on a dynamically determined conflict resolution rule. In this use case example, this means that if the access request is to read a degree certificate, the conflict resolution rule is grant overrides, but if the access request is to read the scholarship awards, the conflict resolution rule is deny overrides.

3   Related Works

Nicole Dunlop et al. [6] have classified the conflicts of policies into four different categories. They have proposed different strategies for when and how to resolve conflicts. With the Pessimistic Conflict Resolution approach preventive steps are taken to resolve conflicts so that conflicts do not arise. With the Optimistic Conflict Resolution approach different conflict resolving steps are taken when conflicts do arise such as: new rule overrides old rule, assigning explicit weights or priorities to rules and so on. However the strategies are static i.e. the conflict resolution strategy is not chosen at run time.

Chen-hia Ma et al. [7] have defined a way for static and dynamic detection of policy conflicts. For resolving conflicts a *conflict_resolution_policy* is used which has a number of *priority_rules* that actually define different precedences. These *priority_rules* are tried one by one until the conflicts are resolved. In comparison, our proposed system chooses one combining rule based on the request context and uses that to resolve all conflicts.

Various conflict resolution strategies have been discussed in [8-10]. However, all those strategies are static. Mazzoleni et al. [11] argued that XACML policy combining algorithms are not sufficient to integrate policies where there is no centralised control and presented a system to integrate policies for different organisations. Nevertheless, their policy combining algorithm is static.

Apurva Mohan et al. [12] have argued that the static composition may not be suitable for dynamic environments where there is need to adapt the policies dynamically with the environment. They proposed a dynamic conflict resolution strategy that chooses an applicable policy combining algorithm based on a set of environmental attributes. But the problem with their system is that the policy combining algorithm (PCA) rules have to be mutually exclusive. If more than one PCA rule is evaluated to be applicable then an error is generated. This is not suitable where multiple parties provide individual PCAs and ensuring mutually exclusive PCAs in such a dynamic environment would be difficult. The conflict resolution strategy of our system is such that individual PCAs are provided by different authorities and one PCA is selected based on the precedence of the authority.

4   An Overview of the XACML Policy Combining Algorithm

The highest level element of an XACML (v2 and v3) policy is the *Policy set.* A *Policy set* can be a combination of *Policy* or *Policy sets*. **Policy** is the basic unit used by the PDP (Policy Decision Point) to form an authorisation decision and it can have a set of **Rules**. XACML defines a set of rule-combining- algorithms and policy-combining-algorithms which form a single authorisation decision from the set of decisions obtained by evaluating either a set of rules or set of policies respectively. The standard combining algorithms of XACML v2 and v3 are defined as:

- Deny-overrides (Ordered and Unordered),
- Permit-overrides (Ordered and Unordered),
- First-applicable and
- Only-one-applicable.

In the case of the Deny-overrides algorithm, if a single Rule or Policy element evaluates to "Deny", then, regardless of the evaluation result of the other Rule or Policy elements, the combined result is "Deny". For the Ordered Deny-Overrides the behaviour of the algorithm is the same except that the order in which the collection of policies is evaluated will match the order as listed in the policy set.

Similarly, in the case of the Permit-overrides algorithm, if a single "Permit" result is encountered, regardless of the evaluation result of the other Rule or Policy elements, the combined result is "Permit" and the obligation attached to the policy or policy set forming the decisions is also returned with the "Permit" decision. For the Ordered Permit-overrides the behaviour of the algorithm is the same except that the order in which the collection of policies is evaluated will match the order as listed in the policy set.

In the case of the "First-applicable" combining algorithm, the first decision encountered by the Rule, Policy or PolicySet element in the list becomes the final decision accompanied by its obligations (if any).

The "Only-one-applicable" policy-combining algorithm only applies to policies and ensures that only one policy or policy set is applicable by virtue of their targets. The result of the combining algorithm is the result of evaluating the single applicable policy or policy set. If more than one policy or policy set is applicable, then the result is "Indeterminate".

In XACML v3 some other combining algorithms are also defined, such as Deny-unless-permit (which returns Deny only if no Permit result is encountered; Indeterminate or NotApplicable will never be a result), Permit-unless-deny (which returns Permit only if no Deny result is encountered; Indeterminate or NotApplicable will never be a result)

In XACMLv2 a policy or policy set may contain one or more obligations. In XACML v3 a rule, policy or policy set may contain one or more obligation expressions which are evaluated to obligations when such a rule, policy or policy set is evaluated. For each combining algorithm the "Obligation" that was attached to the rule, policy or policy set that returned the decision is also returned with that final decision. In both XACMLv2 and XACMLv3 an obligation is passed to the next level of evaluation only if the effect of the rule (for v3), policy or policy set being evaluated matches the values of the FulfillOn attribute of the obligation. An obligation will not be returned to the PEP if the rule (for v3) policy or policy set from which it is drawn is not evaluated.

5   An Overview of Our Policy Combining Strategy

Our authorisation system was described in [13]. Here we provide a brief overview only. Our system receives an independent access control policy and conflict resolution policy from each policy author. Four types of policy author are supported, in decreasing order of precedence: the legal authority, the data issuer, the data subject and the data controller. A conflict resolution policy comprises an ordered set of Conflict Resolution Rules (CRRs), and each CRR comprise a Decision Combining Rule (DCR), plus the rule for which access requests this DCR applies to. The access request is received by the Policy Enforcement Point (PEP) (step 1 of Fig 1). The PEP passes the request to the Master PDP (step2 of Fig 1). The Master PDP determines which DCR applies to the current request by evaluating the CRRs of the various authors, in order (Fig 2).

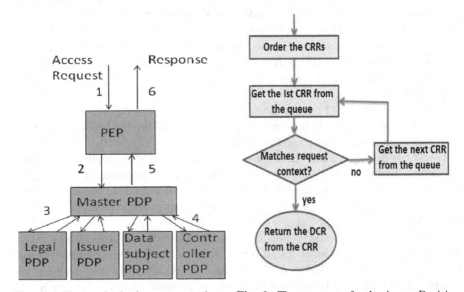

Fig. 1. The authorisation system in a simplified form

Fig. 2. The process of selecting a Decision Combining Rule (DCR) by the Master PDP

Our implementation currently supports 3 DCRs: FirstApplicable, DenyOverrides and GrantOverrides which have their standard XACML meanings, but in principle any conflict resolution algorithm can be supported.

The Master PDP collects all the CRRs defined by the different policy authors as well as having one default rule (which is configurable). From the request context it knows the data issuer and data subject and so can determine the ordering of the CRRs. It orders the CRRs of the legal authority, data issuer, data subject and data controller sequentially. For the same author the CRRs are ordered according to their times of creation so that the latest CRR always comes first in the author's list.

All the conditions of a CRR need to match the request context for it to be applicable. The CRRs from the ordered CRR queue are tested one by one against the request context. If a CRR's conditions do not match the request context the next CRR from the queue will be tested. The default CRR is placed at the end of CRR queue and it will only be reached when no other CRR's conditions match the request context. If a CRR's conditions match the request context the DCR of that CRR is chosen. After obtaining the DCR the PDPs are called (step 3 of Fig 1) and the Master PDP gathers the responses from them (step 4 of Fig 1). The final result is computed according to the chosen DCR as described below.

If DCR=FirstApplicable the Master PDP calls each subordinate PDP in order and stops processing when the first Grant, Break the Glass (BTG) [14] or Deny decision is obtained. If none of these is obtained, then Indeterminate is returned if at least one PDP returned this, otherwise NotApplicable is returned.

For DenyOverrides and GrantOverrides the Master PDP calls all the subordinate PDPs and combines the decisions using the following semantics:

- DenyOverrides – A Deny result overrides all other results. The precedence of results for deny override is Deny>Indeterminate>BTG>Grant>NotApplicable.
- GrantOverrides – A Grant result overrides all other results. The precedence of results for grant override is Grant>BTG>Indeterminate>Deny>NotApplicable

When a final result returned by the Master PDP is Grant (or Deny) the obligations of all the PDPs returning a Grant (or Deny) result are merged to form the final set of obligations.

In our system the policies of the different authors remain independent of each other and are independently evaluated. This also helps to enforce them in a distributed system, when they are transferred as "sticky policies" to other systems along with the data they control. The receiving system does not need to employ complex processing algorithms in order to create an integrated complex 'super' policy from the received policies and the organisation's own policy; it only needs to start an independent PDP and order the incoming CRRs along with its existing ones.

6   Policy Creation and Integration Strategy Comparison

In this section we shall first look into the strategy that can be taken to convert the previous example use case scenario into policies for our system and then the same into one XACML 'super' policy.

While forming the conflict resolution policy the conflict resolution rules (CRRs) obtained from legislation [15] come first, then come the CRRs from the issuer, then from the data subject and then from the controller and finally the default one.

For the scenario of our use case example the issuer has 2 different CRRs to contribute to the conflict resolution policy. The CRRs of the issuer are:

1. If resource_type=scholarship_info, DCR=DenyOverrides
2. If resource_type=degree_certificate, DCR=GrantOverrides.

We assume the first CRR was written after the second CRR, as they are ordered according to their times of creation.

The issuer has an access control policy saying "for resource_type = scholarship_info, effect = Permit and for resource_type = degree_certificate, effect = Deny". These apply to all accessors i.e. the public.

Suppose that the data subject is embarrassed to have been given a hardship assistance scholarship. He has a policy saying "for resource_type = scholarship_info, scholarship_type = hardship assistance, effect = Deny".

The data subject can have any conflict resolution rule and that CRR will come after the CRR of the issuer on the ordered list of CRRs and so it will only be evaluated if there is no CRR from the law or the issuer matching the request context. However, as we have already seen, the issuer does have two CRRs that will match.So the CRP will have the following CRRs in order:

1. CRR from the law: none.
2. CRR from the issuer (CRR no. 1. If resource_type = scholarship_info, DCR=DenyOverrides; CRR no. 2. If resource_type = degree_certificate, DCR=GrantOverrides).
3. CRR from the data subject: <anything>.
4. CRR from the controller: none.

Suppose that a request to view a student's scholarship information has arrived. The Master PDP will evaluate the ordered list of CRRs. The law has no CRR regarding this [15]. The next CRRs on the list are the CRRs from Issuer. The CRR no. 1 of issuer will match the request context for which the DCR=DenyOverrides. So the DCR=DenyOverrides is chosen by the Master PDP. The Master PDP now calls the independent PDPs of the law, issuer, data subject and controller. In this case the legal PDP always returns NotApplicable, and the issuer PDP always returns Grant. The data subject PDP will return Deny when the scholarship_type=hardship assistance otherwise it will return NotApplicable. There is no controller PDP for this use case scenario as the controller and issuer are the same for this use case (i.e. the university). So in case of scholarship_type= hardship assistance the final result will be Deny (according to the DenyOverrides DCR). For other types of scholarship information the DCR will remain the same i.e. DenyOverrides. The legal PDP returns NotApplicable, the issuer PDP returns Grant, the data subject's PDP returns NotApplicable. Therefore, the final decision becomes Grant.

Suppose that a request to view an alumni's degree certificate has arrived. The Master PDP will evaluate the ordered list of CRRs. The law has no CRR regarding this [15]. The next CRRs are the CRRs from the issuer. Issuer CRR no 2 will match the request context which has a DCR=GrantOverrides. So it chooses the DCR=GrantOverrides. The Master PDP now calls the independent PDPs of the law, issuer, data subject and controller. In this case the legal PDP returns NotApplicable, the issuer PDP returns Deny. The data subject PDP will return NotApplicable. So according to the GrantOverrides DCR the final result will be Deny (unless the alumni specifically grants the access in his/ her policy).

Now if we try to combine the policies from the law, issuer, and data subject under one XACML PDP policy the policies from the different authors can't remain independent anymore. In order to make sure that the law always has the highest priority the top policy combining algorithm can't be DenyOverrides or GrantOverrides as the decision of the legal policy can then be overridden by the other authors. To give the legal policy the highest priority the top combining algorithm needs to be first applicable with the legal policy coming first. To implement our example policies the policies from the issuer and data subject need to be combined under the DenyOverrides algorithm for one case (for resource_type=scholarship_info) and under the GrantOverrides algorithm for the other case (resource_type= degree_certificate). This means it requires splitting the policies of the different authors and then combining them together into PolicySets based on the resource type. This may require manual interpretation and implementation depending on the needs of the organization and the complexity of the legal, issuer and subject policies. The integration of polices from different authorities into one 'super' policy may not be impossible but it is not an easy task and might be difficult or impossible to fully automate. It will certainly damage the integrity of the individual policies by splitting them up and may make it more difficult to prove compliance with data protection legislation. In contrast, our system keeps the policies written by the different authors integral and independent of each other, and makes it easier to show compliance with the law and to transfer them to remote systems as sticky policies.

7   Integration of Obligations

Each XACML policy document contains one Policy or PolicySet element as a root XML tag. A PolicySet can contain a number of Policies or PolicySets. A Policy represents a single access control policy, expressed through a set of Rules. Each Policy or PolicySet or Rule (for v3 only) element can define Obligations which can contain a number of Obligation elements. Each Obligation element has an Obligation ID and a FulfillOn attribute. XACML's obligation combination strategy can be viewed as a vertical procedure where the Obligations of a contained Rule/Policy/PolicySet are combined with the Obligations of the containing Policy/PolicySet. An Obligation associated with a Rule or Policy is returned with a decision only if the effect of the Rule or Policy being evaluated is the same as the FulfillOn attribute of the Obligation. If the Policy is contained in a PolicySet, the Obligations associated with the PolicySet having a FulfillOn attribute value matching the effect of the PolicySet are combined with the returned Obligations of the contained Policy. For example, if policyset A has obligation o1 and it contains policy A with obligation o2 and policy B with obligation o3 then the final obligations returned could be o1 and o2 or o1 and o3 (assuming they all have the same FulfillOn attribute) depending upon the combining algorithm (see below) and the order in which policy A and B are evaluated. This procedure continues recursively.

The limitations of the XACML obligations combining algorithm is that if a rule, policy or policy set is not evaluated then no obligations from them are returned to the

PEP [5 (p82), 4 (p87)]. With XACML's GrantOverrides / DenyOverrides combining algorithms as soon as a Grant/ Deny decision is encountered the Grant / Deny is returned without evaluating the rest of the policies. Also with the FirstApplicable combining algorithm as soon as a decision (Grant/Deny) is obtained it is returned. This strategy of obligation combination may result in losing important obligations that ought to be returned. For example, if the controller's policy said that every time a Grant decision is returned, there is an obligation to "log the request" whilst the data subject's policy had a similar requirement that when a Grant decision is returned there is an obligation to "e-mail the data subject"; then if these policies are combined in a single XACML PolicySet with a GrantOverrides combining algorithm, then one of these obligations will always be lost. In light of the above one can see that the integration of polices from different authorities into one 'super' XACML policy is more complex than simply splitting the policies of the different authors and then combining them together into PolicySets based on the resource type, as this may result in the loss of obligations..

In contrast to XACML, our system's policy evaluation and obligation combination strategy can be viewed as a horizontal procedure. In our system for both GrantOverrides and DenyOverrides all the PDPs are evaluated and the final decision is chosen based on the DCA. The obligations that are returned by all the PDPs that have a decision equal to the final decision are combined. For example if the controller PDP returned a decision Grant with an obligation to "log the request" and the data subject's PDP returned a decision Grant with an obligation to "e-mail the data subject" and the final decision is Grant; then in our system the returned obligations will be the combination of the obligations attached to the Grant decisions. If the policies are implemented in a single XACML PDP with either a GrantOverrides or DenyOverrides combining algorithm, the returned obligation(s) will only be the obligation(s) attached to the policy that was encountered first and that contributed to the final decision.

8   Implementation and Testing

The authorisation system is implemented as a standalone web service using JAVA which runs in a servlet container (apache Tomcat). The present implementation can choose a DCR dynamically from a fixed set of configured CRRs. Each CRR is a policy either written in XACML or PERMIS [16] and the DCR is obtained as an obligation. The correct functioning of the system was validated using over 100 test cases based on different use case scenarios [18].

It can be argued that increasing the number of PDPs will unduly affect the system's performance, so we ran some performance tests to determine the scale of this. The authorization infrastructure was installed in a single machine running Ubuntu 10.04 whose configuration was: duel core processors each with cpu speed = 2993.589 MHz; cache=2048 KB; and 2GB total memory. The configuration of the client machine that made the authorisation decision requests was: Duel core processor with 2.53 GHz CPU speed, 2.98 GB memory and running Windows XP. The client software was

SOAPUI [17]. The client was operating across a local area network. Two series of tests were performed. The first set tested the reduction in performance for an increasing number of PDPs running inside the authorization service. The second set tested the reduction in performance as the number of rules in a policy is increased for a single PDP inside the authorisation service.

Table 1. Time (in ms) to make an authorization decision for different number of PDPs

Test	Mean	Std Dev	% Discarded	Mean PDPi – Mean PDPi-1
1 PDP	5.27	0.51	4.07	
2 PDPs	6.34	0.74	2.47	1.07
3 PDPs	14.82	1.47	2	8.48
4 PDPs	22.64	1.53	2	7.82
5 PDPs	30.37	1.9	1.4	7.73
6 PDPs	38.30	1.99	1.6	7.93
7 PDPs	46.47	2.32	1.2	8.17
8 PDPs	54.26	2.28	2.4	7.79
9 PDPs	62.51	2.59	0.8	8.25
10 PDPs	69.61	2.55	1.2	7.1

In this first series of tests the authorization server was configured with an increasing number of policies/PDPs, each containing 1 rule. In the first test the authorization server only had 1 policy configured into it (the legal PDP with 1 rule). In the second test the authorization server was configured with the legal policy and the data controller's policy/PDP (with 1 rule). In the third test the authorization server had 3 policies/PDPs: the data subject's sticky policy (with 1 rule), and the legal and controller's configured policies. In the subsequent tests an additional sticky policy PDP with 1 rule was added.

In each case we measured the time taken for an authorization decision to be made when the client asked to read a data record, and a grant result was obtained. This necessitated all configured policies being interrogated and the Master PDP determining the combining rule (GrantOverrides was chosen) the overall decision and set of returned obligations. The tests were run 100 times and results lying more than two standard deviations from the mean where discarded as outliers. The results are shown in Table 1.

From the results one can observe that there is a decision making overhead of approximately 8 ms per additional sticky policy PDP. The reason the 1st PDP was only 5ms and the 2nd PDP only added 1 ms is that they are both built in PDPs and not sticky policy PDPs (which are added dynamically).

For the second set of performance test the authorisation system is configured using only one PDP. The number of rules is increased at each test and the time to get a response for a request is measured. Each test was run 100 times and the outliers (> 2 standard deviations) were discarded. The results are shown in Table 2.

Table 2. Time (in ms) to make an authorization decision for different number of Rules

Test	Mean	Std Dev	% Discarded	Additional Time per rule
1 Rule	5.9	0.7	5.2	5.9
10 Rules	15.58	0.9	5.2	1.07
100 Rules	69.26	1.59	4.2	0.64
1000 Rules	581.19	8.12	0.98	0.58

We can see that as the number of rules increases, the time taken to reach a decision reduces per rule until we reach a steady state of approximately 0.58ms per rule (for our implementation and configuration). For our particular implementation and configuration, the effect of adding a new sticky policy PDP to the authorisation server running in a PC, in the worst case is approximately equal to adding 14 new rules to an existing PDP, and in the best case only 8 rules.

Taking our earlier use case example, policies for the law, controller/issuer and data subject contain 15, 2 and 1 rules respectively. The complete legal policy that enforces the European Data Protection Legislation can be found in [15]. The combined 'super' policy contains 18 rules. Using tables 1 and 2 we can calculate that the time taken to evaluate the 3 separate policies (using 2 configured PDPs and 1 sticky PDP), for our particular implementation and configuration, would be approximately 31 ms (20+2.5+8.5) whereas the time taken to evaluate the 'super' policy would be approximately 23 ms. So whilst there is a performance overhead of approximately one third in this use case, this should be offset against the complexity needed to create a combined 'super' policy which always returns the correct decisions and obligations.

9   Conclusions

In this paper the policy combining strategy of our system is compared with the static policy combining approach of XACML. Our strategy allows the policy engine to dynamically choose different combing algorithms based on the request context while allowing the policies written by different authors to remain separate, integral and independent of each other. The separation of policies facilitates the easy integration of "sticky" policies into the system allowing personal data to be transferred to a different domain along with its policies. Furthermore, our system allows the return of combined obligations written by different authors, which the current XACML policy combining strategy is unable to do when keeping the policies of individual authors intact. However, further work is still needed to see how easy it might be to integrate the polices from different authors into one 'super' policy, as an alternative to the approach presented here.

References

1. Karjoth, G., Schunter, M., Waidner, M.: Privacy-enabled services for enterprises. In: 13th International Workshop on Database and Expert Systems Applications, pp. 483–487. IEEE Computer Society, Washington, DC (2002)
2. Mont, M.C.: Dealing with Privacy Obligations: Important Aspects and Technical Approaches. In: International Conference on Trust and Privacy in Digital Business, Zaragoza (2004)
3. Ardagna, C.A., Bussard, L., Vimercati, S.D.C., Neven, G., Paraboschi, S., Pedrini, E., Preiss, F.-S., Raggett, D., Samarati, P., Trabelsi, S., Verdicchio, M.: PrimeLifePolicy Language. In: Workshop on Access Control Application Scenarios, W3C 2009(2009)
4. OASIS XACML 2.0. eXtensible Access Control Markup Language (XACML)Version 2.0, http://www.oasisopen.org/committees/ tc_home.php?wg_abbrev=xacml#XACML20 (October 2005)
5. OASIS XACML 3.0. eXtensible Access Control Markup Language (XACML) Version 3.0, http://docs.oasisopen.org/xacml/3.0/ xacml-3.0-corespec-en.html (April 16, 2009)
6. Dunlop, N., Indulska, J., Raymond, K.: Methods for Conflict Resolution in Policy-Based Management Systems. In: Proceedings of Seventh International Enterprise Distributed Object Computing Conference, pp. 98–109. EEE press, New York (2003)
7. Ma, C., Lu, G., Qiu, J.: Conflict detection and resolution for authorization policies in workflow systems. Journal of Zhejiang University Science A 10, 1082 (2009)
8. Russello, G., Dong, C., Dulay, N.: Authorisation and conflict resolution for Hierarchical Domains. In: Eight IEEE International Workshop on Policies for Distributed Systems and Networks (2007)
9. Syukur, E., Loke, S.W., Stanski, P.: Methods for Policy Conflict Detection and Resolution in Pervasive Computing Environments. In: Policy Management for Web Workshop in Conjunction with WWW2005 Conference, Chiba, Japan, May 10-14 (2005)
10. Lupu, E.C., Sloman, M.: Conflicts in Policy-Based Distributed Systems Management. IEEE Transactions on Software Engineering, 852–869 (1999)
11. Masoumzadeh, M.A., Jalili, R.: Conflict detection and resolution in context-aware authorization. In: 21st International Conference on Advanced Information Networking and Applications Workshops (2007)
12. Mohan, A., Blough, D.M.: An Attribute-based Authorization Policy Framework with Dynamic conflict Resolution. In: IDtrust, Gaithersburg, MD (2010)
13. Chadwick, D.W., Fatema, K.: A Privacy Preserving Authorisation System for the Cloud. Journal of Computer and System Sciences, vol 78(5), 1359–1373 (2012)
14. Ferreira, A., Chadwick, D., Farinha, P., Correia, R., Zhao, G., Chilro, R., Antunes, L.: How to securely break into RBAC: the BTG-RBAC model. In: Annual Computer Security Applications Conference, Honolulu, Hawaii, pp. 23–23 (2009)
15. Fatema, K., Chadwick, D.W., Van Alsenoy, B.: Extracting Access Control and Conflict Resolution Policies from European Data Protection Law. In: Camenisch, J., Crispo, B., Fischer-Hübner, S., Leenes, R., Russello, G. (eds.) Privacy and Identity 2011. IFIP AICT, vol. 375, pp. 59–72. Springer, Heidelberg (2012)
16. Chadwick, D., Zhao, G., Otenko, S., Laborde, R., Su, L., Nguyen, T.A.: PERMIS: A modular authorization infrastructure. Concurrency and Computation: Practice and Experience 11(20), 1341–1357 (2008)
17. SOAP UI, http://www.soapui.org
18. Fatema, K.: Adding Privacy Protection to Policy Based Authorisation Systems:PhD thesis, University of Kent, UK (to appear, 2014)

Evolving Computational Intelligence System
for Malware Detection

Konstantinos Demertzis and Lazaros Iliadis

Democritus University of Thrace, Department of Forestry & Management of the
Environment & Natural Resources, 193 Pandazidou st., 68200 N Orestiada, Greece
kdemertz@fmenr.duth.gr, liliadis@fmenr.duth.gr

Abstract. Recent malware developments have the ability to remain hidden
during infection and operation. They prevent analysis and removal, using
various techniques, namely: obscure filenames, modification of file attributes,
or operation under the pretense of legitimate programs and services. Also, the
malware might attempt to subvert modern detection software, by hiding running
processes, network connections and strings with malicious URLs or registry
keys. The malware can go a step further and obfuscate the entire file with a
packer, which is special software that takes the original malware file and
compresses it, thus making all the original code and data unreadable. This paper
proposes a novel approach, which uses minimum computational power and
resources, to indentify Packed Executable (PEX), so as to spot the existence of
malware software. It is an Evolving Computational Intelligence System for
Malware Detection (ECISMD) which performs classification by Evolving
Spiking Neural Networks (eSNN), in order to properly label a packed
executable. On the other hand, it uses an Evolving Classification Function
(ECF) for the detection of malwares and applies Genetic Algorithms to achieve
ECF Optimization.

Keywords: Security, Packed Executable, Malware, Evolving Spiking Neural
Networks, Evolving Classification Function, Genetic Algorithm for Offline
ECF Optimization.

1   Introduction

Malware is a kind of software used to disrupt computer operation, gather sensitive
information, or gain access to private computer systems. It can appear in the form of
code, scripts, active content, or any other. To identify already known malware,
existing commercial security applications search a computer's binary files for
predefined signatures. However, obfuscated viruses use software packers to protect
their internal code and data structures from detection. Antivirus scanners act like file
filters, inspecting suspicious file loading and storing activities. Malicious programs
with obfuscated content, can bypass antivirus scanners. Eventually, they are unpacked
and executed in the victim's system [1].

L. Iliadis, M. Papazoglou, and K. Pohl (Eds.): CAiSE 2014 Workshops, LNBIP 178, pp. 322–334, 2014.
© Springer International Publishing Switzerland 2014

Code packing is the dominant technique used to obfuscate malicious code, to hinder an analyst's understanding of the malware's intent and to evade detection by Antivirus systems. Malware developers, transform executable code into data, at a post-processing stage in the whole implementation cycle. This transformation uses static analysis and it may perform compression or encryption, hindering an analyst's understanding. At runtime, the data or hidden code is restored to its original executable form, through dynamic code generation using an associated restoration routine. Execution then resumes as normal to the original entry point, which marks the entry point of the original malware, before the code packing transformation is applied. Finally, execution becomes transparent, as both code packing and restoration have been performed. After the restoration of one packing, control may transfer another packed layer. The original entry point is derived from the last such layer [2].

Code packing provides compression and software protection of the intellectual properties contained in a program. It is not necessarily advantageous to flag all occurrences of code packing as indicative of malicious activity. It is advisable to determine if the packed contents are malicious, rather than identifying only the fact that unknown contents are packed. Unpacking is the process of stripping the packer layers off packed executables to restore the original contents in order to inspect and analyze the original executable signatures. Universal unpackers, introduce a high computational overhead, low convergence speed and computational resource requirements. The processing time may vary from tens of seconds to several minutes per executable. This hinders virus detection significantly, since without a priori knowledge on the nature of the executables to be checked for malicious code all of them would need to be run through the unpacker. Scanning large collections of executables, may take hours or days. This research effort aims in the development and application of an innovative, fast and accurate Evolving Computational Intelligence System for Malware Detection (ECISMD) approach for the identification of packed executables and detection of malware by employing eSNN. A multilayer ECF model has been employed for malware detection, which is based on fuzzy clustering. Finally, an evolutionary Genetic Algorithm (GA) has been applied to optimize the ECF network and to perform feature extraction on the training and testing datasets. A main advantage of ECISMD is the fact that it reduces overhead and overall analysis time, by classifying packed or not packed executables.

1.1   Literature Review

Dynamic unpacking approaches monitor the execution of a binary in order to extract its actual code. These methods execute the samples inside an isolated environment that can be deployed as a virtual machine or an emulator [3]. The execution is traced and stopped when certain events occur. Several dynamic unpackers use heuristics to determine the exact point where the execution jumps from the unpacking routine to the original code. Once this point is reached, the memory content is bulk to obtain an unpacked version of the malicious code. Other approaches for generic dynamic unpacking have been proposed that are not highly based on heuristics such as PolyUnpack [4] Renovo [5], OmniUnpack [6] or Eureka [7]. However, these methods are very tedious and time consuming, and cannot counter conditional execution of unpacking routines, a technique used for anti-debugging and anti-monitoring defense [8]. Another common approach is using the structural information of the executables to train supervised machine-learning classifiers to determine if the sample under analysis is packed or if it is suspicious of containing malicious code (e.g., PEMiner [9], PE-Probe [10] and Perdisci et al. [11]). These approaches that use this method for filtering, previous to dynamic unpacking, are computationally more expensive and time consuming and less effective to analyze large sets of mixed malicious and benign executables [12] [13] [14].

Artificial Intelligence and data mining algorithms have been applied as malicious detection methods and for the discovery of new malware patterns [15]. In the research effort of Babar and Khalid [3], boosted decision trees working on n-grams are found to produce better results than Naive Bayes classifiers and Support Vector Machines (SVM). Ye et al., [16] use automatic extraction of association rules on Windows API execution sequences to distinguish between malware and clean program files. Chandrasekaran et al., [17] are using association rules, on honeytokens of known parameters. Chouchan et al., [18] used Hidden Markov Models to detect whether a given program file is (or is not) a variant of a previous program file. Stamp et al., [19] employ profile hidden Markov Models, which have been previously used for sequence analysis in bioinformatics. The capacity of neural networks (ANN) to detect polymorphic malware is explored in [20]. Yoo [21] employs Self-Organizing Maps to identify patterns of behavior for viruses in Windows executable files. These methods they have low accuracy as a consequence, packed benign executables would likely cause false alarm, whereas malware may remain undetected.

2   Methodologies Comprising the Proposed Hybrid Approach

2.1   Evolving Spiking Neural Networks (eSNN)

eSNN are modular connectionist-based systems that evolve their structure and functionality in a continuous, self-organized, on-line, adaptive, interactive way from incoming information. These models use trains of spikes as internal information representation rather than continuous variables [22]. The eSNN developed and discussed herein is based in the "Thorpe" neural model [23]. This model intensifies the importance of the spikes taking place in an earlier moment, whereas the neural plasticity is used to monitor the learning algorithm by using one-pass learning. In order to classify real-valued data sets, each data sample, is mapped into a sequence of spikes using the Rank Order Population Encoding (ROPE) technique [24] [25]. The topology of the developed eSNN is strictly feed-forward, organized in several layers and weight modification occurs on the connections between the neurons of the existing layers.

The ROPE method is alternative to the conventional rate coding scheme (CRCS). It uses the order of firing neuron's inputs to encode information. This allows the mapping of vectors of real-valued elements into a sequence of spikes. Neurons are organized into neuronal maps which share the same synaptic weights. Whenever the synaptic weight of a neuron is modified, the same modification is applied to the entire population of neurons within the map. Inhibition is also present between each neuronal map. If a neuron spikes, it inhibits all the neurons in the other maps with neighboring positions.

This prevents all the neurons from learning the same pattern. When propagating new information, neuronal activity is initially reset to zero. Then, as the propagation goes on, each time one of their inputs fire, neurons are progressively desensitize. This is making neuronal responses dependent upon the relative order of firing of the neuron's afferents [24], [26], [27].

The aim of the one-pass learning method is to create a repository of trained output neurons during the presentation of training samples. After presenting a certain input sample to the network, the corresponding spike train is propagated through the eSNN which may result in the firing of certain output neurons. It is possible that no output neuron is activated and the network remains silent and the classification result is undetermined. If one or more output neurons have emitted a spike, the neuron with the shortest response time among all activated output neurons is determined. The label of this neuron is the classification result for the presented input [26], [27], [28].

2.2   Evolving Connectionist Systems (ECOS)

ECOS [29] are multi-modular, connectionist architectures that facilitate modeling of evolving processes and knowledge discovery [26]. An ECOS is an ANN operating continuously in time and adapting its structure and functionality through a continuous interaction with the environment and other systems according to: (i) a set of parameters that are subject to change; (ii) an incoming continuous flow of information with unknown distribution; (iii) a goal (rational) criterion (subject to modification) applied to optimize the performance of the system. The evolving connectionist systems evolve in an open space, using constructive processes, not necessarily of fixed dimensions. They learn in on-line incremental fast mode, possibly through one pass of data propagation. Life-long learning is a main attribute of this procedure. They operate as both individual systems, and as part of an evolutionary population of such systems. [26] [30]. ECOS are connectionist structures that evolve their nodes and connections through supervised incremental learning from input-output data.

Their architecture comprises of five layers: input nodes, representing input variables; input fuzzy membership nodes, representing the membership degrees of the input values to each of the defined membership functions; rule nodes, representing cluster centers of samples in the problem space and their associated output function; output fuzzy membership nodes, representing the membership degrees to which the output values belong to defined membership functions; and output nodes, representing output variables [31].

ECOS learn local models from data through clustering of the data and associating a local output function for each cluster. Rule nodes evolve from the input data stream to cluster the data, and the first layer W_1 connection weights of these nodes represent the coordinates of the nodes in the input space. The second layer W_2 represents the local models (functions) allocated to each of the clusters. Clusters of data are created based on similarity between data samples either in the input space, or in both the input space and the output space. Samples that have a distance to an existing cluster center (rule node) N of less than a threshold R_{max} are allocated to the same cluster N_c. Samples that do not fit into existing clusters, form new clusters as they arrive in time. Cluster centers are continuously adjusted according to new data samples and new clusters are created incrementally. The similarity between a sample S = (x, y) and an existing rule node $N = (W_1, W_2)$ can be measured in different ways, the most popular of them being the *normalized Euclidean distance* given by equation 1, where n is the number of the input variables. $d(S,N) = \frac{1}{n}\left[\sum_{i=1}^{n} |x_i - W_{1N}|^2\right]^{\frac{1}{2}}$ (1).

ECOS learn from data and automatically create a local output function for each cluster, the function being represented in the W_2 connection weights, creating local models. Each model is represented as a local rule with an antecedent –the cluster area, and a consequent– the output function applied to data in this cluster.

2.3   Evolving Classification Function and Genetic Algorithms

ECF, a special case of ECOS used for pattern classification, generates rule nodes in an N dimensional input space and associate them with classes. Each rule node is defined with its centre, radius (influence field) and the class it belongs to. A learning mechanism is designed in such a way that the nodes can be generated. The ECF model used here is a connectionist system for classification tasks that consists of four layers of neurons (nodes). The first layer represents the input variables; the second layer – the fuzzy membership functions; the third layer represents clusters centers (prototypes) of data in the input space; and the four layer represents classes [30], [26]. A GA is an evolutionary algorithm in which the principles of the Darwin's theory are applied to a population of solutions in order to "breed" better solutions. Solutions, in this case the parameters of the ECF network, are encoded in a binary string and each solution is given a score depending on how well it performs. Good solutions are selected more frequently for breeding and are subjected to crossover and mutation. After several generations, the population of solutions should converge on a "good" solution. The ECF model and the GA algorithm for Offline ECF Optimization are parts from NeuCom software (*http://www.kedri.aut.ac.nz/*) which is a Neuro-Computing Decision Support Environment, based on the theory of ECOS [29].

3   Description of the Proposed Hybrid ECISMD Algorithm

The proposed herein, hybrid ECISMD methodology uses an eSNN classification approach to classify packed or unpacked executables with minimum computational power combined with the ECF method in order to detect packed malware. Finally it applies Genetic Algorithm for ECF Optimization, in order to decrease the level of false positive and false negative rates. The general algorithm is described below:

Step 1: The train and test *datasets* are determined and formed, related to n features. The required classes (packed and unpacked executables) that use the variable *Population Encoding* are imported. This variable controls the conversion of real-valued data samples into the corresponding time spikes. The encoding is performed with 20 Gaussian receptive fields per variable (Gaussian width parameter beta=1.5). The data are normalized to the interval [-1,1] and so the coverage of the Gaussians is determined by using i_min and i_max. For the normalization processing the following function 2 is used:

$$x_{1_{norm}} = 2 * \left(\frac{x_1 - x_{min}}{x_{max} - x_{min}}\right) - 1, \quad x \in R \tag{2}$$

The data is classified in two classes namely: **Class 0** which contains the unpacked results and **Class 1** which comprises of the packed ones. The eSNN is using modulation factor m=0.9, firing threshold ratio c=0.7 and similarity threshold s=0.6 in agreement with the vQEA algorithm [28] [27]. More precisely, let A = { a_1 , a_2 , a_3 ... a_{m-1} , a_m } be the ensemble of afferent neurons of neuron i and W = { $w_{1,i}$, $w_{2,i}$, $w_{3,i}$ ... $w_{m-1,i}$, $w_{m,i}$} the weights of the m corresponding connections; let mod $\in$ [0,1] be an arbitrary modulation factor. The activation level of neuron i at time t is given by equation 3: $Activation(i,t) = \sum_{j \in [1,m]} mod^{order(a_j)} w_{j,i}$ (3) where order(a_j) is the firing rank of neuron a_j in the ensemble A.

By convention, order(a_j)=+8 if a neuron a_j is not fired at time t, sets the corresponding term in the above sum to zero. This kind of desensitization function could correspond to a fast shunting inhibition mechanism. When a neuron reaches its threshold, it spikes and inhibits neurons at equivalent positions in the other maps so that only one neuron will respond at any location. Every spike triggers a time based Hebbian-like learning rule that adjusts the synaptic weights. Let t_e be the date of arrival of the Excitatory PostSynaptic Potential (EPSP) at synapse of weight W and t_a the date of discharge of the postsynaptic neuron.

If $t_{e<}$ t_a then $dW=a(1-W)e^{-|\Delta o|r}$ else $dW=-aW$ $e^{-|\Delta o|r}$ (4). Δo is the difference between the date of the EPSP and the date of the neuronal discharge (expressed in term of order of arrival instead of time), a is a constant that controls the amount of synaptic potentiation and depression [24]. ROPE technique with receptive fields, allow the encoding of continuous values [26] [27]. Each input variable is encoded independently by a group of one-dimensional receptive fields (figure 1). For a variable n, an interval $[I^n_{min}, I^n_{max}]$ is defined. The Gaussian receptive field of neuron i is given by its center μi and width σ by equation 6.: $\mu i = I^n_{min} + \frac{2i-3}{2} \frac{I^n_{max} - I^n_{min}}{M-2}$ (5) $\sigma = \frac{1}{\beta} \frac{I^n_{max} - I^n_{min}}{M-2}$ (6) where $1 \leq \beta \leq 2$ and the parameter β directly controls the width of each Gaussian receptive field. Figure 1 depicts an encoding example of a single variable.

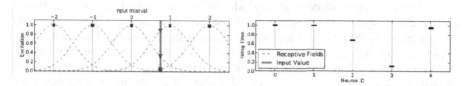

Fig. 1. Population encoding based on Gaussian receptive fields. Left Figure: Input Interval – Right Figure: Neuron ID

For an input value v=0.75 (thick straight line) [27] the intersection points with each Gaussian is computed (triangles), which are in turn translated into spike time delays (right figure) [27].

Step 2: The eSNN is trained with the *packed_train* dataset vectors and the testing is performed with the *packed_test* vectors. The procedure of one pass learning is described in the following Algorithm1 [26] [27].

Algorithm 1: Training an evolving Spiking Neural Network (eSNN) [27]

Require: m_l, s_l, c_l **for a class label** $l \in L$

1: initialize neuron repository $R_l = \{\}$

2: **for all** samples $X^{(i)}$ belonging to class l **do**

3:   $w_j^{(i)} \leftarrow (m_l)^{order(j)}$, $\forall j \mid j$ pre-synaptic neuron of i

4:   $u_{max}^{(i)} \leftarrow \sum_j w_j^{(i)} (m_l)^{order(j)}$

5:   $\theta^{(i)} \leftarrow c_l u_{max}^{(i)}$

6: **if** $\min(d(w^{(i)}, w^{(k)})) < s_l$, $w^{(k)} \in R_l$ **then**

7:   $w^{(k)} \leftarrow$ merge $w^{(i)}$ and $w^{(k)}$ according to Equation 7

8:   $\theta^{(k)} \leftarrow$ merge $\theta^{(i)}$ and $\theta^{(k)}$ according to Equation 8

9: **else**

10: $R_l \leftarrow R_l \cup \{w^{(i)}\}$

11: **end if**

12: **end for**

For each training sample i with class label $l \in L$ a new output neuron is created and fully connected to the previous layer of neurons resulting in a real-valued weight vector $w^{(i)}$ with $w_j^{(i)} \in R$ denoting the connection between the pre-synaptic neuron j and the created neuron i. In the next step, the input spikes are propagated through the network and the value of weight $w_j^{(i)}$ is computed according to the order of spike transmission through a synapse j: $w_j^{(i)} = (m_l)^{order(j)}$, $\forall j \mid j$ pre-synaptic neuron of i.

Parameter m_l is the modulation factor of the Thorpe neural model. Differently labeled output neurons may have different modulation factors m_l. Function order(j) represents the rank of the spike emitted by neuron j. The firing threshold $\theta^{(i)}$ of the created neuron I is defined as the fraction $c_l \in R$, $0 < c_l < 1$, of the maximal possible potential

$$u_{max}^{(i)} : \quad \theta^{(i)} \leftarrow c_l u_{max}^{(i)} \quad (7) \quad u_{max}^{(i)} \leftarrow \sum_j w_j^{(i)} (m_l)^{order(j)} \qquad (8)$$

The fraction c_l is a parameter of the model and for each class label $l \in L$ a different fraction can be specified. The weight vector of the trained neuron is compared to the weights corresponding to neurons already stored in the repository. Two neurons are considered too "similar" if the minimal *Euclidean* distance between their weight vectors is smaller than a specified similarity threshold s_l (the eSNN object uses optimal similarity threshold s=0.6). All parameters of eSNN (modulation factor m_l, similarity threshold s_l, PSP fraction c_l, $l \in L$) included in this search space, were optimized according to the Versatile Quantum-inspired Evolutionary Algorithm (vQEA) [28]. Both the firing thresholds and the weight vectors were merged according to equations 9 and 10:

$$w_j^{(k)} \leftarrow \frac{w_j^{(i)} + N w_j^{(k)}}{1 + N}, \forall j \mid j \text{ pre-synaptic neuron of i} \qquad (9)$$

$$\theta^{(k)} \leftarrow \frac{\theta^{(i)} + N \theta^{(k)}}{1 + N} \qquad (10)$$

Integer N denotes the number of samples previously used to update neuron k. The merging is implemented as the (running) average of the connection weights, and the (running) average of the two firing thresholds [27]. After merging, the trained neuron i is discarded and the next sample processed. If no other neuron in the repository is similar to the trained neuron i, the neuron i is added to the repository as a new output.

Step 3: If the result is unpacked then the process is terminated and the executable file goes to the antivirus scanner. If the result of the classification is packed, the new classification process is initiated employing the ECF method. This time the malware data vectors are used. These vectors comprise of 9 features and 2 classes malware and benign. The learning algorithm of the ECF according to the ECOS is as follows:

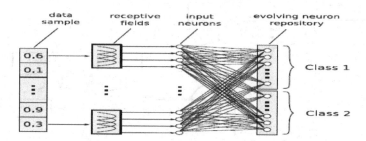

Fig. 2. The Evolving Spiking Neural Network (eSNN) architecture

a. If all input vectors are fed, finish the iteration; otherwise, input a vector from the data set and calculate the distances between the vector and all rule nodes already created using Euclidean distance. **b.** If all distances are greater than a max-radius parameter, a new rule node is created. The position of the new rule node is the same as the current vector in the input data space and the radius of its receptive field is set to the min-radius parameter; the algorithm goes to step 1; otherwise it goes to the next step. **c.** If there is a rule node with a distance to the current input vector less than or equal to its radius and its class is the same as the class of the new vector, nothing will be changed; go to step 1; otherwise. **d.** If there is a rule node with a distance to the input vector less than or equal to its radius and its class is different from those of the input vector, its influence field should be reduced. The radius of the new field is set to the larger value from the two numbers: distance minus the min-radius; min radius. New node is created as in to represent the new data vector. **e.** If there is a rule node with a distance to the input vector less than or equal to the max-radius, and its class is the same as of the input vector's, enlarge the influence field by taking the distance as a new radius if only such enlarged field does not cover any other rule nodes which belong to a different class; otherwise, create a new rule node in the same way as in step 2, and go to step 1 [33].

Step 4: To increase the level of integrity the Offline ECF Optimization with GA is used. ECF system is an ANN that operates continuously in time and adapts its structure and functionality through a continuous interaction with the environment and with other systems. This is done according to a set of parameters P that are subject to change during the system operation; an incoming continuous flow of information with unknown distribution; a goal (rationale) criteria that is applied to optimize the performance. The set of parameters P of an ECOS can be regarded as a chromosome of "*genes*" of the evolving system and evolutionary computation can be applied for their optimization. The GA algorithm for offline ECF Optimization runs over generations of populations and standard operations are applied such as: binary encoding of the genes (parameters); roulette wheel selection criterion; multi-point crossover operation for crossover. Genes are complex structures and they cause dynamic transformation of one substance into another during the life of an individual, as well as the life of the human population over many generations. Micro-array gene expression data can be used to evolve the ECF with inputs being the expression level of a certain number of selected genes and the outputs being the classes. After the ECF is trained on gene expression rules can be extracted that represent packed or unpacked [34].

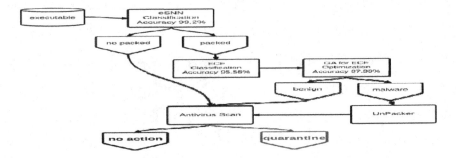

Fig. 3. Graphical display of the ECISMD Algorithm

Step 5: If the result of the classification is benign, the executable file goes to antivirus scanner and the process is terminated. Otherwise, the executable file is marked as malicious, it goes to the unpaker, to the antivirus scanner for verification and finally placed in quarantine and the process is terminated.

4   Data and Results

To prove generalization ability of our classification approach we need a reliable dataset. The full_dataset comprised of 2,598 packed viruses from the Malfease Project dataset (http://malfease.oarci.net), 2,231 non-packed benign executables collected from a clean installation of *Windows XP Home plus*, several common user applications and 669 packed benign executables. It was divided randomly in two parts: 1) a training dataset containing 2,231 patterns related to the non-packed benign executable and 2,262 patterns related to the packed executables detected using unpacked software 2) a testing dataset containing 1,005 patterns related to the packed executables that even the most well know unpacked software was not able to detect. These datasets are available at http://roberto.perdisci.googlepages.com/code [11].

The virus dataset containing 2,598 malware and 669 benign executables is divided in two parts: 1) a training dataset containing 1,834 patterns related to the malware and 453 patterns related to the benign executables 2) a test dataset containing 762 patterns related to the malware and 218 benign executables. In order to translate each executable into a pattern vector Perdisci et al [11] they use binary static analysis, to extract information such as, the name of the code and data sections, the number of writable-executable sections, the code and data entropy.

In both classifications described below, *Training Accuracy* reports the average accuracy computed over 10-fold cross-validation. *Testing Accuracy* refers to the percentage of packed executables that were correctly detected by each classifier in the *Packed_Test_Dataset* and in the *Virus_Test_Dataset* respectively.

In the first classification performed by the ECISMD, the eSNN approach was employed in order to classify packed or not packed executables. The results for testing are: Classification Accuracy: 99.2% No. of evolved neurons: Class 0/867 neurons - Class 1/734 neurons, In order to perform comparison with different learning algorithms the *Weka software version 3.7* was used (http://www.cs.waikato.ac.nz/ml/weka). Table 1 reports the results obtained with *RBF ANN, Naïve Bayes, Multi Layer Perceptron (MLP), Support Vector Machine (LibSVM), k-Nearest-Neighbors* (k-NN) and *eSNN*.

Table 1. Comparison of various approaches for the Packed dataset

Packed Dataset		
Classifier	Train Accuracy	Test Accuracy
RBFNetwork	98.3085%	98.0859%
NaiveBayes	98.3975%	97.1144%
MLP	99.5326%	96.2189%
LibSVM	99.4436%	89.8507%
k-NN	99.4436%	96.6169%
eSNN	99.8%	99.2%

In the 2nd classification performed by the ECISMD the ECF approach was employed in order to classify malware or benign executables. The ECF model has the following parameter values: MaxField=1, MinField=0.01, number of fuzzy membership functions MF=1; number of rule nodes used to calculate the output value of the ECF when a new input vector is presented MofN=9 (number of neighbors to consider when evaluating nearest node); number of iterations for presenting each input vector Epochs=6. The results for the *test_dataset* are: Classification Accuracy: 95.561%, Correct Samples: 933/980, Accuracy/Class: 82%/ Class 0 - 98% /Class 1. For the ECF parameter optimization during training, the following parameter value ranges were used: Min Field: 0.1, Max Field: 0.8, membership function: 9, Value for the m-of-n parameter: 3, Generation: 6 and Population: 4. For the optimized value of the ECF, 30% of the data was selected for training and 70% for testing. The classification accuracy in test_dataset after the optimization was 97.992%.

Table 2, reports the results obtained with 6 classifiers and optimized ECF network (RBF Network, Naïve Bayes, MLP, Lib SVM, k-NN, ECF and optimized ECF). The best results on the testing dataset were obtained by using the eSNN classifier, to classify packed or not packed executables and the optimized ECF (in the 2nd classification) which classifies malware or benign executables.

Table 2. Comparison of various approaches for the virus dataset

Virus Dataset		
Classifier	Train Accuracy	Test Accuracy
RBFNetwork	94.4031%	93.0612%
NaiveBayes	94.0533%	92.3469%
MLP	97.7551%	97.289%
LibSVM	94.6218%	94.2857%
k-NN	98.1198%	96.8367%
ECF	99.05%	95.561%
Optimized ECF	99.87%	97.992%

The average time for the classification of a pattern vector on a 3.06GHz Intel P4 processor was about $t = 0.00016$ seconds per executable. These results are much smaller than the ones of Perdisci et al [11] in which on a 2GHz Dual Core AMD Opteron processor was about $t=0.001$ seconds per executable.

5   Discussion - Conclusions

A new Evolving Computational Intelligence System for Malware Detection (ECISMD) was introduced. It performs classification using eSNN to properly label a packed executable and ECF with GA to detect malware and to optimize itself towards better generalization. An effort was made to use minimum computational power and resources. The classification performance of the eSNN method and the accuracy of the ECF model were experimentally explored based on different datasets. The eSNN was applied to an unknown dataset and reported promising results. Moreover the ECF model and the genetically optimized ECF network, detects the patterns and classifies them with high accuracy and adds a higher degree of integrity to the rest of the security infrastructure of ECISMD. As a future direction, aiming to improve the efficiency of biologically realistic ANN for pattern recognition, it would be important to evaluate the eSNN model with ROC analysis and to perform feature minimization in order to achieve minimum processing time. Other coding schemes could be explored and compared on the same security task. Finally, the ECISMD could be improved towards a better online learning with self-modified parameter values.

References

1. Yan, W., Zhang, Z., Ansari, N.: Revealing Packed Malware. IEEE (2007)
2. Cesare, S., Xiang, Y.: Software Similarity and Classification. Springer (2012)
3. Babar, K., Khalid, F.: Generic unpacking techniques. In: Proceedings of the 2nd International Conference on Computer, Control and Communication (IC4), pp. 1–6. IEEE (2009)
4. Royal, P., Halpin, M., Dagon, D., Edmonds, R.: Polyunpack: Automating the hidden-code extraction of unpack-executing malware. In: ACSAC, pp. 289–300 (2006)
5. Kang, M., Poosankam, P., Yin, H.: Renovo: A hidden code extractor for packed executables. In: 2007 ACM Workshop on Recurring Malcode, pp. 46–53. ACM (2007)

6. Martignoni, L., Christodorescu, M., Jha, S.: Omniunpack: Fast, generic, and safe unpacking of malware. In: Proceedings of the ACSAC, pp. 431–441 (2007)
7. Yegneswaran, V., Saidi, H., Porras, P., Sharif, M.: Eureka: A framework for enabling static analysis on malware, Technical report, Technical Report SRI-CSL-08-01 (2008)
8. Danielescu, A.: Anti-debugging and anti-emulation techniques: Code-Breakers J. (2008)
9. Shafiq, M.Z., Tabish, S.M., Mirza, F., Farooq, M.: PE-Miner: Mining Structural Information to Detect Malicious Executables in Realtime. In: Kirda, E., Jha, S., Balzarotti, D. (eds.) RAID 2009. LNCS, vol. 5758, pp. 121–141. Springer, Heidelberg (2009)
10. Shaq, M., Tabish, S., Farooq, M.: PE-Probe: Leveraging Packer Detection and Structural Information to Detect Malicious Portable Executables. In: Virus Bulletin Conference (2009)
11. Perdisci, R., Lanzi, A., Lee, W.: McBoost: Boosting scalability in malware collection and analysis using statistical classiffication of executables. In: Proceedings of the 2008 Annual Computer Security Applications Conference, pp. 301–310 (2008) ISSN 1063-9527
12. Kolter, J.Z., Maloof, M.A.: Learning to detect and classify malicious executables in the wild. Journal of Machine Learning Research 7, 2721–2744 (2006)
13. Ugarte-Pedrero, X., Santos, I., Bringas, P.G., Gastesi, M., Esparza, J.M.: Semi-supervised Learning for Packed Executable Detection. IEEE (2011) 978-1-4577-0460-4/11
14. Ugarte-Pedrero, X., Santos, I., Laorden, C., Sanz, B., Bringas, G.P.: Collective Classification for Packed Executable Identification. In: ACM CEAS, pp. 23–30 (2011)
15. Gavrilut, D., Cimpoes, M., Anton, D., Ciortuz, L.: Malware Detection Using Machine Learning. In: Proceedings of the International Multiconference on Computer Science and Information Technology, pp. 735–741 (2009) ISBN 978-83-60810-22-4
16. Ye, Y., Wang, D., Li, T., Ye, D.: Imds: intelligent malware detection system. ACM (2007)
17. Chandrasekaran, M., Vidyaraman, V., Upadhyaya, S.J.: Spycon: Emulating user activities to detect evasive spyware, IPCCC. IEEE Computer Society, 502–550 (2007)
18. Chouchane, M.R., Walenstein, A., Lakhotia, A.: Using Markov Chains to filter machine-morphed variants of malicious programs. In: 3rd International Conference on Malicious and Unwanted Software, MALWARE 2008, pp. 77–84 (2008)
19. Stamp, M., Attaluri, S.: McGhee S.: Profile hidden markov models and metamorphic virus detection. Journal in Computer Virology (2008)
20. Santamarta, R.: Generic detection and classification of polymorphic malware using neural pattern recognition (2006)
21. Yoo, I.: Visualizing Windows executable viruses using self-organizing maps. In: VizSEC/DMSEC 2004: ACM Workshop (2004)
22. Schliebs, S., Kasabov, N.: Evolving spiking neural network—a survey. Evolving Systems 4(2), 87–98 (2013)
23. Thorpe, S.J., Delorme, A.: Rufin van Rullen: Spike-based strategies for rapid processing. Neural Networks 14(6-7), 715–725 (2001)
24. Delorme, A., Perrinet, L., Thorpe, S.J.: Networks of Integrate-and-Fire Neurons using Rank Order Coding B: Spike Timing Dependant Plasticity and Emergence of Orientation Selectivity. Published in Neurocomputing 38-40(1-4), 539–545 (2000)
25. Thorpe, S.J., Gautrais, J.: Rank order coding. In: CNS 1997: Proceedings of the 6th Annual Conference on Computational Neuroscience: Trends in Research, New York, NY, USA, pp. 113–118. Plenum Press (1998)
26. Kasabov, N.: Evolving connectionist systems: Methods and Applications in Bioinformatics. In: Yu, P.X., Kacprzyk, P.J. (eds.) Brain Study and Intelligent Machines. Springer, NY (2002)

27. Wysoski, S.G., Benuskova, L., Kasabov, N.: Adaptive learning procedure for a network of spiking neurons and visual pattern recognition. In: Blanc-Talon, J., Philips, W., Popescu, D., Scheunders, P. (eds.) ACIVS 2006. LNCS, vol. 4179, pp. 1133–1142. Springer, Heidelberg (2006)

28. Schliebs, S., Defoin-Platel, M., Kasabov, N.: Integrated feature and parameter optimization for an evolving spiking neural network. In: Köppen, M., Kasabov, N., Coghill, G. (eds.) ICONIP 2008, Part I. LNCS, vol. 5506, pp. 1229–1236. Springer, Heidelberg (2009)

29. Song Q., Kasabov N.: Weighted Data Normalization and Feature Selection. In: Proc. of the 8th Intelligence Information Systems Conference (2003)

30. Huang, L., Song, Q., Kasabov, N.: Evolving Connectionist System Based Role Allocation for Robotic Soccer. International Journal of Advanced Robotic Systems 5(1), 59–62 (2008) ISSN 1729-8806

31. Kasabov, N.: Evolving fuzzy neural networks for online supervised/ unsupervised, knowledge–based learning. IEEE Trans. Cybernetics 31(6), 902–918 (2001)

32. Kasabov, N., Song, Q.: DENFIS: Dynamic, evolving neural-fuzzy inference systems and its application for time-series prediction. IEEE Trans. 10(2), 144–154 (2002)

33. Goh, L., Song, Q., Kasabov, N.: A Novel Feature Selection Method to Improve Classification of Gene Expression Data. In: 2nd Asia-Pacific IT Conf. vol. 29 (2004)

34. Kasabov, N., Song, Q.: GA-parameter optimization of evolving connectionist systems for classification and a case study from bioinformatics. In: Neural Information ICONIP 2002 Proceedings of the 9th International Conference on, IEEE ICONIP, 1198128 (2002)

35. http://www.kedri.aut.ac.nz/

36. http://malfease.oarci.net

37. http://roberto.perdisci.googlepages.com/code

38. http://www.cs.waikato.ac.nz/ml/weka

Lightweight Formal Verification in Real World, A Case Study

Andrea Atzeni, Tao Su, and Teodoro Montanaro

Dip. Automatica e Informatica
Politecnico di Torino, 10129 Torino, Italy
{shocked,tao.su}@polito.it, teodoro.montanaro@studenti.polito.it

Abstract. To security oriented large-scale projects, formal verification is widely used to assure the satisfaction of claimed security properties. Although complete formal verification and validation requires a great amount of time and resources, applying lightweight formal methods to partial specifications reduces the required efforts to a convenient amount, while can still uncover sensitive software design problems. This paper describes our experience of applying lightweight formal verification to the authentication system of *webinos*, a substantial cross-device software infrastructure developed in a large scale EU funded project. The paper details the approach, the properties analysed, the lessons learned and concludes with possible recommendations for practitioners and designers about how to use lightweight formal verification in real world projects.

Keywords: lightweight formal methods, authentication system, web-based platform, security properties, model checking.

1 Introduction

In computer science, formal methods are used under the expectation that the mathematical models will help to find out the errors hidden in system design. However, they are also considered techniques requiring high level expertise. For this reason, they are mostly considered for strong safety-demanding projects, like space applications [1], or for sensitive security building blocks, like cryptographic protocols [2].

In most real world projects, only a few properties are critical, and performing formal analysis on the complete system is expensive. Lightweight formal methods are promising solutions to this problem: only partial specifications and focused properties can be verified, rather than the complete system model.

This paper describes our case study where we applied lightweight formal verification to the authentication system in the *webinos* platform [3], which aims to provide a secured platform for various types of web-enabled devices.

In our study, the experience of generating formal models and the lessons learned during the formal analysis process are more valuable than the end result. They can make recommendations to practitioners and designers in similar situations, in particular the approach of assigning the lightweight formal verification work to the testing group as higher-level testing work.

L. Iliadis, M. Papazoglou, and K. Pohl (Eds.): CAiSE 2014 Workshops, LNBIP 178, pp. 335–342, 2014.
© Springer International Publishing Switzerland 2014

Testing is cost effective, flexible and widely used, but it is inefficient when dealing with security properties and small probability errors. Thus, we introduced a formal verification process in our work to provide cost-efficient coverage of the key security domains correctness. As a positive side effect, this process also brought a deeper understanding of the previous in-place testing procedures.

2   Related Work

Lightweight formal methods are popularly used to analyse critical security-building blocks as well as strong safety-demanding applications.

Zave [4] applies lightweight formal modelling and analysis techniques to check the correctness of the Chord protocol, a well known DHT algorithm. She analyses the ability of the nodes to maintain a single ordered ring given ample time and no disruptions while it is working. The result shows Chord is not correct: there are cases where the ring may break and never repair itself. In the paper, the author claims the usage of lightweight methods increases the quality of specifications and implementations, taking only a very convenient amount of efforts to detect most problems. Our work reaches the same conclusion. The main differences lie on the approach: Zave's work analyses whether the proposed global invariant is preserved, while our work checks all paths of the available system states, until the proposed properties are satisfied or falsified.

Taghdiri and Jackson [5] present how they use lightweight formal methods on the Pull-Based Asynchronous Rekeying Framework (ARF), a solution proposed for the scalable group key management problem in secure multicast. They agree that lightweight formal methods are feasible and economical. During the analysis, the authors build a model which is less than 100 lines, and check some critical correctness properties. As a result, they detect several hidden flaws, including a serious security breach. Compared with our work, Taghdiri and Jackson use the tick-based modelling idiom, while we use the global-state modelling idiom. They further generalised their model to a structure that can be reused in checking a class of secure multicast key management protocols. The report of using the same structure to validate Iolus protocol can be found in [6].

The researches described above use lightweight formal methods, but do not answer the question of how to smoothly integrate formal methods into real world projects without excessive cost. Researches along this vein exists in the industrial world, where the systems involved are much more complex and only part of the system is formally analysed. This is consistent with the concept of lightweight formal methods, so it is sensible to mention approaches tried out to make formal verification an accepted industrial practice. In this context, the authors of [1] present a case study of using partial formal models for verifying the requirements of FDIR system in space station. They proposed to consider formal verification and validation as intermittent "spot checks" executed by an additional independent formal methods experts. They argue this is a viable way to introduce formal methods into real world projects. With this idea in mind, the authors also present the case studies for spacecraft fault protection systems [7]. They suggest that lightweight formal methods can offer an effective way to improve the quality of specifications, and consequently the end product. While our approach of considering formal verification as part of abstract level testing work brings both advantages and disadvantages, it is suitable for projects with limited resources, i.e. when hiring an additional independent team of experts is not a sustainable solution. Moreover, "re-using" the testing group during the verification process allows for a deeper understanding of the specifications and the system, and this will benefit the future testing work. The drawback comes from the lack of experience of the testing group, which could have a limited knowledge of formal methods techniques.

3 The Case Study

The formal verification work started after a comprehensive testing system was built [8]. The goals were finding the system flaws as well as highlighting the potential misunderstandings in system specifications [9].

3.1 *webinos* Platform

The *webinos* project focuses on constructing a secured platform that can be accessed by multiple types of web-enabled devices.

The architecture of this platform centres on the concept of *Personal Zone*, which is one-to-one correlated with the user. The *Personal Zone Hub* (PZH) is the focal point of the zone. The other devices in the zone are called *Personal Zone Proxies* (PZPs), which support and expose standard JavaScript APIs for accessing devices features, such as camera, geolocation, networking etc. The devices can communicate with each other with or without the PZH after they pass the challenges of the authentication system.

3.2 Authentication System in *webinos*

The authentication system consists of user authentication process, device authentication process and third-party authentication process.

Users are primarily authenticated through their OpenID [10] credentials, such as Google or Yahoo! accounts. This operation only allows a user to connect through the PZH web interface. Devices are authenticated through the possession and use of an RSA private key. For devices which are generally used only by a single user (e.g., smartphone), this credential can be used as an authenticator for many privileged operations. For shared devices (e.g., smart TV), the PZH needs to check the user's presence and identity before this credential can be further used for authentication. Third-party authentication is executed via OAuth 1.0 [11], which requires an additional trusted developer-provided server to hold on the developer's OAuth credentials. This server is accessed by client-side JavaScript of a *webinos* application in order to sign OAuth requests and gain access to third-party resources. In *user authentication* and *device authentication*

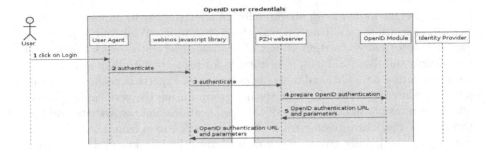

Fig. 1. Partial *webinos* user authentication sequence diagram. Reprinted from [9].

processes, there are three isolated sub-processes corresponding to different situations. For example, in the device authentication process, there is a *device-held private key* sub-process detailing how the user can get the RSA key from the *Keystore Manager* to authenticate the current device.

In *webinos*, the workflow of each process is expressed using sequence diagrams, with some additional explanations written in natural language. For example, part of the user authentications process diagram is illustrated in Fig. 1, and the detailed requirements that *"OpenID login MUST be requested using the PAPE extension and set* `max_auth_age=0` *in order to prevent authentication caching"* are attached in the end. The other processes are expressed in the same way.

The authentication process is further detailed by an incomplete authentication state machine (i.e. without *presence checking* state), which helps to understand the state transitions, and several entity authentication tables outlining how different entities are authenticated by the others.

3.3   Approach

webinos platform is quite complex. A complete formal verification is neither feasible nor cost-effective with respect to our goals. Our chosen approach is thus practical and straightforward, as detailed in next steps:

1. clarifying the specifications logic and understanding the sequence diagrams;
2. translating the diagrams into corresponding formal models;
3. selecting the need-to-check properties;
4. analysing the results and finding possible improvements.

We used NuSMV [12] model checker. The principals in the authentication system were modelled using *VAR* variables, each operation was presented as a parameter of the *VAR* variable. And an additional *system_status* was inserted to present the snapshot of the system. The transitions between each state of the *VAR* variables were assigned with *ASSIGN* variables based on the switch-case logic. To be consistent with reality, we added non-determinism into the models. User interacts with the system, thus we put two additional states, the *send_wrong_password* state and the *reject_authorisation* state into user's status representing the unexpected user behaviour. Availability is another concern, with the potential occurrence of DoS attack. Thus the *busy* state was inserted into the models, representing the situation where the module stops working after it finishes its previous work. An example of state transitions of the *User Agent* module is shown in Fig. 2. In any transition, with half probability either the module proceeds to the next work or it enters the *busy* state.

```
init (useragent_status):= idle;
next (useragent_status):= case
    system_status = login_request & useragent_status = idle:
        {send_auth_req , busy};
    system_status = load_auth_url & useragent_status = idle:
        {send_identity_provider_url_req , busy};
     TRUE : idle;
esac;
```

Fig. 2. An example, partial state transitions setting of *User Agent*

The need-to-check properties were defined using *SPEC* variables, which fell into the following classifications:

- *completeness*: it is always true that the final state of the system will be the correct one with the corresponding initial state.
- *correctness*: it is always true that the correct final state of the system can be achieved with the corresponding initial state.
- *security properties*: the user who sends too many wrong credentials will be stopped; the user who fails to pass authentication challenges will be blocked for privileged operations; the affect of unexpected situations will be deleted or mitigated by corresponding countermeasures.

3.4   Results

This study formally analysed the authentication system with 18 pages specifications, and built 5 models for the isolated processes. The total effort amount was approximate to 1.5 person months. The efforts mainly came from the translation from sequence diagrams to formal models, and the work of learning how to use NuSMV. During the verification process, the following issues were reported:

- *ambiguities and inconsistencies*: although the specifications are mainly expressed in sequence diagrams, minor ambiguities and inconsistencies still exist. For example, in the "entity authentication tables", the term *"PZPs"* refers to the devices in the third table, but in the sixth table, *"PZPs"* is used to refer to the personal zone proxies.

- *incompleteness*: the specifications lack several key factors, resulting misleading for the implementation. For example, there are no details of how many requests each module can take in the authentication system, and how they will react with multiple requests. This issue leads to an ultimate challenge to build a "perfect" model which shows the exact properties of the authentication system. The method we chose to solve this problem was by adding a second request which is concurrent with the first one, and setting that the modules to work only when they are in *IDLE* state. This solution is a better approximation of real behaviour, but has a very poor scalability.
- *missing assumptions*: the system designers only assume all the modules will work as established, without considering unexpected situations. This error is found in the model checking results, in which the checker reports the *completeness* property cannot be satisfied because of the unexpected situations introduced in the models.

4   Discussion

During our work of applying lightweight formal verification to the *webinos* authentication system, we strictly followed the pragmatic principle: *we only modelled a high-level abstraction of the system, without considering the other parts of the platform*. Still, some important problems were found. Several lessons worthy sharing have been learned, which can give practitioners recommendations on how to introduce lightweight formal methods into real world projects.

4.1   Lesson 1: Choose the Right Tool

The expensive requirement of expertise is the main obstacle between the formal methods and real world projects. A suitable tool can greatly reduce this expense. In our case, NuSMV is a fairly easy-to-use tool with respect to state exploration.

However, one major flaw of NuSMV was found in the verification process. If user sends a wrong password, OpenID scheme will redirect the browser back to the login webpage. NuSMV thinks this operation is a loop, and it raises an error. The same happened when the user rejects the authorisation request.

From another point of view, when a user sends too many wrong credentials, it is likely impersonated by a machine that is trying to perform a brute force attack. OpenID scheme has already adopted the CAPTCHA [13] technique as the countermeasure for this attack. So, in the model, a threshold was added to limit the number of times a user can send the credentials to the OpenID server. Hence, the problem was circumvented with strict consistency to reality.

4.2   Lesson 2: Assign the Verification Work to the Testing Group

Another important question is, who should perform formal verification work to bring greater benefits with less costs? Our answer is: to the testing group. Compared with hiring an independent formal verification experts team, assigning the verification work to the testing group is cost friendly. Moreover, the testing group already has a deep knowledge of the system, so the errors in the formal models can be directly correlated to the system, even to the specific code points. As a positive effect, this would make more robust traceability between the models and the system. Since the testing group is experienced with errors, another important issue of prioritising the errors is also solved by this approach. Finally, the experience in verification improves the testing group capacity to generate test cases, since it brings a deeper understanding of the system

4.3 Lesson 3: Focus Only on Crucial Properties

Focusing on crucial properties is a key argument in lightweight formal methods.

In our case, the authentication system consists of distributed modules and uses different authentication methods for different resources, it is thus rather complex with respect to the need-to-check properties. However, since the connections are established on top of secure channels, we only analyse the system in an abstract level, i.e. the properties relative to message content are not considered. For this reason, only the properties listed in 3.3 are concerned, which are strictly related to the system functionality. These properties are shared by many authentication schemes, thus our models can be generalised and applied to different authentication systems.

4.4 Lesson 4: Adopt OpenID over a Self-developed Module

In the case of building an authentication system for the web-related software, OpenID is more thorough and secure than a "re-invented wheel".

In our case, the designers of the authentication system did not consider user's misbehaviour. As stated in Subsection 4.1, lacking CAPTCHA technique will leave space for brute force attacks. Furthermore, at present the open-source OpenID server implementation is available, allowing for organization-specific configurations, thus the scheme can be used even in case of specific requirements.

5   Conclusion and Future Work

Lightweight formal verification technique minimises the gap between formal methods and real world projects. In our work, several major issues were found with very limited resources. Another important aspect is that this verification work was done by the testing group of the project, allowing for positive feedback in the development of a refined testing suite.

However, to make formal verification an accepted industrial practice, there is still a lot of work ahead. This method should be tested to a broader range of security properties and on other security-critical domains in the platform. Also, the most effective formal model should be identified. We plan to analyse the same system with different formal languages, to assess which language and specifically which language capability is optimal in the concept of lightweight formal methods.

Acknowledgements. The research described in this paper was funded by the EU FP7 *webinos* project (FP7-ICT-2009-05 Objective 1.2).

References

1. Easterbrook, S., Callahan, J.: Formal methods for verification and validation of partial specifications: A case study. Journal of Systems and Software 40(3), 199–210 (1998)
2. Mundra, P., Shukla, S., Sharma, M., Pai, R.M., Singh, S.: Modeling and Verification of Kerberos Protocol Using Symbolic Model Verifier. In: 2011 International Conference on Communication Systems and Network Technologies, pp. 651–654. IEEE (June 2011)
3. Fuhrhop, C., Lyle, J., Faily, S.: The webinos project. In: Proceedings of the 21st International Conference Companion on World Wide Web - WWW 2012, p. 259. ACM Press, New York (2012)
4. Zave, P.: Using lightweight modeling to understand chord. ACM SIGCOMM Computer Communication Review 42(2), 49 (2012)
5. Taghdiri, M., Jackson, D.: A lightweight formal analysis of a multicast key management scheme. In: König, H., Heiner, M., Wolisz, A. (eds.) FORTE 2003. LNCS, vol. 2767, pp. 240–256. Springer, Heidelberg (2003)
6. Taghdiri, M.: Lightweight modelling and automatic analysis of multicast key management schemes. Master's thesis. MIT (2002)
7. Easterbrook, S., Lutz, R., Covington, R., Kelly, J., Ampo, Y., Hamilton, D.: Experiences using lightweight formal methods for requirements modeling. IEEE Transactions on Software Engineering 24(1), 4–14 (1998)
8. Su, T., Lyle, J., Atzeni, A., Faily, S., Virji, H., Ntanos, C., Botsikas, C.: Continuous integration for web-based software infrastructures: Lessons learned on the webinos project. In: Bertacco, V., Legay, A. (eds.) HVC 2013. LNCS, vol. 8244, pp. 145–150. Springer, Heidelberg (2013)
9. webinos group: webinos authentication system specifications (2012), http://www.webinos.org/content/html/D033/Authentication.htm
10. Recordon, D., Reed, D.: OpenID 2.0. In: Proceedings of the second ACM workshop on Digital identity management - DIM 2006, p. 11. ACM Press, New York (2006)
11. Hammer-Lahav, E.: The OAuth 1.0 Protocol (2010), http://tools.ietf.org/html/rfc5849
12. Cimatti, A., Clarke, E., Giunchiglia, F., Roveri, M.: NuSMV: A reimplementation of SMV. In: Proc. STTT 1998, pp. 25–31 (1998)
13. von Ahn, L., Blum, M., Hopper, N.J., Langford, J.: CAPTCHA: Using hard AI problems for security. In: Biham, E. (ed.) EUROCRYPT 2003. LNCS, vol. 2656, pp. 294–311. Springer, Heidelberg (2003)

Security Requirements Analysis
Using Knowledge in CAPEC

Haruhiko Kaiya[1], Sho Kono[2], Shinpei Ogata[2], Takao Okubo[3], Nobukazu Yoshioka[4],
Hironori Washizaki[5], and Kenji Kaijiri[2]

[1] Dept. of Information Sciences, Kanagawa University, Hiratsuka 259-1293, Japan
kaiya@kanagawa-u.ac.jp
[2] Dept. of Computer Science, Shinshu University, Nagano 380-8553, Japan
[3] Institute of Information Securiry, Kanagawa 221-0835, Japan
[4] National Institue of Informatics (NII), Tokyo 101-8430, Japan
[5] Waseda University, Tokyo 169-8555, Japan

Abstract. Because all the requirements analysts are not the experts of security,
providing security knowledge automatically is one of the effective means for
supporting security requirements elicitation. We propose a method for eliciting
security requirements on the basis of Common Attack Patterns Enumeration and
Classification (CAPEC). A requirements analyst can automatically acquire the
candidates of attacks against a functional requirement with the help of our method.
Because technical terms are mainly used in the descriptions in CAPEC and usual
phrases are used in the requirements descriptions, there are gaps between them.
To bridge the gaps, our method contains a mapping between technical terms and
noun phrases called term maps.

Keywords: Requirements Engineering, Requirements Elicitation, Security Requirements, Structured Knowledge.

1 Introduction

Because an information system is embedded and used in some social activity such as
business or entertainment, knowledge of the social activity, i.e., domain knowledge is
crucially necessary for eliciting the requirements for the system. Knowledge of information technology such as Internet and mobile devices is a kind of domain knowledge
because our daily activities cannot be performed without such technologies.

Especially in security requirements elicitation, knowledge related to technologies
plays an important role because actual attacks are achieved by means of the technologies and most countermeasures are implemented in the same way. We thus expect requirements analysts have enough knowledge of security and related technologies when
he/she elicits security requirements. Apparently, it is unrealistic expectation because the
knowledge of security and related technologies is too huge for all requirements analysts
to understand it. In addition, such knowledge is always updated every day. Providing
the knowledge of security and related technologies automatically is one of the helpful
ways to satisfy this assumption.

In this paper, we proposed a method for eliciting security requirements on the basis of Common Attack Patterns Enumeration and Classification (CAPEC), which is

L. Iliadis, M. Papazoglou, and K. Pohl (Eds.): CAiSE 2014 Workshops, LNBIP 178, pp. 343–348, 2014.
© Springer International Publishing Switzerland 2014

machine-readable and up-to-date knowledge for attacks. CAPEC consists of attack patterns, and the patterns are usually increased when CAPEC is updated. In the method, candidates of attacks against a function (a use case) are automatically selected from the knowledge. Although requirements analysts have to examine whether each candidate actually threatens the function, they do not have to learn all the knowledge in advance.

Because attacks using concrete technologies such as scripting and database queries are focused in CAPEC, most descriptions in CAPEC consist of technical terms. However, a description of a function such as a use case description in a use case model is usually implementation-independent. To bridge the gaps between CAPEC descriptions and requirements descriptions, a mapping between technical terms and noun phrases called "term map" is used in our method. Although we have to manually prepare the term map, we assume we can gather and improve the term map step by step during its usages.

The rest of this paper is organized as follows. In section 2, we review related works using domain knowledge for eliciting requirements. In section 3, we present a method for eliciting security requirements. We finally summarize our current results and show the future issues.

2   Related Work

The importance of the domain knowledge is widely accepted in requirements elicitation and even in software engineering in general [10]. We can thus find a lot of requirements elicitation methods using domain knowledge. One of the significant problems of the methods is that there is no guarantee to develop or acquire the domain knowledge. There are a few methods for developing the domain knowledge for requirements elicitation [3], [6]. Using existing structured knowledge is another solution to solve this problem. Several methods [8], [2] use Common Criteria (CC) as such knowledge.

Even when we can obtain domain knowledge, the knowledge is not always machine-readable. For example, CC documents are normally written in PDF format and we cannot sometimes access the texts in the documents due to the security settings in PDF.

We can find some public and machine-readable knowledge base such as CAPEC, CVE or CWE. Common Vulnerabilities and Exposures (CVE) is a dictionary of publicly known information security vulnerabilities and exposures. Common Weakness Enumeration (CWE) is a set of software weakness. Although all of them seem to be useful for eliciting security requirements, we first use CAPEC in our research.

3   Method for Eliciting Security Requirements

The goal of this method is to support security requirements elicitation using CAPEC, which is structured and machine-readable knowledge resources. Although security experts should examine elicited security requirements after applying this method, this method enables them to save effort. We mainly explain our method in this section. In addition to CAPEC knowledge, we have to prepare a mapping between noun phrases in requirements descriptions and technical terms used in CAPEC. We also explain how to prepare such a mapping.

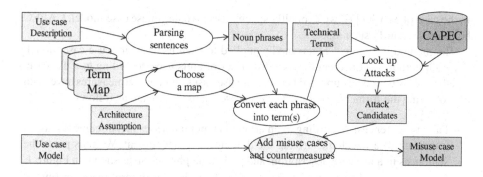

Fig. 1. Data flows among this elicitation method

3.1   Elicitation Method

Figure 1 shows the data flows among our requirements elicitation method. Boxes and cylinders correspond to data stores, ovals correspond to processes and arrows correspond to data flows in the figure. The inputs of the method are as follows.

- Use case description: In the method, we assume requirements are represented in a use case model and a use case description specifies each use case in natural language sentences. Security requirements elicitation is then performed for each use case. In this sense, a use case description is the main input of the method.
- Term maps: As mentioned at the beginning of this section, we have to prepare a mapping between noun phrases in a use case description and technical terms used in CAPEC because technical terms such as "SQL" or "buffer" are not directly used in use case descriptions. We thus have to prepare the mapping to bridge the gap between the noun phrases and technical terms. We call such a mapping "term map" in this paper. Because technical terms usually depend on a specific architecture or implementation, we prepare the mapping for each architecture assumption.
- Architecture assumption: Even at the requirements elicitation stage, some architecture assumptions such as client-server or cloud platform are considered. Such architecture assumptions give large effects on security issues because actual attacks and their protections are usually achieved on the basis of such assumptions. We assume such architecture assumptions are provided before requirements elicitation. Such assumptions correspond to an element "Technical_Context" in an attack pattern in CAPEC.
- Use case model: Because the output of the method is misuse case model [9] or MASG [7], we prepare a use case model as one of inputs.

The output is a misuse case model as mentioned above. The following elements in the model are elicited on the basis of an attack pattern.

- Misuse cases: An attack pattern itself directly specifies a misuse case.
- Countermeasure(s): In a misuse case model, a countermeasure is represented as a use case, and there exists a mitigate- or avoid-relationship between the use case and a misuse case. Countermeasures can be found in an element "Solutions_and_Mitigations" in CAPEC an attack pattern.

In the case of MASG [7], we explicitly specify assets (data) in use case model. CAPEC helps us to identify such assets.

The method in Figure 1 is repeatedly applied to each use case in a use case model. For each iteration, a different the use case description is used according to a use case, and the use case model is updated because misuse cases and countermeasures have been added during the former iterations. The processes in the figure are as follows.

- Parsing sentences: According to an article [1], noun phrases in a document play an important role for characterizing the domain of the document. We thus parse the sentences in a use case description, and pick noun phrases up as shown in Figure 1.
- Choose a map: We assume we have already had libraries of term maps for several architecture assumptions. We simply choose one of them on the basis of the description of the architecture assumption. We expect such a description is provided in the same form of "Technical_Context" element in CAPEC.
- Convert each phrase into term(s): As mentioned above, technical terms used in CAPEC are not usually used in use case descriptions. We thus convert each noun phrase into technical terms on the basis of a term map.
- Look up attacks: We look up attack patterns on the basis of technical terms. We assume attacks in the patterns can be applied to a use case specified in the use case description. We thus call the looked up attack patterns "attack candidates".
- Add misuse cases and countermeasures: For each attack candidate, we have to manually examine whether it can be really applied to the use case description. If it can be applied, we add misuse cases and their countermeasures to the use case model on the basis of the candidate.

Except "Add misuse cases and countermeasures", processes above can be performed automatically.

3.2 Preparing Term Maps

A term map is used for bridging the gap between phrases in requirements descriptions and technical terms in CAPEC. As we stated above, technical terms used in CAPEC are not usually used in use case descriptions. We thus have to bridge the gap between phrases in use case descriptions and technical terms by using the term map. Figure 2 shows an example of a term map for web applications and its usage. In this example, we have an architecture assumption that a system will be implemented as web application. We thus use this term map. At the left top of this figure, a part of use case description is shown, and two phrases "data" and "display" are focused. These phrases are converted into four technical terms "SQL", "schema", "database", "web page". These terms are used for finding attack patterns in CAPEC.

Although term maps should be manually gathered, they will be reused and improved step by step during their usages. We had experiences to gather this kind of domain knowledge [5], and we have empirically validated that we could improve the quality of such knowledge [4]. We thus assume we can also gather and improve the term maps in the same way.

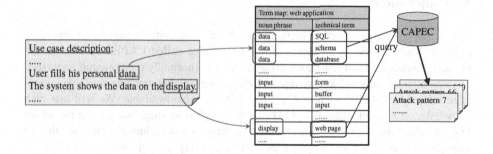

Fig. 2. An example of a term map for Web applications and its usage

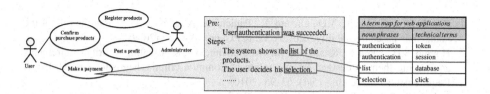

Fig. 3. A use case model, a use case description and a term map for web applications

3.3 Example of Applying the Method

We show a small example of applying the method. The example is about a web application for shopping. In figure 3, we show the use case model, a use case description and a term map used in this example. Because the system is implemented as a web application, a term map for web applications is used. In a use case description of a use case "Make a payment", three noun phrases "authentication", "list" and "selection" are identified. On the basis of the term map in Figure 3, these noun phrases are converted into four technical terms "token", "session", "database" and "click". Attack_Prerequisites of the following attack patterns contain each technical term as follows.

- token 4 patterns:
  - 102 Session Sidejacking
  - 36 Using Unpublished Web Service APIs
  - 39 Manipulating Opaque Client-based Data Tokens
  - 461 Web Services API Signature Forgery Leveraging Hash Function Extension Weakness
- session 11 patterns: 102, 103, 196, 21, 222, 226, 462, 467, 59, 60, 61
- database 3 patterns: 108, 109, 470
- click 2 patterns: 103, 222

Basically, all the patterns above become candidates of attacks. When we have to prioritize the attacks, we can refer to the values of other elements such as "Pattern_Completeness", "CIA_Impact" and "Typical_Severity".

4   Conclusion

In this paper, we proposed a method for eliciting security requirements. Because machine-readable and up-to-date security knowledge called CAPEC is used in the method, this method can reduce the effort of its user (normally requirements analysts).

Currently, we only use knowledge in CAPEC, but related machine-readable knowledge related to CAPEC such as CVE and CWE is also available. We will use such knowledge sources in addition to CAPEC. Although term maps seem to be useful for bridging the gaps between requirements descriptions and technical terms, we do not validate we can gather and improve the term maps step by step. We will continue to apply the method to various kinds of requirements descriptions to validate this point.

References

1. Capobianco, G., Lucia, A.D., Oliveto, R., Panichella, A., Panichella, S.: On the role of the nouns in ir-based traceability recovery. In: ICPC, pp. 148–157 (2009)
2. Houmb, S.H., Islam, S., Knauss, E., Jürjens, J., Schneider, K.: Eliciting security requirements and tracing them to design: An integration of common criteria, heuristics, and UMLsec. Requirements Engineering 15(1), 63–93 (2010)
3. Kaiya, H., Shimizu, Y., Yasui, H., Kaijiri, K., Saeki, M.: Enhancing domain knowledge for requirements elicitation with web mining. In: APSEC, pp. 3–12 (2010)
4. Kaiya, H., Suzuki, S., Ogawa, T., Tanigawa, M., Umemura, M., Kaijiri, K.: Spectrum analysis for software quality requirements using analyses records. In: COMPSAC Workshops, pp. 500–503 (2011)
5. Kaiya, H., Tanigawa, M., Suzuki, S., Sato, T., Kaijiri, K.: Spectrum analysis for quality requirements by using a term-characteristics map. In: van Eck, P., Gordijn, J., Wieringa, R. (eds.) CAiSE 2009. LNCS, vol. 5565, pp. 546–560. Springer, Heidelberg (2009)
6. Kitamura, M., Hasegawa, R., Kaiya, H., Saeki, M.: A Supporting Tool for Requirements Elicitation Using a Domain Ontology. In: Filipe, J., Shishkov, B., Helfert, M., Maciaszek, L.A. (eds.) ICSOFT/ENASE 2007. CCIS, vol. 22, pp. 128–140. Springer, Heidelberg (2008)
7. Okubo, T., Taguchi, K., Yoshioka, N.: Misuse cases + assets + security goals. In: CSE, vol. (3), pp. 424–429 (2009)
8. Saeki, M., Hayashi, S., Kaiya, H.: Enhancing goal-oriented security requirements analysis using common criteria-based knowledge. International Journal of Software Engineering and Knowledge Engineering 23(5), 695–720 (2013)
9. Sindre, G., Opdahl, A.L.: Eliciting security requirements with misuse cases. Requir. Eng. 10(1), 34–44 (2005)
10. Zhao, Y., Dong, J., Peng, T.: Ontology classification for semantic-web-based software engineering. IEEE Transactions on Services Computing 2, 303–317 (2009)

Author Index